Miracle,
Solution
and System

Miracle, Solution and System

Solution-focused Systemic Structural
Constellations for Therapy and
Organisational Change

By Insa Sparrer

solutions
books

First published in Great Britain in 2007 by
SolutionsBooks
26 Christchurch Road
Cheltenham
GL50 2PL
United Kingdom
www.solutionsbooks.com

Originally published in German as 'Wunder, Lösung und System' by
Carl-Auer-Systeme Verlag, 2001 (ISBN 978-38967020-4-3)

ISBN 978-0-9549749-5-4

Translated by Samuel W.F. Onn
Illustrations by Matthias Varga von Kibéd and Insa Sparrer
Cover Design by Cathi Stevenson
Design, typesetting and production by
Action Publishing Technology Ltd
Printed in Great Britain

Contents

Preface

It is often said that science, armed with the scalpel of rationality, has eliminated the idea of miracles from natural events. I say: Quite the contrary! Science has given miracles a new depth. For anyone who wants to learn how to be amazed, rather than scared, Insa Sparrer's miraculous miracle book is highly recommended reading.

Heinz von Foerster
Pescadera, CA, USA
25th October 2000

Foreword

Systemic therapy deals with a large spectrum of human reality: from the micro-level of cooperative relationship forming to perspectives spanning many generations, which place people at the intersection of deep connections and loyalties. Is it not fascinating how many paths can (and need) to be searched for and discovered, in order to bring us closer to what lies behind human suffering and to find the ways in which we can help give impetus to constructive change? In this matter, Insa Sparrer's book offers something special: it provides a creative and original differentiation of systemic practice, worthy throughout of the status of an original model, which occurs not through isolation but integration, linking. I think this is the most sensible way to speak (and write) about the 'object' of psychology: by integrating and combining perspectives, and by consciously recognising diversity as a quality. The word 'object' implies an image: something standing in front of us, presenting itself to us as a recognisable object.

However, the 'object' of psychology cannot be 'found' or 'discovered', since there is no given thing that can be identified as such.[1] Rather, all talk of mental coherences requires an 'anthropological pre-understanding', i.e. a human model, an answer to the question 'What is man?' No psychological theory can be formulated in the absence of a kernel of assumptions about the 'essence' of what it is to be human, i.e. the premises of every theory of man. These assumptions are chosen and established in a more or less explicit decision process. This process simultaneously contains a statement about the observer him or herself: I cannot have an idea of man that is not connected with my idea of myself. This makes psychology into a particular science, and psychotherapy a very specific profession: the observer of the human psyche, the soul-mapper, is also always an observer of him or herself – and the model he or she has of the soul is therefore simultaneously a model of him or herself. He or she speaks of the soul in the same way as about him or herself.

For this reason, I find the final chapter of this enthralling book by

[1] Herzog, W. (1984): Modell and Theorie in der Psychologie. Goettingen (Hogrefe), p.92

Insa Sparrer of great importance. She makes it clear that a systemic solution-focused perspective is also a way of life. The ideas expressed in this book apply to us all – the development of our idea of man always involves a development and change of our idea of ourselves. Systemic therapy and systemic theory development are already familiar with this idea: one's own position and one's own idea of man are continually reflected, one's own premises are critically questioned within a continual process of self-referencing. The variety of perspectives, the variety of approaches, the possibility that everything could 'also be completely different' – all these are known characteristics of lateral thinking, of the gaze more oriented towards what could be than what 'is'. Nevertheless, systemic therapy is still not immune from processes of dogmatisation, factional disputes about whether an approach 'is' now systemic or not. As a result, it is not uncommon for systemic-phenomenological and systemic-constructivist approaches to take up escalatory and contrary positions in the discussion: one is in danger of talking about 'truths', the other of defending 'pure doctrine', and both are in danger of falling prey to a culture of reciprocal devaluation. Suddenly the field finds itself again embroiled in torturous language games similar to those played in other areas of our society: 'That's not scientific!' – as was recently said about systemic therapy. 'Scientific', 'systemic' – words degenerate into 'medals' awarded or denied at the discretion of those with the power of defining.

This is disappointing, and therefore I am pleased that there exist books such as this one, where we are not dealing with 'linguistic medals' but orientation and integration. Systemic and Solution Focused Therapy, (Structural-) Constellation Work and the approach of Virginia Satir, verbal and nonverbal approaches – all this is shown in this book to be not only teachable and learnable, but also, above all, reducible to a coherent logical structural which, in an impressive manner, integrates the different modes of thinking, the different approaches to human 'realities'. Systemic-phenomenological and systemic-constructivist approaches need not be contradictory – we do now need to have the right membership book in order to belong.

Rather, against the background of these considerations, all the therapeutic approaches we find appear as *descriptions*, which afford a reduction in complexity. The author of this book has succeeded in providing a description that preserves this complexity while still formulating it in words in a way that for many readers – including myself – untangles contradictions and relieves tensions. Systemic and meticulous, while at the same time also readable, lively and exciting, this book introduces a complex world, a world in which solution oriented therapy based consistently on the concrete goals of the client combines with constellations work spanning many generations. Systemic-constructivist and systemic-phenomenological descriptions of human life contexts hold out their hands to one another in this book. What comes out of this type of 'marriage' can be judged by all those who have experience of the author – a proven master of her subject over many years in both fields – in action: a vast abundance of options, therapeutic possibilities suited to a wide range of situations in which people are looking for therapeutic help.

What do I expect of this book? I hope that after reading it the reader will find it easier to abstain from the ornamental use of names. If someone says they work according to the Insa Sparrer method, that person has not understood this book. (Equally, the book has not been understood if the sources used are not specified with the same care as is the case here.) It is all about using the perspectives, not so as to restrict, but to develop, in an inventively creative process, the only perspective we are able to develop: our own. One of my Gestalt Therapy teachers, Alfred Dürkop, used to say: 'It's always better to be an original – be it a small one, than a transfer picture, be it a large one!' I hope that the creative originality with which this book was written will help many readers to become a little bit more helpful, systemic and solution oriented in their work than before. That would be a good goal – and its realisation would be a 'miracle'.

Arist von Schlippe
First Chairman of the Systemic Association
Osnabrück, February 2001

Foreword

Ingenious. The Systemic Structural Constellation work developed by you and Matthias has helped me enormously to combine what I learnt from our common teacher Virginia Satir with what I find so fascinating in the work of Bert Hellinger. Attending your inspiring courses was a real pleasure and, after my long and more or less exclusive occupation with NLP, has brought me very close again to systems and their 'positioned' living metaphors. This alone was a great gift to me.

Your achievement in terms of integration, by extending constellations work to create Solution Focused Systemic Structural Constellations, increases the value of this gift beyond measure. Your impressive demonstrations of the solution geometric interview and other solution focused interventions and constellations, which I was able to witness first hand in your courses, showed me in the most pleasant way that there was again something critically new for me to learn. I worked through your book with relish and it has deepened the experience of amazement and miracles I gained from the practical experience of your work – and that's not something that can be taken for granted with the cognitive sorting and theoretical training of miracles.

I was therefore also very happy with your innovative and lively work, for, in the way you apply the De Shazer miracle question in the representative system, I see something wrapped up in systems that I had in mind for the development of the PeneTRANCE model for individual clients: namely, to hypnotise them through questioning into the state of goal achievement.

The idea of doing this with an entire system had not occurred to me. And doing this in the representative system I find simply ingenious. I am very grateful to you for this way of having initiated me into the miracle of the miracle question: I found your demonstration of its enormous effectiveness in the representative system thoroughly convincing.

Asking the miracle question in the representative system in a constellation was not a revelation to me simply because I found in it something that was important to me in NLP (as I practise it). It was also a revelation because with your miracle integration work you managed, through the third pole, the miracle pole, to reconcile further in me the poles of the systemic work of Satir and Hellinger. Had she been able to sit in on your demonstrations, Satir would have been overjoyed. (And if she, where she is now, is also practising Hellinger's work, this work will come all the easier to her after taking a look at Matthias' and your seminars.)

Your book also helped me a lot in following what I have seen you implement in your practical applications with such brilliance and ease. I wish your book many thoughtful readers – from the systemic world, the constellations world, and other worlds, including that of NLP. Many practitioners of NLP have a lot to gain from reading it – not only because they will be amazed by (perhaps for the first time) entering into the world of constellations. They will also benefit from the highly convincing way in which the effectiveness of the miracle question is demonstrated and aided by the classification of the constellations phenomena. Your clear action-based comments on the application of the miracle question in constellations will also help them to balance the widespread 'goal fetishism' of NLP: this book helps take us a good distance away from the delusion of feasibility – and towards a mindset in which we don't stand unnecessarily in the way of miracles.

Thies Stahl
Quickborn, January 2001

Foreword to the English edition

This is a book about **miracles**. When I speak of miracles I do so not in terms of content, but in terms of **structure**, i.e. in terms of the nature of the connection between content-related aspects. Over the years it has become increasingly clear to me that the notion of solution, as well as that of problem, cannot be understood in terms of content. A particular content, a specific situation, can be experienced either as a problem or as a solution. It is not the problem in itself that represents the problem. Rather the problem or solution arises through the manner in which we view or deal with the situation – just, for example, as we might perceive a glass to be either half-full or half empty.

Initially the miracle is to be understood in terms of the answer to the **miracle question** as used in the solution focused conversation:

Picture yourself this evening going to bed as usual and falling asleep ... Assuming a miracle occurs during this night, and the miracle would be that everything that you currently see as a problem, is solved ... just like that ... that would be the miracle ... and if it happens so fast that really would be a miracle! ... Now if no one tells you that the miracle has happened, how would you know? ... What would be different? ... What would you do differently? ... Would you think differently? ... Or would your sensations change? ...

This question cannot be answered without a partial experience of the solution. The question is therefore not a question in the normal sense of the word, but a trance induction into a particular state, the solution-state. While answers to miracle questions reflect content-related information, the miracle, through content, points towards a fundamental change:

A change in perspective

The miracle does not exist on the same level as the problem and the goal. A goal is often described as a kind of opposite to the problem, the relationship between problem and goal often being analogous to that between the negative and the print of a photo: one can be derived from the other.

This is not true of the miracle! The problem and the miracle exist independently of each other. Entirely new topics, for example, often occupy centre stage in the miracle. After the miracle occurs, it is not that *something* is different, but that *everything* is different: the world is perceived in a new way. 'The world of the happy man is different from that of the unhappy man,' as Wittgenstein said in his early work, the *Tractatus*. The miracle occurs first within us and then shines out into the world by giving us new impulses and actions.

A fundamental change takes place with the miracle that affects all areas of life. Put another way: the miracle is like a colourful bouquet of flowers that can be continually enriched by adding an extra flower; the flowers are like individual events unconnected by a chain of cause and effect. The miracle, therefore, helps us to break free from the world of causality, from captivity and bondage, and to enter into the world of the solution.

This book deals with solutions that carry in them this power of change, solutions:

- As a dissolution of problems
- As a release from attachments
- As a re-entry into the process of life.

Miracles, like solutions, remind us of our resources. The solution is always present as a possibility, but is nonetheless often overlooked.

Problems and goals are generally described in content-related terms, and understood as such. Miracles and solutions also encompass content, but this content is not essential to their make-up. Rather, they are more like by-products of the new perspective; the solution is revealed far more through the experience of the miracle. The interventions and procedures presented in this book are designed to facilitate such experiences. They remind us of something we already know but have forgotten.

Six years have passed since the publication of the German edition of 'Miracle, System and Solution' ('Wunder, Lösung und System'), and the different forms of the Solution Focused Systemic Structure Constellations I developed and described in this book have since been successfully implemented on many occasions. They have become a central and permanent component in the application of Systemic Structural Constellations (SySt®). **SySt**, which I developed together with Matthias Varga von Kibéd, are a group of different formats bound together by a common grammar.

The different formats allow the client's problem to be transformed into a spatial-pictorial representation, using people and symbols as representatives for systemic elements and allowing us to gain additional information from beyond the verbal discussion. Systems are thus simulated by positioning people in the room, and changes made to a system – by means of rearrangements, additions and rituals – can provide indications of possible steps towards a solution.

Readers of this book may well be unfamiliar with Systemic Structural Constellations (SySt). However, it is not required that the reader have any knowledge or experience of structural constellations and group simulation procedures, and those unfamiliar with this material will be welcomed into this subject area. The descriptions below of the different roots are primarily aimed at readers already familiar with group simulation procedures such as psychodrama, reconstruction and sculpture work or structural constellations. That said, those with no such experience will still benefit from reading this foreword, which provides an overview of the origins and different possibilities of SySt.

The *Solution Focused SySt* I developed form a subgroup of SySt representing the translation of the solution focused approach to the practice of systemic structural constellations. The constituent elements of solution focused constellations – for example, the *goal*, the *miracle* and *exceptions* – become elements of the SySt format. This gives rise to the *Solution Constellation*, the *Goal Approximation Constellation*, and the *Nine* and *Twelve Square Constellation*. We find the simultaneous use of verbal solution focused language and the *transverbal language of* SySt in the *Solution Geometric Interview*, as shown in a solution focused conversation with a group of representatives positioned in a constellation.

Solution Focused Systemic Structural Constellations (SfSySt) have seen a number of **further developments** over the years. For more details see the Postscript at the end of the book.

In SySt, Matthias Varga von Kibéd and I have both increasingly come to emphasise the aspect of language. We conceive SySt as a *transverbal language* that can be 'spoken' in the most diverse of fields and which provides additional information to verbal language, incorporating both knowledge in the form of the individual's bodily experience and that which exists between us.

We consider the following to be the **roots of SySt**:

- *Group simulation procedures*, i.e. procedures based around working with people arranged as symbols representing the elements in a client system. All of these procedures originate from Moreno's *Sociometry* and *Psychodrama*, where we encounter the idea of implementing role-play from the world of the theatre in a form of lay theatre designed for healing purposes. With the help of precise information, the client introduces a role-player to the role. The client watches the role-play as an observer. In doing so he or she experiences a form of externalisation: the client is able to observe his or her 'problem' from outside. After role adoption, new life concepts for the client can be put to the test with the help of role expansions (by the role-players or at the request of the client).

In the *Family Reconstruction* and *Sculpture Work* of Virginia Satir, Moreno's concepts are adopted, and highly detailed role-play is complemented and abridged using symbols and ritual. Satir also sees role-playing as central. Her goal is less a matter of new life concepts and more to do with a reconciliation within the family, gaining understanding and an ability to leave the past behind.

In Bert Hellinger's *Family Constellations*, the place of role-playing is taken by the representation of people etc. Role-players become representatives who symbolise people. Representatives express what they perceive, see, hear and think. They are given no role description and no longer act out a role. Hellinger speaks instead of the 'foreign feelings' perceived by the representatives.

In SySt we introduced the term *representative perception*. We interpret the different perceptions arising among representatives as a perception phenomenon and not as a translation of feelings as per Hellinger. Although we also speak of representatives, we only ask them about the changes in their bodily sensations in order to minimise interpretation. We ask about what is 'better', 'worse', 'the same' or 'different', in order to gain an indication of the direction in which things should proceed. This allows us to perform purely hidden work.

– The **solution focused approach** of the school of Steve de Shazer and Insoo Kim Berg, from which we adopted the following:
  - Difference-based work. For example, we ask representatives, about differences and not their absolute feelings.
  - Future-oriented work. Solution construction, rather than problem analysis, is our objective.
  - The inclusive and not knowing attitude. The 'leader' – we tend to say 'facilitator' or 'host' – of a SySt is an expert in methodology, while the client is adept at content. Working with a group of clients, the facilitator does not decide who is right or wrong; rather he or she adopts a multi-directional position vis-à-vis the entire group, highlights contradictions and consequences, takes no decisions. The search for guilt and innocence, right

and wrong, is replaced by the search for solutions appropriate to the entire group.

- The holding of a solution focused conversation before and after the structural constellation. In principle, SySt should always be cloaked in a therapeutic or counselling process.

- The **hypnotherapeutic approach of Milton Erickson**, from which we adopted the following:

  - The diligent approach to language: observation of word associations, the emotional and psychological effects of words and implicit statements

  - Different forms of pacing and leading

  - Different forms of reframing. For example, among representatives we distinguish those with intended reframing. These are representatives who, between the first and the final (solution) picture, pass through a process of transformation and become something else. *Obstacles*, for example, can become *protective walls*, and then, in the solution picture, *helpers*; a hidden benefit can first be transformed into *the price that must be paid for the solution* before finally becoming the *preciousness* . Another form of reframing occurs in the host's echoing, in which he or she changes unappreciative answers by the representatives so that they suggest possibilities for the desires that lay behind them or recontextualises them through the introduction of a given perspective – for example, 'From the perspective of X, Y is perceived to be so and so.'

  - The observation of the constellation event as a trance phenomenon. For example, this allows us to observe in the representatives of a SySt such things as age regression, changed time perception, amnesia, analgesia and perception changes such as sharper memories.

  - Different forms of utilisation. For example, the trance phenomena of the representatives are utilised to map systemic elements. The idea of symptoms as trance elements can be traced back to the hypnosystemic approach of Gunther Schmidt, whose systemic enhancements of Erickson's hypnotherapy played an important role in the development of SySt.

- The **systemic approach**. From our perspective, SySt should preferably be imbedded in the framework of systemic/solution focused therapy, counselling or mediation. We therefore also emphasise an initial context and case clarification and follow-up sessions to work with systemic/solution focused approaches.

- **The philosophy of Wittgenstein** as a philosophical background to SySt.

–   Charles Sander Peirce's **theory of signs**, George Spencer-Brown's **concept of distinction**, the **syllogistic square** of Aristotelian logic and the **idea of the negated tetralemma** from the work of Nagarjuna (the founder of Madhyamika Buddhism) as a basis for specific SySt formats.

'Miracle, Solution and System' makes many references to the **family constellations** of Bert Hellinger. However, the paths between his and our work have diverged increasingly. Structural constellations work was from the beginning clearly different to family constellations. For a while we hoped that, with the influence of Gunthard Weber, family constellations would take on a form that was compatible with a constructivist human and worldview – for Gunthard Weber is indeed one of the co-founders of the Helm Stierlin constructivist school. However, Hellinger's own work took an entirely different course to ours, and we did not share his basic concept: while we were working on a solution focused, constructivist, difference-based and low interpretation basis, Bert Hellinger was emphasising the aspect of the given, of reality as seen by him, of expert knowledge, and developed a content-based teaching about orders and dynamics.

Hellinger has increasingly moved away from the original family constellations. He now positions representatives himself and often works with trained representatives. This makes it harder for the observer to see that representation is a basic human ability, and that in principle anyone is able to access the knowledge that exists between us, not just well trained elite. In his 'Movements of the Soul' Bert Hellinger allows the representatives to move slowly and according to their own impulses, in order to reveal the dynamics rooted in the past. The focus of his work thus shifts to the past, dramatic art and entanglement.

SySt lead us in a different direction. Whenever possible we try to perform hidden work and pay close attention to differences in order to reduce the risk of interpreting. We leave the interpretation of the constellation events to the client.

We work through the client's case, while allowing the client to position the representatives him or herself, allowing the client's vision to 'flow' into the constellation. And, as opposed to Hellinger, we are very interested in scientific investigation and encourage this activity.

In the meantime, we are now working increasingly in other **fields**, as, for example, in the creative fields of film, music and text, as well as mediation and peace work. In the field of organisational counselling we have developed specific methods for the internal application of SySt. Frequent *representative exchange*, for example, goes a long way towards preventing subsequent counter-transference phenomena, while the *constellation without constellator* allows us to work with more than one focus at the same time. For those interested in these further developments I recommend my book 'Systemische Strukturaufstellungen: Theorie und Praxis' , which provides a detailed overview of the current status of SySt.

The most observant readers may notice that the original chapter XI concerning integration of the systemic-phenomenological and systemic-constructivist approach using details from the philosophy of Edmund Husserl has been omitted form this edition. It can still be found in the German edition.

Insa Sparrer
Munich, 27.4.2007

Acknowledgements

I would like thank my husband, Matthias Varga von Kibéd, who gave me the impetus to write this book, was a continuous source of motivation and inspiration, and read the manuscript with a view to stylistic improvements. Without the development of Systemic Structural Constellations in the first place, there would have been no Solution Focused Systemic Structural Constellations, and as such a significant contribution is also attributable to him.

My many thanks also to Thies Stahl, who gave me many valuable tips on the meta model of NLP.

Above all, I would like to thank the many clients and seminar participants without whose help this book could not have been written. In particular, I would like to thank those participants who helped with the revision of the descriptions of their constellations and gave their consent to the publication of their constellation sessions.

Many thanks also to Susanne Kessler and Katharina Wille, who read the manuscript and whose insightful questions and comments led to improvements.

Many thanks also to the clients who, due to my pre-occupation with this book over the last months, have had to do without me.

For the English edition, I would like to take the opportunity here to extend my sincere thanks to Petra Müller-Demary, who established contact with my translator, Samuel W. F. Onn, and further coordinated contact between translator and proofreader. I would further like to thank Samuel W. F. Onn, who translated this book in a highly independent manner and with remarkably little need of consultation, as well as Vivian Broughton, whose extensive editing and stylistic revision made possible the current form of the book, and Mark McKergow and Jenny Clarke at SolutionsBooks for their work on the format and the translation. I would also like to thank Miles Bailey and his team at Action Publishing Technology for their work in rendering this complicated text into print.

Insa Sparrer
Padua
18.7.2007

To put you in the mood:

Learn to be amazed again at everyday and surprising things

*Make the path to the goal easier through the **miracle** of sudden change*

*Look forward to **solutions**, even if this requires you to let go of this or that **problem** (to which you are attached)*

*Discover new contexts that can fundamentally change the current **system***

Chapter I

Introduction

This is a book about miracles. Miracles that are achievable. It is also about the capacity to be surprised by new things and open to solutions. The first part of this book looks at the way we find and devise solutions. How we confront these solutions, how we come into contact with and experience them, will be discussed in the following sections.

The term 'miracle' refers in this book to the miracle question method, one core element of the solution focused approach. In the 1970s, together with their team from the Milwaukee BFTC institute, Steve de Shazer and Insoo Kim Berg developed **Solution Focused Therapy** (hereafter referred to as SFT). SFT is characterised by its orientation towards solutions. This method focuses on future and resource orientation as well as action, as opposed to internal processes. It is a method of discussion in which the discussion leadership acts as hypnotherapeutic trance induction for the discovery of solutions. This means that while SFT takes place as a discussion, its aim is in fact to create experiences.

Surprisingly, this approach dispenses entirely with problem analysis, to such an extent that the therapist does not even need to know the problem. How is this possible? How can this type of procedure lead to long-term stable improvements? In this book I will answer these and other questions, showing among other things how, even when there is a constant focusing on the solution, the problem is not neglected and its usefulness is taken into account.

This book will combine the constellations method, which many of you will know from Bert Hellinger's **Family Constellations**, with the solution focused approach of the Milwaukee centre, based on Systemic Structural Constellations. Some twenty years ago Bert Hellinger developed his version of Family Constellations. His method typically places representatives of people from the family system in the room, so that the external picture of the spatial arrangement mirrors the internal picture of the client. The method focuses on this externalisation of an internal image, using representatives, and finding a solution image by means of rearrangement and ritual. The constellations method is primarily nonverbal. It focuses on the physical sensations and experiences of the representatives and the experience of verbal and nonverbal ritual.

Unlike solution focused procedures, the family constellations approach is problem oriented: it deals with problematic family events, such as death, divorce, family secrets, asks about excluded family members, examines the existence of 'identifications' and the transference of guilt, and checks if anyone is likely to follow another family member to their death.

All these questions suggest implicit assumptions, such as: 'Excluding members always has damaging effects on the system' instead of 'As a rule, where there are disturbances, it is worth keeping an eye open for the possibility of reversing an exclusion'. In this way, the procedure creates the impression that past burdens must be uncovered prior to a solution.

The **Systemic Structural Constellations** I developed with Matthias Varga von Kibéd after 1989 build on a range of group simulation procedures, including the Family Constellations of Bert Hellinger. Above all, it is to Hellinger that we owe our thanks for the original lean and sparse form of the constellation (which contain no gesticulations or props) and insights into forms of systemic principles.

On the other hand, Systemic Structural Constellations were also influenced by many of Virginia Satir's procedures: by her image of man and her therapeutic attitude, as well as the constructivist approaches, such as those of the Heidelberg School (H. Stierlin, G. Weber, G. Schmidt) in their theoretical approaches. Systemic Structural Constellations are a method of translating and extending the fundamental principles involved in understanding the family system to other systems, for example to conflict mediation, organisations, bodily systems, value systems, internal components, screenplays etc. They differ from Family Constellations in part in that they are built on a systemic grammar and can be effective simultaneously on different levels, they give primacy to process work and predominantly involve syntactic work in which it is possible to abstain largely from interpretations, which in turn makes 'hidden' work possible. Abstract systemic elements as well as *representatives*, *locations* and *free elements* can be brought into the constellation (described in detail in III.1.1.2.3). This extension also allows temporal and spatial aspects to be factored in.

The **Solution Focused Systemic Structural Constellations** presented in this book build on the grammar of Systemic Structural Constellations and integrate Solution Focused Therapy in the following different ways:

  – By an iterative application of SFT and Systemic Structural Constellations

- By introducing different elements to the constellation from SFT (SFT as a constellation)
- By means of a solution focused dialogue with the representatives (the constellation as a solution focused interview)

Constellations work (in some of its earlier versions) and solution focused brief therapy are two forms of systemic therapy that belong to two **opposing approaches**: the systemic-constructivist and the systemic-phenomenological approach. At first glance, these two forms appear to be irreconcilable, for the following reasons:

- Constellations work deals with earlier generations
- Solution focused brief therapy refrains from all problem analysis
- Constellations work is centred around dissolving entanglements and reconciliation with the past
- SFT is centred on the search for solutions
- In the constellations procedure systems are simulated using spatial arrangements and people, and the bodily experiences of the representatives are used in order to gain insight into the structural dynamics of the client system.
- The leader of a solution focused conversation withholds herself entirely and asks only solution focused questions

Solution Focused Systemic Structural Constellations represent my attempt to develop a constructive link between the two procedures. They integrate the **advantages of both methods** and thus forge a new whole in that:

- They make it possible to bring together continual and sudden change through the use of a timeline as, for example, in the goal approximation constellation and the nine and twelve square constellations. This therefore represents a method of trans-continual change. The experience of the solution in a constellation joins with the continual application of the solution process in everyday life.
- Through inclusion of the concept of loyalty, and despite the strin-gent solution focused procedure, they also manage to make room for reconciliation with the past.
- The twelve and nine square constellations facilitate dialogue with both internal and external systemic components, such as people, groups, fields etc.
- With the solution geometric interview it also becomes possible to identify and include other types of exclusion such as defocused

topics, neglected values, suppressed emotions and overlooked consequences. Solution Focused Systemic Structural Constellations not only allow participants to experience consistent feelings with respect to alien (other than their own) systems, they also provide linguistic access to new information about the represented (their own) system.

Solution Focused Systemic Structural Constellations represent a novel combination of conversation and constellation. They allow the aspects of reconciliation work and the dissolving of entanglements to be integrated into a solution focused approach without diminishing it. The constellations method thus becomes, through the integrative expansion of SFT, a more complete therapy and consultancy method in which conversation and constellation freely merge into one another.

   The focus on solutions in Solution Focused Systemic Structural Constellations helps:

- Improve from the start the atmosphere between systemic parts in a particular system and in the group.
- Overcome large differences in understanding between people present, as in conflict situations in smaller or larger systems (such as mediation processes in institutions, companies, political conflict situations), because our differences manifest in problems, while we resemble each other in solutions. A study by the Brief Family Therapy Center (BFTC) found that answers to the miracle question were the same in all cultures, while problems can be formulated in very different ways.
- Avoid re-traumatisation where clients have suffered severe trauma due to experiences in war, or of torture or rape.
- Formulate solutions more concretely. Working with a timeline is particularly helpful here as it represents a translation of the scaling work of SFT into constellations work.
- Establish a framework for the constellation that is protective and strengthening. The goal approximation, as well as the twelve and nine square constellation can, as *meta-constellations*, make resources accessible more quickly and thus strengthen the client *before* she has solved her problem.

The **integration of the constellation into the solution-focused discussion** allows:

- Absent people to be taken into account appropriately, whose perspectives then become clearer

- The client to adopt a meta-position vis-à-vis her present situation through the externalisation of the systemic structure in the constellation.
- The indirect benefits of the problem to become clear and consequently nurture a sense of meaning, which boosts the stability of the results (according to research by Grawe (1998) and other therapy disciplines).
- Entanglements to be dissolved improving the SFT process.
- Loyalty issues to be taken into consideration and steered towards a solution.
- Room to be made for work on reconciliation with the past.

This book is written both for advanced learners and those who are as yet unfamiliar with the two techniques. **Chapters II and III** provide an introduction to the methods that underlie **Solution Focused Systemic Structural Constellations** (SFT and Systemic Structural Constellations) for which no prior knowledge is required. Still, the constellations method, with its complexity and effects, is difficult to understand based on a written description alone. To gain a fuller understanding normally requires *experiencing* a constellation as an observer or, better still, as a representative. If you have already witnessed a family constellation, however, the description of Solution Focused Systemic Structural Constellations in this book will be clear and intelligible.

The latter section of the third chapter provides an overview of the types and scope of Systemic Structural Constellations. This is designed more as a reference section, to which you will be able to resort later on in the book to find out more about the systemic structural constellations mentioned in the text.

The presentation of SFT diverges significantly from the descriptions found in specialist literature, and those familiar with the field may discover new aspects in this section. The book provides many answers to questions the reader may not yet have asked but which crop up after many years of practising this method. The overview of Systemic Structural Constellations is very densely written and at some points expands on the description already given in *Ganz im Gegenteil* (Varga von Kibéd & Sparrer, not translated as yet).

It is helpful to have read the first two chapters before moving on to the following chapters, though should you skip these chapters, cross-referencing is provided at the appropriate places, allowing you to refer back for more information where necessary. 'Speed readers' will find some explanations repeated in individual chapters.

Chapters IV, X, and XI are theoretical chapters which can be treated as additional reading and are not required in understanding other chapters. They address the philosophical background to Solution Focused Systemic Structural Constellations and describe the differences, similarities and equivalents of SFT and Solution Focused Systemic Structural Constellations. The final chapter is intended as a practical extension to daily life.

Chapters V to IX present the different forms of Solution Focused Systemic Structural Constellations, each chapter containing a theoretical part followed by detailed case studies. The details of the case studies – names, locations, professions etc. – have been changed for confidentiality reasons. Unless otherwise specified, the constellations were performed by the author.

Masculine and feminine person designators are used throughout in an unsystematic manner so as to include both of the two groups of readers.

Italics and **bold type** have different functions. *Italics* are used for the following:

- *Specialist terminology* that is used differently from in everyday speech, such as *locations*, which we use to define a symbolic category but which otherwise describe localities in a country.
- *Names* of representatives, for example *mother* for the *representative* of the client's mother and not the mother herself. The same name is printed normally as soon as it refers to the actual person or thing being represented.
- For *emphasis*

Bold type, besides titles, is used for the first mention of **key terms or phrases**.

Chapter II

Brief Description of Solution Focused Therapy (SFT)

Describing what Solution Focused Therapy comprises is not easy. Steve de Shazer who, together with Insoo Kim Berg and his team, developed Solution Focused Therapy (SFT) at the Brief Family Therapy Center (BFTC) in Milwaukee, denotes this form of therapy with the word 'it'. He sees SFT as an unconventional form of therapy, for the following reasons:

- it is based only on a rudimentary personality concept.
- despite often being effective in resolving psychotherapeutic issues, the exploration of these is not the main goal of SFT.
- its aim is not to provide a cure, but to produce changes in a solution-state with the help of the 'miracle question' (described in detail in II.1.5.9.)
- the solution-focused method of questioning is non-specific, e.g. it makes no fundamental differentiation between different diagnoses.
- it is not based on a cause and effect model.

Knowing this, the reader may then well wonder what SFT actually is. This 'it' in Solution Focused Therapy is hard to describe positively; it is in fact easier to characterise in terms of difference from other processes that make use of changes in human behaviour.

In contrast to other forms of therapy, in SFT there is no fixed, circumscribed human image. Steve de Shazer does not speak of a process of healing or inner development, since there is no process that is oriented towards an *absolute* goal. The solution-focused process is entirely oriented towards the specific goals of the client. In this respect SFT takes place systemically – it does not assess the goals of the solution-focused process itself, rather it takes for granted that, in the end, the client will be aware of what is good for her. The client's 'knowing' appears through the hypnotically induced solution-state formed by the miracle question.

The therapist facilitates the client's search processes by posing questions that help the client find their own solution more easily. He thus can be seen as a facilitator who endeavours to become more and more superfluous to the client, as in the following Buddhist teaching that describes the relationship between teacher and pupil (from de Mello 1996):

A pupil asks a teacher to take him on as his pupil. The teacher answers: 'You are a pupil because your eyes are still closed. When the day comes that you open them you will see that you cannot learn anything from me or from others.' 'But why then does one require a teacher?' asks the pupil in amazement, to which the teacher replies: 'In order to recognise that you don't need him.'

SFT is therefore not a process in which the therapist chooses to move in a particular direction, but one that places complete trust in the client's capacity for self-healing and self-organisation as soon as a suitable context is established. Still, the therapist does act as a model for the client to the extent that she adopts a non-judgemental position towards the client and displays her trust, and this, as an approach towards the world, also helps the client in giving up fixed opinions. It is, however, not the goal for the client to imitate the therapist. This is well described by another Buddhist teaching (ibid.):

A teacher says to his pupil: 'If you take me as a role model you will damage yourself, for then you will refuse to see things for yourself.' After a pause, he adds: 'And you will also damage me, for in this way you refuse to see me as I am.'

This comes from the search for solutions, and is therefore in opposition to all the therapeutic procedures that prefer to search for the causes of symptomatic behaviour.

II.1 Different forms of solution

SFT does not ask the question 'why', which is replaced by asking, 'What exists instead of the problem?' – the purpose being to find and design solutions. Questions based on exceptions (see II.1.6) and elements of the miracle question (see II.1.5.9) help to recover solutions that already exist but have been forgotten. The solutions developed in SFT are not arbitrary; rather they are always embedded in the context of what is given by the client. I will speak more on this point later, when I discuss questions pertaining to the context of miracles (II.1.5.9).

II.1.1 A Change of Paradigm

The term homeostasis plays an important role in many forms of systemic therapy. It is assumed that systems try to maintain a condition of homeostasis, often at the expense of long-needed change and adaptation to the environment. An attempt is made to disturb this equilibrium in the status quo by using therapeutic methods in order that – after a period of subsequent chaos – a process of change is unavoidably induced.

With SFT however, it is assumed that things are constantly in motion and that nothing remains the same. The therapist does not try to disturb the existing situation, but rather she tries to draw out what the situation might offer in terms of useful behavioural traits and convenient moments. It is not a matter of disturbing the homeostatic condition, as in the Palo Alto School (Bateson, Beavin, Jackson, Watzlawick among others) or perhaps the Milan School (Boscolo, Checchin, Prata, Palazzoli); rather it is a matter of finding something positive in what seems negative. I call this process the search for solutions in the present. Similarly, solution-states are also looked for in the past – that is the conditions that surrounded any exceptions to the problem. Instead of hindering or reversing that which is unwanted or problematic, SFT focuses on all that is positive and useful in the situation, so that this can be perceived and proliferated.

SFT's main emphasis is on active solution building. Steve de Shazer and his team even went so far as to introduce this process without being aware of the client's problem. This approach is radical in terms of the stringency with which he channelled the focus towards a solution.

In my view, SFT comprises four parts:

- solutions in the present
- solutions in the past
- solutions in the future
- designing and prescribing tasks

This classification is somewhat different to that found elsewhere in the literature. I have chosen to use it because I think it brings a coherence to the wide diversity of SFT questions.

Steve de Shazer and his team created an exercise for clients who were on their waiting list. The therapist wanted the client to use the waiting time before the first session to achieve some positive change, and since the therapist knew nothing of the client, the exercise inevitably had no connection with the problem. This led to the development of the **first session formula task**, which sought to find the most detailed answers possible to the following questions:

'What things are you happy with at the moment?'
'What things can remain as they are and should not be changed by our working together?'

To their amazement, the BFTC team discovered that their clients were able to report clear improvements in their situation by the time of their first session. This led Steve de Shazer and his to team to conclude that the therapist does not even need to know the nature of the problem in order to help bring about change. Armed with this knowledge they began to focus entirely on building solutions, which effectively led to a change of paradigm in therapy terms: away from problem analysis and towards locating solutions.

From then on, the BFTC team began to look for other methods that focus on solutions – regardless of the nature of the problem in question – and no longer turned initially to problem analysis or cause identification.

At this point, the reader may well ask how it is possible that, with no prior knowledge, the problem can still be solved successfully and reliably. We are in fact so used to discovering the actual situation, analysing it and asking about its causes, that any approach that does not contain these elements can appear absurd. However, it is precisely this shift of focus – away from cause analysis towards solutions – that is surprising and effective in solution-focused processes.

I will now, as on many occasions later, make a philosophical remark about SFT in order to explain the context of solution-focused processes.

In the works of Ludwig Wittgenstein we find the philosophical background to SFT. For this reason I have chosen to quote from his two main works, *Tractatus Logico-Philosophicus* (Wittgenstein 1989b) and *Philosophical Investigations* (Wittgenstein 1989a). In the *Tractatus*, section 6.4321, we find:

'The facts all contribute only to setting the problem, not to its solution.'

Here Wittgenstein points out that problems and solutions are entirely different, and that one cannot be deduced from the other. This does not mean that problem and cause analysis will never be of help in finding solutions, it says only that problem and cause analysis is not a necessary condition for the discovery of solutions – though, naturally, those elements of problem analysis that are helpful in achieving change should also be taken into account in solution-focused processes.

II.1.2 How is the value of the problem-oriented approach incorporated into SFT?

When a problem in therapy is thoroughly analysed and investigated it causes a certain appraisal of the client to be expressed. Here the therapist is saying indirectly that

- she is devoting her time to the client
- she recognises the magnitude of the client's problem
- there is nothing wrong if the client has not yet solved her problem

An external trigger from a neutral perspective is often needed to help develop new ideas in the problem solving process. Being troubled by a problem remains a condition only as long as the person with the problem remains entangled with it.

This form of client appraisal in problem-oriented forms of therapy finds its equivalent in solution-focused processes in **stressing the magnitude of the problem**. If the therapist makes frequent references to the severity of the client's problem, the client begins to value this and is more inclined to act in a way that favours change; clients need their conversation partner to recognise their difficulties as a prerequisite for their willingness for change.

Change that happens too fast can be experienced by the client as a loss of face, as if they were themselves not capable of finding the solution on their own (the client believes the solution was easy to find because the change took place so quickly). The following Jewish story describes an affectionate way to help someone save face (Singer 1999, S. 145):

The Letter of Recommendation
A merchant addresses Rabbi Kestenmacher, a man known for his bonhomie, on the following matter. He had taken a young boy into his employ as a helper. In general the boy had conducted himself very well and had been loyal and honest, and he (the merchant) had been able to rely on him. However, he had learned that the boy had for some time taken to selling hundredweight sacks of bones behind his master's back and pocketing the money for himself. He had thus been forced to send the boy away. The boy however had requested a letter of recommendation and asked that the fraud not be mentioned lest he find no other position. What is a man to do in this situation without violating the truth? Rabbi Kestenmacher replies: 'You should write in the reference: "he was honest – to the bone".'

Some of a client's so-called 'resistance' merely indicates that this first step – appraisal of the problem – has been missed or insufficiently dealt with. Resistance at this stage shows that the therapist has overlooked something or has proceeded too quickly. Resistance, therefore, becomes a signal for the therapist during the process of interaction, or 'a communication on the part of the client to the therapist in order to reconfigure the therapeutic context', as the Ericksonian therapist Gunther Schmidt from Heidelberg puts it.

A problem orientation often has reconciliation as its goal – the reconciliation of the client with her biography for example. Many clients, for instance, find it difficult to put troublesome events behind them, and this leads to the focus falling not on the solution, but on the events involved, and gives rise to questions as to why the events happened. One way of making letting go easier is for the client to understand the perspectives of the other people involved, and thereby recognise that the impulses of the others were not altogether ill intentioned. With the help of this reframing, we are sometimes able to put past events behind us more easily bringing the matter to a close. In solution-focused processes, we turn immediately in the direction of solutions by asking:

'How would you recognise that … is no longer a problem for you?
'What would be different for you then?'

Here the therapist enquires about the circumstances in which the client would be able to leave the past behind, what evidence would exist for this, and what the client would notice that would demonstrate that this change of perspective – from problem to solution – had been possible; or how the client would recognise that they had achieved reconciliation with the past. Again, Wittgenstein has something to say on the matter in *Tractatus* (6.521):

'The solution of the problem of life is seen in the vanishing of the problem.'

Thus, the problem is to an extent done away with and in its place appears the solution. Here the solution is a new experience, another way of being. The solution appears, it is not made. Solutions are not created, but appear through the disappearance of the problem. We recognise solutions, but we are not able to describe them, we can only suggest.

A similar thing is true with the meaning of life: no sooner do we recognise it than the question of the meaning of life itself disappears; it is, however, difficult to describe what it comprises.

Seen in this light, the key question changes from 'How do I create a solution?' to 'How do I come into contact with a solution?' By asking what it is that alerts us to the appearance of the solution, we enter into contact with this other state of being; to an extent we become familiar with this other side of life and we ourselves change as a result; by 'coming into contact'. Thus, I prefer to speak of 'coming into contact with' rather than the creation of solutions.

We can also compare this 'coming into contact' with Buber's I-Thou relationship. Buber differentiates between an I-It relationship and an I-Thou relationship: the I-Thou relationship is characterised by 'entering into contact' with the other, while the I-It relationship is characterised by 'manipulating' the other. While questions relating to goals require the client to pursue an I-It relationship, she enters into an I-Thou relationship with the solution at the moment she experiences the solution by answering the miracle question (see II.1.5.9).

We can also see problems as obstacles in the stream of life from which we learn something by the process of overcoming them, and which only become currents in the stream of life at the moment they join the river and disappear into it. Steve de Shazer used the metaphor of a key that fits the lock of the gates to the castle. We know how to open the lock, but do not need to know what the key was made of, nor why this particular key fits the castle lock.

II.1.3 Therapeutic Attitude

SFT takes place as a conversation. The therapist asks questions but offers no content-related direction. The therapist is the specialist in the asking of questions, while the client is the specialist in the development of the content of the solutions. This requires the therapist to act with the utmost caution. Even when she thinks she knows what is best for the client, the therapist still needs to be confident that the client possesses all the resources required, even though they may not be immediately to hand. This becomes particularly difficult if the client expresses suicidal thoughts or admits to ideation of or actual behaviour that may endanger others. Indeed, it calls for a high level of trust in the client's resources if the therapist, at this point, is to move on to new topics and refrain from getting involved; rather he should be asking questions about the likely consequences of the client's behaviour.

Adopting a state of ignorance and a non-judgmental stance will help the therapist hold back her own opinions. By adopting a purely questioning mode and benevolently accepting all the client's answers, the therapist gives the client sufficient space without having to fear judgment. It is important that the therapist is able to listen properly to the client otherwise the therapist runs the risk of imposing her own view on the client, as the following story demonstrates (De Mello 1998, p.22):

'Well, haven't you changed Henry! You used always to be so tall, and now you seem so small to me. You used always to be so stout, and now you look so slim to me. You used always to be so pale, and now you are so brown. What is the matter with you, Henry?' And Henry says: 'My name is not Henry at all, my name is John.' – 'Oh, so you also changed your name!'

The therapist poses questions, but does not interrogate; the therapist leads the conversation with the help of questions, but does not manipulate since no particular answers are expected. In other words, the therapist allows the client to express herself freely, to say things that elsewhere would not be permissible; things they fear or that would be socially unacceptable. It is at this point in solution-focused brief therapy that forbidden topics are addressed, some of which may be mentioned for the first time. And it is precisely this that will be different from the client's previous experiences and will create the space for something new.

Since the therapist gives the client no contextual clues, the process of change has to start with the client. This strengthens the client's sense of autonomy and deters the development of dependency on the therapist. It is also important for the therapist never to be a step ahead of the client – she should always be one step behind – otherwise the client may feel forced to move in a direction determined by the therapist.

The therapist's questions should be presented as part of the appraisal in order that the client does not feel she is being interrogated or pressurised. The therapist can express the appraisal by expressing acceptance in the following ways:

'Yes.' (next question)
'Hmm.' (next question)
'(Nod)' (next question)

This lets the client feel they are appreciated, and not as if they are being 'treated' by a specialist.

The therapist verifies whether the client's answers are leading towards his goal by asking the client about the possible consequences of what they are proposing that they should do in the given situation.

This procedure is based on the hypothesis that 'unethical' proposals for action by the client will have negative consequences for the client himself, based on or caused by that action. That the therapist is acting well is seen in that the client remains loyal to himself and does not limit his possibilities. To an extent bad action holds within itself its own punishment, as Wittgenstein shows in the *Tractatus* (6.422), when he writes:

'… At least these consequences are not allowed to become events… There must indeed be some kind of ethical reward and punishment, but they must reside within the action itself.'

If the consequences are to be found within the action itself, it is likely that frequent 'unethical' acts will be damaging to the person in the long run. Consequently, when we learn to observe and understand the long-term consequences of our actions, we are taught what is good for us by them. Ultimately, these consequences not only show us what is good for us, they also show us what is good for us within our community, because egotistical behaviour has long-term negative effects on our relationships. It changes the stance we take towards the world, and changes for us the world as a whole. Even if others know nothing of our negative acts, they can still detect in our stance if we have changed. And so the punishment lies within the action itself.

Returning to the stream metaphor: negative acts correspond to the currents within the stream of life, and the long-term consequences of these acts correspond to the broader context in which the currents are found, that is, the stream of life itself.

Providing that the questions posed relate to a time sufficiently far ahead in the future, we can see whether the possibilities of the client are likely to increase or decrease (possibly due to negative consequences). Wittgenstein (*Tractatus* 6.43) says the following:

'If the good or bad exercise of the will does alter the world, it can alter only the limits of the world, not the facts – not what can be expressed by means of language.

'In short: the effect must be that it becomes an altogether different world. It must, so to speak, wax and wane as a whole. The world of the happy man is different from that of the unhappy man.'

The switch from problem-state to solution-state, to use Wittgenstein's expression, is a transition from the world of the unhappy person to the world of the happy person. The client does not change individual events, but changes his attitude towards the world. The client's world then becomes entirely different; not only has some-*thing* changed, change has also happened to the *whole*. Sometimes a small change in behaviour can lead to a change in attitude and consequently, a change in the client's own world. Of course this does not mean that all the client's problems will be solved, it only means that a door to solutions has been opened; moreover this does not give us permanent access to solutions, we must continually re-open the door that leads to them.

An important element of solution-focused procedures is the **multi-directional attitude** adopted by the therapist. The term **'multi-directional**, especially **multi-directional partiality'** comes from Ivan Boszormenyi-Nagy (1973), and is used to mean a position in which the therapist takes a firmly inclusive stance in relation to both the client and the client's loved ones, including other third parties involved, and so does not act in a partisan manner. The Milan school speaks here of the 'neutrality' of the therapist. However, this is somewhat misleading in that the therapist naturally has feelings and opinions; however, she should not act in accordance with them. As soon as the therapist adopts a particular behaviour out of her own opinions, or begins to take sides, the client loses the sense that he is being fully understood and seen. The client needs his position to be understood without any partisan attitudes by the other. This absence of partisanship calls for a high level of tolerance, absence of judgement and trust in the client's own resources by the therapist.

This attitude is the opposite of saying 'I know better' or 'He or she is right'. Thus, the therapist's practice of solution-focused discussion leadership is also an exercise in tolerance, absence of judgement and vigilance; it is not only the client who learns from this process, but to an extent so does the therapist.

The client learns that:
  – she can receive complete attention
  – her problems are understood
  – hope exists
  – solutions already exist
  – the therapist trusts her – she herself is trustworthy
  – her time will be used to achieve change
  – she is allowed to take decisions
  – she is entrusted with finding a solution
  – knowledge resides with the client

The therapist learns:
  – not to direct the process of change according to her own wishes
  – to abstain from judgment
  – to put her own opinions last
  – to tolerate difference
  – to trust the client to find solutions
  – to trust in the possibility of a solution
  – about another's life

The solution-focused conversation is a reciprocal learning process for both the client and the therapist. As the therapist listens to the client and accepts what she says without judgement, something new is learnt by both parties: the client discovers that she has something to say, while the therapist gains knowledge of a possibly unfamiliar world. Both experiences together produce something that is new and greater than the sum of the parts. We are dealing here with a kind of tetralemma that combines the view of the client with that of the therapist to create a new 'both' form (for more on the tetralemma, see III.1.1.2.3). It is within this process of interaction that solutions arise; the implementation and the process of change start with the client.

When I speak here of 'solutions' I am not referring to what goes into determining a 'solution'. 'Solution' here means more than that something is solved. The experience of mourning or the acknowledgement or assumption of personal responsibility can be a solution. Even if this is uncomfortable, it is often described by the client as 'better'.

Steve de Shazer stated that 'We can understand what *better* means without knowing what *good* means', indicating that we do not actually need to be able to describe what it *is* that needs to be achieved; instead it is sufficient to be able to see when the situation has improved. This also means that therapists do not need to know the details of their clients' goal, it is sufficient for the clients themselves to know the direction things should move in and be able to recognise when things are improving.

Solutions include not only convenient, pleasing and happy conditions, but also difficult situations that breathe life back into a stagnating process. In this situation, the therapist should exercise a certain amount of neutrality towards what goes into devising a solution. The following teaching makes this clear (de Mello 1996, p. 27):

Spiritual relief
A master once taught that no words in themselves were bad, so long as they were used in the right context. On being told that one of his pupils had a foul tongue he said: 'Profanities are sometimes known to provide a form of spiritual relief where prayer fails in the task.'

The *multi-directional* attitude is clearly not a matter of technique, but an inner attitude and approach towards life. The individual solution-focused questions that I will highlight in the following section are always to be understood in this way and failure to do so will lead to reduced effectiveness.

II.1.3.1 Experiments 1 and 2
Experiment 1
The following should be tried at the next available opportunity:

When you next have an argument, conflict or difference of opinion with your partner (or someone else), and are convinced that it is he or she who is in the wrong, adopt an exaggerated *multi-directional* approach towards him or her. Behave towards them as if you find their arguments and position convincing and try to see the issue from their perspective. Then adopt a position from which you can represent both your side and their side of the argument. Observe whether the argument is any different when you adopt both sides in this way.

In doing this you are to an extent rehearsing the constellations method, which will be discussed in detail in the next chapter. It is only possible to adopt an *multi-directional* attitude if we are able to place ourselves in the position of the other party; however to do this we have to try to understand the other party's position, which is precisely what happens in the constellations process. Solution-focused processes are in part a 'constellation of thoughts', and it can be seen here how closely these two methods are linked.

Experiment 2

The next time you are left with the impression that your partner has done something wrong, you should act as if you believe he or she possesses all the skills needed to solve the problem themselves. Support them with questions, but give no advice. Finally observe what difference this approach makes in comparison with previous similar situations.

II.1.4 Solutions in the present

The SFT process is usually split into questions that relate to the goal, questions that relate to exceptions to the problem, and the miracle question. It involves a solution-focused process for which there exist different forms of solution. I have therefore differentiated between different types of solution in this form of therapy, which can be identified with the help of a specific questioning technique:

1. Solutions to which we already have access in the present
2. Solutions that we have already experienced in the past
3. Solutions which will become possible for us in the future

The solution-focused interview can thus be arranged into three groups of questions:

1. What is the client happy with? What would she change?
2. When did solutions already exist?
3. What tells the client that the solution has already occurred?

Steve de Shazer usually began the first interview with one of the following questions:

'What do you do during the day?'

Or

'What do you do for a living?'

Clients normally answer such questions by listing their abilities – that is they say what they do during the day, usually including activities they find easy to perform and are in control of. These introductory questions initially aim to discover something about the context of the client's life and then to find out about the client's current resources. These can also be seen as 'solutions in the present'.

We can also gain access to solutions in the present by means of the **first session formula task**. As already mentioned above, the *first session formula task* can be set as early as the initial registration by the client – for example, where there is a long waiting time before the first meeting – in order that the client can start doing something useful for himself before the therapy begins. By asking the questions 'What things are good in my current situation?' and 'What should definitely remain as it is?' the exercise focuses attention on all current positive events, relationships with other people, situations and objects. This expands the possibilities for the client, since positive things are generally suppressed in problem situations. However, what has been suppressed now re-surfaces through this exercise and can influence the client, in the form of solutions that were previously inaccessible.

We often experience a situation as a problem because we no longer see, or perhaps have forgotten, how many positive things currently exist in our lives; so the *first session formula task* acts as a reminder of current resources.

It may seem at this point that SFT provides a schema for the therapist's behaviour. Indeed Steve de Shazer initially thought of simulating solution-focused processes using computer-controlled analysis techniques; in effect replacing the therapist with a computer! However, he later gave up on this idea. The schema described in this chapter should not be understood as a mechanical process; it does not dictate what the next step in the therapy would be. From an observational perspective the process can be viewed as a schema; however during the therapy it is the process of interaction between therapist and client that determines what happens next. The described process should be understood as a description, not a prescription.

II.1.4.1 Experiment 3
First answer the following questions:
- What good relationships and professional opportunities do you currently have?
- What makes you happy?
- What do you have that helps you?
- What do you do to have fun?

Make any notes on these questions here:

....
....
....

Observe any change in your experience after doing this exercise.

II.1.5 Solutions in the future
This section will deal with future solution-states: for example, achieving the goal and discovering that the problem has disappeared. First we will look at goal clarification.

II.1.5.1 Clarifying the goal
The goal can be clarified by asking the client what it is that they would like to achieve and by the posing of the miracle question. In solution-focused approaches the therapist can only work with the **client's goal**, not with those of the referral agent or the client's loved ones. The client can only speak for his own goal. The goals of referral agents and loved ones must, however, still be taken into account in order for SFT to bring about a reliable result. When referral agents – for example parents or the courts – pay for the session themselves, they are usually particularly keen that their goals feature as part of the results of the therapy. Misunderstandings in terms of goals are most common when, for example, clients are sent by a youth welfare office, psychiatrists or loved ones. *Multi-directional* behaviour by the therapist is important here to prevent him from taking sides, while including the perspective of all. The following questions can be helpful in discovering the client's goal:

'What is your concern?'
'What brings you here?'
'What would you like to change?'

The answers to these questions most often will focus on what would be *absent* if the solution existed, for example:

'I would no longer feel pain.'
'The fear would be gone.'
'My husband would no longer ...'
'I would no longer drink.'

These types of answers need further scrutiny, since one cannot conclude from them what has replaced the now absent problem. For example when fear has disappeared there may be a feeling of relaxation, elation or activity in its place. This is not something fixed, however, and may vary according to the perspective adopted. The false assumption that the opposite of a problem-state is something that is fixed reinforces the hypnotic problem-oriented perspective. By stressing the absence of something this absence, and not the desired solution, will become the focus of the client's perception. At this stage the following question can be helpful in encouraging the client to **formulate** her goal more **positively**:

'What is there instead?'

Some clients find it hard to answer this question. In such cases, the therapist remains silent and waits. Offering help too early can quash the client's own initiative and send the answers in an inappropriate direction.

Hastily and frequently given advice makes clients more passive, receptive and dependent. Long **silent pauses**, however, pass responsibility for continuing the conversation back to the client, thereby maintaining a situation in which the client is more active and more quickly becomes independent of the therapist.

After each clear pause in speech the turn of the next conversation partner begins, being indicated through the silence; the client understands that it is his turn to talk. Silent pauses are thus a highly effective part of the solution-focused process.

II.1.5.2 Small digression on silence

There are many types of silence: silences that distance; silences that bring together; silences that burden; and silences that allow a person to come to themselves. This last form is described well by Michael Ende in his book *Momo* (1973, p.15 f.):

'What little Momo could do that no other could do was listen. That's nothing special, some readers might say, everyone can listen. But there you are mistaken. There are only a few people who can really listen. And the way Momo knew to listen was something altogether unheard of.

Momo was able to listen in such a way that simple people would suddenly come upon bright ideas. And not because she said or asked something that led them to have such thoughts; no, she just sat there and listened, giving her complete attention and empathy. At the same time she would behold the other person with her big, dark eyes, who would then feel the thoughts suddenly surface within him, thoughts he never knew were there. She could listen in such a way that helpless or undecided people immediately knew precisely what it was they wanted, the shy suddenly felt free and courageous, the unhappy or gloomy optimistic and cheerful. And when someone said their life was an outright failure and meaningless and that he was but one among millions, on whom nothing whatsoever depended, who could be replaced as fast as one replaces a broken pot –when he went to tell all of this to little Momo, it became clear to him, by some mysterious means, that he had been wholly mistaken and that among all the people in the world there was only one person like him, just as he was, and therefore in his own unique way he was important for the world.

That's how well Momo could listen!'

In solution-focused procedures it is important to be silent in a way that the client will feel he is not alone, that the therapist gives her full attention and accompanies the client's thought processes in a nonverbal way. The amount of time that needs to pass for the silence to be taken as a cue is 3.6 seconds in America, 4.5 seconds in Germany and 17.8 seconds in Norway according to an oral statement by Steve de Shazer at a seminar we hosted at SySt. For Steve de Shazer silences represented an important component of his consultations, since silences force the client back on himself and enable him to find the next step on his own.

An entirely different dimension of silence is demonstrated in the statement given by a master, as quoted by Anthony de Mello in his collection of stories *Zeiten des Glücks* (1994, p. 156):

Silence
Said the master:
'While you were still in the womb, you were silent.
Then you were born and began to speak, speak, speak –
until the day comes you are laid in your grave.
Then you will be still again.
Capture this silence that existed in the womb and will exist in the grave and even creeps in to this interval of noise that is called life.
This silence is your deepest being.'

Using silence in the right way can be something or an art, and mastering that art may not come naturally, as is also true of the art of telling a joke. For example, a famous Jewish joke goes as follows:

Two old friends are sitting in a compartment and telling jokes. Since they have known each other a long time, each time instead of telling the whole joke, they started to use numbers to represent the jokes. A traveller enters their compartment and hears the pair calling out numbers and laughing heartily on each occasion. Not wishing to be left out, the traveller calls out a number of his own. This, however, is met by silence, and no-one laughs. The traveller asks why they haven't laughed at his number – to which he gets the answer: 'It's the way you tell it!'

II.1.5.3 Clear and realistic goals
It is important that the client formulates his goals realistically and clearly. Should this not occur, the therapist may ask:

'On a scale of 0 to 10, where 0 means "would never happen" and 10 means "would definitely happen", how realistic would you rate this goal?'

Clients nearly always answer this question realistically. If the answer does not seem realistic, however, the following can be added:

'Oh, really?'

The therapist can then ask what is different after the goal has been achieved:

'Assuming you have achieved your goal, what is then different for you?'

In this way, the therapist learns more about the client's goal and what he would like to happen if the utopian goal were achieved, and allows us to gather information as to what end is this goal is a means to. Goals arrived at in this way can say more about what the client actually wants than do answers to direct questions about the goal. In this way we can learn about the client's underlying goal.

Complex goal descriptions should be split up into **smaller steps** so that the client can verify more quickly when he is approaching his goal. It is an important part of the therapeutic learning process that the client receives this kind of fast and regular feedback. This is comparable to a biofeedback process, in which people learn to use the feedback from their own bodily systems to improve their health.

II.1.5.4 Multi-directional attitude of the therapist despite the client's 'unethical' goals

The following somewhat dramatic case helps clarify what can be achieved by adopting a neutral attitude and simply asking about the likely consequences in cases where the initial goal statement is not ethically or morally acceptable, to the therapist.

One of my clients, who lives in a temporary shelter for the homeless, came to the session one day in an angry mood and told me of her wish to hire a hit man to kill an alcoholic who had been constantly harassing her, despite her having called the police on many occasions. Knowing this client had strong connections to the underworld I was at first frightened but tried to remain calm, and asked the client what would be different if she were to go through with her plan. The client described to me how she would finally have some peace, how she would be able to sleep again and how she would be able to leave her apartment without fear. With further questioning about the change that would occur, the client explained that she would have to take precautions so as not to be found out, and that she would have to live with the fear of being held responsible by the police.

Again I asked what would be different if the murder were to take place. The client began to name the professional goals and further education she would like to pursue afterwards. I asked some more specific questions related to this.

The initial fury and aggressiveness of the client disappeared and the idea of murder did not come up again in this or any subsequent sessions. Somehow following this session the client started to deal better with her housing situation and became more active in terms of changing her professional situation.

In this session, my client acted as my teacher; from the way she reacted to my questions I learnt more than I did in many other sessions. It became clear to me that even in the most aggressive cases, the underlying goal – the real wish – of the client can be something positive. I experienced just how worthwhile it is to refrain from passing judgment and to continue asking questions, even in cases in which the stated goal was ethically unacceptable to me.

Sometimes the choice of method can be wrong; however this does not mean that the actual goal is in itself unethical. If we continue to ask questions for long enough the real goal underlying the initially stated goal will show itself, and this more often than not will be life-affirming. It is a mistake to assume that the initially stated goals are causally linked with those that appear later; in fact they usually having nothing to do with each other and such connections are therefore not usually worth pursuing. By dealing directly with the underlying goal however, we can in most instances dispense with the means employed in reaching the initially stated goal.

On this issue, Wittgenstein has the following to say, in the *Tractatus* (5.1361):

'Belief in the causal nexus is *superstition*.'

Cause-and-effect thinking assumes the existence of a linear causal chain. In this type of chain, however, the cause of the last link in the chain cannot be clearly determined: do we take the first event as the cause, the last event before the situation occurred, or one of the events in between?

The following story may serve to highlight the difficulty of determining causes:

A Sufi teacher and his pupil walk past a gallows, and the teacher ask his pupil: 'What was the cause for which this man was hanged? Was it his carelessness that led to his capture? Was it the decision of the court, without which it would not have been possible to hang him? Did it happen because he was a bad man? Or was it because the murder was discovered and the relatives had called for revenge?'

This shows that, even in cases when the casual chain is known, establishing cause is still an arbitrary decision. Thus, according to Wittgenstein, thinking in terms of cause and effect is in fact a form of superstition.

Causal thinking often makes us narrow and rigid, since the future appears to be partially determined by the present and we may overlook many possibilities because we act on the basis of past causal chains.

An effective method used in therapy, therefore, is that of pattern disruption: the breaking up of causal chains previously thought – subjectively – to be mandatory. By changing a sequence, the whole pattern changes: small changes can give rise to much larger changes. This means that SFT, as a systemic process, operates on the basis of **circular causation** in that effects can recur retroactively upon the initial stimuli , ie cause and effect determine each other.

This is even true in cases where a healing effect is present: the healing effect does not indicate the cause, for example: a headache is not caused by a lack of aspirin.

II.1.5.5 Using scales as a way of dealing with the impossibility of understanding others precisely

Even where the therapist believes she knows the client's goal, it is again important to make sure the goal has been **clearly formulated**. When a client formulates her goal it is helpful to check if the goal has been understood correctly – for example, if the goal is stated as being a state of 'contentment', the same word can mean different things to different people. Steve de Shazer spoke of the need to create useful misunderstandings based on the fact that the individual use of language differs so widely that 'correct understanding' becomes highly problematic. Here he draws on Wittgenstein's theory of language games. Wittgenstein said (*Philosophical Investigations 43*):

'For a *large* class of cases – though not all – in which we employ the word "meaning" it can be defined thus: the meaning of a word is its use in the language.'

And

'Let yourself be *taught* the meaning through use.'

Given that the meaning of words is first generated through their use, it is then somewhat unlikely that the same word will mean precisely the same thing to two different people. With this in mind it is often better to ask more rather than fewer questions. A statement by the client should be understood in the context of the client's day-to-day use of words. Goal formulation has thus been interpreted properly when the client gives an indication (possibly a nonverbal cue) that her goal is clear.

The purpose of the interview is for the client to develop a clear and detailed image of what her goal is – this is necessary so that the therapist can recognise when this goal has been achieved (although the therapist need not know the details of the goal).

In order to be able to recognise progress while moving towards the goal, the therapist should establish a number of smaller, measurable steps (with larger goals, for example that of seeking a partner, the client finds it hard to recognise small improvements).

The **use of scales** helps in the detection of partial goals. For example the therapist can ask the client the following questions:

'On a scale of 0 to 10, where 10 means "Your goal is fully achieved" and 0 means the opposite, where would you place yourself now?'
'What was it that helped you get from 0 to n?'
'How would you recognise that you had advanced from n to n +1?'
(In place of n write the client's current position on the scale)

Scales have the advantage of being pragmatically specific: the subject-matter of the goal is not specified but allowed to remain vague. The use of scaling questions means the client is urged to become more specific, while the therapist is able to keep the subject open. In this way precision in stating the subject matter by the client is attained through a simultaneous contextual vagueness on the part of the therapist.

Scaling questions are a means of communicating something without needing to know the precise details of the matter at hand. As previously mentioned, at a SySt seminar in Munich on the use of scaling questions, Steve de Shazer said: 'We can understand what "better" means without knowing what "good" means.'

To understand language means **understanding change**, not absolute values. This allows us to understand something about relevant differences which, if formulated directly, would remain incomprehensible. (Differentiation as a basic principle can be found in the work of Gregory Bateson and also later in the work of George Spencer Brown.)

Similarly our sensations are also the product of differences. For example we possess no absolute ability to perceive 'warm' from 'cold' other than as difference. If we hold one hand in cold water and the other hand in hot water, and then afterwards hold both hands in a tub of warm water, we perceive a different water temperature in both hands, despite their being placed in the same vessel. What happens is that each hand measures the *difference* in temperature and not the *absolute* temperature of the water. It is precisely this fact of perceived difference that scales employ and they are thus particularly suited as a way of reaching agreement.

Asking questions involving relevant difference can make agreement possible without the need for the conversation partners to know precisely what the other understands by his formulation. Scales may also be of help in determining progress made during the course of therapy, as illustrated by the following example:

One of my clients began her first three therapy sessions each time by listing all the things with which she was not yet satisfied. This left me with the impression that for her nothing had changed since the first session, and I began to doubt whether our conversations were of any use to her. When I asked her to say where she saw herself today on a scale of 0 to 10, she answered '6' much to my great surprise. In answer to my follow-up question – 'What indicates to you that you are a "6"?' – she provided me with a list of improvements. Her habit of starting all the previous sessions by listing all the things she was not yet satisfied with had left me with an entirely false impression.

When a client gives a value on a scale from 0 to 10 we should not, however, assume we know what she means by it. The following example, taken from a seminar with Steve de Shazer in which he performed live interviews, makes this point.

One of my clients answered de Shazer's question as to where he would place himself on a scale of 0 to 10 – where 0 meant 'the point when he was asking for therapy on the phone' and 10 meant 'the miracle' – by saying he was a 2. I was surprised that he gave such a low number. Steve then asked the client: 'How do you see the difference between 0 and 1?' The client answered: 'Well, the step from 0 to 1 is the largest.' De Shazer then asked: 'What is the difference between 1 and 2?' To which the client replied: '2 is twice as large as 1.'

The client was not wrong: the step from 0 to 1 is in effect the largest, in that it is the step from problem-state to the beginning of the solution-state, and the step from 0 to 2 is twice that of 0 to 1.

In most cases, the client's scale is not used in this way. Normally 1 is understood to mean 'one small step' and 2 'still at the beginning'. What we recognise here is that 2 is further along the scale than 1 regardless of whether we use the first or the second sense of the scale. As soon as we focus on differences however, the absolutes of the scale become secondary .

It is often not a good idea to use 0 for the worst situation as this can cause the scale to be taken for an absolute scale. By taking 0 to mean the moment it was decided to start therapy on the other hand, we emphasise the fact that differences are going to be measured.

Given the impossibility of knowing one another exactly, teaching in many traditions has been – and still is – performed through story telling. A story provides a context for the information it is supposed to communicate, as well as for what it can communicate, often through its many layers. A story provides an extract from life and as such, approaches the whole more than isolated bits of information. This is illustrated in the following oriental teaching:

A master taught his pupils though stories and allegories. Some listened enthu-
siastically while others were unhappy for they considered the stories trivial
and longed for something deeper. Their pleas for wise words and secrets
however were rejected by the master time and time again. 'You should understand that the shortest path from a man to the truth is a story,' he said. After a
pause he added: 'Just as a lost coin can be found with a small candle, so the
deepest truth can reveal itself to you through a simple story.'

II.1.5.6 Transition from the semantic to the syntactic procedure

The switch from absolute values to scaled values is also a **change from
the semantic to the syntactic procedure**. Questions relating to compre-
hension of the current situation are replaced by questions probing
relevant differences. We ask 'What is better?' and not 'What does this
situation mean for you?' Our questions are thus **process-oriented**. In
asking about differences we facilitate a process and do not enquire
about a condition. This, of course, also supports the occurrence of
change; questions about conditions – how and why something is the
way it is – serve only to stabilise and preserve those states, whereas
questions about difference promote movement and change. The world
is in a permanent state of flux and as such categories that express
change fit better with the idea of 'describing' the world than do categories that express states which are more fixed.

II.1.5.7 Behaviour-related goal formulation

Finally I would like to point out that it is useful for the client to describe
her goal in **behavioural terms**, since the more types of behaviour the
client mentions, the more prepared she will be to act in a way that will
help achieve her goal. Changes in behaviour in the form of goal statements from the therapist and the client also help to create an observable
yardstick for both the client and the therapist. It is then easier to devise
an exercise at the end of the session that helps the client implement the
behaviour patterns listed in the miracle (see II.1.5.9). The more often the
client names behaviour that she exhibits when her problem is solved,
the more options she has to achieve her goal.

  When we have a problem we often feel like victims, however as it
becomes clear to us that we can contribute to the achievement of our
goal, we feel less helpless and consequently more optimistic. The shift
from the problem state to the solution is often a change from being a
victim to being proactive.

II.1.5.8 Experiment 4

Think of a problem in which you would like to change something, and ask yourself the following questions, in each case using the lines below to make notes:

'How would you recognise that your problem had been solved?'

....
....
....

'What would be there instead of the problem?'

....
....
....

'How would you recognise this?'

....
....
....

'What would you then do that you would not normally do?'

....
....
....

'What else would be different?'

....
....
....

'On a scale of 0 to 10, where 10 represents your goal and 0 represents your position before you began this exercise, where would you place yourself now?'

....
....
....

'What changed from when you were 0?'

....

....

....

II.1.5.9 When a miracle occurs

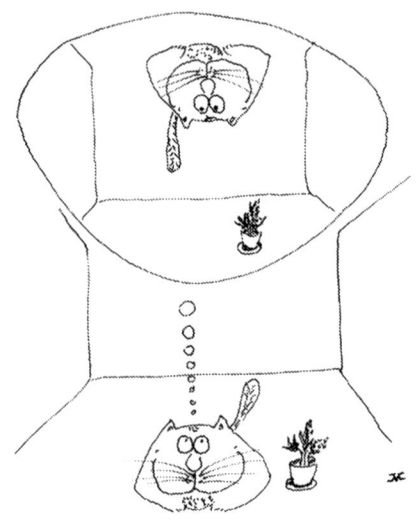

There are many types of miracles (after Fiddy 1990)

... but what we mean here are possible miracles! (after Fiddy 1990)

The conventional way of approaching a desired change involves clarifying the nature of the current goal. This clarification of the goal can provide an image of a solution in the future. However it takes place entirely from the perspective of the problem-state: as the client thinks about what her goal is, she comes closer to her goal through her thoughts, but still experiences the problem-state. The **miracle question** represents a completely different way to approach solutions in the future.

The miracle question lies at the core of SFT, and by answering it the client reveals what it is that she really desires – or more precisely, how her life will change when the solution takes place. In contrast to goal clarification this does not result in a fixed goal, but instead provides an insight into the client's 'form of life' ('form of life' is understood here in the sense of late Wittgenstein – the habitual activities and responses which form the background to any use of language). This question thus reaches much further: answering the question pinpoints the consequences, relationship effects and interdependence which usher in a change on the way to the solution. We will also discover something about the price the client will have to pay if she relinquishes her problem-state – in other words we discover the benefit of the problem remaining unsolved. This 'benefit' is mostly unrecognised at first, but taking it into consideration can contribute significantly to the client's ability to sustain the solution. It often takes the form of a habitual way of doing something, the advantage of which is that it doesn't require much energy to do, whereas a new and unfamiliar behaviour would.

The miracle question represents a hypnotic induction of a solution-state from within which the question can be answered. As long as the client remains in the problem-state she will be unable to answer the miracle question. This also means that the therapist will only know *a posteriori* if she has posed the miracle question, for it is only when the client experiences a subsequent solution-state that the miracle question can be said to have really been asked. Asking the miracle question thus obviously involves interaction between the therapist and the client.

The experiments performed at the BFTC involved a comparison of the effectiveness of asking the miracle question orally as opposed to in writing. It was found that the written form was significantly less effective than the oral version. This result among many others, supports the idea that the act of asking the miracle question is not a technique. The miracle question must be adapted to the context in which it is asked and articulated in a truly interactive manner. To this end, after the subsequent written formulation of the miracle question, I also give some indications as to what should be included in the formulations.

It should be noted that *formulating* the miracle question is a different process than *asking* the miracle question. The therapist recognises that she has properly asked the miracle question only when the client experiences the miracle – that is when the client is able to perceive, in the present, future experiences related to a time after the disappearance of the problem.

If the client is still in the problem-state after the *formulation* of the miracle question, the therapist has not yet really *asked* the miracle question. This difference was referred to by Steve de Shazer in his lecture to the 1998 conference in Heidelberg, *Ways of World Making*.

The miracle question thus leads to an experience in which we become certain that a solution is possible. Having therefore gained this certainty, the first step towards taking action can then follow. As Steve de Shazer said: 'Doing is knowing.'

One of the countless ways of formulating the miracle question is shown in the following example.

'I will now ask you what is, perhaps, a somewhat unusual and also difficult question. You will need to use a certain amount of imagination to answer it. Suppose you go home after this session ... and you talk to your family, eat your evening meal and maybe do something else ... and then at some point you become tired and go to bed ... and at a certain moment ... you fall asleep ... and ... suppose that during the night a miracle happens ... and the miracle would be ... that all the problems that brought you here today are solved ... at one fell swoop ... just like that ... and that really would be a miracle, wouldn't it? ... and you wake up early the next morning ... and no one you that this miracle has happened ... how would you know that this miracle had occurred?'

The pauses used in this question, denoted by '...' are important, since without them there is no guarantee that the client can follow the question in her thoughts and bodily experience and so be directed towards the miracle-state. Asking the miracle question is done in different stages, each of which represents a fundamental component in the induction of the 'miracle trance'.

We can use the following introductory words:

'I will now ask you what is perhaps a somewhat unusual, and also difficult question. You will need to use a certain amount of imagination to answer it ...'

This anticipates the client's commonly cited objection that the question is too difficult to answer or that they are incapable of answering it. If this objection is still raised, the therapist can then fall back on what she in fact said at the start – namely:

'Yes, exactly. That really is a difficult question.'

The following part places the question within the context of the client's every-day experience:

'Suppose you go home after this session ... and you talk to your family, eat your evening meal and maybe do something else ...'

This insertion of the question into the every-day life of the client is important in ensuring that the client does not propose something that is completely unrealistic for the miracle situation, but rather connects with her every-day life while answering the question.

The miracle is then introduced by saying:

'... and then at some point you become tired and go to bed ...'

The use of the word 'suppose' in the subsequent part indicates an imaginary, surprising moment, and as such leads smoothly on to the word 'miracle':

'... suppose ... during the night ... a miracle happens ...'

The client's curiosity about the miracle has now been awakened and the following pause encourages the client's search process, which is now beginning to set in. Only after this does the therapist continue, by explaining the miracle:

'... and the miracle would be ... that all the problems that brought you here today ... are solved ... suddenly ... just like that ...'

This final pause should be made to last a little longer, because the client at this moment needs some time to imagine how it would be if all the problems she has brought with her had been solved. In doing this it is important to use the formulation 'all the problems that brought you here today', because this allows the problem to be isolated, but also without specifying it too much – if the client's problems were to be spoken about too precisely at this point, the subsequent miracle would only correspond to this specific situation and not the client's general situation, which is far more encompassing. However, if we say that *all* the problems have been solved, without the specification that they are the problems that brought her here today, the miracle becomes unrealistic. New problems in life are constantly appearing. Seen as a solution that can encompass all problems, therapy then becomes a life-long programme – in effect, a kind of permanent therapy. But this is not the task of therapy, and for this reason it is important to isolate the problem with this specification.

The transition in the formulation from the subjunctive – '[and the miracle] would be' – to the indicative – 'are solved' – is intentional. Linguistically speaking, this triggers the transition from the idea of possibility to one of reality and thereby encourages the client to believe she can already experience possible future changes in the here-and-now.

The next insertion is made to facilitate the client's acceptance of the word 'miracle'. Many clients answer by saying, 'I don't believe in miracles', and so to avoid any discussion about the existence of miracles, I relate the miracle to the sudden transformation of the problem into a solution, using the words:

'– and that really would be miracle, wouldn't it? –'

That this sudden turnaround is a miracle has been confirmed by all my previous clients to this day.

This is then followed by an implementation of the miracle in the day-to-day life of the client, with the words:

'– and you wake up early the next morning – and no one tells you that this miracle has happened – how then would you know this miracle had occurred?'

It is advisable at this point to make it clear to the client that no one will be informing her when the miracle occurs. This invites the client to look for herself for signals that the miracle is present. Naturally, the client can only identify these signals if she is already in a certain sense experiencing the miracle.

We find a detailed form of the miracle question in Milton Erickson's Crystal Ball technique (de Shazer 1995), albeit involving an extremely comprehensive trance induction in the near future (in one week, in one month) and distant future (in one year, in two years, when the therapy is finished). Erickson often connected this form of **pseudo-projection in time** with the induction of amnesia in the client. He himself took notes of everything the client mentioned in terms of changes, improvements and assistance and then implemented these things in subsequent therapy sessions.

The advantage for the therapist of the crystal ball technique, as shortened in this way by Steve de Shazer, is ease of application. The client, on the other hand, benefits by learning that it is *she*, and not the therapist, who will be doing all the work, affording her more confidence and independence from the therapist.

Should the client begin her answer to the miracle question by describing her feelings, thoughts or actions, the therapist can encourage further articulation of the differences using the following question:

'And what else?'

It is important here that the individual elements in the answer to the miracle question are conjoined with an 'and', and not linked together with an 'if ... then', which would imply a chain of cause and effect and construe earlier changes as preconditions of subsequent changes. The component parts of the miracle do not determine each other; rather, like a colourful bouquet of flowers, they point to the independent opportunities in the world of miracles. The idea of a chain of causally connected events narrows our minds, lessens our opportunity for perception and leads us to believe that changes are dependent on prior events. The abundance of individual events, at the time of the miracle, on the other hand, enriches our experience and affords us new freedoms: we go beyond the self-established borders of our own world and by doing so facilitate the realisation of previously excluded parts of the miracle.

I like to use the word 'miracle' in connection with the miracle questions, since it implies that:

- Inconceivable things can occur.
- The miracle is a gift and not something we can manufacture ourselves.
- We are allowed to say 'irrational' things and thereby avoid unconscious and restrictive belief sentences.
- The answers we find come at a cost.
- Feelings of gratitude and amazement can be triggered.

At the moment we are able to express gratitude we again find ourselves in a state of being given a gift and of richness that is incompatible with the problem-state.

If a client still rejects the word 'miracle', the therapist can react paradoxically, such as:

'Yes, for you it really would be a miracle if something surprising were to happen, don't you agree?'

Or, by saying:

'So what should we call something that is very surprising and joyful? Maybe we can call it the great surprise?'

If the client gives an account of the day after the night the miracle occurred, she often returns to her problem-consciousness, especially in cases where negative outcomes appear. In this case, the therapist can ask the following question:

'Now the miracle occurred during the night. How do you react now?'

With this question the therapist aims to help the client to continue focusing on the miracle. It is often necessary to recall the miracle; this shows that this type of change cannot be taken for granted.

In addition to the direct changes for the client, the context and consequences of these changes should also be looked into. This can be done using the following questions:

'Has anyone apart from you noticed this miracle?'
'Who, apart from you, would notice this miracle?'
'Who, apart from you, would be the first to observe that this miracle has occurred?'
'Is there anyone else who has noticed this miracle?'
'What might others observe that would indicate that the miracle has taken place?'

If the client describes negative reactions from family members, friends, acquaintances and colleagues, the therapist should then clarify the client's response to these negative reactions. Sometimes the client will once again display the old, problematic behavioural patterns when faced with the negative reactions – envy, annoyance, etc. If this occurs, it can be useful to once again recall the miracle and ask how she (the client) would react if the miracle had just occurred. Surprisingly, more sensible reactions then normally occur to the client. This again shows that the client in fact already possesses the resources but forgets how to access them.

II.1.5.10 Motivation through visions vs. motivation through suffering

If at this stage of the interview – i.e. after the miracle question – the client is asked about her strategy for coping with emerging problems in the context of the miracle, she then has more energy and hope at her disposal with which to deal with such problems. We can also understand the solution-focused approach in the sense that the client, with the help of the questions about goals, exceptions and miracles, is initially brought into a state of increased hope before starting to solve the connected difficulties. With problem-oriented procedures, on the other hand, it is expected of the client that she come to terms with her situation, and the amount of energy to which she has access in this moment, is relatively low and does not increase as a result of coming into contact with her problems. If the miracle-state is touched upon prior to tackling the problems, however, the client has far more access to her own energy and resources and will be more successful in solving her emerging problems. It is also to be expected that, in this state, the client will have less need of help from the therapist. (In the problem-state, conversely, she would be much more dependent on the help of the therapist.)

Problem-oriented approaches place strong emphasis on the suffering of the client, with the aim of raising their 'energy level' and, to an extent, providing motivation. This is the equivalent of the heightened performance of a wounded soldier in a dangerous situation who marches for days on end. In solution-focused procedures, on the other hand, the client is motivated by her goal and through the experiencing of the solution with the help of the miracle question. This is the equivalent of increased performance due to visions, such as when the founders of companies or projects have an initial clear idea of their achievable goals before taking the initial steps in that direction. Both procedures involve the mobilisation of resources; the second, however, is surely more pleasant than the first.

When the therapist inquires as to the reaction of the outside world to the change in the client's behaviour after the miracle, this can sometimes reveal all the positive reasons for leaving the problem unsolved. In the context of the miracle, we find the mirror image to the causes of a problem when we understand that it is the causes that are obstructing the solution.

If a new goal appears during the following session, it is then important to integrate this into the miracle; the miracle gives access to the solution, it affects the whole situation, and encompasses more than just the solution of the problem stated by the client. The path to the miracle thus reveals something *general,* not just a *specific* way of achieving the solution for a specific problem. The client learns how she can find solutions and is given a small taste of the solution. She is then able to recognise when something of this nature occurs again and to recall her goal.

Some clients return to Steve de Shazer many years later. Since this is something that does not happen very often, his first question is usually the following:

'What have you forgotten?'
'What have you forgotten that was working before?'

During an investigation at the BFTC in Milwaukee, Steve de Shazer and his team discovered that answers to the miracle question in different cultures showed no significant differences: while cultural differences were visible in the description of problem-states, the people's answers tended to resemble each other when it came to solutions.

Through the miracle question we gain access to a solution-state that tells us something about the essence of the solution. For this reason, recalling this solution-state helps engender further solution impulses.

II.1.6 Solutions in the past

After clarification of the goal, or after the miracle question, the therapist may ask whether there was a time at which the goal or the miracle, or at least some parts thereof, had already been achieved. Here she is essentially looking for exceptions to the problem. These I see as solutions in the past that the client has already achieved. If the client is able to locate examples of exceptions in the past, this will give her some hope of being able to achieve her goal – or at least parts of the miracle situation – since exceptions in the past can, to a certain extent, act as proof that improvements for the client are possible.

In terms of the exceptions, it now becomes essential to discover the differences from the situation in the present, for these differences can indicate to us what things will be of help in bringing about similar situations again. Situations which the client can help to re-occur are naturally more useful than those which occur accidentally or over which the client had little or no influence. These latter situations are of the following types: 'in which … was still alive' or 'when my husband still had his job' etc. If such situations are mentioned, the therapist should simply continue asking about other exceptional situations; when unusable situations are mentioned by the client it is better to continue questioning than to comment on these situations. This is done based on the following principle, from the *I Ching* (Wilhelm 1956, p. 163):

'The best way to combat evil is through vigorous progress in the name of what is good.'

In the literature on SFT, asking questions about exceptions comes after goal clarification. However, since the answers to the miracle question are more decisive, it can be more useful to ask the questions related to exceptions after asking the miracle question. This enables the miracle to be integrated into daily life in yet another way, since the client becomes aware when parts of the miracle have already occurred, and the miracle, therefore, is no longer solely part of the future. The therapist can now encourage this integration with the following questions:

'Can you recall any situations in which parts of the miracle have already occurred?'
'Have any of the things you just mentioned after the occurrence of the miracle already happened?'
'Has there been a time before when something like this miracle happened?'

At this point scaling questions are often of help, such as:

'On a scale in which 10 represents the miracle and 0 represents the state you were in when you called me to arrange the time for this session, where would you now place yourself?'

The therapist can also use a scale of 1 to 10. This has the advantage that a client that would have placed herself at 0 (on a scale of 0 – 10) would then scale herself at 1. This is often seen as meaning 'something', as opposed to 'nothing', and therefore not rock-bottom. However, in most cases, clients place themselves higher than 0. This can be seen as evidence of progress and can be accompanied by the following question:

'What has helped you to move from 0 to *n*?' (where n is between 0 and 10)

With patients who are in pain it is important to ask about small improvements, since larger changes are likely to be denied. The following questions can be used:

'Were there times, moments, when you felt just a little bit better?'
'Were there moments when very small parts of the miracle had already occurred?'

Scaling questions can now be used to elicit exceptions in the past, such as:

'Have there already been situations in the past in which you were higher on the scale than *n*?'
'What's the highest value on the scale of 0 to 10 that you have reached in the past?'

After this it again becomes necessary to ask the relevant questions about the differences between situations that were exceptions and the present situation.

Recalling past situations where the problem was either completely or partially solved helps the client to recall her resources as well as contexts and people that were helpful. In essence this is a matter of 're-remembering' the fact that we already possess all the resources we require – instead of focusing on what is missing, we highlight instead our inner riches, our contact with people that offer support and those things that make us stronger. Because the therapist in SFT holds back from making concrete suggestions, this form of therapy can also be seen as an approach that encourages the process of remembering. Even the miracle is compiled from moments in the past and their effects. Thus we are only able to imagine something within the limits of our possible experience.

When we look again at the picture of the currents in the stream, the currents now appear to have less reality than the stream of life, for although they are moving within the stream, they are moving in a circular fashion and not in a straight line. But even then they point towards the direction of greater flow, and consequently we can approach the thing that is standing in our way – the problem – as an opportunity for learning. Like the currents in the stream, the problem has a lower level of reality than the stream of life within which it exists. This broader context provides us with the framework within which we experience the problem. It is thus possible to reinterpret a problem as a useful opportunity for learning and as such, we experience it in the broader context of the stream of life. We only experience it as a problem when we forget this broader context. So experiencing the broader context frees us from adherence to a temporary difficult reality, and can help reduce suffering. Every context can also be experienced within a broader context, however, meaning that we are dealing with a spiral of contexts around whose twists and turns we ourselves are moving.

SFT widens the context in which the client experiences her problem. This happens by

- Expanding the temporal (sequential) context by asking goal questions and the miracle question
- Expanding the perspective by means of the first session formula task mentioned in section II.1.1 (expansion of the spatial (simultaneous) context)
- Transition from causal thinking to experiencing the moment (parts of the miracle as independent possibilities).

We can view SFT as a **method of deconstruction**. Problems already being dissolvable by a mere change of perspective, their inherent character of being only constructs is clearly apparent. When we go beyond the constructs, we come into contact with the stream of life. When we try to hold on to whatever we come into contact with, we begin to construct a reality and in the end become prisoners of our own constructs. SFT's method of deconstruction helps to free us from this and to experience the moment. From this point of view, it can be seen ultimately as a spiritual method.

II.16.1 Experiment 5
Now look at your problem again from the beginning and ask yourself the miracle question in the following form:

'When you finish reading this – and set about doing your daily chores or maybe planning something enjoyable – and then later in the evening you become tired and go to bed – and – assuming – during this night a miracle takes place – and your problem is solved – how – in the morning – do you know that the miracle has happened?'

Make a note of what occurs to you:

....
....
....

'Who else notices the miracle?'

....
....
....

'How do they react to the change in your behaviour or your new attitude?'

....
....
....

'How do you yourself react? Remember that the miracle has now happened!'

....
....
....

'Who else has noticed changes after the miracle?'

....
....
....

'What else is different when the miracle has happened?'

....
....
....

'Who at your place of work would notice that the miracle has happened?'

....
....
....

'How do your colleagues react to the change in your behaviour after the miracle?'

....
....
....

'How do you yourself react to their reaction now that the miracle has happened?'

....
....
....

'How do your friends react to the miracle you have experienced? Do you notice this?'

....
....
....

'How do you react to the reactions of your friends?'

....
....
....

'Have any of your relatives noticed the miracle?'

....
....
....

'How do they react?'

....
....
....

'How do you react to their reactions after the miracle has happened?'

....
....
....

II.2 'Visitors', 'complainants' and 'customers' as stages of a development process

Steve de Shazer and his team introduced the terms visitor, complainant and customer as interactional descriptions of client readiness. This makes it easier for the therapist to decide on suitable exercises for the client, while at the same time emphasising the nature of the interaction of the therapist-client system. If a client acts like a 'visitor' with one therapist, she may well act like a 'customer' with another therapist. Understanding these terms as interaction descriptors also means that a client can move from being a 'visitor' to being a 'customer' in the course of a single therapy session. This is therefore not a question of the client's attributes, as is often assumed in superficial interpretations of SFT, but rather of the client's possibilities of reaction to the therapist's behaviour.

This differentiation between 'visitors', 'complainants' and 'customers' can also be seen as an interactive process between the client and the problem. Approaching the situation in this way, it becomes clearer *why* a client behaves like a 'visitor', 'complainant' or 'customer'. Steve de Shazer's aim was to emphasise the **interactive process** between client and therapist.

I would like now to highlight my approach in which the stages of 'visitor', 'complainant' and 'customer' can be seen as variations of a natural process of development of the client in interaction with their topic.

A client behaves like a 'visitor' in situations where she does not know what she would like to change and is unsure even whether she has a problem. By contrast, the 'complainant' provides a clear picture of her goal but plays the role of the helpless victim from which she sees herself as unable to escape. The 'customer', on the other hand, knows her goal and has some idea of what she needs to do in order to achieve it.

Answers to the miracle question will indicate in which category the client's behaviour comes. The 'visitor' is completely unable to answer the miracle question; the 'complainant' initially refers to the miracle in terms of changes in their feelings and physical sensations, as well as changes in the behaviour of other people (eg partners, children, colleagues, friends etc.); and a 'customer' clearly talks of action that she would take after the miracle had occurred.

In my opinion, 'visitor', 'complainant' and 'customer' as terms for client readiness can also serve to describe the stages of an everyday process of change. Every self-initiated change presupposes a motive for changing the current situation. The first stage – that of the 'visitor' – can be seen as a stage in which the client begins to feel dissatisfied with their current situation. She begins to wish for a change, but does not yet know what direction that change should take and is as yet unable to specify her discomfort; she senses the need for change, but is unable to articulate any goal – all she knows is that she longer wants ... to be there. This describes precisely the situation of a 'visitor'.

In the next stage, the 'visitor' may experience something that gives her an idea of what kind of change she is looking for and so she becomes a 'complainant'. Something happens at the margins of her world which she finds new and attractive; it becomes clearer to her what it is that she would like to have 'instead', but she still doesn't know how to get there. In this respect she feels like a victim trapped in her position who can do no more than complain about her situation.

The 'complainant' then becomes a 'customer' at the moment she gets an idea of how she can contribute to achieving the new desired goal-state. From this moment on she can start to show her own initiative and start to act. The victim has begun to take action and is therefore no longer a victim.

Thus by catching a glimpse of new ways of acting we become 'customers'. All three stages are necessary to the development process – the first two stages may be short in duration, but in most cases they are necessary. By understanding this the therapist may be able to be more tolerant towards their clients.

Clients come to us in any one of the three stages. With 'visitors' it is important that they learn that something else exists beyond the world that they have known through their experience, and so the therapist needs to help her identify a broader context. For the therapist to be able to do this it is important to assess the severity of the problem so the 'visitor' will feel she is being taken seriously. Observations, such as 'Have you ever tried to do such and such...?' are of little help because the 'visitor', not knowing which direction to take, is unable to act. It will help the 'visitor' however if the therapist picks up on each positive event mentioned making observations such as:

'Ah, how did you manage to do that?'
'Ah, that's a good idea!'

Expressing surprise in this way helps sow the seeds for ideas about which things are good for the 'visitor' and would be useful to continue doing. Insoo Kim Berg gave a wonderful example of this at a seminar:

She had a client for whom everything had gone wrong: she had lost her job; her partner had left her; she had gained a lot of weight and no longer looked after herself to the extent that she smelled badly, felt sick and desperate. Kim Berg listened long and hard to this client until one day the client mentioned that she had three dogs that always liked her, regardless of what she might do. 'Wow!'

said Kim Berg upon hearing this. 'It is very important to have such a dog, and you even have three of them!'

The highlighting of positive things helps the client to recognise things that are good for her and to develop ideas for possible goal-states. At a later stage the therapist can ask questions about the differences that would bring about a solution to the problem, for example:

'How would you recognise that your problem was solved?'
'This must have made a difference to your current situation, mustn't it?'

The questions aid the process of identifying goals, though they should not be asked too early to avoid overburdening the client.

While it is useful during the initial 'visitor' stage to touch on solutions in the present that can act as models for parts of a goal, in the second 'complainant' stage it is useful to refer to solutions from the past, which can serve as examples for the client's own ability to act. In this way, the client can see that she is in fact not actually as helpless as she feels. Exceptions to the problem in the past prove that solutions are possible, while differences in the present situation reveal which things the client can do differently, and which people or places can provide her with help and support.

The miracle question can be asked during any of these stages, since it does not require the client to be willing to act. Indeed the fact that, when faced with a seemingly unsolvable situation, a desired change suddenly becomes possible is itself part of the essence of the miracle contained in the miracle question. And while a 'visitor' can only provide very unspecific answers to this question – eg, 'I feel better in a way, but I can't say quite how' – this does nonetheless indicate a certain orientation on her part.

With some types of 'visitors' however even asking the miracle question is inadvisable. This is mainly the case when the client is a 'visitor' and does not wish see any change, preferring instead to accept her fate. The following example may serve to clarify this.

A client came to me whose daughter had committed suicide while in the psychiatric ward. Since her daughter's death everything had seemed to have gone wrong for the client. She argued with her friends and the people she knew, spoke badly of them, and talked about all the bad things that had happened to her. According to her version of events nothing around her was good. Drawn in by her constant complaining, I asked her the miracle question. She was appalled by the question and said there could never be any miracle, given how mean the others were to her, and that her daughter's suicide had affected her so much that nothing could ever go well for her. In response to this I asked her what it was she was hoping to achieve through therapy, if not even a miracle would suffice to allay her suffering. After a long pause she said that she didn't know and that it was her friends who had advised her to try therapy.

In such cases the therapist can only wait until the client is ready to want change. The **miracle question** can also serve as a **test** of whether a desire for change does exist, and then to identify the earliest moment at which change could occur. The following example shows how even the ability to describe the workings of the miracle does not necessarily imply that the client possesses a willingness for change.

A client couple came to me. They had been living together for a number of years and were now considering whether or not they should separate. I began the session by asking the miracle question and had each answer the question separately. The man explained to me how he would again become close to his wife, how in the morning they would look at each other with different eyes and they would sleep with one another again. He said his wife would react with happiness to his new behaviour and they would do things together again, visiting friends who would be pleasantly surprised at what they witnessed. The miracle as described by the woman was quite similar: she also spoke of more intimacy between them, more attentiveness and helpfulness from her husband, more joint activities and the surprise their friends would show. As they began to speak of the miracle, they began to glow and looked at each other in a friendlier way. At the end of session I told them that for two days a week they were to act as if the miracle had occurred and observe what difference this made. Each was to guess when the 'miracle day' of their partner was.

When they came to the next session I asked them to tell me what things had changed. The man began by saying that for him the following day had been a 'miracle day'. He had been able to look at his wife with different eyes, had been friendlier to her, done this and that, which had pleased her. However, each time he would approach his wife physically she would turn him away. At this point I gave a questioning look to the wife. She answered: 'Yes, my husband has changed completely, but I still can't just pretend that nothing has happened. He has done so many things to me in the past I'm not able to get closer to him yet.' I asked her to tell me when she thought the miracle might be able to take place. She said: 'At the earliest, in four months.'

Since the husband was going to be away from home for a while for work reasons, I suggested that we stop the therapy for a time and that they call me when they want to continue the sessions or to let me know when the miracle had occurred.

Some miracles should not be allowed to happen too soon. A miracle requires a willingness to leave behind bitterness and abandon feelings of revenge.

Solution-focused questions help to make 'visitors' into 'complainants' and 'complainants' into 'customers'. This all takes place in the context of the enquiring, open, *multi-directional* and supportive approach of the therapist. Through the syntactic and non-semantic approach of the therapist a process of change is stimulated within the client. In this the therapist belongs to the client's system, meaning that the reactions of the client take place within the interactive process between the therapist and the client – in an interactive process with another therapist the client might exhibit other behaviour. The solution-focused approach is thus an effective and supportive means for use in processes of change (though, of course, it provides no actual guarantee of change).

As a systemic method, Solution Focused Therapy desists from diagnosis precisely because at the moment the therapist encounters the client she becomes part of that client-system. The interactive patterns of the 'visitor', 'complainant' and 'customer' help in the designing of exercises for the client, and in this sense they act as a paradigm for classifying the *current* situation. Emphasis is placed on the word 'current' since this interactive classification is not a diagnosis with any value in terms of prognosis; rather, it serves solely to help create client exercises.

II.3 Designing exercises

At the end of the session the client is usually assigned an exercise by the therapist. At the BFTC, Steve de Shazer and Insoo Kim Berg usually worked with a team that sits behind a one-way mirror. This emphasises the separation between observers and the acting therapist. When working with a team it can be a disadvantage to remove this separation as this sometimes adds to the confusion of the client. Together, the therapists and the team devise an exercise, which is then passed on to the client by the therapist.

In order to make the exercise easier to accept it is introduced by means of giving between one and three *compliments*. These compliments help in the construction of a 'Yes-set' (in the sense of Milton Erickson) such that the client says 'yes' internally to the compliments and thus finds it easier to say 'yes' to the exercise. In this sense, the compliments prepare the ground for the exercise. Naturally, only compliments that both the team and the therapist find convincing may be chosen. Giving compliments does not imply flattery, and the compliments must always be coherent for both the therapist and the client. Compliments should be understood as appreciative observations about resourceful client behaviour.

The most important aspect of the exercise is that it is suited to the client – that is, it does not ask too much of the client, it is pleasurable to the client and is experienced as providing support for the client. In finding such a well-suited exercise, it is helpful to split clients into 'visitors', 'complainants' and 'customers' such that:

– 'Visitors' can at best only be assigned the 'first session formula task'

- 'Complainants' are given an observation exercise
- 'Customers' are given an action exercise.

The first session formula task is suitable for the 'visitor' since the 'visitor' does not yet know in which direction a change might occur. Observation exercises are suited to 'complainants' since they are as yet unable to act; however they are able to make observations, finding contexts in which action becomes possible.

'Customers' on the other hand mention action in their answers to the miracle question, and so it is possible to assign action exercises.

According to Steve de Shazer, SFT has two meta-rules:

- If something works, do more of it.
- If something doesn't work, do something different.

These meta-rules not only apply to the designing of exercises, but also to the therapist's own approach. When something in the interaction with the client proves worthwhile, it is sensible to continue doing it. But when steps in the direction of a solution are not well received then 'doing something different' becomes applicable. This, for example, can sometimes be the case when the client talks for the first time about something that for her was a traumatic situation. In this case, the talking itself can represent a solution for the client. A solution-focused approach therefore does not mean blindly asking solution-focused questions; on each occasion, the context must be verified first in order to decide on an approach that is suitable in that given moment.

When devising exercises, all 'exception' situations (according to the first meta-rule) can now be used where the relevant difference from the current 'problem' situation is determined by the fact that the client herself has performed some action. If the client has acted in the past and thereby solved her problem, it is advisable that she should continue to do so in the future. The therapist can then create exercises for the client from these actions by:

- assigning the easiest action
- proposing that the client choose and perform one of the actions on two days in the week, and observe the difference between days the action is performed, and the days when it is not and she behaves as usual
- naming the relevant actions of the 'exception' situations, and asking the client to decide on two days of the week by throwing a die which action she performs on that particular day .

Do more of the things that prove their value…

… and use the resources at your disposal! (after Fiddy 1990).

The exercises described above are suited to a 'customer'. If we are dealing with a 'complainant', however, the therapist can use the 'exception' situations mentioned in the interview as model situations for observation exercises. This leads to the following suggestions for observation exercises:

- The client observes when person X and person Y behave as in the desired 'exception' situations and what makes these situations different from the situations when X and Y behave as in the problem situation.
- The client observes when these 'exception' situations occur and observes what things increase the likelihood of their occurrence.
- The client observes when parts of the 'exception' situation occur and to what extent they then behave differently.

According to the second meta rule, the following exercise type can be created for 'customers':

'Are you doing something differently now than before?'

This exercise is particularly helpful when the same interaction patterns between pairs, such as parents and children, occur on a continual basis, as in the following example.

A client came to me suffering from extreme anxiety, depression, insomnia and various psychosomatic complaints. The situation in her marriage had come to a head: for no apparent reason and on many occasions each week her husband would be struck by fits of jealousy in which he would swear at her and verbally abuse her, sometimes leading to violence. Divorce was out of the question for my client, since she feared her husband would kill her in such an event. Her wish was that they could live together in peace.

I praised her for having held out for 40 years and not yet having given up, despite the difficulty of the situation. I added that she must be important to her husband, as otherwise he would not react with jealousy. Even if his way of showing his love was extremely disagreeable, it also showed that he too would prefer to live together peacefully with her. Her reaction to the fits of jealousy, the physical pain and insomnia she suffered gave her husband reason to fear she might leave him, which could only have heightened his jealousy still further. I told her that the next time her husband is jealous she should behave differently than before.

During the following session, four weeks later, I asked what she had changed. She said that her husband was now only suffering from fits of jealousy once a week. 'How did you manage that?' I asked her, totally surprised. 'The first time he had one of his fits of jealousy I banged the table with my fist. This amazed my husband so much that he stopped what he was saying and stared at me. Now I know I need no longer be afraid of him. Now I can sleep again.' The client's situation improved rapidly. Over a half-year period the frequency of the husband's fits of jealously dropped further still, such that they only occurred once every two months. The client was no longer affected by his attacks and was able to continue living with him.

In this case it was important to allow the client to make her own choice of what she would like to do differently, since it is the client herself that is best able to judge the situation at any given moment. It could easily have been judged too dangerous to assign the client the exercise of thumping her fist on the table. However, the client knew her husband and was intuitively better able to judge his reaction.

Other patterns the therapist can use to create action exercises include the following:

'Next time do … instead of doing … as you usually do.'
    'Choose whichever is the easiest for you from the following actions and adopt this behaviour next time … occurs.'

'Roll a die every day and when the situation … occurs adopt the behaviour corresponding to the number thrown from the following list.'

Further examples of action exercises can be derived from the answers to the miracle question, as follows.

'Select one of the actions mentioned in the miracle and perform it twice per week. Observe whether, on the days when you perform this action, this makes any difference to you.'

The following exercise can be given in situations where the client is highly motivated to act:

'Select what is the easiest action for you and observe whether it makes a difference to you when you perform this action.'

When the therapist feels that the client is encountering difficulties performing a certain action, but is nonetheless motivated to change her situation, then performing only the easiest action can be sufficient. Where the therapist is doubtful, however, it is better to assign the client an observation exercise, such as:

'Choose two days every week on which you act as if the miracle had already happened. Observe if this makes a difference to you.'

The *as-if* action takes the client into a condition in which she behaves as if the miracle had already happened. It builds a bridge between the present situation and the miracle condition, and by passing over this bridge by acting 'as if', the possibility becomes reality. Change takes place when the client begins to see the actions contained in the miracle as possible for herself, and then contemplates performing them.

Partners can be assigned a common exercise and each can be asked to evaluate the other on their respective 'miracle days'. If the proposals of the partners do not concur there is also an option of following one partner's proposal on odd days and the other's proposal on the even days.

Each of these exercises can also be combined with an **element of chance**, such as choosing which exercise to do on the throw of a dice or a coin. This is useful mainly in cases where a playful element might improve the client's mood, or where the chance elements fit in with the client's general view of the world.

The following are examples of observation exercises.

1. 'Before going to bed, think about what the next day would be like if it were to be a 'miracle day'. Estimate and make a note of where you think you would place yourself on a scale of 0 to 10, where 0 means 'the miracle did

not occur at all' and 10 means 'the miracle occurred fully'. In the evening of that day make a note of where you were on the scale and then estimate your position for following day.'

Comparing the estimated and observed values indicates which days were better and which days worse than expected. The better days point to things the client found helpful and, conversely, the worse days will indicate those things that were not helpful.

2. 'Observe what is different on the days when the symptom is not present. What are you doing differently on these days?'

The associations of this exercise are similar to those found in 'exception' exercises: days when there are no symptoms present represent exceptions to the problem and consequently are a solution in the present or the past.

3. 'Estimate how often you think the symptom will be present on the following day. Check the accuracy of what you estimated on that day and then repeat the procedure for the day after that.'

This exercise works in the form of biofeedback: the client rapidly receives feedback on her assumptions from which she can learn both consciously and unconsciously.

II.3.1 Structure of the therapy sessions

Steve de Shazer often began the second therapy session with the following question:

'So, what's better?'

He does not ask about the exercises so the client does not feel she is being disciplined if she has not completed the exercise; if she has performed the exercises, she will mention her experiences of these in her answer to this question.

I normally begin the second session with the question:

'What things have changed?'

This is more neutral. Some clients react to the question about improvements with denial, since by focusing on things that are still not working how they want them to they can show that further sessions are still needed. Over subsequent sessions, however, improvements are often mentioned.

If the client responds by saying that no improvements have occurred, the therapist can react by saying:

'What did happen then? – (long pause).'

In most cases clients begin to mention improvements following this comment, but if this is not the case the therapist can ask:

'How did you feel after the last session?'

By this stage the client normally begins to mention positive changes.

If however it transpires that the exercise was not useful to the client, it is advisable not to set any further exercises, since this can detract from the search for useful actions. It can be more useful, for example, to continue examining those things that had proved helpful.

If the problem has worsened it is often also useful to ask one of the following questions:

'How do you manage to keep on going?'
'How do you cope with that?'
'What helped to prevent things from getting worse?'

By the time of the third session, the therapist can use the following question, as used by Steve de Shazer:

'Has enough improved yet?'

Followed, in the fourth session, by:

'How would you recognise that you don't need any more sessions?'

In my experience, clients in Germany tend to expect a longer course of therapy, and when this question is asked as early as the fourth session they are left with the impression that the therapist would like to get rid of them. For this reason, I only ask this question after a discussion with the client suggests that a sufficient number of significant improvements have been achieved. At the BFTC in Milwaukee, for example, the average number of sessions is three, while 97% of cases involve fewer than 10 sessions.

II.4 The limits of SFT

SFT is an enclosed system that works. It has its limitations, however, and these will be discussed in the following subsection.

II.4.1 The principle of not acquiring new abilities

SFT is a method of therapy in which it is assumed that the client already has all the resources she needs. Thus when difficulties arise that call for the acquisition of new skills, SFT as a method is no longer applicable. These situations call for **psycho-educative approaches**.

An example may clarify this difference. If someone is in pain, it can be helpful for them to learn some relaxation techniques. In doing so, the client acquires a new ability which she can apply again in the future – i.e. she learns to use a general method, one that is not specific to her.

Solution Focused Therapy would bring a different approach to this case. In SFT the therapist would ask about the times when the client experienced a lower level of pain and elicit information about what the client did differently at those times. In this way, the client becomes aware of the things she is already doing that reduce her pain or discovers what can help her to feel better – i.e. she learns which things, specific to herself, can help her.

Both methods are helpful in reducing pain: in the first the client learns a new skill, in the second she learns to recognise how she was already helping herself. SFT is a method for self-help in which the client quickly becomes independent of the therapist.

Another relevant difference between these two methods is the distinction between **problem** and **difficulty**. A difficulty is when the client only needs to acquire new information in order to reach a solution. With problems however this information, though it could well resolve the difficulty, is of no use to the client.

For example, when someone enters a state of panic because a snake is climbing up their leg, but this same person's fear disappears when someone explains that the snake is not dangerous, we can then say that that person had experienced a difficulty vis-à-vis the snake, but not a problem. However, if the fear persists, despite the information that it is harmless, then we are dealing with a problem. SFT helps in the second situation. In the first situation, the provision of information is sufficient on its own.

Many other therapeutic methods, besides making the client aware of her resources and setting exercises, also teach the client new abilities and provide her with new information. This is true of behavioural therapy, Neuro Linguistic Programming (NLP), family therapy and others. SFT, on the other hand, limits itself to triggering and facilitating a process of change. Other functions commonly associated with therapy – accompanying a client through difficult situations in her life, such as when the client is suffering from a fatal illness; teaching functions; and giving information – in the strict implementation of SFT are left for others.

This does not mean that these other functions are not useful; it means only that they are not essential to the process of change. Thus, while they can still be associated with SFT, the therapist should separate and specify each of them – that is, the therapist should indicate which are necessary for change to occur and which superfluous to the process. The client will become independent more quickly when forced to fall back on her own resources. Instead of concentrating on acquiring new abilities, solution-focused brief therapy focuses upon the **re-remembering** of our own resources: it points out that we already possess what we need; it indicates the ways in which we are already 'whole'; and helps us to discover the wealth we have within us.

A teaching relationship can continue over many years, and since a pupil will learn a lot from a good teacher, she will often return to him or her. The goal of SFT however is for the client to become independent of the therapist as quickly as possible, and for this reason the therapist endeavours to become superfluous to the client as soon as possible, by withholding information and refraining from teaching the client new abilities, leaving the work of achieving change entirely to the client. In cases where an insurance company has agreed to a fixed number of hours of therapy, the therapist may be inclined to comment:

'I am impressed by the progress you have made… I wonder if it might be a good idea to use our remaining time on another project?'

The client might then decide that she wishes to acquire new abilities, or the therapist might help the client through a longer process – thus the client can take the decision herself as to whether to continue with the therapy, without being led to believe that she needs to do so in order to solve her problem. By separating therapy, teaching, facilitating and other exercises the client is able to become independent more quickly, and can decide herself whether to accept any further offers of help without seeing them as essential to solving her problem.

II.4.2 Only client goals can be aimed for
In the section on clarifying client goals, I pointed out the importance of the therapist understanding what it is the client wishes to achieve. Goals of the client's loved ones, referring agents, third parties and the therapist can all be taken into account but should not be seen as the actual goal of the therapy. From experience, requests for therapy that do not come from the client herself mostly give rise to difficulties.

If a client is obliged to attend therapy – for example, to verify a client's fitness for work in view of an application to enter early retirement or as a condition for early release from prison or a measure taken by parents in raising their children – it should not necessarily be assumed that the client herself is motivated to undergo therapy. Extraneous, imposed goals are not simply adopted by a client. At this point, we should clarify what it is the client desires and how the referring agents would react if the client were to achieve her goal. In SFT change is mediated by the therapist's questions which enable the clients to make up their mind about new ways to achieve their goals. The therapist does not change the client – he can only help the clients achieve their goal by asking suitable questions.

Let us assume a child is sent for therapy by her parents who are hoping for an improvement in her behaviour. In this situation we could ask the child the following questions:

'Your parents have told me that you are having some problems. They would like the constant arguments to come to an end. I know what they would like to see. But what would you like?'

If the child says something to which you know the parents would react to angrily, the following questions can be asked:

'How do you think your parents would react to that?'
'What do you do when your parents become angry?'
'What would you have to do in order for your parents to allow you to do ...?'

Or

'How could you arrive at a situation in which you are getting along well with your parents, despite doing ...?'

The therapist can also verify any objections that might occur to her that might happen after the child's goal has been achieved, by asking

'When ... has occurred, how can you be sure that ... does not happen?'

It is important that the therapist helps the client to achieve her own goal – only then can the therapist assume the client is actively participating in the therapy.

Similar problems exist in psychiatry: the psychiatrist can only work with the client's given goals, not with the psychiatrist's own goals which might well differ from those of the client. The following example should serve to clarify this.

On a a psychiatric ward where patients who had already spent more than 20 years in hospital underwent therapy to prepare them to live in shared accommodation, an attempt was made to transfer a patient to shared accommodation who did not himself actually want to be discharged from the hospital. On the day before the planned move to the new accommodation, the patient destroyed a television set in the communal area and ran around screaming. This answer to the impending discharge was noted by the doctors and the patient was placed in the hospital's intensive care ward.

Progress is not always approved of by the client, especially where it implies an increased level of responsibility on their part. For the patient in the above example, who had already spent two decades in hospital, the thought of going back to live outside the hospital was terrifying, whereas the transfer to intensive care ensured that he could spend the rest of his life in the protection of the psychiatric ward.

In this situation SFT could have helped by taking the patient's wishes into account at an earlier stage – and protected the television set. At the same time progress towards achieving the goal of the hospital staff – self-reliance of the patient – cannot be made in SFT if the patient does share the same goal.

If the therapist were to work with the hospital staff – and not with the patient – she could help them work towards reaching their goal of increasing the self-reliance of the patient, albeit within the limits agreed to by the patient. The following questions could be useful to the hospital staff:

'How would you recognise that the patient is behaving in a more self-reliant way?'
'In which situations is he acting in this way already?'
'What is his goal?'
'Does he agree to being placed in shared accommodation?'
'If you place him in shared accommodation, how do you expect he will react?'

SFT is a method that does not allow any manipulation. In this respect it is a fully comprehensive method, but one in which the therapist has no goal or ambition except that of helping the client to achieve her goal.

II.5 Common confusions with SFT

Some elements of SFT are often misinterpreted and confused with other methods. In order to clarify how SFT should be understood, I will now provide some examples of the differences between SFT and these methods.

II.5.1 SFT and positive thinking

With positive thinking, as with many applications of what we call 'affirmations', unlike SFT, the consequences of established goals are not investigated and the context of the goal is therefore not taken into account. Positive results are dependent on the particular context. Something positive for person A can be negative for person B. Positive thinking thus reveals nothing about the content of the goal, but only serves to show that the person in question sees their goal as positive. What one person sees as a positive goal is only really clarified when the consequences of the goal are observed at its realisation. Goals with unpleasant side effects or consequences are not experienced as positive, even if the name of the goal itself appears to promise positive things. The following story from the oral Tassawuf tradition clarifies this point.

A knowledge-seeker set out for a distant village in order to locate a Sufi master known for his wisdom. When he arrived in the village he was told that the master lived on the other side of the mountain. Although darkness was setting in, the pupil nonetheless set off across the way. Upon seeing a bright light burning in the distance the pupil became sure that he would find the Sufi master. His surprise was all the greater then when he reached the source of the light only to find an oil lamp around which a swarm of moths was fluttering. Then, as his eyes became accustomed to the darkness, he noticed a faint light up ahead. He moved up to this light and found the Sufi reading by the light of a candle.

'Why are you sitting here in the candle light, when down below a much brighter light is burning?' asked the knowledge-seeker.

'As you can see,' replied the Sufi, 'the bright light is for the moths that allow me to read here in peace.'

If the context of a goal is not taken into account the result may be the opposite of what is intended. That goals have *frequently* shown themselves to be useful does not mean they will *always* do so, as shown in the following teaching (after Singer 1999):

A successful businessman came to a master and boasted in his presence of his successes and his theory of economic development. After a while the master, who at first had listened silently, objected asking: 'Is growth the only benchmark you use in your theory?' 'Yes, all growth is good in itself,' answered the businessman. 'Oh,' replied the master, 'but isn't that also the way cancer cells think?'

II.5.2 SFT and NLP

II.5.2.1 The difference between goals and miracles

As with NLP, clarifying the client's goals in SFT is also an important aspect in the process of discovering solutions. As we have seen, the miracle question contributes on a more fundamental level to finding a solution than does asking questions about goals – only with the miracle question does it become clear what it is the client actually wants and how the realisation of her goal in her every day life appears.

A goal can be thought out and planned; the client's real wishes will appear through the miracle. The miracle question also reveals the client's entire form of life (in the sense of Wittgenstein), including all the consequences of achieving the goal for the client as well as for her resulting relationships with family members, colleagues, employers, friends and acquaintances.

We arrive at the goal by making a concerted effort. The miracle on the other hand, comes to us as a gift and as such cannot be planned; we can only receive the gift and then marvel at it.

II.5.22 Solution-oriented vs. solution-focused

From the wide range of techniques and approaches classified under NLP, the NLP Meta Model and the well-formedness criteria for goal definition can be useful in drawing a comparison between NLP and SFT.

A) Comparison of the meta model and the solution-focused approach
The NLP Meta Model for discussion leadership borrows from Chomsky's language model, which differentiates between the surface and deep structure of language, where the surface structure is represented by spoken language and the deep structure by the removal of deletions, generalisations and distortions (among other things).

By 'deletions' Chomsky means the relationship of the original elements of the deep structure with the transformed (into surface) structure – that is the process through which, in the transformation of deep structure into surface structure, elements of the deep structure are lost. 'Generalisations' refer to specific information in the deep structure that become unspecific in the surface structure and thus generalised. 'Distortions' are erroneous connections within the surface structure. Deletions, generalisations and distortions are thus the processes that lead to an impoverished model of the world, reduced choice and limited belief sentences.

In order to satisfy the client and provide them with a wide variety of choice, it is useful to remove the deletions in the client's statements, specify her generalisations and disentangle her distortions. In their meta model, Richard Bandler and John Grinder (1998) developed a specific questioning technique to aid this procedure. Since then NLP has developed far beyond the original meta model.

In order to clarify the difference between the approaches of SFT and NLP (in many respects the differences are still large), the following list gives a side-by-side comparison of possible follow-up questions to client statements for both the NLP Meta Model and SFT.

'In fact I never feel good.'

NLP	SFT
'Really? Never at all?' 'In every conceivable moment?' (Questioning the universal quantifier) 'In what way don't you feel good?' (Questioning the unspecific verb) 'Measured against what don't you feel good?' (Questioning the deleted comparison)	'Are there times when you feel just a tiny bit better?' 'On a scale of –10 to 0, where –10 represents your worst state, where would you place your self at this moment?'

'My husband's behaviour still drives me crazy'

NLP	SFT
'How does he do that? Through brainwashing? Solitary confine-ment?' (Drastic questioning of the causal link as a semantic malformedness allows, where successful, for a humorous distancing from the cause and effect perspective) 'What behaviour? And whom is it directed towards?' (Questioning the casual link) 'To whom does your husband behave in this way? What things do *you* then do to drive yourself crazy?' (Questioning of special deletions and the unspecific relation and simultaneous denominalisation and questioning of the casual link)	'How would you notice…?' 'When do you and your husband get along a tiny bit better?' 'Suppose that tonight – after you eat your evening meal – and eventually go to your bed – in the middle of the night a miracle occurs – such that your husband's behaviour was no longer a problem for you – how would you notice this? What would you do then?'

'It was so bad – I've not felt well ever since.'

NLP	SFT
'What, of the things you have noticed, have you taken to be the cause for the deterioration in the situation?' 'What was it that was bad, for whom, and in what way?' 'How, when, where and in relation with whom do you feel bad? Measured against what?' (Questioning of the deletions: missing references, unspecific verbs)	'Recently, were there any times, in which you felt better?' 'Where there any differences? Were there times when things were not as bad?'

'I know I will never find the right partner.'

NLP	SFT
'How and in what way do you know that?' (Questioning the unspecific verb) 'Never? With not one single exception?' (Questioning the universal quantifier) '"Right" for whom?' (Questioning the deleted comparison) '"Right" in what way?' (Questioning the deleted judgment procedure) '"Right" measured how and against what?' (Questioning the deleted benchmark criteria) '"Right" according to which criteria for which period of time?' (Questioning according to deleted specifiers) 'In what way do you mean "find"?' (Questioning the unspecific verb)	'How would you notice that a partner was right for you?' 'How would you notice that a suitable partner for you could turn up?' 'Assuming you had found a suitable partner, what would then be different for you?' 'What would you then do that you don't already do?'

'It has always been like that.'

NLP	SFT
'What has always been like that, and for whom?' 'And in what circumstances was this the case?' (Questioning the deletions)	'How would you notice that something was changing?'

'Nothing at all is changing.'

'Nothing at all? Not even the smallest of changes? In your whole life does nothing ever change?' (Questioning of the universal quantifier) 'For whom has there been change and in what way in particular, and in what way have things not changed?' (Questioning the unspecific references) 'What has not changed?' (Questioning the unspecific subject) 'How have you noticed that nothing at all has changed?' (Questioning the unspecific verb)	'How would you notice that something is beginning to change?'

'Whenever my mother says … I become so furious it spoils my day.'

NLP	SFT
'Really every time?' (Questioning the universal quantifier) 'What part of what your mother says makes you furious, and in what way does she say it?' (Questioning the unspecific verb and the causal link) 'In what way do you become furious?' (Questioning the unspecific verb)	'Can you remember a situation when you were not at all, or less, angry when your mother said…?'

If we compare the questions asked in NLP with those of SFT, we see that the NLP questions aim to complete and specify the statements by the client. When the statements of the client are problem-oriented, the problems are then analysed in more detail. The SFT questions, however, are always oriented towards solutions and probe the client about exceptions to the problem and how solutions can be recognised. Both methods are solution-oriented. SFT, however, immediately moves in the direction of solutions, while NLP often begins with problem analysis. Nonetheless, when the client is asked about or mentions exceptions to the problem (for example, through the questioning of the universal quantifier or modal operators), the questions in the meta model can be used to help specify and clarify them.

B) Comparison of well-formedness criteria for goal definition and the solution-focused approach
In NLP, when the client is asked for her goal, the therapist continues to question the client's statements until the 'well-formedness criteria' for defining the client's goal have been met. The most important of these criteria are as follows:
   The behaviour stated by the client as representing her goal – i.e. the client-defined goal-state – must:

  - be under the client's control – i.e. the client must be able to initiate and sustain it (this means the goal needs to be realistic).
  - be well contextualised – i.e. the client must specify when, where and in relation with whom she would like to realise the respective behaviour or state (the goal must therefore be stated in highly situation-specific terms and described in the form of new behaviour for the client).
  - be stated precisely and in terms of sensory perception – i.e. the client should say what the goal-state or goal behaviour is in as precise a way as possible and how she will perceive its realisation sensually.
  - be formulated positively (linguistically) – i.e. not described in terms of an absence of something ('I will no longer be afraid' might then become 'I will take a deep breath').
  - contain no comparisons with deleted references.

In SFT, simplified versions of these useful well-formedness criteria tend to be incorporated implicitly, without being formulated in the same detailed way. The opening question 'What is your goal?' is not asked in SFT; instead SFT asks: 'What is your concern?' or 'What brings you here?' This encourages the client to expresses a number of wishes, rather than a selected goal statement. Focusing on the socially accepted goal statements brought to the therapy session by the client for example, could make it more difficult for the client to come into contact with the solution and for change in the form of life – from the world of the problem, to that of the solution – to take place. This way of questioning also makes it easier for the client to see what she desires less as an ultimate goal or final solution, and more as the start of something new which cannot be formulated like a rewritable 'goal', but which remains open and allows for future creative metamorphosis and expansion.

Goal clarification tends not to last very long in the solution-focused interview – the goals given by the client only suggest a direction, and the miracle question is asked as soon as possible to reveal the client's true goal.

NLP and many systemic schools ask the following types of questions:

'What do you need to move from your current state to the goal-state?'
'What do you need to believe in order to move from your current state to the goal-state?'
'What can you do in order to achieve the goal-state?'
'What could definitely prevent you from achieving your goal?'

These questions are not asked in SFT, however, since they adhere to a problem-state perspective and make the road to the goal-state appear cumbersome and long. Thanks to the miracle question, the path to the goal can be travelled in an instant, elegantly and with no effort. The client is able to describe this path in detail from the perspective of the goal.

The exercises at the end of the first session are offered to the client so that she realises in her every day life the goal she has already experienced through the miracle question. This will require an amount of hard work and determination, which is why SFT uses scaling questions at this point to clarify the steps taken and progress achieved. Otherwise, the thought of reaching the goal only after having followed a long and tiring path often prevents any contact with the goal on an intellectual level.

The following types of questions are not asked directly in SFT:

'What is good about your current state?'
'What will you give up when you achieve your goal?' ('What is the price of achieving your goal?')

We learn something indirectly when we enquire about the context of the miracle. What is good in the current state (and which would have to be given up in solving the problem) *can* cause difficulties for realising the miracle. The following question can help in this situation:

'And if the *miracle* had occurred now, how would you *then* deal with this problem?'

If questions are asked directly about the price of the solution, the power of the solution (when the miracle is experienced) can be diminished, and the thought of having to give something up can push the client back in the direction of the problem. The use of selective goals, as described above and used widely in the practice of NLP, can be balanced with an exploration of the client's meta goals or meta needs ('What will be ensured for you when you have achieved goal XYZ?'). The NLP well-formedness criteria can thus be utilised in SFT.

In terms of the fundamental logic of the approach, which transforms 'to have goals' into 'to be in the solutions-state', the PeneTRANCE model developed in NLP by Thies Stahl (1988) comes closer to Steve de Shazer's application of the miracle question. For more information, see Appendix 1.

Chapter III

Brief introduction to Systemic Structural Constellations (SySt)

I developed systemic structural constellations work together with Matthias Varga von Kibéd in the years after 1989. The main aspect of this method is the process of working with the constellation itself. The style, approach and attitude adopted in SySt were influenced by hypnotherapy, systemic therapy, solution focused therapy and family therapy.

In contrast with the traditional practice of family constellations which usually only represents people, systemic structural constellations 'positions' a highly diverse range of systems from different fields – body systems, decision structures, goals, resources, alternatives and internal parts. 'Positioned' is used here to mean the process whereby representatives for individual systemic elements are chosen out of a group of people, and then placed in the room according to how the client views the relationship of these elements. The constellation picture is therefore the externalisation of an internal image. The advantage of setting up this picture as externalised is that (unlike an internal picture) it can thus be changed so that the individual systemic parts can feel more comfortable. The resulting 'solution picture' can then retroact positively on the problem situation.

III.1 The basic principles of the constellations method

Constellations should be understood horizontally . . .

and not vertically!

In the method of constellations that we use in SySt, the representatives are placed having been given no information about any features or behaviour of the person they are representing. It suffices merely to indicate who belongs to the particular system, and the level and type of relationship that exists between the various elements of that system. For example, with family constellations, the client places representatives from the group as people belonging to her system according to her internal sense of her relationship to them. This allows the client to externalise her internal image of her family. Family members, for example, who have died or are not spoken of in the family, are thus more likely to be placed on the edge of the constellation and often facing away from it. This method of positioning representatives (i.e. those representing the members of the system), without making any statements, gestures or giving any specific details, was perhaps first used by Thea Schönfelder in an application with psychiatric patients. Bert Hellinger then took this method and adapted it in his family constellations.

The resource of role-playing has been a long established practice in psychotherapy. In psychodrama, for example, scenes are re-enacted in detail and new solutions sought for the problems presented. The difference between this and constellations is that the former provides far more detailed information about the people from the start. Of course, typical constellations effects also occur with psychodrama, but they are difficult to differentiate from the data already supplied to the role-players. Stepping into the role of a counterpart – e.g. a murderer steps into the role of the victim – has thus already been used in psychodrama to help understand other positions and perspectives.

Virginia Satir also used the portrayal of unknown or alien systems using people in her development-oriented family therapy work. She introduced symbolic postures (including the four Satir categories: placater, blamer, hyperrational, irrelevant) and symbolic forms, which can be used to present situations concisely. Examples of this include the *Virginia Steps*: a small step or stool which enables a child to reach the same eye level as his parents; or a role-player as a symbol of a childbirth procedure, who stands with her legs spread such that the representatives of the children can pass through. As in psychodrama, Virginia Satir also provides a lot of information from the beginning – again in order to make the context of past events more visible and easier to understand. For example, she asks about the financial, political and personal situation of parents and relatives in order that clients, as well as the role-players, can picture more effectively their parents and their parents' ability to manoeuvre in a given situation.

Virginia Satir developed family reconstruction, family sculpture and many other dynamic constellations-style procedures. In family reconstructions, important family scenes are re-enacted in order to gain insights into the parental situation and understanding of any problematic behaviour on the part of the parents. Family sculpture, on the other hand, is a static procedure in which the client creates a sculpture of her family using role-players whom she instructs to adopt typical postures and gestures for each family member and whom she provides with statements. The four Satir categories can also be used with the sculpture:

- *blamer*: standing upright, one hand pointing at someone in disapproval
- *placater*: kneeling on the floor, hands imploringly thrust upwards
- *hyperrational*: sitting upright in a chair, stiff, arms folded
- *irrelevant*: standing in room with legs crossed, arms pointing in different directions.

Because of giving the role-players so much information, this procedure does not allow role-played and represented roles to be easily differentiated, the difference being that role-players are doing just that: playing a role, with a great deal of direction about character and attitude, whereas representatives are simply placed to represent the person without any attitudinal or content information about the person to influence their experience. It is then their here-and-now experiences in the particular constellations configuration that is relevant, and is known as 'representative perception'.

III.1.1 Basic aspects of systemic structural constellations (SySt)

Family constellations and SySt both use constellations. However, in terms of their grammar, therapeutic posture and interpretation of constellations events, the two methods are quite different. Systemic structural constellations have more in common with the constructivist-systemic approach and build on the hypnotherapy work of Milton Erickson. This means that a lot of attention is paid to pacing, the client's own language is used and her problem, as formulated by her, is positioned in the constellation – for example, a tetralemma constellation is used for a decision situation and a structural body constellation, placing the relevant body parts, for a physical illness. Bert Hellinger's family constellations, however, are more provocative and more clearly related to the depth psychology perspective.

III.1.1.1 Typical subjects of SySt

We will now look at the typical subjects of constellation work, especialy SySt, and highlight some differences between SySt and other constellation work (in III.1.1.2)

III.1.1.1.1 Representative Perception: an opportunity for experiencing others

Both the procedures mentioned are founded on the constellations method. The surprising thing about representative perception is that it allows systems to be represented using people, where those people know nothing about the system that is to be represented. The people in the constellation, whom we will call '**representatives in the narrow sense**', are asked to describe just their bodily sensations and experience when standing in the position in which they have been placed by the client. We call this **representative perception**. Hellinger used the concept of *foreign feelings*.

In SySt, the representative's body becomes an organ of perception that can be used to experience the sensations, attitudes, emotions and thoughts of the member of the unknown system. The people in the constellation describe just the differences in their state compared to their experience having been placed in the constellation. Interpretations or opinions about their perceptions should not be expressed at this point. The experiences that belong to the unknown system perceived through the representative's body, will disappear as soon the representative moves out of the constellation and sits down.

Representative perception normally kicks in as soon as the person has been chosen as a representative (or at the latest when they are properly placed in the constellation) while experiences specific to their own personal situation are not affected. These people now stand in for the people they are representing. This provides us in some sense with the possibility of experiencing and knowing someone else's psychic state. The statements made by the representatives show a high level of congruence with the represented person's actual condition. They express relationship structures. They are not absolute correlations: rather, in terms of content, they feature the represented elements of the system, contain typical statements of the represented elements of the system or point to clear similarities in the changing process.

At what moment representative perception begins depends on how it has been introduced by the facilitator before the constellation implicitly or explicitly. If the facilitator states that the representative sensations begin as soon as the representatives have been placed, then 'standing' and 'sitting' will serve to differentiate between 'belonging to the constellation' and 'not belonging'. However, another criterion for differentiation can be introduced verbally: for example, 'sitting in the surrounding circle of the constellations room' and 'being inside the circle'.

The act of transformation from person to representative occurs verbally through the naming of the representative: for example, 'you represent X'. A name can also be assigned at this stage, though numbers serve equally well. Moreover, a range of experimental constellations designed to identify the minimum requirements for representation to occur has clearly suggested that not even the name need be given in order that the representatives, immediately after being positioned, can experience the sensations appropriate to the person they represent and give meaningful responses.

To release the representatives from their roles (de-roling), words can again be used, e.g. having the representatives say their own names to themselves. Other possibilities include:

- Shaking out of arms and legs
- Walking around
- Client releases the role player using words
- Cold water on face and arms
- Shower

III. 1.1.1.1.1 Perception of other people's experiential states, not re-incarnation or past-life states

The notion of representative perception presupposes no concept of a soul as some sort of entity or field. It only points to the generation of specific information states similar to those created by processes of perception in the usual sense. It is therefore used as a guiding metaphor for the thematic handling of certain phenomena in group situations and should not be unnecessarily obscured by concepts like reincarnation, or specific ideas about souls of system elements, abstract things or whatever.

The fact that other people's psychic states can be experienced under certain conditions can sometimes give rise to wild speculation about the process this entails. Some people have speculated that in family constellations the souls of ancestors initiate a form of contact. However, this can be disproved. In structural body constellations, body parts are positioned and the representatives perceive sensations appropriate to the individual body parts of the client. To speak of the 'soul' of a toe or the heart would have little meaning here, given our use of language.

Similarly, in abstract constellations, as in belief polarity constellations, the presentation of a 'soul' for the systemic elements of 'knowledge', 'love', and 'order' would be particularly strange. When we use reincarnation as an explanatory hypothesis in representative perception, we serve only to mystify constellations unnecessarily. The idea of a new opportunity for perception is thus simpler and contains no assumption of entities such as souls in the elements of the system or abstract concepts.

III.1.1.1.2 The constellations process

With family constellations, Bert Hellinger emphasises that the constellation should be positioned with complete attention in order to ensure that the first constellation picture can be experienced by the client, as opposed to a merely rational understanding. We often support the constellation setting-up process with variations of the following words:

'Concentrate on your breathing. Feel how the soles of your feet touch the floor – and notice how your hands touch the representative's back – feel where your hands are leading you. Follow the movement that arises.'

These trance-inducing words interrupt the client's thinking so that, in the resulting confusion, she is able to connect with her intuition more.

As stated before, sometimes representation begins at the moment a role is assigned (and not during the initial constellation set up). This indicates that the decisive process in inducing representation is that of role assignment, where as mentioned the role can be named only by a number. The words, 'You are now…', or the selection of representatives by the client, initiates the constellations process. Words or an according action induce a process in which what is in another's psyche can be perceived.

Of course, this does not mean that representatives no longer have any access to their own feelings. Taken-on feelings from the person represented can resonate with the representative's own feelings, and we call these **individual resonance feelings**. Sometimes the individual's own feelings may even disappear after they have been assigned a role. This can sometimes mean, for instance, that a headache disappears during a constellation, though in most cases it will return after de-roling.

III.1.1.1.2.1 What can be learned from constellations
Constellations teach us that people do not exist separately from each other, as we tend to believe in most situations. If people are able to feel the bodily experiences in what for them is an unknown system with such accuracy as soon as they are positioned in the constellation, then we also know more about our own families than we think. The common assumption that we exist separately from one another as individual entities, and can only really experience our own selves, must therefore be brought into question.

If, on the other hand, we begin with the assumption that we are **connected with each other at a fundamental level,** and that due to internal and external influences our ordinary level of reciprocal perception has been weakened, then constellations can serve to show us how we could again perceive more fully. Mutual understanding would then be readily available and could only be disrupted by internal or external influences. It would no longer be a question of 'How do we establish contact?' but more a matter of: 'What do we need to avoid doing in order that the contact remains intact and uninterrupted?'

This has also been demonstrated by further observations of constellations. It has been shown on frequent occasions that family members, although not present during the constellation, nonetheless experience change in the same way as the representative in the constellation. For example, an uncle in America, who had been shunned by his family, and with whom he had had no contact for the last ten years, suddenly called one of my clients within a few days of a constellation. In another example, after a woman's constellation at which her mother was not present, without being prompted the mother began to talk with her daughter about a matter that had been a taboo subject between them for the previous twenty years.

Since we normally assume that we exist separately from each other, we will ask ourselves how a certain piece of information can be transmitted to someone else. I would suggest that this is perhaps the wrong question. If, for example, we start from the assumption that there is a connection between people, the question then becomes: 'What is it that separates people?' We are then forced to find out why we no longer have contact with each other. The question of receiving information from one another is now no longer valid.

We also learn from constellations that feelings and emotions do not belong to us as individuals in the way that we think. If new feelings and emotions can appear within us during the constellations process and then disappear equally quickly after de-roling, this tells us that bodily feelings and emotions are not stable attributes belonging to us – they visit us like fluttering birds and then leave us again.

Constellations can provide a certain amount of training in 'letting go'. During the constellations process, the representatives learn how they can disengage from emotions, feelings and thoughts. As soon as we define ourselves through our feelings, emotions and thoughts, we become their slaves and thus make any form of change more difficult to achieve.

III.1.1.1.3 The difficulty of not performing constellations: constellations as a daily process

From the SySt point of views, constellations occur all the time during our daily lives. Indeed, it is very difficult *not* to perform constellations. For example, our **gestures**, when talking to someone, often have the character of a constellation. If you say 'On the one hand …' while making a gesture with your right hand, followed by '… and on the other hand …' accompanied by a gesture with the left hand, you are pointing to two different positions and as such have performed a small constellation. Frequently, your conversation partner adopts a different posture unconsciously, according to each of the positions indicated, and then places himself, by means of this change of location, into each of the two positions – this is especially the case when we emphasise the difference by using our tone of voice and facial expressions.

In principle there is no difference between this and what happens when we are placed in two different positions during a constellation and observe the difference in our physical sensations.

When someone asks us, 'What do you imagine your partner would say about it?' in our thoughts we place ourselves in his position and look to see if, from within, we are able to find an answer. Again we are performing a constellation, albeit only mentally. The same is true of **circular questions**, a method used by the Milan School, in which individual family members are asked about the reactions of other family members to different situations. We are only capable of answering such questions if we place ourselves in the position of the other person. Try answering the following question, and note how you arrived at the answer:

'What would your father say if your mother were to plan to go away on a trip with you?'

Did you feel how you physically transplanted yourself into your father's position? Or maybe you also took up another physical posture? In doing so you have performed a partial constellation in your mind.

Gestalt therapy, for example, uses the technique of the empty chair as a representation for another person. This means a conversation can take place between the client and, say, her mother, by placing two chairs opposite one another. The client sits in each of the chairs alternatively and conducts the conversation from both positions accordingly. The difference from an actual constellation is that the position of the chairs, as the representatives of the client and her mother, are not chosen in the same way, they are simply positioned opposite one another as in a standard conversation arrangement without taking into account the specific distances or angles between the two people. As a result, the geometry of the arrangement is not sufficiently specific for it to be a constellation, although certain constellations-like processes do still occur.

In other words, we gain a better understanding of some of the effects of this type of conversational activity by viewing them from the perspective of a constellation. Given that the client, while sitting in one of the chairs, begins to represent her mother (i.e. behaves as if she were her mother and to a certain extent becomes a part of her), it should not then come as such a big surprise that her answers fit so well with those of the mother. Even the phenomenon reported by clients that their conversation partner (here the mother) also changed accordingly following an implementation of this type of dialogue can be clearly understood from the constellation point of view. We often find that family members, who were absent during a constellation, nonetheless change their behaviour after the constellation has taken place – even in cases where they were told nothing about it. If the representative of the mother is able to become part of what for her is an alien system (i.e. by behaving like the client's mother and making some change), it then becomes clear, using this model of the world, that the represented mother can also make the same change. In a sense, the representative has paved the way for her. Currently we only have a few relevant framework assumptions for this type of world model and no detailed paradigm. Some people take Rupert Sheldrake's morphic fields (1984) as an analogy to this. His experiments – although still controversially discussed in the scientific community – seem to show how teaching subjects – to take an example from education – that have already been studied by certain pupils, facilitate their learning by other pupils – i.e. they can master them faster.

This experience of mental constellations, gestural constellations and constellations using chairs can be put to good use in individual work as we did with SySt. Absent group members can be replaced by symbols, anchors or cataleptic fingers and hands (described below) as impersonal representatives.

Anchors can be used in the following way: the client picks up a symbolic object (e.g. a pair of shoes, a cushion or a sheet of paper with names and direction indicators), moves around the room and intuitively finds a place for the object. She then proceeds to place all the other systemic components in the same way. When all the objects have been positioned, she then takes the place of each of the objects in turn and reports her physical sensations accordingly.

On moving from one anchor-marked position to another, it is important that the client performs a full de-roling by shaking, saying her name to herself, moving around the room, or, if the representation is a stressful experience for her, by rinsing her hands and face in cold water. Through this de-roling process, each associated experience as a systemic member is followed by the recreation of a disassociated meta-position in relation to the represented system. As soon as the client has become disassociated, she can talk with the facilitator about what she experienced in the different representative positions. While in the daily life of her family she belongs to the system, through the constellation, which creates an externalised picture of her family, the client is given the opportunity to observe her family from a meta-position.

The facilitator rearranges the systemic elements and suggests suitable rituals, while changes in the experiences among the systemic members in the constellation are sensed by the client when she stands in the position of the anchor.

Instead of anchors, **symbols** (e.g. dolls or figures) can also be used by placing them on a table. The client can experience how it feels to be in each position by touching the figures with her finger.

This way of working with constellations has the advantage that the client experiences all of the positions from an internal perspective and gains an insight into the perceptions of the individual systemic elements. One slight disadvantage, however, is that the client experiences all the positions in an associated way and is unable to view the constellations process in an entirely dissociated way from the perspective of an observer.

In a non-therapeutic context, a **constellation using a piece of paper and cards** stating names and directions provides a possible form of constellation for organisations. The client can touch the cards with her middle finger, moving them across the sheet of paper intuitively to find the right position. Rearrangements and rituals are proposed by the facilitator, and the changes in perceptions are again verified by the client by touching the cards with her finger (OUR best results were achieved using a **cataleptic** middle finger). We developed this technique building on the hypnotherapeutic use of ideomotor movements.

The most extreme example of the reduction in symbolisation in systemic structural constellations is achieved using a **constellation drawn on paper**. It is necessary to work with a *cataleptic finger* in this instance. The following exercise can help you find out what a *cataleptic finger* is:

Take your right hand (or dominant hand, as the case may be) by the wrist using your left hand (or non-dominant hand) and hold it up in the air. Now release your right hand. It should normally, if you are completely relaxed, fall back down to your lap. Repeat this action a number of times. Now, very slowly, lift your right hand up using your left hand. Slowly and carefully release the grip of your left hand and allow your right hand to remain aloft. Now raise your left hand also. You will notice that both hands feel different. Now make some gestures with your left hand, and afterwards do the same with your right hand. You will notice that your right hand has become partially numb and is difficult to move in comparison with your left hand.

Your right hand has become cataleptic – i.e. you have less direct conscious control over it, as can be seen by the reduced reaction of this hand when it is moved. A cataleptic hand is able to sense feelings and changes without these feelings being spread over the entire body.

The facilitator can use this technique of **the cataleptic hands** as a representative in a constellation – and since she has two hands, we in fact already have two representatives that can be used in individual therapy when we are lacking people. Using a chair and both our hands, we thus are able to represent four positions: that of the focus (the client), which is the first to be taken up by the client herself, as well as three other positions.

Returning to the constellation performed with cards on paper, the client now draws circles and squares – representing the individual systemic elements including arrows to indicate direction – on the paper in positions that she senses are the most appropriate using her finger as gauge. Rearrangements and rituals are again suggested by the facilitator, and the client senses the changes in the various represented images by using her cataleptic fingers.

We can list the aforementioned forms of constellation in increasing order of their level of abstraction, as follows:

1. Constellations using people as representatives
2. Constellations using symbolic anchors
3. Constellations using symbols, performed on table
4. Constellations using cards, performed on table
5. Constellations drawn on paper using cataleptic finger
6. Constellations with no specific role assignment with arbitrary room arrangement (use of chairs for conversation)
7. Constellations using the imagination
8. Mental constellations triggered by circular questions

Surprisingly, in the first five forms there is no appreciable decrease in intensity. The only difference – albeit a substantial one – is that the external picture for forms 2 to 8 is at times experienced in an associated way by the client, who thus at times loses her dissociated observer perspective. The use of people in many respects can be considered a luxury when performing constellations.

III.1.1.1.4 Basic categories of intervention

We can split the different forms of therapeutic intervention found in systemic structural constellations into the following categories:

- positional work
- process work
- tests

By **positional work** we mean all interventions that, by changing the arrangement, lead to an improvement in the experiences of the representatives. This includes the repositioning of representatives, changes in spacing and angles, as well as establishing eye contact between representatives by position swapping and the introduction of excluded people.

By **process work** we mean all interventions designed to bring about an improvement for the representatives using a temporal process. In this the room layout is rarely changed (if any changes are made this is only done to assist the performance of, say, a ritual, after which the original arrangement is restored). Process work includes rituals, the act of making ritual statements, establishing eye contact, finding strength and support by using the family line, clarifying relationships etc. At this point, methods from other therapy schools can be integrated.

When talking about process work, we may also speak of energy or information work. Process work, energy work and information work are used here synonymously, though they in fact emphasise different approaches – the word 'process' stresses the temporal nature of the intervention; the use of 'energy' points to changes in energy states after interventions; and the term 'information' indicates that our 'know-how' changes as a result of the interventions. For example, when we say, 'You are my father' or 'You are my son', the representative will in general be familiar with this type of relationship – what is new here is the experience of *how* it is to be a 'father' and *how* it is to be a 'son'.

When dealing with information we distinguish between '**know-how**' and '**know-what**'. *Know-what* means content, deeds, circumstances and sequences of events, while *know-how* denotes the experiential nature of something. For example, knowing what it is like to have a brother is *know-how*, while the information that someone has two brothers is *know-what*. Constellations, being primarily experiential, relay *know-how*. The representatives take in nonverbal information through their bodies, which, as an experience, constitutes *know-how* that is partially transferred to the client – some information is always lost in the transfer.

By **tests** we mean interventions that are not performed with the intention of improving the representatives' experience, but which only serve to test hypotheses and clarify suspected dynamics and contexts. Interventions in this category include the following:

- allowing one family member to follow another (placing the representatives in line) in order to test for a certain dynamic
- testing whether partial pattern representations are present (a partial representation of an alien systemic pattern or fate) by having the representatives involved switch places

We are dealing with partial pattern representations here rather than 'identifications', since only *some* behavioural patterns are represented but the behaviour of both people is *not identical* whereas 'identifications' in the orginal meaning of the term would be 'made identical', thus requiring the complete pattern. We also find these different forms of intervention in family constellations, albeit hypothesis-testing in family constellations does not occur as explicitly as in SySt.

III.1.1.2 Differences
Besides their similar common subjects, there are many differences between family constellations and SySt, some of which are described briefly below.

III.1.1.2.1 Systemic theory deduction of the basic principles of SySt
Through working with family constellation over a number of years, Bert Hellinger observed the following four basic principles:

–   everyone has the same right to membership of the system
–   in a family, an older child takes precedence over a younger child
–   between an ancestral family and the present-day family, the latter family takes precedence
–   whoever makes the larger contribution takes precedence over a person whose contribution is lesser

These principles are also valid for systemic structural constellations. However, we have given them a systems theoretical basis and added some additional principles. The orientation of a system for existence, growth, propagation, immunisation and/or individuation decides whether the following principles apply.

Our **first principle** states a number of conditions that must be fulfilled in order to ensure the **existence of a system**.

> In order to be able to establish the limits of a system, it is necessary to clarify who belongs to the system and who does not. This is established by means of a number of rules. Breaching these rules leads to disturbances in the system.
>
> fl

The principle of observing membership criteria

In families, membership is established through birth. As a result, no one can be excluded from a family system, since membership by birth is a fact that cannot be denied or changed. An exception to this is made where a family member commits murder. A child belongs to the family by being given life. If the child goes on to commit murder there is then a danger that one of his offspring will have to atone for the murder as a form of compensation – i.e. he or she will carry some of the guilt. For this reason, it is important that the culprit alone carry the burden of guilt. Because of the deed he has committed, a murderer changes his relationship with the members of his family, and it becomes impossible for him, without causing massive disruption, to continue living within the family.

The kinship that he shares with the other family members remains as it is and cannot be taken away from him. It makes no sense, for example, to say that the father no longer exists after he has committed murder. If a father murders another member of the family, however, it can then be very helpful to stop living with him after the event, since all trust will have been destroyed and the relationship will be dominated by fear. A separation from the murderer can also help in many cases to protect the children from carrying the father's guilt.

Within a company, on the other hand, membership and the conditions of membership are determined by contracts, explicit and implicit agreements, and conventions. This means an employee can be fired if he contravenes the rules. If an employee is unfairly dismissed, however, the system acts as if it has a memory. The replacement for the wrongly dismissed employee will often act out some part of the behaviour of his predecessor, or encounter unexpected difficulties in his new position so that his colleagues react to him in a similar way as they did to his predecessor, and the relationship dynamics remains unchanged.

One important difference between organisational and family systems is replaceability. An employee of a company carries out a certain job function, which at another date might be carried out by somebody else, while a family member has a unique position in his or her being related to other family members. Because of this difference, effects of spontaneous representation are even more likely in the organisational context, as an employee of a company already represents a position, while a family member gets their relationships at and by birth rather than by allocation.

The substitution of positions in companies helps make representations a popular topic, and it is therefore extremely important that a predecessor's merits are respected and that no-one is unfairly excluded.

There are some systems for which only this first principle is of any relevance. In such systems, **membership is often determined by a single incident**. These types of systems are unable to grow and propagate themselves – e.g. the system of a group of survivors of an aeroplane disaster or the founding members of a club.

For the facilitator, observing the first principle means she must ask as soon as possible about excluded, unmentioned, rejected or banished members, whom she can then add to the system.

The **second principle** deals with the protection of **growth and propagation**. By growth we refer to what happens when elements within a system multiply, and by propagation we refer to the process by which one system begets another or more new systems. Growth and propagation are thus relative terms as they are defined in terms of the system. Thus, if I define the family as the system, the birth of children can then be seen as growth of the family, and the marriage of one of the children represents propagation since afterwards there are two families.

When a system grows, those who belong to the system lose some space within that system. It is necessary to compensate for this loss of space in order to avoid conflict over the remaining space due to limited resources. Consequently, those already in the system should be accorded a higher value in this respect. This can be achieved by **recognising the order of succession**.

fl

The principle of direct chronology

Within a system, an older systemic member takes precedence over a younger member

With team constellations, for example, the team is often more relaxed and there is more clarity if the order in which members joined the team is respected. Failure to show respect for those that joined the team at an earlier stage often results in a lack of support for those joining later.

When a system propagates itself, the boundaries of the new system are initially weaker than those of the existing system. In order to protect the new system it is necessary that it initially takes precedence over the older system.

fl

The principle of inverse chronology

The new system takes precedence over the old system

An example of this is the creation of subsidiary companies. If a subsidiary company's initial weakness is not shielded from the dominance of the parent system, the subsidiary will have no room to develop. Too early a separation, when the subsidiary company is not yet viable and overestimates its own strength, would be equally detrimental.

A good example of systems that are primarily concerned with **growth**, and not propagation, is that of religious sects. The founder of a sect is not normally pleased when a group of members splits from his sect to form another (propagation), although he is of course keen to see his own sect grow.

Learning groups, on the other hand, are **propagation-oriented**, and not growth-oriented: the number of members of such groups is normally restricted, there is generally no desire to grow in size, and new members are often accepted unwillingly. The purpose of these groups is to pass on specialist knowledge, which in most cases is expected to be passed on to others – i.e. after completion, the members of the group are expected to found new groups themselves. In terms of therapeutic training for example, the first system can be of the teacher-pupil-system type and the following system of the facilitator-client-system type.

To the facilitator, these two sub-principles prove that she can perform rituals within systems for the recognition of the order of succession, and that when faced with two systems, the newer system needs to be protected from the older system.

The **third principle – the regulation of energy flow** – boosts the immune strength and health of a system.

> In order that systems are not weakened by internal conflicts, it is important that contributions made by individual elements be recognised for development of stability and avoidance of destruction by internal disputes. This calls for the regulation of free energy flow within a system.
>
> fl

The principle of precedence for higher contribution

This principle is violated in cases where an element in a body system, for example, becomes ill and other elements in the system start to perform its functions without receiving proper recognition. Just as the inner attitude of a sick person can influence the healing process, for body parts which have taken on an increased work load, there is a need for their contribution to be recognised so that they continue their efforts 'willingly'.

The basic principles we have mentioned above constitute general laws that can be complemented with more specific laws to suit specific systems. For example, the following two additions can be made when dealing with organisations:

1. The recognition of the systemic and official hierarchy
2. The recognition of internal and external influences

At the top of the systemic hierarchy are those informal leaders whose contributions do not normally receive sufficient recognition. The official hierarchy, on the other hand, ensures the organisation's appearance to the outside world. Recognition of internal influences offers protection from sabotage, while recognition of external influences can help with the process of adapting to the environment.

With internal and external influences, we should also differentiate between those influences that are proper and those that are improper. Of course, we should only be dealing here with proper influences, but where a systemic member gains influence by improper means it is still important to develop a certain amount of understanding and establish contact with him so that his wishes can be taken into account in a different way.

An example of an internal influence that deserves recognition could be that of an employee's knowledge about the strengths and ways of his colleagues, from which the whole company benefits despite this not having anything to do with his actual position. External influences can be consultants or acquaintances of colleagues whose knowledge or financial support are of considerable help to the company.

Systems primarily organised around this third principle include clubs. In some clubs, for example, membership is acquired though consistent presence and the payment of a membership fee. However, the contribution made by the individual for the benefit of the club is also important here. Frequent participation, helping other members and making donations all make a member more important to the club. Many clubs are neither growth-oriented nor propagation-oriented, and the level of performance is not always important either. Rather, the working with each other and for each other is of central importance.

The **fourth principle** encourages **maturation among individual members of the system.**

> In order to enable systemic members to develop their own skills and perform services it is important that their contributions be recognised so that, through this, their performance will be reinforced. This supports the differences between systemic members.
>
> fl
> *The principle of precedence for performance and skills*

This principle is often considered before the first three principles in organisations. However, if level of performance is given precedence over contribution, those who have done more for the company will feel discriminated against and will make less effort in the future. Commitment of the members of a system is an important factor in organisations and boosts cohesion and the energy flow within a company.

While recognising performance increases motivation, recognising skills ensures access to resources.

A good example of a system in which individuation, in the sense of individual maturation, is encouraged as a first priority is that of training groups in further education. These groups can mainly be described in terms of the 'learning' motif and performance (also serving as the criteria for membership). They are not concerned with growth and propagation, since each member learns for him or herself and does not plan to pass on what they have learned.

The schema below (Figure 1) gives an overview of the four basic principles with their function for preserving the system, systemic growth, systemic propagation, immune strength creation and individuation.

Overview of the basic principles of systemic preservation (from Sparrer and Varga von Kibéd 2000, p. 170)

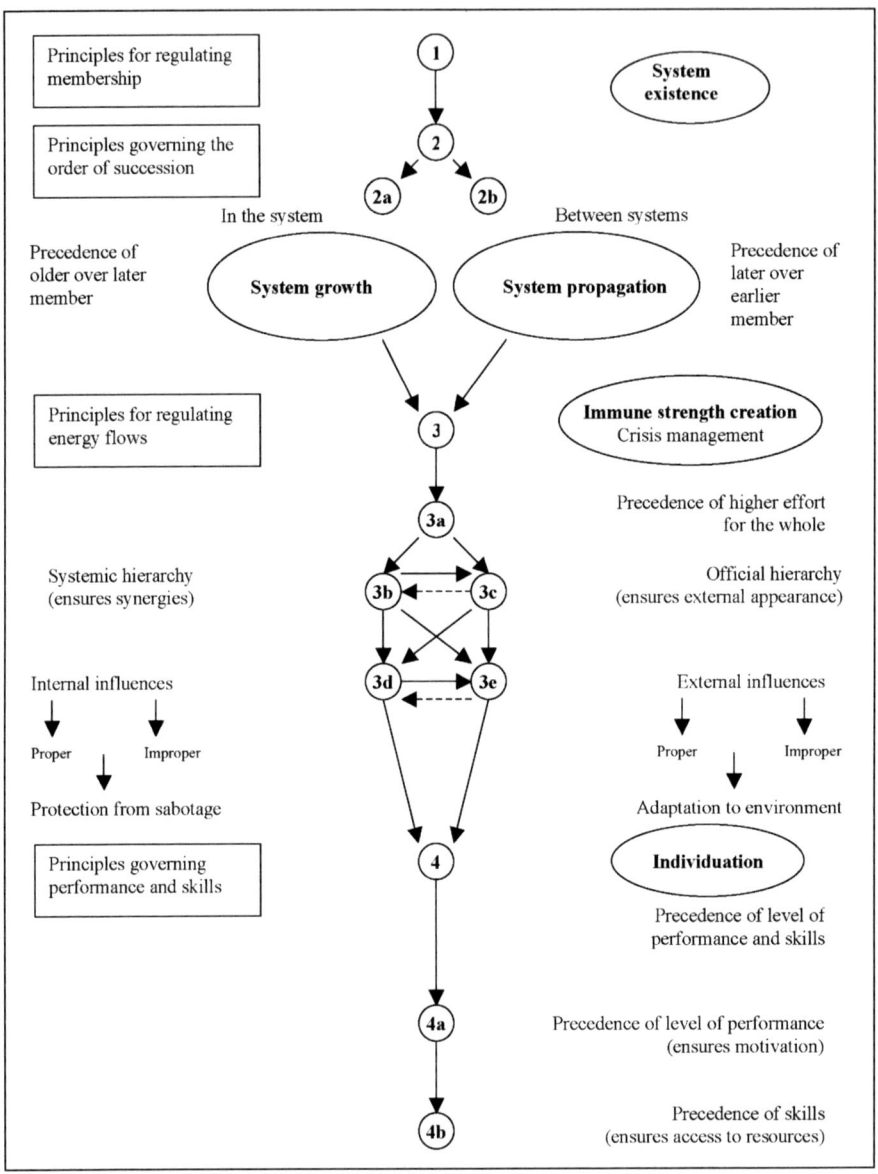

Figure 1: Overview of the basis principles of systemic preservation

The four basic principles that govern membership, the order of succession and energy flow as well as encouraging individuation can be derived from the following **meta-principles**:

First meta-principle: what is given must be recognised. All other principles can be derived from this principle in a specifiable way, since:

- entry into the system is determined by birth or previously established membership criteria. These are 'givens' and only by fulfilling these criteria can a person join the system. Naturally this doesn't mean that the rules cannot be changed in general.
- the order of entry is not determined arbitrarily but takes place over a certain time period and is a given.
- the involvement of a person is seen in their behaviour.
- the performance and skills of a person can be seen in their actions and work.

The difference between things we are able to change and things we must accept as the result of chance is described in the following teaching (de Mello 1996, p.38):

A master said to a woman who was bemoaning her fate: 'You yourself establish your own fate.' 'But I am not responsible for being born a woman,' replied the woman, to which the master said: 'Being born a woman is not a matter of fate – it is a matter of chance. Your fate consists of how you accept being a woman and what you make out of it.'

Systems that do not obey their own rules become unreliable and chaotic, and endanger their own existence. These types of rules normally need not to be mentioned explicitly. The rules often can be seen from the behaviour of the members of the system, that is in their following the rules. Indeed, Wittgenstein emphasises that we first recognise rules through their observance. A rule, therefore, does not exist as such, but shows itself through the effect of its being followed.

These basic principles are to be understood **curatively**. This means they should be understood neither descriptively nor normatively. Instead, they should be understood in the following sense:

When you respect the principles, this contributes to the cure. When you do not respect the principles, this damages you and endangers the system.

Often the basic principles are understood normatively as desired rules and are therefore perceived as a restriction. If they are taken to be curative, on the other hand, they then serve as guidelines for reducing disturbances; and if disturbances are already present, they help with their removal. In this sense, the basic principles are non-judgmental.

The **second meta-principle governs the order in which the basic principles are observed**. It says that

- the principle of system existence has precedence over the principle of system growth and system propagation.
- these principles in turn take precedence over the principle of system immunisation.
- this principle in turn takes precedence over the principle of system individuation.

Systems that must fight for their very existence are not able to deal sufficiently well with their growth and propagation, or have no energy left to do so. Systems in which growth and propagation are endangered are not able to guarantee the creation of immune strength. Systems with weak immune strength must first deal with that weakness before working on individuation. These priorities are summarised in the following schema.

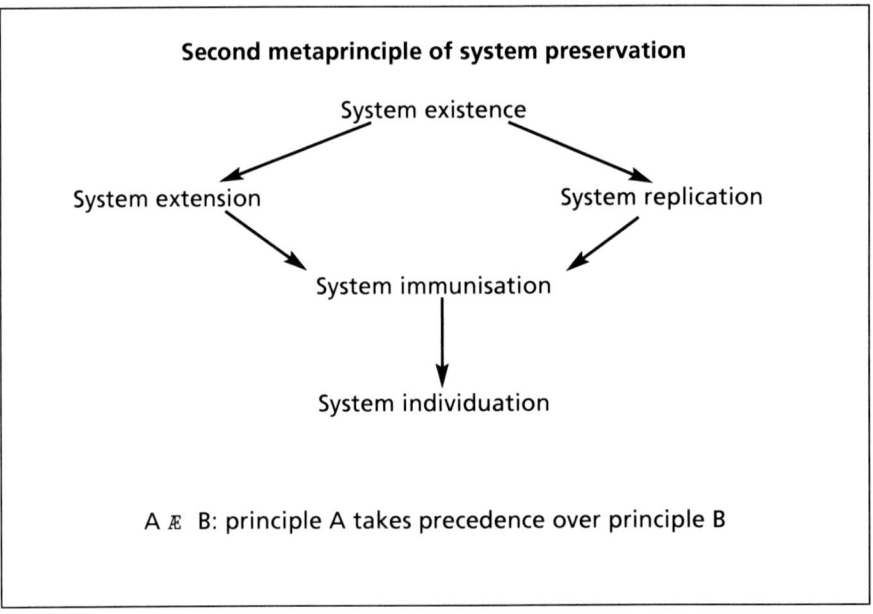

Second metaprinciple of system preservation

System existence

System extension   System replication

System immunisation

System individuation

A Æ B: principle A takes precedence over principle B

This indicates that the basic assumptions take precedence over one another in the given order implying that a breach of the first basic assumption will cause the most damage or produce the severest consequences. It is for this reason that we begin a constellation by asking about excluded members and the first action is to introduce them into the system. We can therefore expect this intervention to have the greatest effect.

Next we need to consider the principle of direct chronology. A breach here counts as the second most severe breach of the basic principles of systemic preservation, and it is only after considering this that we can look to the principles of the level of commitment and performance.

The final principle most commonly comes into play when dealing with organisations. However, from a systemic point of view, it appears only in fourth position, since early consideration of this principle can give rise to conflict.

III.1.1.2.2 Working at different structural levels

Working at different structural levels is typical for systemic structural constellations but does not occur in family constellations. We talk about there being more than one structural level where a constellation of a given system changes into a constellation of another system.

For example, in a 'problem constellation', where an 'obstacle' represents a maternal component, it is possible to change from the problem constellation to a family constellation. The original 'obstacle' component can be renamed 'mother' and the relevant rituals performed with the representative of the mother. We call this an **explicit change of structural level**. If, however, we perform the same ritual with the 'obstacle', but in an abstract, hidden form, we call it an **implicit change of structural level**. Here we are working at the family level but have not previously renamed the 'obstacle' and so we remain explicitly with the problem constellation.

An advantage of implicit changes in structural levels is that it allows **hidden work** (work where the representatives are not named or told what or who they represent and where the topic of the client is not revealed) to be performed. This gives rise to opportunities, especially in non-therapeutic contexts, of working contractually with constellations. For example, it is often essential to have a higher degree of protection for individual employees, since there is no therapeutic contract in these situations, even though therapy-related issues may still arise. *Hidden work* ensures that third party observers are not privy to sensitive information regarding their colleagues. For the colleague, on the other hand, this hidden way of working remains sufficiently explicit to be understood, or if he or she fails to recognise this, the information can still be accepted by his or her unconscious.

A further opportunity offered by changing structural levels is that of working on different levels simultaneously. If we do not rename systemic components explicitly then the rituals performed will act on both levels depending on the type of constellation being performed. For example, in a problem constellation, besides the family level, the work situation will also be affected, meaning that the problem structure and the family structure exist simultaneously. In such cases it is important to formulate the therapeutic interventions in a non-level-dependant manner. For example, in a ritual of giving something back to the place where it belongs for example by returning a burden, a guilt, a responsibility. In the case of an explicit family structural constellation, we might say the following:

'Dear mother – I have received this from you – and have carried it for you for a long time – out of love – I am now giving it back to you, to whom it belongs – and will leave it with you – completely.'

 Instead of this, however, we can say the following:

'It reached me from you – But it belongs to you – And although it is difficult for me – I am now giving it back to you – and am leaving it with you – completely.'

Or, shorter still:

'From you – and back to you – now entirely.'

When different systemic levels are worked on simultaneously in this way, we call this kind of work **systemically ambiguous**. Contrary to clear structural level changes, in systemically ambiguous work we work on different systemic levels simultaneously.

III.1.1.2.2.1 Structural level changes in the example of structural body constellations
I have developed a specific type of constellation in order to make a fluid transition from a body system to family system: this is the **body structural constellation**. In this type of constellation, the body parts, body systems and organs named by the client, are positioned in the constellation. In body structural constellations we distinguish between the following steps:

1.   The client positions in the constellation a representative for herself (we call this '*the focus*'), and the representatives for the body parts, systems and organs which she considers relevant for her specific problem.
2.   If only one of a pair of body parts is placed in the constellation, the facilitator then adds the corresponding part (eg the kidneys). The first part of the pair to be positioned is usually the one that is sick or suffering, while that added by the facilitator is the healthy one. The sick body parts can then express their thanks to each of the healthy parts for their compensatory over-exertion:

'I thank you for your efforts.'

Through this act of recognition, the representatives of the suffering body parts become more willing to carry their burden. This principle of adding the counterpart of the body parts, however, is of secondary importance in comparison with the step described in point 5. This means that step 2 can in fact be performed after step 8.

3. The facilitator asks the representatives about their bodily sensations.
4. When body parts have lost contact with each other, the facilitator reinstates this contact by, for example:
    * repositioning
    * changing line of sight
    * statements, such as, 'Only now I am beginning to perceive you for the first time.'
5. When the representatives mention hints of family members being excluded, the facilitator allows these to be added to the constellation after consultation with the client.

Examples of these hints can be cold shivers, the collective gazing of some of the representatives towards the same position, cold air at ground level, the feeling of a representative or some representatives that someone is missing. This specific combination of body constellations with partial family constellations distinguishes structural body constellations from body constellations.

6. The new representatives are asked about their physical sensations
7. A **return ritual** is performed. The body part that reacts most strongly to particular family members, together with the focus, returns an assumed burden to its rightful place through the placing of, for example, a cushion at the feet of the family member in question, saying:

'We recognise your difficult fate. Its effects reached us and affected us strongly. We received this (the burden) through you. But it belongs to you and your family line and not to us, and we are giving it back to you now and are leaving it with you entirely.'

Having made this statement, they then return to their positions. The family member picks up the symbolic burden and presses it to his chest. By doing this the representative can check whether the symbol feels right being with her, and if this is the case she can say:

'It feels right being with me. Leave it with me.'

If she does not feel that the symbolic burden is in its right place, the representative can then place the symbol behind her at a distance she feels to be fitting. In general, the focus and the body parts now feel relieved. If a body part continues to feel burdened, the return ritual can be repeated.

When all body parts have returned their particular burdens to their corresponding family members most representatives feel better.

8.   Next all family members are positioned outside the body system such that both systems – body and family – are no longer mixed.

9.   Finally, the client takes up the position of the *focus*. The individual body parts can touch her and tell her who they are. Here we again emphasise that they are no longer mixed with the parts of the family system. The client can take in the picture as it now is.

We now have two structural levels in the constellation present simultaneously: that of the body and that of the family. The change of structural level from the body system to the family system starts to occur when hints of excluded family members are perceived. With this type of constellation, family members often appear as introjections within the body system. It is important here that both levels are kept apart – for example, by placing all body parts close together, and keeping the family members separate, outside the body system.

Sometimes, we can see to an extent the client's family standing in the initial arrangement of a **body constellation** (in which only body parts are constellated). In rare cases each body part can be seen as representing a family member. This would be considered an implicit change of structural level. In this case we can continue to work in a structurally ambiguous way. It is also possible that the change of structural level occurs explicitly and we then continue to work on the family level.

An example of this occurred during a further education seminar at which only one participant, of those that had done a family constellation the day before, also chose to enrol for a body constellation. As she positioned her body parts, she in effect drew the picture of a family – i.e. each body part corresponded to a family member and was standing on the same spot as the members of her family in the constellation the day before. We then added to the previous day's constellation picture a body part that had been missing, rearranged the picture according to the model for the family constellation and thus arrived at the solution picture for the body constellation. Her physical symptoms improved immediately after the constellation. The body constellation proved to be a useful addition to the family constellation since the transferral of the improvements after the family constellation to the body system had not occurred automatically.

After a body constellation, the physical symptoms of the client often react very quickly to the constellation – sometimes with immediate improvements and sometimes in the form of a healing crisis that is often followed by improvements compared with the original condition. Body constellations are naturally no replacement for medical treatment. However, they can be helpful where psychological attitudes and forces may be working against healing. This implies that body constellations could be a useful addition to any physical treatment. Helpful interventions in family constellations can also be useful for the corresponding body parts in a body constellation. This can also provide the facilitator with new ideas for interventions when she sees the parallels in these structural levels.

III.1.1.2.3 Categories of symbols in systemic structural constellations

Systemic structural constellations make use of more than the limited number of symbols used in family constellations; their use of a wider ranger of symbols allows the constellations procedure to enjoy an increased range of expressive options. Dynamic processes and different areas can be symbolised. The constellation thus becomes a form of language in which communication takes place, as often in spoken language, by means of symbols. To a certain extent the type of constellation determines the coordinates and therefore the level of differentiation of the problem structure which is indicated. Changing structural levels provides an opportunity, when faced with a low level of differentiation, to switch to a higher level of complexity.

The term '**representative**' is used in different senses. Systemic parts are represented by different people or objects who are then called personal or non-personal 'representatives'. By '**representatives in the narrow sense**' we mean a specific class of symbol in constellations vocabulary: those people representing family members, body parts, problem elements etc. who, once placed in the constellation, are only repositioned by the facilitator.

We have three types of symbols: locations (which retain their position throughout the constellation), free elements (once placed in the constellation, are free to move at will) and representatives in the narrow sense (are repositioned from picture to picture). By '**representatives in the broad sense**' we mean any of these, regardless of whether they represent people or abstract ideas.

The idea of '**representation**' is also used in a third sense: namely, to denote the partial adoption of a pattern from an excluded family member. If a family member has become a taboo subject and is no longer spoken of, someone born later to the family often adopts the same behaviour pattern as that of the excluded member as a kind of compensation. We call this a 'partial pattern representation' – as previously mentioned in family constellations this phenomenon is discussed using the concept of 'identification'.

Apart from *representatives in the narrow sense*, we have also introduced two further symbol types for use in systemic structural constellations: **locations** and **free elements**. By **locations** we mean representatives of locations or areas, who, once positioned in the constellation, remain essentially unchanged in this position for the entire duration of the constellation. **Free elements**, on the other hand, can move around during the constellation. This gives the otherwise static constellation a vitality.

The following table contains the aforementioned three different symbol classes used in systemic structural constellations:

Symbol type	Representatives	Locations	Free elements
Changes in positioning	Within the constellation pictures changed by the facilitator	No changes	Between and within the constellation pictures, can move independently

III.1.1.2.3.1 Use of representatives, locations and free elements in the tetralemma constellation

In the tetralemma constellation we find all three symbol types present. The tetralemma constellation is a systemic structural constellation that can be applied in decision-making situations (more details can be found in Varga von Kibéd and Sparrer 2000). The term 'tetralemma' is a translation of the term *čatuškoti* from Indian logic meaning 'four sides'. This *čatuškoti* was used as a pattern of reasoning in court cases. Four positions can be occupied. The position of the complainant stands opposite to that of the accused. The third position is that of 'both', while the fourth position is that of 'neither of the two'. In the Madhyamika Buddhist tradition, this pattern of reasoning was criticised by Nagarjuna, who emphasised that these four positions were not complete and can in fact be negated . In Buddhist logic, we talk about the quadruple negation: it is neither the first position, nor the second nor third, and similarly not the fourth. However, not even this proposition is taken as a new position. The negation of the four positions together with the denial that this negation itself constitutes a position in its own right represents the fifth non-position of the tetralemma.

We developed a form of constellation based on this pattern of reasoning which lends itself well to the solution of dilemmas. For short, we call this type of constellation the tetralemma constellation, although we are actually dealing with the negated tetralemma. In the tetralemma constellation we position the following parts in the constellation:

— the *focus* as the *representative* for the client,
— the *'one'*, the *'other'*, *'both'* and *'neither of the two'* as *locations* for the different positions
— *'none of these — and not even that'* as a *free element* for the fourfold negation

The first four positions are placed in the constellation as **locations** since they are fixed positions and as such are used to represent sources of power. Initially the locations are not clearly neutral positions as they are mixed with the personal experiences of the client and are so often perceived at first as burdens. The *'one'* position is placed opposite the *'other'* position and *'both'* positioned opposite *'neither of the two'* so that the four positions stand in a square formation in relation to each other. In this way their positions are balanced and they are on an equal footing.

In the flowchart below, none of the positions has precedence over the others. The idea is not to waste time at a position but to move on to the next and so on. The negated tetralemma represents a development process which, once passed through, can be repeated again on a higher level. To a certain extent this is like moving upwards on a spiral, and the tetralemma constellation can help in identifying the next step to be taken in this process.

The fifth 'position' is in fact not a position but a moving, changing, 'non-position'. This is therefore represented by a *free element* which can change itself independently. The *'none'* in *'none of these'* relates to the first four positions and indicates the negation of the first four positions. *'And not even that'* relates to itself reflexively expressing the fact that the fifth 'non-position' is not a new position, but a reflexive pattern disruption.

From the fourth position we can return to the first position without being required to remember the process just completed. We call this a **relapse**. If the fifth non-position is reached but then followed by a return to the first position, we call this a **lap of honour** in which the client verifies whether she really wishes to go to a new first position.

From the fifth non-position therefore it is possible to return to a new, slightly changed first position and then to repeat the same process 'in a different colour'. This is the equivalent of **symptom displacement (1' in Figure 2)**. We can speak of a new first position only when all five positions have been touched and the whole process is integrated in the new one. We then call the change from the 'fifth' to the first position a **creative step (1*)**. The following flowchart should serve to clarify the possible processes occurring in a tetralemma constellation:

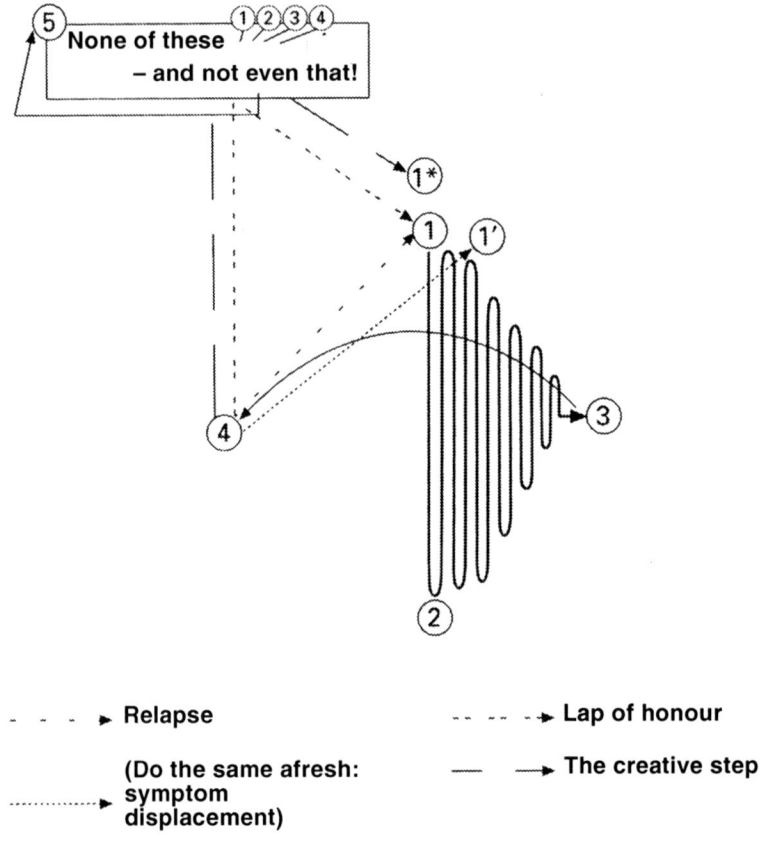

Figure 2: Flowchart for the tetralemma constellation.

At this stage the reader may well ask whether by adding the two other positions and the fifth non-position we aren't simply multiplying the dilemma. However, quite the opposite is true as the third position represents an **internal reframing** showing the **overlooked compatibility** of the first two positions and expanding the situation accordingly. The fourth position represents an **external reframing**, pointing towards the overlooked situation in which the dilemma arose, the situation in which it makes sense, in which we had a blind spot or in which we can see to what extent the dilemma can be useful to us in the future. This expansive reframing first creates a connection between the initial tunnelled vision of the 'either/or' dilemma of the 'one' and the 'other', then moves the focus from this either-or towards a bigger picture. Even this is then moved from its static state allowing a state of animated exchange to be achieved by constant pattern disruptions before a new first position can be taken up again.

III.1.1.2.3.2 Experiment 6
Think of a dilemma in which you often or currently find yourself. Call that side of the dilemma which is closest to you 'the one' side. The other side can then be called 'the other' side. Now think about a context or frame in which both parts of the dilemma are united and check the following:

- can you alternate between the one and the other side?
- is there something you can do that allows a place for both values?
- can one side be a component of the other?
- can you reach a compromise between the two?
- can you allow the power gained by renouncing one side to flow into the choice of the other?
- can you relate the other side to a new attitude?
- can you do the one side and simultaneously also do the other side?
- can you find a third and entirely new alternative?
- can you find a situation in which it is unclear whether you have chosen one side or the other?

Use the lines below to make notes during this exercise
…………………………………………………………………………………..
…………………………………………………………………………………..
…………………………………………………………………………………..

In order to establish the overlooked context, now try to answer the following questions:

'Does your dilemma contain any indications of a blind spot you may have?'
'What could help you to discover this?'
'In what circumstances did your dilemma arise?'
'Has your family also known a similar problem?'
'Can you imagine a situation in which it would make sense to be able not to decide between the one side and the other?'

'Assuming you had solved your dilemma, what would be different?'

Use the lines below for more notes

....

....

....

The fifth non-position allows for an interruption of the pattern. Can you imagine a situation in which you were able to laugh or have already laughed about your dilemma? What does this change for you?

....

....

....

Compare your notes. Has there been any change in your dilemma or in your attitude towards your dilemma? What did you find most helpful?

....

....

....

III.1.1.2.3.3 Sub-categories in the symbol categories of representatives, locations *and* free elements

The categories of representatives in the narrow sense, locations and free elements can be further divided into sub-categories as follows:

1. Marked as provisional to be converted later to this category

Designated locations and/or **designated free elements** are participants that are chosen as locations and/or free elements, but are initially placed by the client as *representatives* in the narrow sense. They only start to function in these different roles in a later picture of the constellation. Designated representatives in the narrow sense are locations or free elements whose function is later to be changed to representatives in the narrow sense. The changes of the designated representatives in the broad sense are intended to change to real locations, free elements and representatives in the narrow sense only after one or more repositionings by the facilitator.

For example, in a free tetralemma constellation, the locations are initially positioned in the space by the client as representatives, and only after the facilitator's first picture re-positioning do they take up the basic position of 'one' opposite 'the other' and 'both' opposite 'neither '. The first picture is thus more characterised by the client's family (and thus is more related to the family situation of the client).

This constitutes an example for designated locations as they are placed like representatives in the narrow sense and only later repositioned as locations.

Similarly, a participant initially positioned as a representative in the narrow sense can be later transformed into a free element, if they are representing a part that is a transpersonal force such as life energy or wisdom. The transformation of the designated representative at a later stage to a representative of the designated category allows us to check how much this part is influenced by the personal history of the client. Thus by using representatives in the narrow sense we get versions of the represented parts that are coloured by the person's history, while the use of free elements rather shows general or transpersonal effects.

2.   As non-personal forms with spatial dimensions

Non-personal locations are those not constituted by people. We call such locations with **spatial dimensions areas**, **fields** and **charged spots**.

In the *nine-square constellation*, which will be described in detail in Chapter VI, we use nine squares which are established using a system of coordinates for time (past, present, future) and context (internal context, border, external context). These fields are marked out on the floor and affect the representatives standing in those fields , e.g. past internal context or present external context, respectively. The facilitator can use her cataleptic hand to check whether the sensations in her hand change when she holds it above each field: if she does feel a reaction, a representative can be positioned accordingly. The representative effect is thus first determined by a position in the room where a representative for this unknown systemic element can then be positioned.

The nine-square constellation also contains a timeline along which the client can position the representative for the miracle (described in detail in Chapter II). The miracle is usually placed in the future/border position and splits the fields into two **areas**: before and after the miracle, which are **abstract spatial areas**.

We speak of **charged spots** in a constellation, where representatives experience different bodily sensations as soon as they occupy a particular spot. Other participants present sometimes may also 'slide' into the constellation from the surrounding circle. Without being positioned, they may experience strong bodily sensations that turn out to be similar to those experienced by a representative when placed on the same spot. In this case, we ask the participant to move to a different seat in the room so that they are no longer an involuntary representative. We then place a representative on the charged spot with the abstract identifier

'That which appeared here.' As already mentioned, we do not need to know any details about the person/element represented on this spot. If we see during the process of the constellation that someone is missing we can position a representative accordingly.

We call **abstract representatives in the narrow sense** with place assignment **symbolic objects**.

These include the **charged objects** that are used as symbols of what is returned during return rituals. This type of object must be renamed, i.e. de-roled, at the end of a constellation. If the facilitator forgets this step, a participant may experience unpleasant symbolic effects when coming into contact with the object at a later time.

In a constellation, for example, we used a cushion to represent a large burden. After the constellation, the cushion was placed carelessly on a chair. When a participant then sat down on this chair, she and the chair both tipped over. Fortunately, the participant was not injured and overcame the shock. Since that event, we now make sure that cushions used as symbols are also de-roled after use. This can be achieved by tapping them with a hand or shaking them.

We call **non-personal** and **personal free elements** with flexible spatial dimensions **migratory areas**.

Free elements are dynamic, and if they possess a spatial dimension they are also **variable** in that their space can increase or decrease. If during a constellation a **migratory area** is not occupied by a representative, the facilitator must then ask the other representatives to sense where it is in the room, or use her cataleptic hand to do the same herself. A personal free element of this kind could be constituted by several people holding hands in a loop to represent the boundaries of the area, and the moment they are constellated being permitted to freely follow their impulses.

3.   As a temporal form

In terms of **locations** we call this temporal form a **timeline.** This is a linear non-personal location.

The aforementioned *nine-square constellation* contains a timeline. A timeline is established by having the client position her focus and then asking her where in the rooms she locates her future, and where her past. Future and past need not always be represented in a straight line – they can lie on a crooked line, where the present is often found at one of the bends on this curve.

Another possibility is for the facilitator to establish the timeline herself, thereby establishing the coordinate system. An advantage of this second form is that it allows the facilitator to see from the client's positioning of the *focus* where the client is positioned at that moment: for example, in the present or future, and the direction in which the focus is facing, e.g. in the present looking towards the past. An advantage of the first form is that the client does not have to adapt to a pre-defined timeline, but instead can choose her own form of timeline, since not all time lines run in a straight line. If we allow the timeline to be chosen by the client, we experience a part of the client's experience of time; if we decide ourselves on the timeline, we are able to see where the client places herself in time. The constellations process happens intuitively, and often even the clients themselves are surprised at where they position their representatives.

We call representatives for which the time factor is taken into account **evolutionary representatives**. When representing a person, representatives can sometimes represent the different developmental stages of this person simultaneously. For example, a representative may experience a sudden feeling of being a four-year-old. In this case, we normally place a second representative to represent this childhood part. The facilitator can then integrate the two aspects by saying:

'It is good to know – you are the four-year-old – and you are the adult – and you can be both – at the same time.'

We took this procedure from Stephen Gilligan, who highlights this possibility of being able to embody different elements at the same time in his practice *Self Relations Psychotherapy*. This method involves the integration of the neglected parts of a personality called *neglected selves*.

Sometimes in such a situation, the client is reminded of traumatic experiences. If this happens, it is important to separate the childhood situation from that of the adult. We normally do this by adding a representative to represent the event, and then asking this representative to withdraw slowly until he is finally able to sit down. Events pass and therefore representatives of events do not stay in the picture, and when they leave and sit down this, in the language of constellations, means that the situation has truly passed. Using this method, we can give an experience of traumatic events having passed, e.g. war, accidents or serious illness.

We call the temporal form of *free elements* a **dynamic timeline** because it changes in terms of dimension and form. The **free element** in this case can again be represented as personal or non-personal. With a **non-personal dynamic timeline**, the facilitator, using her cataleptic hand and changes in sensation, must again check where the *dynamic timeline* is located or ask the *focus* to say where she senses the *dynamic timeline*. With a personal form, on the other hand, the *dynamic timeline* can be represented by a number of people holding hands and following their own impulses. The representatives can then indicate the way in which the temporal space has changed.

4. Borders

When dealing with **locations** in this subcategory we speak of a **static border**. This is a **non-personal location** found between two areas or at the end of an area.

In the nine-square constellation for example, we can take the line between the areas before and after the miracle as one such **static border**.

With **representatives in the narrow sense**, we call the borders **variable borders**, since the representatives can be repositioned from stage to stage. *Variable borders* can again be represented as personal or non-personal. An example of the non-personal form is given by a shoe placed on the floor as a representative for a *variable border*, the position of which may be altered by the facilitator. In the personal form, on the other hand, a number of people can again be chosen who hold hands and can be repositioned by the facilitator between pictures.

When dealing with **free elements** in this subcategory we then speak of **dynamic borders**. These can be represented by many people placed in a line, and who are free to move but must stay together. This can be achieved by holding hands. For the fifth non-position in the tetralemma constellation for example, more than one person, or a number of people can also be used. The fifth non-position would then be represented by a variable border. This is useful where a number of aspects in the fifth non-position need to be taken into consideration.

5. As symbols with intended reframing

Locations with intended reframing could be locations such as towns, for example, where the value of the town changes. The location known as 'town' can first refer to a specific town but then during the constellation change to the value that it represents to the client – for example, 'home'.

Representatives in the narrow sense with intended reframing occur in problem constellations. In this case, initial *obstacles* change into *protective barriers*, and then change again to become *helpers*. Since representatives in this situation do not have neutral names, these must be changed explicitly during the process if they are to continue to signify that which they actually evolve to represent, and to be integrated in their evolved role. In the solution picture, each systemic element has its own place and value, and therefore any originally negative names that are no longer suitable will have needed to be explicitly changed appropriately.

A further example of *representatives in the narrow sense with intended reframing* is given by the role of the *benefit* in the problem constellation. This element first changes into *the price that must be paid if the problem disappears*, and then changes into *the preciousness created when a high price has been paid*.

Free elements with intended reframing can be found in the tetralemma constellation. Here, the *fifth non-position* is able to change into *wisdom*. This sometimes gives rise to a simultaneous change in structural level, from the tetralemma constellation to a belief polarity constellation (see Chapter III.2.1).

6. **As chosen (not yet positioned) representatives in the broad sense**

The symbols of all three symbol categories – **locations, representatives in the narrow sense** and **free elements** – are first chosen by the client and only later positioned in the constellation picture. Even where this does not happen, the client's choice may still have an influence on the constellation. Positioning *representatives in the broad sense* only at a later stage can lead to an initial reduction in complexity.

With constellations we normally build up in stages – i.e. initially we only place the essential elements, and the excluded and additional elements are added later. This, for example, means we can check how relevant the individual excluded elements are to the problem that has just been worked with. In family constellations often there exist many excluded family members, though rarely are all relevant to the question at hand. By building up in stages or layers, differences are introduced by means of adding the people to the constellation successively. As a result, in the sense of Bateson, the information is increased.

7. **As ambiguous representatives in the broad sense**

Ambiguous representatives in the broad sense have more than one meaning at the same time. When in systemic structural constellations an implicit change of structural level occurs – i.e. the representatives in the broad sense are not renamed explicitly – they belong simultaneously to different structural levels and therefore have an ambiguous meaning. If we work in a systemically ambiguous way, some of the representatives in the broad sense placed in the constellation become ambiguous representatives.

With evolutionary representatives, an ambiguous form may also exist. This occurs when there is no change in stage of life from adult to childhood, but where the representative embodies both stages simultaneously.

The following table gives an overview of the **symbol categories used in systemic structural constellations**:

Characteristic features in the generation of the subcategories	Location	Representatives in the narrow sense	Free elements
Provisional with later conversion to this subcategory	Designated locations	Designated representatives	Designated free elements
Non-personal forms with spatial dimensions	Areas, fields, charged spots	Symbolic objects	Migratory areas
Representatives in the broad sense with a temporal form	Timeline	Evolutionary representatives	Dynamic timeline
Borders	Static borders	Variable borders	Dynamic borders
As symbols with intended reframing	Eg: 4th position in the tetralemma constellation fi systemic loyalty	Eg: Obstacles fi Protective barrier fi Helpers	Eg: Regressive 5th position in the tetralemma constellation fi client as child
As chosen (not yet positioned) representatives in the broad sense	Chosen locations	Chosen representatives in the broad sense	Chosen free elements
As ambiguous representatives in the broad sense	Ambiguous locations	Ambiguous representatives in the narrow sense	Ambiguous free elements

Figure 3: Table of symbol categories used in systemic structural constellations.

This differentiation between symbol categories expands the scope of application for systemic structural constellations considerably. The different symbol categories allow dynamic aspects, the passage of time and semantically loaded areas to be taken into account during constellations. This affords systemic structural constellations a much broader grammar and higher level of variability in application and design when compared with classic organisation and family constellations.

III.2 Classification of systemic structural constellations

In the first of the following two sections I will describe the different forms of systemic structural constellations, list the parts to be set up in the constellation and briefly explain their grammar. I will then present the 'types' and 'areas' as two superordinated categories in the classification of systemic structural constellations.

III.2.1 Forms of systemic structural constellations

The different **forms** of systemic structural constellation are related to each other by common basic grammatical assumptions and meta-principles (see also Chapter III.1.1.2). Each form of constellation highlights a different aspect, often has specific solution pictures and uses different procedures, which are also determined by the different symbols used. The individual forms of systemic structural constellations are given below with the author of each constellation form given in brackets.

Problem constellations (Sparrer/Varga)
In problem constellations, those parts we see as belonging to the 'grammar' (in the sense of the later Wittgenstein) of the word 'problem' are positioned, as follows:

Focus
It is the *focus* that carries the problem. This can be an individual or a group. The *focus* is required, for without someone to carry the problem it would be of no relevance to anyone, purely an academic exercise without any context..

Goal
If we did not have a goal we would have an unclear situation similar to that of the visitor in SFT. With every problem, we must assume that there is a desired goal that cannot yet be achieved. Of course, a goal may also be that there will be no change in a situation.

Obstacles

If we listen to a problem, our first thought is of obstacles. Without obstacles there would generally be no problem, nothing would be standing in the way of achieving the goal. With problem constellations we normally use between one and three obstacles. If there are more than three obstacles we combine them into three groups.

The *obstacles* change during the constellation into **protective barriers** and then **helpers**. An internal reframing takes place during the constellation and therefore we speak of **representatives with intended reframing**.

Resources

In systemic structural constellations, as with SFT, we start from the assumption that the client already possesses all the resources needed to solve the problem. If we need to learn something (e.g. acquiring new skills) before solving the problem, we tend to call this a 'difficulty' rather than a problem. With psychological problems the solution characteristically lies within us, we already posses the necessary resources to solve the problem, and therefore do not need to learn anything new.

Benefit

The benefit is what is useful about the problem not yet having been solved. The benefit is often not known and may simply be a matter of saving energy. As long as the problem exists, we don't have to change anything and can continue with our life as it is. Solving the problem involves a change, which means to give up our routine, and it requires strength and concentration. This is often more difficult to achieve than simply carrying on with the problem.

Since this benefit in its present form must be given up in exchange for a solution to the problem, it thus becomes the **price that must be paid** for the dissolution of the problem. However, it is still important to take this into consideration in some form in the solution, and in doing so it becomes the **preciousness** now regained. The benefit is also included in problem constellations as a **representative with intended reframing**.

Future task

After the goal has been achieved, there is normally a new task that needs to be performed. With some problems, the second step is taken before the first. If this occurs, this is a case of the future task being confused with the goal.

Consideration of the future task is still necessary where the future task creates even larger problems for the client than that of achieving her goal. We come across this kind of constellation in cases of final exams, where more demands are placed on the student by the uncertainty of the job hunting process than by revising for the exams themselves. In such cases, achieving the goal can become a problem due to nerves or a sense of dread in respect of the upcoming job hunting process. The future task in this case clearly is the context of the goal.

All of these parts are positioned in the problem constellation as *representatives in the narrow sense*. The problem constellation is also a background grammar for some other SySt constellations. This means that these constellations can be complemented by, or implicity understood as, aspects of the problem constellation.

Given their very general grammar, problem constellations are suited to nearly all issues, since most issues can be reconstructed as problems. We can see problem constellations as a coordinate system, whose coordinates are given by the individual parts in the problem constellation. Other systemic structural constellations provide other coordinates which can be used to represent the client's problem; our choice of coordinates depends on the problem at hand. Some problems can often be well represented in different forms of systemic structural constellations.

Linguistic surface structural constellations (Sparrer/Varga)

Here statements from the client's world view are placed into the constellation. We allow the client herself to summarise or express her problem in one or two statements, or extract a particularly striking formulation from her problem description. The grammatical segments of this statement are then positioned as representatives. Problem constellations, sometimes a partial family constellation, tetralemma constellation or constellation of the defocused topic can serve as a good background grammar for this. We often see parts of a problem constellation in segments of the central statement by the client. The *benefit*, normally not present at this stage, can be added by the facilitator.

This type of constellation is particularly suitable for use when the client presents different problems , because when required to combine his problems into two statements, he is forced to concentrate on the essential issue. Even where clients identify a particular statement as a recurring pattern in their problems, the linguistic surface structure constellation may still provide the right structure for this problem.

Constellation of the defocused topic (Sparrer/Varga)

This constellation places the following parts in the constellation:

- *focus*
- *official topic*
- *defocused topic*

The *official topic* is the problem as given by the client, while the *defocused topic* is 'something also touched on by the official topic'. We used to call this type of constellation the 'constellation of the real topic'. However, the real topic is not one that comes before the official one or points to a deeper understanding. We therefore changed its name to the neutral sounding 'constellation of the defocused topic'.

The three parts in the constellation of the defocused topic can alternatively be viewed in parallel with the three parts of the problem constellation:

- focus, goal, obstacle; or
- focus, goal, benefit; or
- focus, goal, future task

The benefit, obstacle, or future task can also represent an excluded family member. The grammar of the constellation of defocused topics can often be understood by means of a partial family constellation. It is sometimes also helpful to use the problem constellation as a background grammar to the partial family constellation and even the tetralemma constellation. The constellation of defocused topics is particularly useful in hidden work.

Tetralemma constellation (Sparrer/Varga)

This type of constellation builds on the negated tetralemma, a form of argument originating in Indian logic. As already mentioned, the tetralemma or čatuškoti is a form of argument that was used in court cases. It is used to distinguish between the position of the complainant, the accused, the position in which both are right, and the position in which neither is right. The negated tetralemma stems from Nagarjuna, the founder of Madhyamika Buddhism, who criticised the tetralemma form of argument by negating all four of these positions. When asked whether in doing this he would not be adopting a new position, he said, 'I've never taken a position.'

The four positions – 'the one', 'the other', 'both' and 'neither of the two' – and the 'fifth, non-position' constitute the starting point for the tetralemma constellation. The four positions are placed as locations, while the 'fifth non-position' is placed as a free element. The person representing the client is also placed (for further details see Chapter III.1.1.2.3). We have complemented the arguments schema from Indian logic with an operational sequence based on this tetralemma constellation. This is particularly suited to either-or situations in which two poles can be seen as 'the one' and 'the other'. The 'both' position represents the overlooked compatibility of the two poles, and the 'neither of the two' represents new possibilities. The 'fifth non-position' represents a basic pattern disruption which can be achieved, for example, through use of humour, earnestness or refraining from giving a judgment or appraisal.

In comparison to other SySt constellations, the tetralemma constellation is dominated by the process work. None of the four positions, and not even the 'fifth non-position', is better than any of the other positions, though the 'fifth non-position' has the advantage of being less rigid. The tetralemma constellation is used to find the next step in a developing process. After the 'fifth non-position', a new first position can be adopted again, for the 'fifth non-position' challenges its own existence. The 'fifth non-position' can lead to the adoption of a whole new attitude. Even when we are dealing with the steps in a developing process, it is still not a matter of there being a best position to be in, but a matter of which steps are the most favourable in the given situation.

Sometimes, after the 'fifth non-position' is reached, the process passed through up to that moment is forgotten, and the original first position is returned to. We call this a **relapse**. Seen from a neutral place, we can say that the right moment for change has not yet arrived. Even where someone, after reaching the 'fifth non-position', again takes up the original first position, despite remembering the process passed through, this can be seen as necessary to the integration and achieving of steps towards a stable change. This we call a **lap of honour** after Heidelberg Ericksonian therapist Gunther Schmidt, who introduced this term in one of his seminars.

If during a **lap of honour** someone does not repeat the process as before but goes through the same process 'in another colour', we are then dealing with what we call **symptom displacement**. This can also be an important step in gaining insight into the development process. It is only after the 'fifth non-position' is followed by a creative step to a new level with an entirely new first position that we speak of **a new first position**. The next suitable step for the client is that which is the largest possible for her in the given context.

The tetralemma constellation is used in dilemmas, decision situations and the mediation of two conflicting parties. We distinguish between **free and fixed tetralemma constellations**, depending on whether we position *locations* or use *designated locations* in the initial picture of the constellation. If we are working with two conflicting parties, we often use two foci in the tetralemma constellation.

Polar decision constellation (Sparrer/Varga)
This type of constellation is essentially the same as a partial tetralemma constellation. It is sufficient for clarification to just move from 'the one' to 'the other'.

Multiple decision constellation (Sparrer/Varga)

Multiple decision constellations involve more than two alternatives. The individual alternatives and the focus are positioned as representatives. This type of constellation clarifies how the decision for the individual alternatives is experienced as well as the consequences of the decision. Instead of *both* we use *all of this*, instead of *neither of the two* we use *none of these*.

Belief polarity constellation (Sparrer/Varga)

This can be traced back to the division of religious systems according to their primary didactic emphasis by Frithjof Schuon (1981). For example, we can distinguish between the Jnana, Bhakti and Karma types of yoga in terms of whether the basic concept of the religion is characterised by knowledge, love or order (duty).

In belief polarity constellations, a triangle is described with the *locations* knowledge, love and order into which the *focus* is placed as a representative. The goal of this constellation is for the *focus* to able to take freely from these three sources of power. This does not normally happen at first, since access to these sources is often barred by upbringing or other biographical effects. These barriers are lifted during the constellation, and, without asking questions about the barriers, the access to the sources is opened.

As in the tetralemma constellation, we distinguish here between **free and fixed belief polarity constellations**, depending on whether the client is instructed at the start to position *locations* or use *designated locations* in the constellation.

We use belief polarity constellations mainly to **modify belief sentences**. To do this we instruct the client to whisper the relevant belief statement into the ear of her *focus*. The *focus* is asked frequently about this belief statement during the constellation, which allows us to see directly how, when and by which ritual the sentence changes. Sometimes the *focus* simply forgets the problematic belief sentence.

The belief polarity constellation can also be used as a **meta-constellation** in that the belief polarity constellation provides the framework for a subsequent constellation. For example, a family or organisation constellation could take place within a belief polarity constellation. This has the advantage that the intensity of the conflict within the represented system is attenuated by the power sources, which create a resourceful space that does protect the representatives.

The belief polarity constellation can always be used to find resources and strengthen individual behaviour.

The remaining constellations in this section are less frequently used, and may be safely skipped by the first-time reader.

Core transformation constellations (Sparrer/Varga)

This has its origins in the core transformation process developed by Conirae, Steve and Tamara Andreas for NLP, adapted by Siegfried Essen for use in work on fundamental beliefs as part of his systemic work with spiritual matters. We transformed this process into a constellation.

The constellation involves the *focus* together with a restrictive fundamental belief (or symptom or problem), which are normally placed in front of four good intentions, using representatives. The last intention behind the *focus* generally represents a deep spiritual source on which all other representatives can feed. This type of constellation is also used to find resources and transform symptoms.

Solution-focused SySt constellations:
  - **Nine and Twelve-square constellations (Insa Sparrer)**
  - **Goal approximation constellation (Insa Sparrer)**
  - **Solution constellation (Insa Sparrer)**
  - **Solution geometric interview (Insa Sparrer)**

These four types of constellation all represent a direct combination of SFT and SySt constellations. They are described in detail in chapters IV to IX of this book

Syllogistic constellation (Matthias Varga von Kibéd)

This form of constellation can be traced back to Aristotle's square of opposition. In order to represent a recurring situation in the client's problem, the parts 'for all', 'not: for all' (the logical negation of 'for all'), 'for some' and 'not: for some' are placed in the constellation as representatives. A variation of this form might use the parts 'always', 'never', 'sometimes' and 'sometimes not' in a similar way. The logical labelling of Aristotle's square of opposition – contrary, contradictory, subcontrary and subaltern – provides the basis for the process work used in syllogistic constellations. This constellation is particularly suited for use in waiving generalisations, discovering exceptions, inspecting entrenched behaviour and revealing prejudices.

  - **Semiotic constellations (Sparrer/Varga)**
  - **Keno-Pythagorean constellation (Sparrer/Varga)**
  - **Constellations of main aspects of signs (Sparrer/Varga)**
  - **Constellations of classes of signs (Sparrer/Varga)**

These types of constellations are based on the basic concepts of sign theory / semiotics found in the work of Charles Sanders Peirce (1983).

In keno-Pythagorean constellations, the so-called keno-Pythagorean categories of firstness, secondness and thirdness are positioned as representatives. This type of constellation provides us with the qualities, structures and dynamics of the client's problem.

In **constellations of main aspects of signs**, we chose type (legisigns in the terms of Peirce), token (sinsigns) and tones (qualisigns), then symbol, index and icon, as well as argument, dicent and rhema as representatives. Here we differentiate how the signs itself is given, how its relation to its object is given and how it is related to the person, each threefold: either can be a possibility, a reality or a rule-based connection. This constellation type, by using the coordinates of sign theory (semiotics), provides us with an alternative way of viewing the problem.

In **constellations of classes of signs**, the ten compatible combinations of the main aspects of signs are chosen as representatives. This provides us with concrete solution-related indicators in terms of experience of perception and external events, in terms of bodily sensations and moods.

Enneagram constellation (Sparrer/Varga)

In this constellation, the nine different personality types are placed as locations in the constellation so that they form the shape of a enneagon (nine sided figure). The client's *focus* is then placed within this field. The centre of these personality types can then be added as a **free element**. In this type of constellation, tendencies become visible and imbalances equilibrated.

Simultaneous group topic constellation (Matthias Varga von Kibéd)

This type of constellation is particularly suited for use with groups that are highly inhomogeneous or in a state of protracted conflict but which nonetheless wish to improve their situation. Initially, the group chooses representatives of the different parts of the group, who then choose *representatives in the broad sense* for the constellation.

It is not necessary that the group agrees on a topic – parts of the group may, however, position their respective topics in the constellation as *representatives in the broad sense* by means of symbols (using readily available objects). The topics can also be identified by commonly-agreed letters, if a good name for a particular topic proves hard to find. The topics themselves are identified using group brainstorming. If many topics are identified, it is useful to divide these into smaller clusters, which can then also be labelled with letters.

Each part of the group chooses one or more *foci* from the overall group, which they then position together. Different symbols are then chosen for the different topics and positioned as *representatives in the narrower sense*. In order to introduce an element of humour to this kind of group, it is recommended that the representatives themselves be allowed to choose one or more of the free elements from the group, who can then, when placed in the constellation, move around in any way they wish.

It then becomes possible for the members of one part of the group to become acquainted with the topic of another part of the group. They achieve this by standing on or over the symbols representing the different topics and feeling the changes in their physical sensations. By means of process work, a better reciprocal understanding in the group is made possible.

Individual participants can also stand in the positions of the *foci* and the **free elements** in order to become acquainted with them. Care should be taken to ensure that the positions of the *foci* and the *free elements* are always occupied by at least one person.

By asking participants about their experiences when in the positions of the different topics, *foci* and *free elements* a lot of the processes existing in the group become clear, while the adopting of different perspectives helps promote reciprocal understanding and respect.

Constellations of psychosomatic problems:

Body constellation (Sparrer/Varga)
In this type of constellation, individual body parts, organs and body systems thought by the client to be relevant to her problem are placed into a constellation as representatives. At the suggestion of the facilitator, these are complemented in the second stage by any excluded body parts, organs and body systems. External influences and aids (medicines, crutches, medical treatment) can be added using representatives depending on the nature of the client's problem. The constellation helps reveal the relationship of the parts to each other and enables improved communication as well as supportive processes to take place between them. It also helps identify a good position for external aids within the internal image and shows which external influences may cause damage or have a supportive role. Medical treatment can be effectively complemented in this way. Body constellations are not a replacement for medical treatment but can support any treatment as well as help identify other useful aspects.

Body structural constellations (Insa Sparrer)

Here, as opposed to body constellations, additional excluded family members relevant to the client's problem are added to the constellation. As such, the body structural constellation is a combination of a body constellation and a family constellation. It centres on return rituals between body parts and family members and the dissolving of entanglements. Body structural constellations are described in more detail in Chapter III.1.1.2.2.

TCM constellation (Sparrer/Varga)

This constellation uses representatives for the five functional circles in TCM (traditional Chinese medicine) and then views physical sickness through this coordinate system. The first picture of the constellation can indicate to practitioners of TCM where they should insert their acupuncture needles. Amazingly, however, the state of the meridians is seen to change during the constellation even without the insertion of needles. By working together with practitioners of TCM, and with the help of pulse and tongue diagnostics, empty meridians are seen to have become fuller following a constellation. The process work involved follows the basic principles of TCM and structural level changes to the family system are frequent.

Homoeopathic systemic constellations (Matthias Varga von Kibéd and Friedrich Wiest)

This type of constellation is a combination of the following:

- client symptom constellation
- guiding symptom constellation
- family structural constellation (usually a birth family constellation)

Analogies can be found between the structural level of the client symptoms, that of the guiding symptoms of the remedy picture, and that of the family. This makes a structural level change from one system to another much easier. These constellations help to release blockades in homoeopathic treatment, undo entanglements and allow the mental component of a psychosomatic illness to become more visible and be solved.

Chakra constellation (Sparrer/Varga)

This type of constellation uses representatives for the *focus* and the seven chakras and a free element for the kundalini energy. Structural level changes to the family constellation are frequent.

III.2.2 Types of systemic structural constellations

The individual forms of systemic structural constellations can be implemented in different ways, which we call **types**, as follows:

Hidden constellations

These constellations use abstract representatives, *locations* and *free elements*, and use exclusively abstract, non-specific names for the individual parts. For example: 'What the *focus* is looking at', 'What emerges for …(e.g. the goal)', 'What is missing here', 'What is really important' etc. This enables us to work with the elements in the constellation without the need to become explicit.

This is particularly useful when working with organisations, where the situation often doesn't allow personal details to be used explicitly. Despite the lack of explicit names for the parts in the constellation, the person for whom the constellation is being performed is often able to understand and interpret the scenes.

Sometimes during this type of constellation there is also a change of structural level, but even here hidden work is still possible. The facilitator is able to work implicitly on the structural levels, while explicitly maintaining the given names for the elements in the constellation. This could mean, for example, working implicitly with the father while working explicitly with the boss.

Mixed symbolic constellations

These constellations do not use the grammar of any particular constellation form; rather, depending on the client's problem, they use a highly diverse range of elements, such as abstract ideas, people, objects, animals, values, resources, alternatives and groups. The disadvantage of this type of constellation is that the facilitator is unable to follow any standard form. The incredible grammatical complexity that arises in the interaction between different systemic levels and symbol types means this type of constellation is only used by the most experienced constellations facilitator.

This system must also be known to be *complete*, either in terms of content or intuitively. This is not something given by its structure alone, as with logical structures such as the tetralemma constellation. It is important for the structure to be 'complete' insofar as excluded parts can be identified more easily when we know which things do actually belong to the system.

Multi-focus (multi-perspective) constellation

This constellation involves the positioning of more than one *focus*, giving us access to different perspectives. It is particularly suited to group conflict situations.

A different *focus* can be used for each party so that the different perspectives are visible in the constellation. This can also be used with a very large group with a clearly defined problem, where for each part of the group that has adopted a position in respect to the problem a focus is positioned in the constellation. A solution picture has been achieved when, in respect to the goal and the different aspects of the problem that have been placed in the constellation, the different *foci* are standing in a supportive relationship to one another.

A further application of this is the supervision constellation. Here the counselling team (or counsellor) or the therapeutic team (or facilitator) and the system that is to be counselled (or receive therapy) is placed in the constellation. This type of constellation has a minimum of two foci: the system that provides counselling (therapy) and the system being counselled (receiving therapy). If different groupings exist within the systems being counselled (receiving therapy) these can similarly be represented by different foci.

Constellations with structural level changes

These types of constellations include all systemic structural constellations in which one or more of the elements in the constellation show new aspects which lead to another systemic level. For example, when 'the one' and 'the other' of the tetralemma constellation show aspects of the client's mother and father as part of the constellation. In such cases, the client can rename 'the one' and 'the other' explicitly as mother and father, thereby introducing an **explicit change of structural level**. Alternatively, the facilitator may choose to continue working at the initial structural form of constellation (in our example, the tetralemma constellation), but ensure that the ritual statements used are suited to both levels. In this way, the facilitator can work at different structural levels simultaneously. This reveals a natural transition to systemically ambiguous constellations, which are described in the following section.

When we work on different levels simultaneously, we trust that the client's unconscious will select the appropriate structural level. Constellations with this kind of **implicit change of structural level** are particularly well suited to organisations, since the personal level may play a decisive role but there is normally no contract to work on this level, and yet this can still be taken into account using an implicit change of structural level.

Systematically ambiguous constellations

In this type of constellation, the facilitator starts by considering more than one structural level from the very beginning, or encourages the client to see the therapeutic change not only from the perspective of the chosen structural level, saying, for example:

'The X part is showing you Y as well as other things apart from that'
'X and what ever else it refers to ...'
'X and whatever also emerges with it ...'

These statements show that the systemic part X can also contain other aspects than those which are explicitly seen. It is essential here that any statements used in the process work speak to more than one systemic level equally and simultaneously. It is helpful to use highly abstract sentences, implicit presuppositions and quasi-tautological statements. Suggestions as in the statements given above can elicit unconscious processes which can help build links to other contexts and increase the transfer of solutions to other areas. The procedure in this type of constellation shows the proximity of systemic structural constellations to hypnotherapeutic work.

Constellations of compound systems

Compound systems come in the form of families in which one or both partners of a married couple had been married previously and there are children from earlier marriages (or companies considered along with their subsidiaries, etc). In these constellations, a decisive role is played by the previous partner and the second basic principle of systems – i.e. 'Later systems take precedence over earlier systems.'

Constellations of compound systems are particularly useful when it comes to family businesses, which provide a good example of the interaction between a family and an organisation, and the possibility of reciprocal entanglements.

Combined constellations

This is given by a combination of different forms of constellation – for example, the constellation of a defocused topic complemented with elements of a problem constellation, or a linguistic surface structure constellation expanded with elements of a problem constellation. In any such combination, the grammar of the main system dominates that of the smaller system.

Where the systems used are equally important, the facilitator may start working in one system and then change to the other system later on, or the main focus of the work can be shifted from one system to the other. In this case, the constellation method is determined by the system currently being worked in.

Partial (forms of) constellations

These are constellations in which not all the elements of the system have been positioned, but only those at first glance relevant to the problem. For example, in a problem constellation, initially we need only place the *focus*, *goal* and *obstacle*. During the constellation it will become clear whether other parts are missing which can then be added. Partial constellations are thus abridged forms of the given type of constellation.

Constellations in layers

This type of constellation refers to the way a constellation can proceed. The facilitator builds up the constellation in layers, not placing all the elements into the constellation at the beginning. Instead, initially she has the client place the fewest possible number of parts of the relevant system – i.e. the focus and one or two other parts. In the second picture, any excluded elements are added to test what effect they have. In the third picture, a further relevant systemic component can be added, and, if necessary, another in a fourth picture. The differences, and therefore also the information, increases from picture to picture. As Bateson would say, the greater the number of differences established, the more information becomes available. This means that we do not have the whole complex system in the first picture, but can understand the specific effects with each addition. From the client's point of view, this way of proceeding is normally more manageable and comprehensible.

Constellations using alter egos

With some constellations it can be useful for the client to be placed in the constellation picture himself in addition to his *focus*. The *focus* thus takes on the role of the alter ego. This is particularly useful when the *focus* turns out to be an *evolutionary representative* and represents the client as a five-year-old child, for example. When the client then enters the constellation she is able to speak to the five-year-old child she used to be, embrace it and thus integrate this part of herself.

Supervision constellations

Supervision constellations are able to draw on all forms of systemic structural constellations as soon as a double *focus* is used.

In principle, this type of constellation includes the system that is to be supervised (client system) and the supervisee (or counsellor/therapist). This means that there is always a minimum of two systems – and we have representatives for the client and his system and the supervisee and his system. If we had more supervisees there would of course be more representatives. The question to be answered refers to the relationship between these two systems. For the system to be supervised we can use family structural constellations, organisation structural constellations, conflict constellations, problem constellations etc.. This type of constellation can help answer the following questions:

- What is the best position for the supervisee in relation to the system that is to be supervised?
- How does the client see the supervisee?
- What does the client's system need?
- What has been overlooked by the supervisee in the client's system?
- What could a next step be for the client's system?

Meta constellations (a constellation within a constellation)
Here we are dealing with a hierarchically superior and a hierarchically subordinate system. The hierarchically superior system provides the framework for the hierarchically subordinate system. Suitable meta constellations are belief polarity constellations, goal approximation constellations, nine and twelve-square constellations and tetralemma constellations. These can define a context within which other constellations – for example, family, organisation or political structural constellations – can be performed. Meta constellations have the following advantages:

- with belief polarity constellations the poles act as resources and offer protection and power as soon as they are purged of personal elements. They can then act as compensatory sources of power for the constellation that is within the belief polarity constellation.
- With goal approximation constellations the timeline provides a direction so that a simulation of steps into the future can be taken.
- With tetralemma constellations the different positions represent the steps of a process.

III.2.3 Systemic structural constellations used in different fields
Besides these different types of constellations, we also differentiate between **constellations for use in different fields**. In these fields we can perform different types of structural constellations or variations of family and organisation constellations. In the following, I describe the individual fields for which we have developed different forms of constellation.

Constellations in the organisational field
Some of the first ideas for organisational constellations came from Bert Hellinger. Their basic forms were substantially extended by Gunthard Weber. Brigitte Gross, Siegfried Essen, Guni Baxa, Christine Essen, Friedrich Wiest, Thomas Siefer, Gerd Metz and Werner Messerig added new insights to this approach. Then Matthias Varga von Kibéd and I developed the application of SySt to organisations. These constellations build on some of the basic principles of family constellations and share a similar grammatical structure.

The **organisational structural constellations** we developed differ from conventional organisational constellations in many aspects, including the following:

- apart from representatives, they can also include *locations* and *free elements,*
- abstract systemic components are also placed in the constellation,
- they allow for hidden and ambiguous work,
- the constellations process takes place simultaneously on more than one structural level and as such is based on ambiguity,
- the work on the level of content (semantical) gives way to syntactical work.

For our organisational structural constellations we developed specific forms to deal with different situations. Except where stated, the following forms were all created by Insa Sparrer and Matthias Varga von Kibéd.

We distinguish between the following forms of organisational structural constellations:

Hierarchy level constellations (Sparrer/Varga)
This constellation takes into account the individual hierarchical levels of an organisation (using *representatives in the narrow sense*). Each individual hierarchy level is represented by a single person, while hierarchical levels about which different opinions and beliefs are held are represented by more than one person. The number of hierarchical levels represented in the constellation depends on how relevant the differences are to the client's problem.

Team structural constellations
This constellation contains representatives of a team (*representatives in the narrow sense*). Where appropriate, *values* (*representatives in the narrow sense* or *locations*) and *goals* (*representatives in the narrow sense*) are added.

Internal team constellations

Hidden work with SySt constellations also allows us to perform constellation work for individual problems using teams or groups of managers and colleagues within a company. The four main forms of this are

1. constellation with repeated exchange of the representatives
2. constellation without a facilitator
3. context clarification constellation
4. solution-focused dialogue with inaudible answers in combination with a solution constellation.

1. **Constellation with repeated exchange of the representatives** (Matthias Varga von Kibéd)
    In this constellation the representatives are continually exchanged. The constant exchange helps the representatives to free themselves from their own theories and to perceive more easily their spontaneous bodily sensations in each position. Another advantage is that this exchange helps to reduce overlaps between people and their recent roles, and avoids potential confusion of the representatives after derolement. It is also helpful because people in a department are representing their colleagues and they can learn to view the question at hand from different perspectives.

2. **Constellation without a facilitator** (Matthias Varga von Kibéd).
    In this form of constellation, team members place themselves in the constellation as if they were being placed by an imaginary facilitator for the team problem. Interestingly, the participants exposure to a representative's perception of themselves now reveals a different perspective to that previously perceived and brings completely new aspects into view, of which some of the team members had been totally unaware. We call this reflexive representative perception, or representative perception for yourself.

3. **The context clarification constellation** (Sparrer/Varga).
    This constellation serves to clarify within organisations whether the client's issue is related to the organisational context and/or to their private context. This constellation contains the following:

    *   a *focus* (*representative in the narrow sense*)
    *   the *problem* (*representative in the narrow sense*)
    *   the *professional context* (*representative in the narrow sense*)
    *   the *private context* (*representative in the narrow sense*)

4. **The solution-focused dialogue with silent answers combined with a solution constellation** (Chapter VIII) (Insa Sparrer).
   This constellation starts with a solution-focused interview in which the client thinks their answers to the questions but does not say them aloud. The facilitator can tell from the client's body language when she has answered a question and whether she is still in the problem-state or has moved to the solution-state. Then the *focus, goal, miracle,* people, groups of people, as well as situations in the context of the miracle and exceptions, where applicable, are positioned in the constellation. This procedure enables the constellation to proceed in an entirely hidden way, which is often very useful when dealing with organisations.

Project constellations
Here, besides the project team members (*representatives in the narrow sense*), goals (*representatives in the narrow sense*), resources (*representatives in the narrow sense*), values (*representatives in the narrow sense* or *locations*) and market requirements (*representatives in the narrow sense*) are also positioned in the constellation.

Value polarity constellation (Sparrer/Varga)
The value polarity constellation follows the basic pattern of the belief polarity constellation. The *values* are positioned as *locations* and the people relevant to the problem are positioned as *representatives in the narrow sense*. This form of constellation is particularly suited to work involving the basic values of a company philosophy.

Simultaneous double tetralemma constellation with dual focus (Matthias Varga von Kibéd)
This constellation uses two foci, one for each party. Position A corresponds to one of the parties, position B to the other. The third and fourth positions then correspond to the third and fourth position for both parties. This form of constellation is particularly useful when dealing with conflict situations in organisations.

Multi-perspective constellation for the defocused topic (Sparrer/Varga)
This constellation is also suitable for conflict situations. Each of the parties involved in the conflict is allowed to place their own focus in the constellation. A common focus is then chosen collectively by the two parties. Additionally, the official topic and the defocused topic (both *representatives in the narrow sense*) are then placed in the constellation.

Simultaneous group topic constellation (Matthias Varga von Kibéd)
This constellation can even be used in long-term conflict situations and with groups that are strongly divided. The number of *foci* used in the constellation corresponds with the number of conflict topics – for example, two *foci* for men and one for women, where the number of men is greater than that of women and this is an important aspect of the topic. Each party of the conflict places its topics into the constellation, with a *common task* (*representative in the narrow sense*) being added in an organisational contexts. If the participants are unable to agree on the names of the topics, we use numbers or letters for the respective representatives. If there are too many topics, they can be clustered into groups. The *foci* and the *common task* are then placed in the constellation together with people as *representatives in the narrow sense*, with objects (*representatives in the narrow sense*) being commonly used for individual topics. If they wish to do so, all the group members can move into the different positions of the representatives and symbols and acquaint themselves with the perspective of the others (cf. Chapter III.2.1)

The constellation of the absent team (Insa Sparrer)
This is a special case of the solution geometrical interview. Where the team is only partially present, this form of constellation facilitates a solution-focused dialogue using representatives as if the entire team were present. A more detailed description of this form of systemic structural constellation is given in Chapter IX.1.

Constellations in the creative fields
These are mainly the result of our collaboration with film directors and professional writers/storytellers, which led to the development of different forms of constellation for screenplays and stories. As opposed to family constellations and most other therapeutic and counselling applications of SySt constellations, with **script constellations** (screenplays and stories for books – for more details see Varga von Kibéd and Sparrer 2002) the goal is generally not to achieve a quick and simple solution to a problem. On the contrary: interesting, hidden and deep conflicts are essential components of many a good script. Consequently, a central question here relates to what action arises from a starting place and what could make a suitable back-story.

With script constellations there is no therapy or counselling. Script constellations are more a matter of exploring different rearrangement possibilities of pre-existing characters and parts, the introduction or omission of characters, questions as to the coherence or overloading of ideas, as well as the different ways to develop a story etc. Building on the grammar of systemic structural constellations, script constellations also allow us to try out experimental procedures, which, in a therapeutic or counselling application, would prove highly problematic or unsatisfactory. It was thus only after we started working in this field that we discovered a number of the rules governing script constellations.

As a special technique for script constellations, we developed **simultaneous, partial spontaneous modification by the representatives themselves**. Here all the representatives are asked, on hearing an acoustic signal and within certain restrictive conditions, to follow their spontaneous impulses for change. We observed the following pattern of effects with surprising consistency:

- If we allow a fifth, sixth or smaller part of the spontaneous impulse to be acted out, we obtain miniature scene changes, which essentially represent an analogy of a *frame-by-frame analysis*.
- If we allow a quarter of the spontaneous impulse to be acted out, we generally get larger relevant sequences or main parts of a scene.
- If we allow a third of the spontaneous impulse to be acted out, we generally get the next scene.
- If we allow a half of the spontaneous impulse to be acted out, we normally reach the end of the screenplay or spill over beyond the end.
- If, after allowing half of the spontaneous impulse to be acted out, further spontaneous partial change takes place, the story as a rule will exceed the plot development and often becomes boring.
- If we allow the entire spontaneous impulse to be acted out, the story exceeds the limits of possible change and we obtain absurd episodes.

The observation of these relatively consistent effects of this simultaneous, partial spontaneous modification induction for representatives (which we have now also applied beyond the narrow field of script constellations) was used as the basis for the 'Varga-Sparrer gearbox' used in simultaneous, partial spontaneous modification of structural constellation images. This uses an instruction to the representatives in the constellation of the following form:

'Now all please think carefully about what in this situation you would like to change – without making the change yet! Give great attention to the impulses to move and desire for behavioural change that arise in you when you look around and notice the others. And then when I clap my hands please act out precisely … (a sixth, a fourth, a third, a half …) of the movement or change that you wished for.'

Using this consistency in the pattern of effects, as described above, we obtain what we call a 'five-speed gearbox'. And by introducing the following formulations to the induction process we can define the different gear changes as shown in the following table:

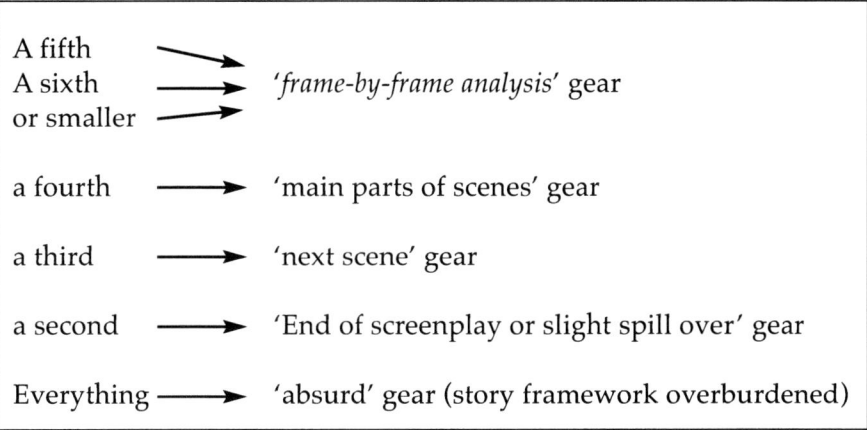

A fifth A sixth or smaller	→	*'frame-by-frame analysis'* gear
a fourth	→	'main parts of scenes' gear
a third	→	'next scene' gear
a second	→	'End of screenplay or slight spill over' gear
Everything	→	'absurd' gear (story framework overburdened)

In **script constellations** we distinguish between the following subtypes (Matthias Varga von Kibéd):

Constellation of the lead and supporting roles
This allows authors to gain an insight into the dynamic web of relationships between their lead and supporting characters

Constellation of the main character traits
This constellation helps authors to improve their understanding of the characters in the screenplay and provides insight into their motivational state and future behaviour. Where the author encounters writing problems, resonances with the author's own system often become clear and can be modified or eliminated as necessary. (This sometimes leads to a crossover between the therapeutic application of SySt constellations and the application used to promote creativity.)

Supervision constellations for writers
Here the author is placed in the constellation together with the characters in the script and her relationship and any possible involvement with the characters in her script become visible.

Multi-perspective script constellations
This type of constellation also takes into account external perspectives, such as the perspective of previous viewers of an already run series, the intended target group for a new film, the producers and financers, the director, the media and critics, as well as the relationship between multiple authors of a screenplay.

Additionally, in working with authors, tetralemma, problem and belief polarity constellations have proved their value in solving creative blocks.

These forms of SySt constellations can also be implemented for film and theatre direction, again using lead and supporting roles, character traits of the main characters, film scenes, and the web of relationships between the actors, the director, the producer and the public, etc.

In **constellations for story tellers** we use

- specific variations of mixed symbolic constellations (story (script) constellations) and
- constellations to clarify the confusion between family conflicts and narrated stories, in the form of combined variations of the story constellation with partial structural family constellations.

Story constellations can also use more than one focus, such as the narrator´s focus, that of the public and that of the author of the story.

Constellations in the political field
As with organisation structural constellations, **political structural constellations** build on the grammar of systemic structural constellations. They emphasise syntactic work and use systemically ambiguous and hidden constellation forms. Apart from representatives, political structural constellations also use *locations* and *free elements* and are therefore to be distinguished from other forms of political constellations.

Political structural constellations use in particular the following aforementioned constellation forms:

Multi-focus (multi-perspective) constellations
This type of constellation is particularly useful when dealing with political situations. A focus can be positioned in the constellation for each conflicting party or group present. This makes clear the different perspectives of the parties.

Mixed-symbolic constellations
These are particularly suitable for use in problems where different kinds of people, values or events, as well as different types of people,

groups of people or countries, play a role. Power sources can be added where necessary for supportive purposes.

Constellations with structural level changes

Structural level changes in political constellations occur most frequently when the client is personally affected by the political situation represented in the constellation. Structural level changes often occur from the entire system to partial systems.

Systemically ambiguous and hidden constellations

This type of constellation is always useful in situations where all parties involved need to save face. Working in a systemically ambiguous way means working on different structural levels simultaneously. If there is a connection between conflict in the group and the family conflicts of individual people, these can be worked on at the same time in a hidden way, with no intrusion into the personal sphere of the person involved. Hidden constellations in which the parts are only mentioned in an abstract way (without any specific names) have the advantage of avoiding specific names for rejected systemic components, thus allowing all systemic parts to receive consideration.

Constellations of combined systems

Combined systems are often used in political situations, since specific conflicts often occur when interlaced systems (family connections, spin-off groups, common organisations etc.) need to deal with a common task.

Combined constellations

Combinations of goal approximation constellations and organisational structural constellations can be used in political situations. Combinations of the constellation of the defocused topic with organisational structural constellations often help in identifying the essence of the problem in a very short time.

Constellations in layers

Building up a constellation in layers is very useful in political situations in order to clarify what is normally a very complex relationship between systems. As systemic parts are added, layer by layer, their influence on the system becomes visible.

Supervision constellations

These are suited for use with advisors to political systems to verify their level of involvement with the system they advise.

Meta constellations
The belief polarity constellation can be used to create a greater context for conflicting political parties, since belief polarity constellations allow resources to be taken from the poles even before the conflict situation has been solved.

Specific constellations for groups
The following two constellation forms are designed for use with groups: the first is mainly for spontaneously occurring and often inexplicable group conflicts; the second improves the atmosphere in a group.

The conflict constellation (Sparrer/Varga)
We developed conflict constellations in order to solve *accidental* constellations. We work on the assumption that constellations occur of their own accord on a daily basis, the only difference being their lack of a uniform group focus. For this reason, different simultaneous constellations tend to cancel each other out.

A uniform focus exists, however, at a seminar, public event or family party, where there is a focusing on one person standing in the centre. It may happen that other, unknown people then 'slide into' this person's system, or the person in the centre may confuse a participant with an excluded person from his system.

We can look at this in the following way: each of us moves around in his or her family with, as it were, empty valences (as in chemistry). The 'holes' represent excluded systemic members or other blind spots. In comparison with projection, we are dealing with a reverse process. Other people can slide into a system with which they have no actual connection. For the owner of the system they thus represent an excluded person. These involuntary representatives start to display unfamiliar behaviour which belongs to the alien system. With projection, on the other hand, a type of behaviour or attribute is projected onto another person, although she does *not* usually actually display the corresponding behaviour or attribute.

The conflict constellation helps us understand the effects of accidental constellations and then to solve the conflicts they give rise to. This is done by placing in a constellation the people involved in the accidental constellation and then checking for any confusions (with another person). This involves working on the following three levels:

- the system in which the conflict arose,
- the client system – in whatever area
- the client's family system into which an outsider 'slides'.

The prismatic Balint group constellation (Matthias Varga von Kibéd)
This constellation is based on the basic principle of Balint group work specially developed by Alfred Drees to deal with the perpetrator-victim problem (Drees 1995). After describing what happened to one of her clients, who had been the victim of violence, the facilitator asked all the other participants what they thought about as they let what the facilitator told them about the client affect them. The answers given by the entire group give a reflection of the client and her surroundings. From our experience of constellations, we can say that the whole group began to represent facets of the client.

In prismatic Balint group constellations, the facilitator or a participant positions one or more representatives into the centre of the participants (sitting in a circle) without saying who the representatives stand in for. The participants then take it in turns to describe the bodily sensations, thoughts or emotions that they feel spontaneously. in this way the facilitator can position positive people or power sources within the circle in order to strengthen the group. The strength of the people in the constellation then affects the whole group.

Another option is to place people in the constellation who act as leading figures for the group. The group can then view these leading figures in a completely new way using the prismatic Balint group constellation.

Constellations used in the field of language learning
Constellation to remove barriers to language learning (Sparrer/Varga)
There has already been some promising work in this field. We are currently working on new forms.

Barriers to language learning may also be connected with loyalty conflicts −not only loyalty to one's family, but also loyalty to one's country. The constellation involves a *focus* and the *ability to speak a language*. The client can stand in the position of this *ability* and observe what things change for her in this position. Her representative then moves towards the *language ability* and reports the spontaneous images and thoughts that occur to her. If excluded parts appear these are also placed in the constellation and the entanglements are solved using process work.

Goal approximation constellation (Insa Sparrer)
This involves a *focus*, a *goal*, a *miracle* and the excluded parts relevant to language learning. These are positioned in the constellation using representatives. A more detailed description of this type of constellation can be found in chapter VII.

Chapter IV

SFT and SySt constellations – similarities, differences and equivalents

Both SFT and SySt constellations are **forms of brief therapy**. This means they use a small number of sessions, but not that the entire therapy process lasts only a short time, as is often wrongly assumed. In both methods, the time between sessions is relatively long, between two weeks and a number of months. Both methods thus emphasise the self-reliance of the client and allow them time to change. With shorter periods between sessions, instead of learning to use their own abilities clients all too often pass the responsibility for change onto the therapist and use the sessions as a permanent counselling facility for conflict situations.

A further similarity between the two methods is that they both mainly use **syntactic procedures** and not, or at least far less, semantic procedures. This can be seen in both cases in the focus on differences and the limited interpretation of individual statements or sensations. 'Syntactic' in this case means that the regularities and structural attributes of the processes are taken into consideration and interpretations are largely avoided. As Steve de Shazer emphasises, we are able to know what 'better' means without knowing what 'good' means. The focus on differences helps limit assessment and interpretation of individual statements or sensations. In other words, it is an elegant way of avoiding value judgements.

The syntactic side also shows itself in systemic structural constellations by the fact that hidden work is possible. This involves positioning abstract systemic parts – e.g. a *goal*, the *miracle*, one or more relevant exceptions etc. – without the client explaining what she means by them. The therapist is able to work in a purely structural way, since she is not aware of any content details at this point. Hidden constellations are described in detail in Chapter VIII.3.

The **therapeutic attitude** in both methods is essentially the same. As far as possible, the therapist tries to adopt a *multi-directional*, open, questioning, interested, non-judgmental attitude.

As opposed to family constellations, the **motivation** to achieve change during a systemic structural constellation is not taken from the level of suffering but **from the vision of a solution**. In this aspect, SySt constellations are similar to SFT, where a vision is used to help deal with the problem and move towards a solution.

We can now see that these initially so extraordinarily different forms in fact display some important similarities, allowing for a close integration of the solution-focused procedure with SySt constellations. For this to succeed, however, we need a clear view of the central differences between the two forms, some of which will be described below.

IV.1 Unknown problem vs. problem dating back more than one generation

At first sight we are most likely to notice the differences between the two methods. While in the constellations method an important role is played by events that can date back generations, in SFT knowing these events is not necessary in order to become familiar with the client's problem. With SySt constellations, although initially we do not normally place family members into the constellation, topics involving excluded family members may appear in hidden form through structural level change. This means that, even where initially a current problem is addressed in the constellation, topics that go back a number of generations can also be touched and also often positioned explicitly in the constellation.

IV.2 Verbal vs. nonverbal

While SFT is to a large extent a verbal method, the focus of the constellations method falls on nonverbal approaches, such as representative perception, the effect of the external pictures and the intuitive positioning of representatives. Even where representatives express their bodily sensations verbally, this method needs only to establish whether they are feeling better or worse, and this can be done in a purely nonverbal way.

The central aspect of constellations work is the experience of *how* something is better. SFT, on the other hand, besides relaying experiences – e.g. using the miracle question – also deals with the acquisition of 'What-Information' (referred to previously as know-what) i.e. content information, as opposed to 'How-Information' (know-how), which relates to the 'how' in the experience of something. I use the term 'information' here in the sense of Gregory Bateson (1985): 'A difference that makes a difference'. As a result, the client gains the following 'What-Information':

- – in which situations he felt better
- – what he contributed to the improvement in his situation
- – which differences exist between the solution- and problem-situations

By answering the miracle question the client obtains information about which new problems may appear when he achieves his goal. At the same time, through his experience of the post-miracle state, he obtains 'How-Information', since he experiences how he would behave, think and feel differently if his goal had already been achieved.

Constellations also show what exists *between* the elements of the system. In doing so, the constellation goes beyond the verbal and nonverbal language of the representatives. We call this *transverbal* language.

IV.3 The impossibility of perceiving other people's psychic states as a 'something' vs. relaying 'How-Information' through representative perception

The most serious difference between SFT and SySt constellations is the use of representatives in the constellations method. An element comes into play here – the simulation of other people's psychic states – which is not resorted to in SFT. Not only does SFT not refer to representative 'perception', initially the method as a whole has no place in the philosophy of SFT.

The philosophical principles of SFT are based on the philosophy of Ludwig Wittgenstein, who, in his *Philosophical Investigations*, indicates how it is impossible to perceive another person's psychic state since this does not exist in the sense that objects exists around us. He illuminates this point by means of the example of perceiving pain (PI 293):

'If I say of myself that it is only known from my own case that I know what the word "pain" means – must I not say the same of other people too? And how can I then generalise the *one* case so irresponsibly?

Now, someone tells me about themselves that *he* knows what pain is only from his own case! Suppose everyone had a box with something in it: we call it a 'beetle'. No one can look into anyone else's box, and everyone says he knows what a beetle is only by looking at *his* beetle. Here it would be quite possible for everyone to have something different in his box. One might even imagine such a thing constantly changing. But suppose the word 'beetle' had a use in these people's language? If so it would not be used as the name of a thing. The thing in the box has no place in the language-game at all; not even as a *something*: for the box might even be empty. No, one can 'divide through' by the thing in the box; it cancels out, whatever it is.

That is to say: if we construe the grammar of the expression of sensation on the model of 'object and designation' the object drops out of consideration as irrelevant.'

If the experience of pain does not refer to *a something*, but the experience of pain shows itself in a particular relationship to the body or is mirrored in a certain relationship structure, it then becomes difficult to speak of perception. We are certainly not perceiving *a something*. At most, we might say that a particular dynamic of a relationship in a constellation has generated an experience of pain.

This, then, is precisely what we try to simulate in constellations. And this is also the way in which something shows itself in a constellation. We do not produce *a something*, but recreate constellations using individual arrangements in which particular sensations arise that *fit* the system represented. Precisely because sensations and mental illnesses are not things but epiphenomena in the dynamic of a structure, they may also disappear if we change that structure. Constellations thus show us which rearrangements, processes and rituals will be helpful in changing unpleasant sensations. Access to the psychic states of others in constellations is given by the fact that such psychic states can show themselves within the representatives' relationship structure and that the representatives are able to access them by perceiving sensations. It is the *differences* in the perception of these representatives' sensations that can indicate which processes are useful in changing the sensations of alien psychic states.

Adhering closely to Wittgenstein's use of language, we can say that the representative perception among the representatives requires a simulation of the space of relevant relationships in which the alien psychic phenomena took place and in which the psychic sensations, cognitions and attitude of alien systems can then show themselves.

The representatives perceive the very specific sensations, cognitions, emotions and attitude in their bodies, which may in part be unknown to the client himself, but which after external verification often proves to fit specifically to the alien system. Time and again participants are astonished to see how precisely and appropriately sensations can be felt by unknown representatives, despite the limited amount, or even total lack, of information about the alien system.

The relation between the representatives' perceptions and the represented system cannot be predicted. If, for example, a representative feels stomach pain, the correspondence in the represented system could be a family member who also suffered from stomach pains or that stomach pains were an issue in the family, or that the stomach pains are merely an indicator that the system requires a change. Which of these possibilities applies, or whether a completely new possibility is is the case, cannot be anticipated just from the representatives' perception. It is important, therefore, not to interpret representative sensations, feelings and cognitions, but only to pay attention to the differences and changes that occur. This is a purely structural procedure.

Sometimes, however, the specific faculty through which representatives react can have a content-related relationship to the represented system, not dissimilar to the example involving stomach pains mentioned above. We call this a weak semantic procedure. This approach is no longer purely syntactic, insofar as the change in the relationship structures in the represented system can no longer be represented by all differences in all sense faculties and sub-modalities in the structural constellation (simply by considering the adequacy of the direction of change). Rather, the sense faculty used in the structural constellation, or even the respective sub-modality, displays a direct equivalence to the represented system. In these conditions, we are able to catch a glimpse of a weak semantic element of the procedure. These conditions also allow for the performance of hidden and, in this sense, syntactic work.

The question often arises during constellations as to how such specific information can be transmitted. This is accompanied by various theses that state that:

- We come into contact with the souls of the deceased
- Telepathic transmission takes places
- Information is relayed via subliminal stimuli

Taking into account Wittgenstein's statements, we can say the following about the transmission of information in constellations:

The observed sensation appears within a structure established by the relationships between the systemic elements of the observed system. As soon as we reproduce this relationship structure in the room, it becomes possible for the corresponding sensations to emerge. It is our hypothesis that this process can be viewed as not being a transmission of information, but that the representative sensations are a consequence of the relationship structure reproduced in the room by the client setting up the representatives. Performing a constellation involves the *intention* of the client, who gives the constellation the perspective from which things are viewed.

There are also some further objections to the theses given above on information transmission in constellations. A counter argument to the idea of making contact with the souls of the deceased is given by the fact that the representative phenomena also appear in constellations of abstract ideas and body parts. It is strange to speak of their having souls, given that we are not adopting the highly particular animistic perspective in which the body parts or animate objects possess 'souls' So 'soul' would have a different meaning than in the sense as 'souls of the deceased'.

The idea that constellations deal exclusively with subliminal perceptions can be disproved using simple experiments. Constellation phenomena also appear when neither the facilitator nor the client is familiar with the represented system. It is possible to set up a completely strange system. Subsequent comparison of the relationship qualities that appeared in the constellation and the relationship qualities of the elements of the represented system show a high level of congruence.

A counter argument to the telepathic transmission argument occasionally proposed as an explanation is given by the fact that sometimes information that is unknown to both the therapist and the client appears and may refer to events that are long since forgotten. This new information can be of the following nature:

- that someone is missing
- how someone who had a hard fate feels
- how someone was injured
- how someone feels who was excluded and now finally is included
- that someone feels they have been unfairly treated
- who feels angry towards whom

When these kinds of sensations appear, we often use statements to express them. This sometimes involves a cautious interpretation of these sensations, which can then be verified by asking the representative if the statement feels right to her. The constellation relays 'How-Information' from which certain 'What-Information' can be derived as necessary. However, during this transformation process from 'How-Information' to 'What-Information' interpretations influence us. It is therefore very important to verify 'What-Information' acquired in this way externally, while 'How-Information' can initially be considered as pure experience with no interpretation. 'What-Information' is always an abstraction of a real situation, while 'How-Information' usually refers to a very particular experience.

In therapeutic situations we mainly deal with 'How-Information' – how someone experiences a particular event, e.g. how it is to be a mother, or how a traumatic situation can now be experienced differently. This is why constellations are so useful in this field of application.

The concept of simulating alien systems using representatives highlights an important difference from SFT, and a real addition to solution-focused procedures. In SFT it is assumed that we are not able to know *how* something is felt by another person. It derives from the fact that sensations are not a *something*, that we cannot experience sensations felt by other people and therefore cannot compare them with our own. During the constellations process, however, quasi-private sensations are made generally accessible in that we are able to conclude from statements by the representatives whether they have feelings similar to those they are representing.

Even in relation to the language used, the assumption is made that a complete understanding is not possible and that the meaning of words is only revealed through their use. Steve de Shazer proposes the construction of useful misunderstandings in situations where a true understanding is no longer possible. As a solution, he introduced scaling, which highlights differences that we are able to understand without needing fully to understand or analyse the exact value structure of the client. As previously mentioned, we are able to know what 'better' means without needing to know what 'good' means.

In SySt constellations we emphasise more the differences between the sensations experienced and less what the representatives sense. This gives a harmonisation between SySt constellations and SFT, as opposed to family constellations where 'What-Information' plays a much larger role. Before performing a family constellation, information about excluded family members is often collected. In SySt constellations, on the other hand, it suffices to place in the constellation a representative for 'the person this is all about'.

IV.4 Temporal vs. spatial differences

SFT focuses on future and resource orientation and uses exercises to transfer experiences and insights gained in the session to everyday life. SFT is a conversation method. It should be noted, however, that the conversation acts as a hypnotherapeutic trance induction into experiencing solutions. This means that while SFT takes place as a conversation, its goal is in fact to bring about solving experiences. At the core of this type of therapy lies the miracle question, which has the role of anticipating a future solution that can be experienced in the present.

The focus on solutions in SFT and SySt constellations occurs through focusing on differences. In the solution-focused interview, differences between the current situation and the exception situation are analysed.

Solution-focused questions are primarily questions about difference, as in the following examples:

'What was different about the situation in which you were feeling better?'
'What is there instead of the problem?'
'From what do you notice that …?'
'What did you do differently (think, feel)?'
'Has anyone else apart from you noticed that the miracle has occurred?'

Systemic structural constellations also take into consideration the differences between different points in time by comparing the feelings experienced by a representative from one constellation image to the next. This comparison corresponds in structure to that of the current situation, the exception situation and the miracle. We ask the representatives, on an image by image basis, whether they feel that something has changed and whether things are now better for them. This syntactic approach further helps to avoid interpretations.

In systemic structural constellations the main focus falls on experience, in particular in the form of representative perception. With the help of representatives, people from the client's system are placed in the room so that the spatial arrangement creates an external picture of the client's inner image. It is the differences that arise from the spatial arrangements of the representatives that are looked for first. These give an indication as to the structure of the relationships between the individual elements of the system. We do not find these spatial differences in SFT.

An advantage of the different spatial arrangements is that experiences in these constellations pictures are relayed in a clearer way than in the mental images triggered by the miracle question in SFT. The relaying of the 'as-if' experience by means of the miracle question is normally weaker than that achieved by entering a constellation picture. With constellation pictures, the step from possibility to reality is easier to take.

Although the differences between SySt constellations and SFT are initially very clear, it is nonetheless possible to find **equivalents** in each for the important concepts contained in both therapy forms.

IV.5 Problem: first constellation picture / context of the miracle

In constellations work, the problem appears in the initial set up picture which the client arranges based on her current condition. In order to stay close to the client's formulation, we developed the specific types of systemic structural constellations.

In starting with the client's current condition, this pacing helps the client to accept the constellation as a natural continuation of the preliminary interview. In the first picture we see the relationship structure of the problem. We don't need to know the content during the constellation work. The constellation pictures that follow correspond to the steps towards the solution.

SFT avoids talking about problems, and instead we find a counterpart to the problem in the context of the miracle. This is where negative reactions from the environment to the changes in the client after the miracle appear. All the obstacles which make a problem a problem may show themselves at this stage. However, in the solution-focused procedure, questions are not asked about the obstacles. Instead questions are asked about how the client manages to overcome the obstacles after the miracle occurs. Within the context of the miracle those parts of the problem appear that need to be overcome for a solution to be possible. This is precisely where we can see the difference from positive thinking. SFT is not only about seeing everything positively, but about *how* the client can *make* things better. The obstacles that appear in the context of the miracle represent the price that the client must pay when giving up the usefulness (i.e. avoidance of obstacles) that creates the state of non-solution. In the context of the miracle, therefore, we to an extent find the negative of the solution.

IV.6 Solution: solution picture / answers to solution-focused questions

Solutions appear in SFT through the client's answers as to:

- what things are good and can remain as they are
- exceptions to the problem
- the client's goal
- the miracle question

The last type of question here (about the miracle question) conveys the solution. We also find this type of experience in SySt constellations in the solution picture, when the client steps into the footsteps of her representatives. The experience in the solution picture of a constellation is nearly always felt more strongly by clients than the experience triggered by the miracle question. The advantage of SFT lies in the specifying of the solution using questions about differences. This gives the client a more accurate content picture of the solution, which can be helpful when implementing the experience of a solution in everyday life.

IV.7 Interventions: positional work, process work and tests / questions and exercises

In SySt constellations, the therapeutic interventions consist of positional work, process work and tests. The therapist reacts in each case to the verbal and nonverbal expressions of the representatives. The reactions of the client are also taken into consideration, though more in the sense of whether she experiences the constellation as fitting. This is very important, since if the client is no longer able or willing to follow the constellation, then the constellation can no longer work for her. The expressions by the representatives guide the interventions. Positional work and process work – similar to the questions used in SFT – lead in the direction of a solution. Both procedures are strongly solution-focused, since they focus attention on differences that lead to improvement: with SySt constellations this occurs through the focus on the changes in sensations felt by the representatives; in SFT it occurs through focusing on differences between exception situations and the different solutions in the future.

An important intervention in SFT is the assigning of an exercise embedded in appreciation and praise to the client at the end of a session. These exercises help the client remember the miracle and, by indicating concrete types of action or observation, facilitate the transition from the experienced possibility of the miracle to the realisation of the miracle. This support in translating what is learnt in the session to daily life is not initially available in constellations; it is therefore very important to integrate this element of SFT into constellations work. This happens in the solution-focused systemic structural constellations, as will be described in detail in the following chapters.

At the end of the constellation, the experience of the solution is present in the solution picture. This leads to a change in attitude from which it is assumed new action can grow. The transfer of the experienced solution to daily life occurs through the impulse that is gained from the experience. Trusting in the new solution picture helps to stabilise the new attitude. The change of attitude is experienced in the solution situation and shows itself in changed behaviour in daily life.

This kind of change of attitude is seen in SFT through the experience of the miracle. Again, the turning point for a change of behaviour is initially provided by a change in attitude. It is therefore not relevant whether the client performs the exercises successfully or not. Ultimately, it is the remembering of a solution situation that is important, not the rehearsal of a certain type of behaviour. It is important that the client remains in contact with her experience of the miracle. Steve de Shazer trusts that the client is herself able to decide whether the exercise is suitable for her or not. His trust proves its worth in his work, as the experience of many therapists working with SFT shows. SFT, then, also works towards a change in attitude from which new behaviours are generated.

Echoing Wittgenstein (1989b, 6.43), we can say that through the miracle question a new world is opened up for the client, the limits of her former world are changed with no change to her environment:

'If the good or bad exercise of the will does alter the world, it can alter only the limits of the world, not the facts …'

This type of change we find again in constellations work in the solution picture of a constellation. As soon as the client positions herself in the solution picture, she can experience how, although her system consists of the same elements, through the new relationship structure the limits of her world have changed. The solution picture in constellations work is thus analogous to the miracle question in SFT.

IV.8 Inclusion of the excluded

Main themes of constellations work are the inclusion of excluded systemic members and the dissolving of entanglements revealed in the client's problem. The main theme of SFT is to find solutions that are initially excluded from the client's world. While SySt constellations attempt to include excluded people and systemic elements, excluded solutions in SFT are found through questions. In both methods, what is missing recovers its place and the limits of the client's world are expanded through the inclusion of solutions.

What is missing and the 'excluded' belong to the system, and the client's 'symptoms' point to this exclusion. The inclusion of the excluded is to a certain extent a 're-remembering'. Since this re-remembering refers to the whole, every solution contains within itself the seed of every further solution. The solution process in both procedures is a model for the generation of further solutions.

Solutions can only show themselves. As a whole, they are not describable and so we should not create concepts for them. If we see something tangible, it points to something more complete for which it is sign – this is not dissimilar to a fractal, where the form of the whole is contained within a part.

While goals are specific solutions to specific problems, the miracle is akin to the gateway to the form of the solution, which contains all possible specific solutions. The miracle can never entirely comprehend this form of the solution, but it can open a door to it. For this reason it is important to link the individual parts of the miracle as reported by the client with an 'and' – just as a flower can always be added to a bouquet of flowers. Access to the miracle opens up a new space, a space for solutions. Consequently, when a client, years after undergoing a course of solution-focused therapy, asks for a further session, this session can be begun by asking: 'What have you forgotten?' The re-remembering can then reopen access to the space for solutions of the miracle. The miracle is an inexhaustible space for resources, a source that connects us to the whole.

Chapter V

Combining Solution Focused Therapy (SFT) with Systemic Structural Constellations (SySt)

Despite the obvious differences between the two methods presented in the last chapter – or maybe precisely because of them – it still makes sense to combine both procedures in order to emphasise the advantages each has to offer.

In this chapter I will demonstrate how both methods can be used consecutively; and in the following four chapters I will show how the solution-focused procedure can be implemented as a systemic constellation so that both methods in effect take place simultaneously.

V.1 Integrating SySt constellations into SFT

Solution-focused brief therapy is a complete and self-contained form of therapy in its own right. Constellations, on the other hand, can only be used in combination with other therapeutic methods. When applying SySt constellations in a therapeutic situation, therefore, it makes sense to use a method that combines different constellations through the means of conversation, and which also asks about and questions the context of the problem, while highlighting, and continuing to use to good effect, the progress made in the therapy. I intend to show how

- elements of SFT and SySt constellations can be applied consecutively during the interview prior to setting up a constellation
- elements of SySt constellations represent a useful extension to SFT
- SFT and SySt constellations can be alternated during therapy

V.1.1 The preliminary interview
Before a constellation can be performed, a level of trust between the

therapist and the client needs to be built up. In addition to this, the context of the problem, and that of a possible constellation, needs to be discussed with the client. If the constellation is to take place in a group, during the first constellations the therapist needs to give some explanations and hints about what should be given attention. In later constellations, as participants´ trust grows successively, the facilitator can work more briefly and directly.

The following description of the preliminary interview can be adapted and shortened where necessary, depending on the circumstances of each case.

The preliminary interview is made up of the following five parts.

1.　Clarification of context

When the client comes for his first therapy session, it is a good idea to find out who recommended therapy to him or who the referring agent was (cf. II.1.5). This information can give an indication of what the client will expect from the therapy and can warn of any possible future conflicting situations the client might be exposed to by achieving his goal. It may also become clear whether there is anybody who might raise objections to the client's achieving his goal or whose reactions may also need to be taken into account. Referring agents can mean parents, partners or doctors, the youth welfare office or a judge, and these may have their own wishes and goals, which may not necessarily be the same as the client's.

Besides the context of the referral, the context in which the client's problem appeared also has to be considered. People suffering from anxiety disorders, for example, see their self-confidence increase considerably after their anxiety problem is solved, which could then cause difficulties in their relationship. In a sense, the client's anxiety had been shielding him from these potential relationship problems.

These sorts of issues need to be clarified before going into the first constellations session, so that the client is prepared to deal with any potentially unpleasant consequences that might occur as a result. Here we ask the question: What will the client do when person X reacts in a particular way to changes brought about by the constellation?

At this point we can use similar questions to those used in describing the context of the miracle in II.1.5.9. Steve de Shazer, for example, often begins a conversation by asking:

'How do you earn your living?'
'What do you do during the day?'

Or, when dealing with children:

'What things are you good at?
'What are you good at in school?'

Through these questions, de Shazer is enquiring about the lives of family members, and this helps identify appropriate metaphors and fitting phrasing for the conversation. By asking about professions and daily activities, he is also addressing areas that are still intact and can demonstrate the existence of resources.

2. Clarifying the goal

The purpose of this stage is to clarify the client's problem. This process is described in II.1.5.1. Again it is important that

- the goal is the client's own goal, and not the goal of the referral agent or family
- the goal is described in positive terms – i.e. in terms of the presence of something (as opposed to an absence of something)
- it is formulated clearly and in detail
- it is subdivided into small steps
- it is formulated in behavioural terms.

3. The miracle question

The miracle question was also explained in II.1.5.9 and can be used as it is described there. Alternatively, the following formulation can be used:

'If now, after asking you a few questions about your family and relatives, your work and your life – we perform a constellation – and if this constellation were to solve your problem miraculously – just like that – and assuming that you then go home – from what would you notice – that the constellation has solved the problem you brought?'

'Who, apart from you, would be the first to notice that your problem is solved?'
'From what would he or she notice this?'
'How would he or she react to this?'
'How would you then react to his or her change in behaviour?'
'Who else would notice?'
'How would others react?'
Etc.

In this way it is possible to verify whether a solution to the problem might itself create new problems. The client can then think about how he would react to any possible unpleasant side effects of the solution. This enables the context within which the constellation takes place to be observed in detail, thereby allowing problems to be avoided that might otherwise arise from the reactions of others from within his environment. This can also verify whether a constellation at this stage would be of any use at all to the client.

In general, the answer we receive to the miracle question has two parts: the client's reaction to the miracle, on the one hand, and the reactions in the client's environment to the change in his behaviour, on the other. Both these parts can be placed in the constellation as the miracle and the context of the miracle, respectively. If, however, the client clearly names negative reactions by specific people which he is unable to deal with, then instead of the general 'context of the problem' I place the representatives for the actual people in question into the constellation.

In the fifth part of the preliminary interview (below) I give an addition to the context of the miracle, namely the reactions of excluded people that belong to contexts in the past, such as childhood, the lifetime of grandparents etc.

4. The introduction of scales and the search for exceptions
After the miracle question has been asked, it can be useful to introduce scaling questions in order to test whether parts of the miracle have already occurred and how much of the miracle has already been achieved (cf. II.1.5.10). Here the following questions may be helpful.

'On a scale of 0 to 10, where 0 stands for 'not at all' and 10 stands for 'the constellation solved my problem completely', where do you currently see yourself?'
'How did you manage to reach ...?'
'Have you previously been higher than ...?'
'When was that? And what was different then?'
'Are there any other differences?'

Answers to these questions can give the therapist ideas for later exercises.

5. Questions about excluded people
Until now we have approached the preliminary interview in the same way as in SFT. We will now look at some of the important questions specific to constellations.

The most important part of a constellations process is the inclusion of unmentioned, excluded and strongly devalued people. The strongest entanglements occur when the first principle that 'everybody has the same right to membership' has been violated and people who join the system later (new members) represent these excluded people (described in more detail in III.1.1.2.1).

Here the system acts like a memory that compensates for past wrongs through the later members of the system – e.g. through succession dynamics or partial pattern representations. The later members of the system take on the behavioural traits and attitudes of the excluded people out of love and loyalty. That love is the connecting force is strongly suggested by experience with constellations, and it is the therapist's task to guide this love in another direction so that the later members act in conscious remembrance or tribute to the excluded people, instead of copying them by denying themselves membership or success.

Excluded family members may already appear as part of the context of the miracle. In general, however, people who appear in the context of the miracle have the tendency to be more from the present, rather than the past. It is therefore advisable to ask the following sorts of questions in order to clarify who still needs to be included and thus ensure stability in the therapeutic results:

'Does anyone in your family have a similar problem?'
'Has this problem already occurred to someone in your family?'

If either of these two questions is answered in the affirmative, it can be assumed that the problem is directly related to the family situation and is being perpetuated by loyalty. If, on the other hand, the client is unable to embrace life fully, stands in the way of her own success or lives her life at minimum energy levels, the problem may be a connection to someone who died young or suffered some kind of injustice. We can ask the following questions to clarify this situation:

'Is there someone in your family you are not allowed to mention or speak of?'
'Did you have any stillborn brothers of sisters?'
'Did someone in your family die at a very young age or in tragic circumstances?'

Of course, these kinds of questions do not guarantee the discovery of excluded family members.

Further indications of excluded people can be found in the initial constellation picture – e.g. in the representatives' sense that there is someone missing, through their sensations of cold shivers, cold air at floor level, charged spots or by the fact that a number of the representatives are all looking towards an empty spot etc.

The detection of excluded family members can also cast the problem in a different light. For example, it may become clear that the client's symptoms can be seen as an echo of those shown by the representative of the excluded person, or that, out of love for the excluded person, the client denies herself something that had been denied to him or her. In this case it is important to appreciate the love involved. Healing can be achieved by redirecting this love so that the unconscious honouring of excluded people, for example, is replaced by the successful action of those who came later, to remember and honour those people.

The following example may serve to clarify this, as well as to show how the preliminary interview paves the way for an initial constellation and how its individual parts are to be implemented.

V.1.2 Case study 1: When loyalty to parents stands in the way of professional advancement (part 1)

Mrs S came to me after she missed her exam for her technical baccalaureate diploma through illness, and then failed to pass at her next attempt, despite intensive revision and mastering the exam topics. She would be allowed only one more chance to repeat the exam, a fact which only made her all the more nervous. The transcript of the preliminary interview to the constellation is shown below.

Facilitator: What brings you to me today?

Client: I have to repeat my exam for my technical baccalaureate, since I missed the exam once due to illness and then failed at the second attempt, and now I'm finding it hard to concentrate. I just can't seem to do my revision – it's just incredibly heavy going.

Facilitator: What gave you the idea to come to me?

Client: My uncle thought I needed help. He recommended that I come to see you. And my mother also thought I should see you – she said I wasn't capable of getting out of the situation on my own.

Facilitator: What do you think?

Client: I agree, I don't know what to do, but I don't know if therapy will help me. I've never done therapy before.

Facilitator: Let's say our conversation here goes well and is beneficial to you: in what ways do you think you'll be able to observe this?

Client: Everything would be less stressful and my nervousness would be gone.

Facilitator: Aha, and what would be there instead?

Client: I'd have more courage and I'd find the revising easier.

Facilitator: How would you notice that your revision had become easier?

Client: I'd be more motivated to do it, and I'd remember what I was learning, and I'd be fiddling around much less.

Facilitator: What would you be doing instead?

Client: I'd sit down in the morning and start learning.

Facilitator: How would you manage that?

Client: I'd open my books and then read and understand what they say, and I'd be able to remember it. Somehow I'd be interested in it.

Facilitator: I'm going to ask you quite a difficult question now. You might need to use your imagination a bit to answer it. If you go home now after this session and eat your evening meal at home – and suddenly become tired and go to bed – then assuming that during that night a miracle were to happen – all the things that brought you here were solved – just like that – and that would after all be a miracle…

Client: *(Client nods to show agreement)*

Facilitator: …When you then wake up the next morning – and no one tells you that this miracle had occurred – from what would you notice that a miracle had happened?

Client: I'd no longer be worried in the mornings.

Facilitator: What would be there in place of the worry?

Client: I'd be looking forward to the day.

Facilitator: What things would you be happy about?

Client: I'd be happy about breakfast and my gym session in the evening.

Facilitator: From what else would you notice that the miracle had happened?

Client: I'd have more energy.

Facilitator: And what would you do then?

Client: I'd get up quicker and have breakfast with my parents and then I'd start revising; it would all be really easy.

Facilitator: Would anything else be different?

Client: I'd be able to look forward to the day, and maybe then I'd again have time to meet one of my friends.

Facilitator: Would anyone else apart from you notice the miracle?

Client: Yes, my mother, and my father, and also my friends.

Facilitator: How would your mother notice that the miracle had happened? And how would she react?

Client: She'd see straight away that I was feeling better.

Facilitator: From what?

Client: I'd be getting up earlier and having breakfast together with my parents; otherwise I sleep late and don't get out of bed.

Facilitator: How would your parents react to this?

Client: They'd be surprised and would ask me what had happened?

Facilitator: And what would be your answer?

Client: I'd say that I was feeling well again and that I'll be able to do the exam.

Facilitator: How would you parents react to this?

Client: They'd be very relieved.

Facilitator: How would your friends react?

Client: They'd be happy for me.

Facilitator: If you are able to start revising again and over time can master your exam topics and this time around manage to pass your exam, what would you do afterwards?

Client: I don't know yet. There are different options. I could go to university, but since I find learning so difficult I'm not sure whether I want that.

Facilitator: And if the miracle had happened and you found learning easy, what would you then do after your exam?

Client: I don't know. Maybe I could do something more artistic. Gold working is also something I'd really like to do.

Facilitator: Is the fact that you don't yet know what you'd like to do afterwards a problem for you?

Client: No. After the exam pressure is gone everything will be easier and I'll have time to make up my mind. I'll drop in on some lectures at university to see what it's like and then do some unpaid work at a goldsmith. I think things will be clearer then.

Facilitator: On a scale of 0 to 10, where 0 stands for 'I can't revise at all' and 10 stands for 'I find revising easy', where would you place yourself at this moment?

Client: at 4.

Facilitator: What helped to get to 4?

Client: Revising together with a friend; and also just imagining that I found it easy to revise – somehow I found that relieving.

Facilitator: That was a good idea, working together with a friend! Maybe you could ask yourself the question more often as to how you would notice you were finding it easy to revise and what things would then be different for you…

Client: That's a good idea. I'll do that.

Facilitator: Were you ever higher than a 4?

Client: Yes, but not when revising for this exam.

Facilitator: Was there ever anyone in your family who also had problems revising or was unable to do a particular job that he or she really wanted to do?

Client: My mother would have liked to have been a teacher but was unable able to go to university because I was already on the way. I think she suffered for a long time from not having learnt a profession.

Facilitator: In a certain way, then, you are being loyal to your mother by not doing your baccalaureate …

Client: *(Client nods).*

Facilitator: Is there anyone else in your family who is affected by the same issue?

Client: No, no one that occurs to me.

The mother was unable to learn the profession that she would have liked to practise since she was already pregnant with the client. This gives us a context for the client's behaviour within her world view. In this we can understand how the client finds it difficult to permit herself something that, in her view, was denied to her mother by her pregnancy (at least this what she had been led to believe).

Through a goal approximation constellation it was possible to transform the client's loyalty in terms of failure towards her mother, so that she learned to allow herself success while also remaining loyal to her mother. (This constellation can be found in VI.4.1).

V.1.3 The inclusion of rituals in the general context of the constellations process

Performing a partial systemic structural constellation is often an appropriate first step to take in an initial individual therapy session, and one which can then be continued in following sessions. In many cases, it is sufficient to weave individual rituals into the therapeutic conversation, which can lead to an entirely natural extension of SFT including systemic structural constellations. Since SFT allows loyalty conflicts to be uncovered and dealt with only in a very indirect manner (e.g. by using the miracle question to identify the reaction of others to the miracle), it often helps to integrate knowledge of loyalties towards excluded people into SFT in the form of questions. This makes one of the core elements of constellation work accessible to the SFT approach.

If the facilitator suspects – or simply seeks clarification – that the client's problem is connected with a sense of assumed guilt or loyalty towards an excluded family member, she can then initially dress up this supposition in a question – e.g.:

'Is there anyone in your family who has a similar problem?'
'Was there anyone in your family who brought guilt upon themselves?'
'Was there anyone in your family to whom wrong was done or you are not allowed to speak of or mention?'

Rituals are thus helpful in recognising and including excluded people, returning assumed burdens and guilt to their rightful place, and clarifying the internal picture of relationships within the family. They allow for a certain amount of correction of the facts. Bert Hellinger has suggested that burden and guilt belong to those that have done wrong (Weber 1997) – only they can make amends for this burden or guilt, and it is only to them that this burden is due. For the others, each act of interference is an affront, for any interference implies that the excluded people are not able to stand up for themselves.

The most important and most common of these rituals will be presented below.

The **return ritual** has already been described in III.1.1.2. It can be employed where the client tries to compensate for guilt or assume burdens that are in fact alien to her. In general, both credit and burden should be left to those to whom they belong. The act of assuming someone else's burden does not mean unburdening that person; rather, it serves only to take away that person's dignity. In attempting to take away someone else's burden, it is as if we say: 'You're not able to do it on your own. You need help.'

In **individual therapy**, rituals can be performed that use anchors, figures and cards as representatives (cf. III.1.1.2). In return rituals, the client first assigns an anchor (or figure or card) to represent herself, and then does the same for the person to whom the guilt or burden is to be returned. A cushion or a bag can be used as a symbol for the burden itself. The client then takes up her own position in the constellation and places the symbol for the burden at the feet of the other person, saying one of the following:

'You are my grandmother (or aunt or great grandfather etc.) – I respect your fate – It touches me – You belong to us – This is something I acquired through you and have carried for you for a long time – but it belongs to you and your life, and – even though this is hard for me, I am giving it back to you – From now on I will honour you in another way.'

'I respect your fate, and I'm leaving it to you now – all of it. In the future I will honour you in another way than I have done till now – I'll make room for you in my heart – and please look upon me kindly – especially when I am faring so well and you did not – In your honour I am letting myself prosper.'

'Your fate/burden/guilt/glory belongs to you alone – I have no claim on this whatsoever.'

'I have carried this for you (out of love) for a long time. Now I have carried it enough. It belongs to you – and not to me – and I am giving it back to you.'

The client now moves into the position of the receiver of the burden, picks up the symbol, pressing it to her upper body to examine whether it feels right in that position and makes her feel good – if this is the case she says:

'Now it's in its right place. It gives me strength. Leave it here with me.'
'With me it's in its rightful place. I feel light.'

If, however, she feels that the burden does not belong to her, she then turns around, looks for the correct position for the symbol, and places it there. Afterwards, she turns towards the position of the anchor that represents her, and says:

'I have brought it to the right place; leave it there, this is where it should be.'

   These ritual statements must of course be tailored to fit each individual situation.
   Ritual statements can also be used in **including and showing appreciation of excluded people**, for example:

'You are my … and I am your … you belong to us. Your fate has touched me a lot. There is a place for you in my heart and it is important that my children (brothers and sisters, relatives etc.) should learn about you.'

   'I am beginning to see you for the first time. I respect you highly.'
   'I can see you. You belong.'
   'I am giving you the place you are entitled to (whoever you are).'
   'We – and you.'
   'Now I am going to forget the bad things they told me about you. You belong, and it is important that my family should learn about you.'

Inclusion of an excluded person or excluded element can also be achieved through **gestures**. For example, the client can first point to herself, then to those people that clearly belong to the system, then to the excluded people, and then back to herself. This short form of inclusion is mainly used when it comes to hidden work. Respect and recognition can also be expressed through the act of bowing.

In cases where the **family relationship is unclear** – such as with half sisters etc. – it is often helpful to say the family relationship out loud during the constellation. These types of **ritual statements** help strengthen the understanding of how things are just as they are, without providing any details – they are more concerned with relaying the nature of an experience than with passing on information. This is demonstrated in the following examples.

'You are my father.'
'You are my mother.'
'You are my brother.'
'I am related to you through my mother.' (e.g. a great aunt on the mother's side of the family)
'We share the same father, but each of us has a different mother.'

The client can alternate between her own position and that of her conversation partner, saying when standing there:

'You are my daughter.'
'You are my son.'
Etc.

Finally, it is at all times possible for the client to state how the relationship or process in question feels to them at a given moment – i.e. naming the given facts:

'That was hard for me – but I survived it and now it's gone.'
'I am resentful of you – even though I know you were not able to behave differently.'
'I need some more time.'
'I am the first, you the second, and you the third.' (The principle of sequential seniority)
'Without you we would not have our business (or fortune) – we have you to thank for that entirely.' (The principle of seniority through commitment)
'We respect your achievements.' (The principle of seniority through performance)

The last five statements can be derived from the second, third and fourth basic principles, which are respected where these have been violated (see III.1.1.2.2 for more detail).

In situations where there is no contact between family members or other elements of the system, we can **establish contact** through eye contact or using the following types of statements:

'I am beginning to see you.'
'I am seeing you for the first time.'

The ritual that establishes contact with family lines is the **strengthening ritual**. For women, representatives of their mothers, grandmothers and great grandmothers etc. are placed behind the client to provide them with strength; similarly, with men, representatives of their fathers, grandfathers and great grandfathers and placed behind the client. If there are no representatives available, the family line can be introduce and temporarily represented by the facilitator using a cataleptic hand.

Where **partial pattern representations** occur in respect to an excluded ancestor of the client then a **dissolution ritual** is used. Bert Hellinger discovered in his own constellation work that excluded people are often represented by family descendants, who in part repeat the pattern of their lives. To a certain extent, therefore, the system does not allow any wrongs to be done without there being consequences.

The dissolution ritual for this type of pattern representation comes in two parts. First, the client marks her position and that of the excluded person using two anchors. She then places herself in her own position, steps out of her role, and then stands in the position of the excluded person. She then checks to see if she feels better in that position. If this is the case it means we are dealing with a *partial pattern representation*.

The second part is the dissolution. The client moves slowly towards the anchor representing the excluded person. When standing just in front of it, the facilitator turns the client round quickly by holding the client's shoulders so that she stands next to the excluded person with a small distance between them, facing in the same direction.

In general, when we cannot see someone, we cannot hold the assumed representation of that person. The facilitator can hold her hand between the head of the client and that of the excluded person, so that the client can no longer see the excluded person, even if she looks sideways. After this, the client goes back to her own position and checks to see if she now feels freer.

It is very helpful in this ritual if the facilitator holds a cataleptic hand over the anchor representing the ancestor. This allows the client to keep the same eye level and means she no longer needs to look down continuously to the floor to see the anchor (this might induce depression).

The ritual for dissolving **partial pattern representations** can also be seen as one specific version of the ritual for removing **a context overlap**, when dealing with contexts such as people, situations, trauma or goal statements. In the meantime we consider the later notion to be the more important concept.

Within a system, the question of **succession** comes up frequently. It should be noted here that succession is often performed out of a sense of duty and loyalty, and with the implicit agreement of the predecessor.

The desire to do things completely differently or better often ends in the opposite result.

The following ritual statements can be used in family constellations:

'Dear mother (father/grandmother…), I will be just like you – but just a little bit different.'

This can be modified for systemic structural constellations:

'I'm doing what you did – but just a little bit different.'
'I'm doing what you did – but in my own way.'
'Just like it was up to now – and only a little bit different.'

A paradoxical form is possible, by saying:

'I'm doing everything my own way – just like you did.'

Here the difference between the other and oneself is also minimised by saying: 'I'm doing everything my own way.' This sequence is far better suited to reaching the goal in a non-provocative way, since the movement happens paradoxically: 'I'm doing what you did: that is, differently from those before me!'

The following story from Anthony de Mello from his collection of stories in *Zeiten des Glücks* (1994, p.96) may help clarify this point.

'Like father like son.
  As the young Rabbi succeeded his father, everyone started to tell him how different he was from his father.
  "On the contrary!" replied the young man, "I'm just like my father. He impersonated nobody, and I impersonate nobody."'

Where difficulties arise in terms of succession arrangements within organisations, the following ritual statement can be useful:

'We have a lot to thank you for and appreciate what you have achieved. You built up this company; we only came afterwards. In taking over from you now, I do so with the highest esteem for you. Please look kindly on me now when I start to lead this organisation.'

Where the **mourning** of a death in the family was **not possible**, this can be made up by means of a ritual. The representative of a child who died young, for example, is placed at the feet of the parents. The parents can then say to the child:

'You are my dear child.'

When both parents touch the head of the *child*, at that moment they experience an inner contact with the child, as well as with their grief. A lack of grieving often leads to a severing of the contact with the dead person and that which we acquired through that person. In this ritual, the representatives of the parents often experience appropriate feelings and start to cry, and it is only in this moment that the child feels acceptance.

In a further stage, the child is taken into the sibling line-up by placing the representative in the appropriate position between the other siblings. The siblings then say, one after another:

'I am your older (or younger) brother (or sister) – you are my younger (older) brother (sister). Even though you are already dead, you belong to us – I will go on living for a while – as long as my life lasts – then I will also die – From now on you will have a place in my heart. Please look kindly on me,while I lead my life.'

In constellations, **confusions of people or of parts** with each other can occur, as in **accidental constellations** or in **belief polarities constellations**. This can be verified as follows: the facilitator holds her hand behind the representative, or behind the hand being held over an anchor, and allows it to become cataleptic; she then asks who or what is seen in the cataleptic hand, or what changes when the cataleptic hand is perceived. The facilitator's hand again acts here as a representative for someone not seen before and often for someone who was excluded.

In **belief polarities constellations** this ritual occurs frequently. With this type of structural constellation, powerful resources – namely 'knowledge', 'love' and 'order' – are arranged in a triangle and an examination of their accessibility is made. The *focus*, as the representative of the client, stands within the field described by this triangle. However, these energy sources are often unavailable to the client due to experiences with her parents. In order to test this, the facilitator holds her hand behind one of the representatives of the energy sources and observes the changes that occur when the hidden element appears. If at this point the *focus* experiences a change, then we know that what is being represented by the hand is important and the following words can be said to the representative of the energy source:

'I have confused you with something (or somebody).'
'I wanted something from you that went beyond what is humanly possible.'
'Only now I am able to see you properly.'

And to the representative hand:

'I now see you for the first time.'
'You belong.'
'From now on I will take from you.'

By using these ritual statements, the knowledge acquired from constellations work can be transferred to SFT as soon as there is any indication of entanglements – e.g. when the behaviour that the client suffers from does not appear to be useful in the given context or seems strange. In the context of loyalty conflicts, on the other hand, this symptomatic behaviour may appear to be useful. The search for entanglements helps the client to build contexts for stable solutions. Approached in this way, it can be seen that SFT and SySt constellations are not based on incompatible basic assumptions.

Another method that we have developed and used systemically is the **Alter Ego Method,** ie working with representatives of the client today and former states of the client in the same constellation picture. We mainly use this method in cases where a representative behaves as if he had relapsed into a stage in the client's childhood. In such cases the *focus* may suddenly react like a small child: his voice changes, he becomes helpless, begins to cry etc. We then ask the *focus* what number occurs to him spontaneously at this moment.

The method of asking about a number was used by Milton Erickson with his clients in order to locate traumatic childhood situations that fit the problem. Unlike Milton Erickson, however, we use this method with representatives.

The number given by the *focus* often corresponds to the age at which something important for the client occurred. We then ask the client if he can think of something important that happened at this age. With extraordinary regularity, the client then usually mentions matching traumatic events that took place at that stage in his life. Although we do not see any causal relationship here between the event and the symptom, this method can be helpful to the client by providing an *as-if* construction that he can use to view his symptoms from a different context.

Since the *focus* behaves as if he is the age of the child, we add the client – i.e. his alter ego – to the constellation to give him support. The client can then hug, console and encourage the *focus*, thereby integrating this child part. Afterwards, the client may take the *focus* by the hand and perform the remaining rituals together with him.

If the *focus* acts as if he has relapsed into a period from the client's childhood, we call him an **evolutionary representative**.

A change of age can sometimes also appear to the *fifth non-position* of the tetralemma –that is if he suddenly becomes weak and helpless. In this case, he is no longer the independent, free, wise fifth non-position of the tetralemma, but rather has become the *focus* at an earlier age. In such cases, we establish a new *fifth non-position* of the tetralemma and rename the original *fifth non-position* of the tetralemma 'the focus at the age of …' Age is again established by asking for a number: the previous *fifth non-position* is asked to name a number that occurs to him spontaneously. The general hypothesis behind this procedure is that the creative child, as the *fifth non-position*, confronts the traumatised child – and it is for this reason that we split the representative of the *fifth non-position* into two representatives: one becomes a new *fifth non-position*, the other represents the damaged childhood part.

For the alter ego we now use the original *focus*, who is then able to take the *'focus at the age of …'* by the hand and give him precisely what he needs. The subsequent rituals are then performed together by these two *foci*.

V.1.4 The use of SFT and SySt Constellations over a longer course of therapy

Until now we have looked at how SySt constellations and SFT can be used interchangeably within a *single* session, and I would like to show now, by means of an example, how a combination of both procedures can be applied over the course of a number of therapy sessions.

V.1.4.1 Case study 2: Problem constellation with follow-up session: a representative-free constellation to release inherited phantom pain

The following example is made up of a preliminary interview with a problem constellation in a group and with an additional constellation in an individual follow-up session four months later.

Mrs I had been suffering from migraines since the age of nine, and intense abdominal pains for the last 17 years, which had been severely aggravated by a serious operation performed some five years ago. In total, she had undergone two abdominal operations and six abdominoscopies. The operations had not been successful, and Mrs I wanted to find out if there were any other options available to her. Her current pain had been diagnosed as caused by abdominal adhesions resulting from the operations, endometriosis in the uterus and intestinal area, as well as a number of ovarian cysts. Not surprisingly, Mrs I was wary of any further abdominal surgery, additionally since her most recent operation had been nearly resulted in her death.

The preliminary interview and subsequent problem constellation is presented below.

Facilitator: What is your current problem?
Client: For years now I've been suffering from recurring migraine attacks and stomach pains, usually one after the other. I'm nearly always suffering from something. I'd like to do a constellation about this and see where the problem is.
Facilitator: Assuming you knew what was wrong and you were feeling better again, what would the difference be?

Client: I'd finally be well again, I'd be free and light. I'd no longer be continually taking things easy and having to lie down constantly.

Facilitator: What would you do instead?

Client: I'd be more relaxed, I wouldn't have to plan so much since I'd have more time. I'd be able to get my work back on track.

Facilitator: How would others react to this change?

Client: They'd be relieved, and I'd be more balanced and would have more time for others.

Facilitator: Was there anyone in your family who suffered a lot, or was frequently or seriously ill?

Client: Yes, my grandfather's mother, on my mother's side of the family. She died while giving birth to him. And my father's mother also died very young.

Facilitator: I propose we do a **problem constellation**. What would you like to call your goal?

Client: Freedom and lightness.

Facilitator: How many obstacles do you want to place?

Client: At least two – my headaches and stomach pains.

Facilitator: Then we'll also add a third unknown obstacle, '*obstacle 3*', to that as well. How many resources do you want there to be?

Client: Two.

Facilitator: Do you want to give them a name?

Client: No, I don't know who they are for sure.

Facilitator: Then we also need a 'benefit', a reason why it is good for you that the goal has not yet been achieved. And we also a need a future task, something you will do when you have achieved the goal. Have you any idea what that might be?

Client: Well, I'd then find work easier and take more pleasure in it, I wouldn't have to rest so much, and I'd have more contact with people again.

Facilitator: OK, now choose someone from the group to be your own representative. It's often easier to find someone if you stand up…

The client chooses a representative for herself. In all the following case studies the representative for the client we call the '*focus*'and will be referred to as such. Also all representatives will be written in *italics*. Obstacle 3 is shortened to *O3*, and the first two resources to *R1* and *R2*. In the diagrams, female and male representatives will be denoted by the symbols ◯ and ◻, respectively, where the cut-out notch indicates the direction they are facing.

Facilitator: Now choose someone for your goal – your obstacles – your resources – your hidden benefit – and the future task.

The client chooses all the parts from the group and begins to place them in the constellation, resulting in the following arrangement:

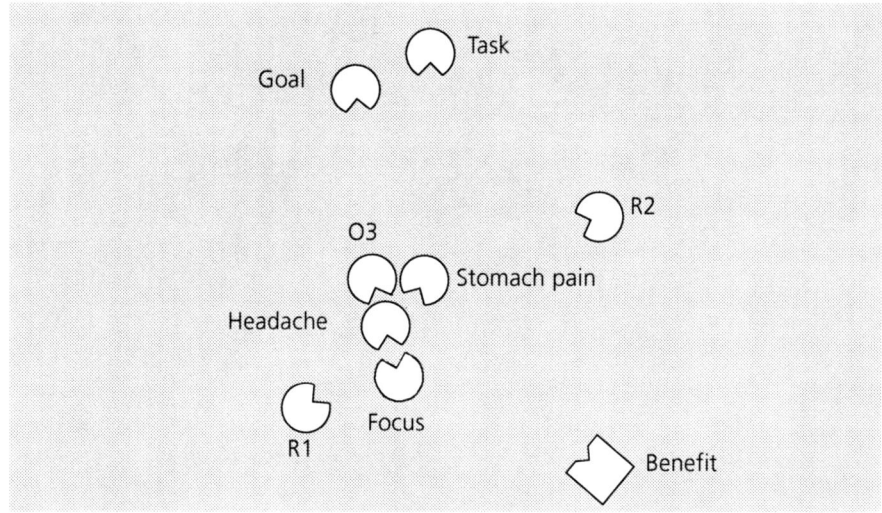

Figure 4

Facilitator: How is the *focus* feeling?
Focus: I find the two obstacles, *headache* and *stomach pain* threatening. My heart is pounding. I find the *goal* interesting and attractive but I can hardly see it. The *second resource* makes things easier for me, but I don't understand the *benefit*. The *future task* really touched me.
Facilitator: Now look behind you. How does that feel?

The focus looks around.

Focus: I feel freer now and can breathe again.
Facilitator (to client): Does this picture say anything to you?
Client: I'm finding it hard to empathise with it.

The facilitator tells the client to exchange places with the *focus*.

Client: Yes, that feels more familiar.

The facilitator tells the client and *focus* to exchange places again.

Facilitator: How are the *obstacles* feeling?
Headache: Relaxed.
Stomach pain: I am the counterweight to *headache*.
O3: Relieved.
Facilitator: The *obstacles* in the first arrangement feel well and strong. During the constellation they will first be 'dethroned', after which they will gradually turn into *helpers*.

The next action is positioning work. The *benefit* and *R2* are placed behind the *focus*, and the *focus* and both the *obstacles* and are turned towards the *benefit* and *R2*, resulting in the following arrangement:

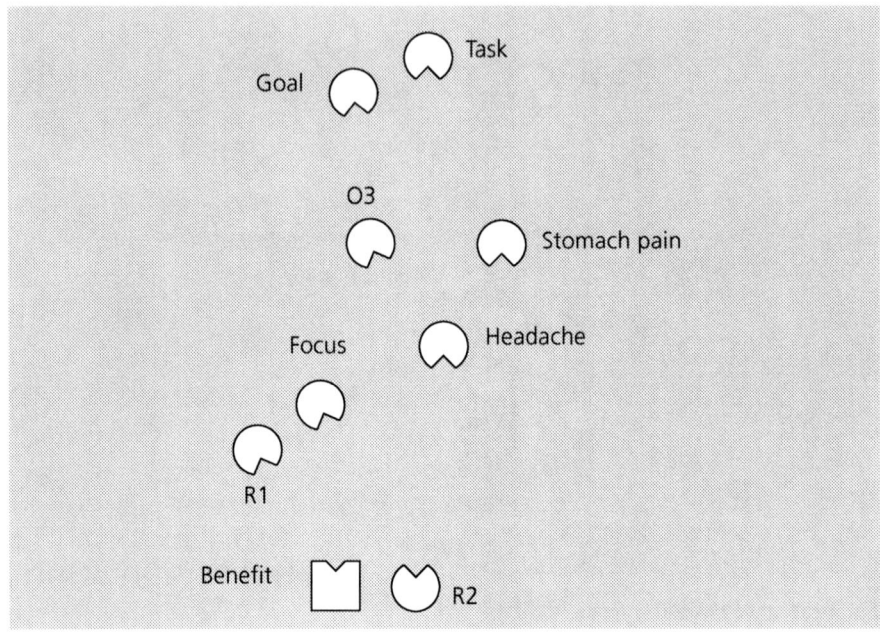

Figure 5

Facilitator: What has changed for the *focus*?
Focus: It is a relief for me when I can see the *benefit* and the *second resource*. It calms me.
Facilitator (to *benefit* and *second resource*): How are you feeling?
R2: I'm feeling fine
Benefit: Wonderful.

The Facilitator tells the *focus* to make the following statements to the *benefit*:

Focus (to *benefit*): You will remain who you are – and as who you are you will remain important – You have helped me find peace – and I allow you to continue to remind me of that – I feel myself strongly bound to you – even without knowing who you are – and you will remain important – even when I look in another direction.
Benefit: That is hard for me.
Focus (to *benefit*, facilitator provides the statements again): Without knowing, I am making room for you – in my heart – and from time to time will look back to you – with love and respect.
Benefit: It is now OK to look in another direction.

The client is highly affected by these words and begins to cry. The facilitator again allows her to switch places with the *focus*. The facilitator then has her say the following words to the *benefit*:

Client (to *benefit*): You will remain important to me – in a different way than before – and you have reminded me of my peace – I will embrace you – but in a different way than before – Look kindly on me when I now turn towards my goal – I hope to receive a signal from you – that does not make me ill – Maybe in the future you could knock more quietly and earlier – I am also taking something from you – even if that is painless.

The client hugs the *benefit*. The facilitator then switches the places of the *benefit* and R2 such that the *benefit* is standing to the right of R2. The *benefit* and R2 agree to this with a nod of the head.

Client (to *R2*): I feel bigger than her.

The *benefit* and R2 can now represent an earlier generation –the constellation suggests that they represent the father and the mother. From this perspective, 'feeling bigger' indicates that the client has been carrying something for R2. The facilitator therefore proposes a return ritual and gives the client a bag as a symbolic object representing the burden that has been carried.

Facilitator: Lay this (the bag) at the feet of R2 and then return to your position.

The client follows these instructions.

Facilitator: The *second resource* may now pick this (the bag) up and press it against her chest.

The therapist instructs the client to make the following statement to R2:

Client (to *R2*): I have been carrying something for you – that does not belong to me – It belongs to you – and I'm now giving it back to you – entirely.

Facilitator (to *R2*): Verify that the burden belongs to you – maybe the *benefit* should be carrying a part of it.

Benefit: I have nothing to do with it.
R2: It doesn't belong to me either.

The facilitator instructs R2 to turn around and place the burden at a place of her choosing after R2 has said the following words to the client:

R2 (to client): This does not belong to you. I will now place in its rightful place.
Client: Now I feel smaller.
Client (to *R2*, prompted by the facilitator): You come before me – I only come after you.

R2 now turns around but finds no suitable place for the bag.

O3: I have the feeling I should be standing behind *R2*.

The facilitator again allows the client to exchange places with the *focus* and places *O3* behind *R2*, resulting in the following arrangement:

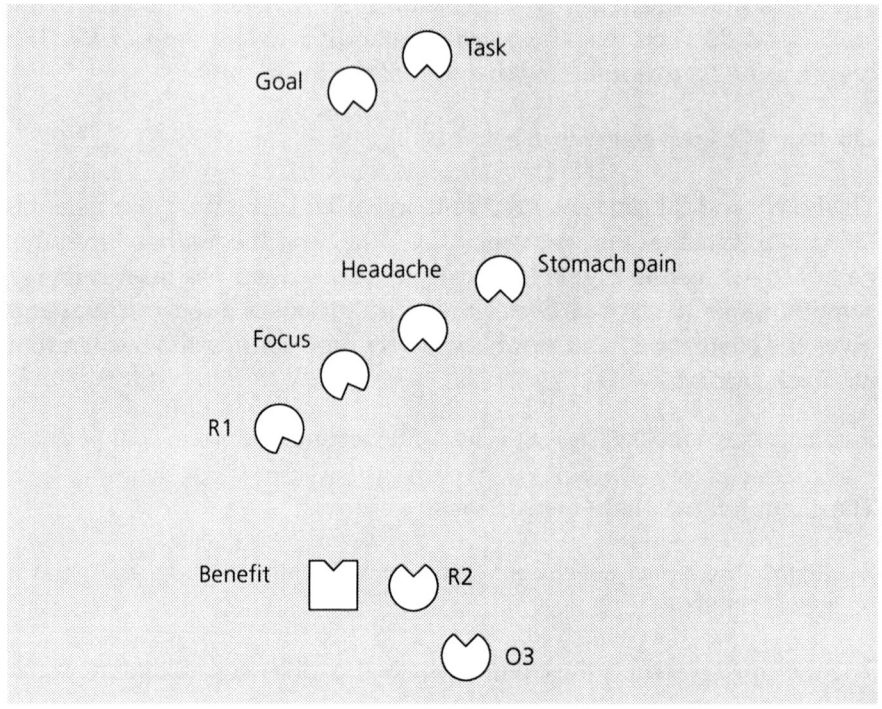

Figure 6

R2 now passes the bag to *O3*. The facilitator then instructs *R2* to say the following words to *O3*:

R2 (to *O3*): It is through you that the burden came to me – I give it back to you now – so you can check where it belongs.

O3 takes the bag, and turns round. The door is opened so that the distance between *O3* and the bag is larger. In this process, both the *focus* and the client have headaches – only when the bag is sufficiently far away do they start to feel better.

Facilitator (to client): The family history could be brought in at this point. Does this make anything occur to you? Who else suffered from headaches in your family?
Client: Apart from me, my mother also suffered from headaches, as did her

mother, both of whose parents also died young: my grandfather during the First World War, my great grandmother from tuberculosis.

Facilitator: Now it's clear which burden you may have received via your grandmother and your mother – how is the *third obstacle* and the *second resource* feeling now?

O3: I'm feeling OK.

Facilitator: How are the other two *obstacles* feeling?

Stomach pain: I'm now helping the *focus*.

Headache: I'm also feeling well.

Facilitator: All *obstacles* have now become *helpers*.

R2 (to *focus*): I feel a warmth and affection for you. You have my goodwill when you look towards your *goal*.

Focus: I feel sad when I see you, and I see there's nothing I can do for you. I thought you were unable to bear your own fate. I see now that overestimated myself.

R2: I require nothing from you.

Facilitator (to *focus*): Now turn around to face you *goal*. How does that make you feel?

Focus: That feels good.

The facilitator instructs her to take a step towards her *goal* and to say the following:

Focus: I am also doing this in your honour (*R2*). You can be pleased for me.

R2: I feel strongly connected with you on this path.

Facilitator How is the *benefit* feeling?

Benefit: I am no longer important.

Facilitator: How is the *first resource*?

R1: I would also like to see the *goal* and accompany the *focus*.

Facilitator: Then turn around. The two *helpers* may also turn around.

This results in the following arrangement (solution picture):

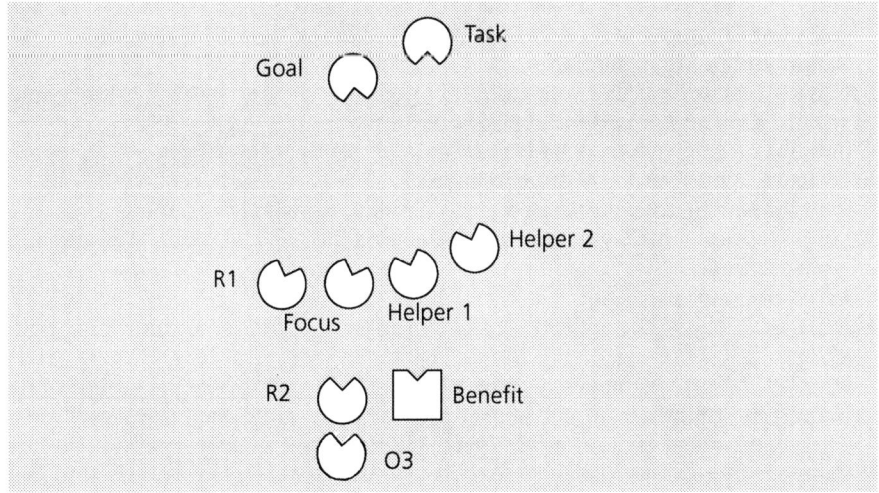

Figure 7

Facilitator: How does the *goal* feel?
Goal: I feel big and strong and really excited when she moves towards me.
Facilitator: How is the *future task*?
Task: I can wait. It's good that she's coming.

The facilitator instructs the client to take the place of her *focus*.

Facilitator: Take a look at them all, also turn to see your ancestors and remember the statements made. See that the burden now lies far behind you. Now bow down a little and turn towards your *goal*. Take a step towards your *goal*. The *first resource* and the *helpers* can accompany her in this step. Now take another step forwards, and while moving take in the overall picture.

Four months later there is a further session. Mrs I explains that her headaches have all but disappeared since the last session. The stomach pains, however, are still as extreme as before. Her doctors suggested she undergo an operation to reduce the pain, but could not say for sure whether it would put an end to her suffering altogether. The operation was not actually necessary from a medical point of view, since her abdominal adhesions and cysts had not exceeded the indicated dimensions, and Mrs I wanted to try another constellation to see whether she might avoid any further medical intervention.

Facilitator: Was there any improvement since we last saw each other?
Client: Yes, now I only rarely get headaches, but the massive stomach pains have not stopped. I have to lie down every day so that I can get through the day.
Facilitator: If our conversation today proves helpful for you, how will you notice this?
Client: I'd be able to work normally again, wouldn't have to lie down continually. I'd simply have more energy. I'd get things back on track. At the moment I'm not sure how I'm going to be able juggle working on my dissertation and going to seminars.
Facilitator: Assuming this was suddenly possible for you – as if a miracle had occurred – from what would you notice this?
Client: I'd no longer have a bad conscience about the things I do.
Facilitator: What would be there instead?
Client: I'd be able to concentrate better; I'd stick to what I was doing.
Facilitator: How would you then split your time between your dissertation and your seminars?
Client: I don't know.
Facilitator: Probably something would be different if you were combining both things…
Client: Yes. Maybe I'd have a regular schedule. I think the most important thing would be my health. If my health problems are gone then things will just sort themselves out on their own, I'll have the energy needed. At the moment I'm always having to take it easy, and that takes up a lot of time; but when I have more energy, then I can do things.
Facilitator: Would others notice if you were full of energy?

Client: Yes. I'd be happier, I'd take part more. I think others would notice that I was approaching them more, and then they'd approach me more too, there'd be more contact.

Facilitator: How would that be for you?

Client: It'd be really great.

Facilitator: Is there someone in your family that was unable to live his life to the full?

Client: Yes, my father.

Facilitator: I propose that we do an additional constellation. Since we don't have a group to use as representatives today we can use playing cards instead, which you can arrange on this sheet of paper. Which body parts do you want to place in the constellation?

Client (after brief consideration): the peritoneum, the uterus with the myomas, the ovaries with the cysts, and the intestines.

Facilitator: Select cards for each of these body parts – and write their names on the cards – and draw an arrow on the cards to indicate the line of sight.

Mrs I selects some cards and labels them. In the first constellation she had found it difficult to follow the arrangement, and now she found it easier to work without representatives.. In such cases it can be helpful to work with symbols (in this case playing cards), and it is now the symbols, instead of representatives, that mark the individual locations.

Facilitator: Now choose cards to represent yourself, your father and your father's mother who died so young. Then touch each of the individual cards in turn using your middle finger to move them over the piece of paper to where you feel is the right place for each of them. Then put yourself and your body parts into position.

After Mrs I has selected and labelled all the cards, she moves each card slowly into its position to produce the following arrangement:

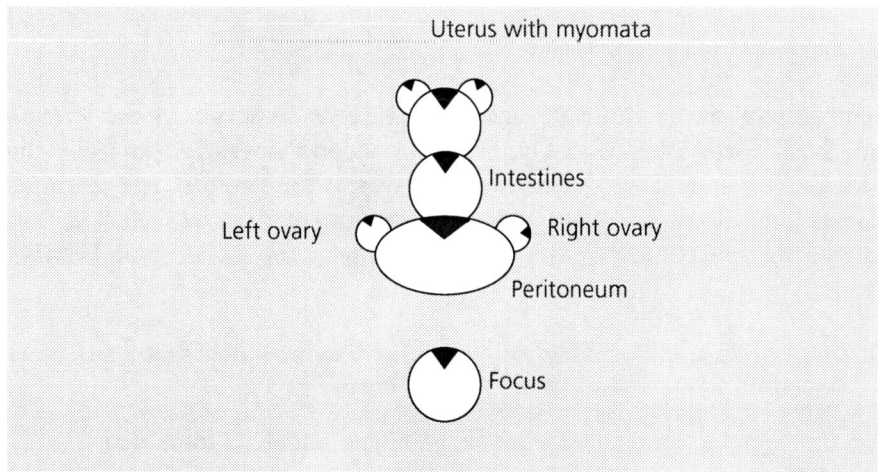

Figure 8

In this picture, the cards representing the peritoneum partially cover those representing the ovaries and the intestines, and the symbols for the myomata have been stuck on to that of the uterus.

Next, all the parts thus positioned are questioned. Since there are no people acting as representatives, the client touches each card in turn with her middle finger and says what it feels like in each position. In order to dissociate the feeling in the finger from that of the remaining upper body, in individual therapy I work with the **cataleptic finger** – that is, I give the client prior instructions as to how to put her hand in this state. In addition, between touching the cards, the client takes herself out of the role by shaking her hand before moving on to the next card. The instructions for entering a role and stepping out of a role are given in each case by the facilitator. In the following transcript, I will talk of the *focus* when the client touches the *focus*-card with her cataleptic finger, and the client when the client is not associated with the role of the *focus* and speaks from her own perspective.

Focus: In this position I feel totally cramped, as if walled-in.
Left ovary: I feel like crying. I am working normally, but I can't move. I feel like a piece of a stocking, I can't stretch myself.

The day after this constellation, the client had a dream about her father's family in which many of the family members where blanked out. Suddenly she understood the meaning of the 'stocking' mentioned by the *left ovary*: her father had lost a leg in the war and every day he would pull a stocking over the stump of his leg and pull the end through the side hole of his prosthesis.

Right ovary: I'm looking the other way, I have to look away. I've been squashed, I was treated roughly, now I'm no more than a lump of connective tissue, I was forced into this position.

The statements of the *right ovary* make sense in terms of the client's medical history. Inexplicably, after her second operation in 1993, the doctors were unable to locate her right ovary. She had lost an enormous amount of blood and the operation took longer than expected. It was after this operation that she began to suffer from extreme abdominal pains.

Uterus: I am fine, still working, but feel isolated because there's too much other tissue and I can't move; when I move, it hurts.
Facilitator: In which direction is the *uterus* looking?
Uterus: I don't know where I'm looking, I'm just looking in front of me.
Myomata: If it hadn't been for the medical treatment we wouldn't be here, but when I move myself I hurt the others.

Intestines: I feel totally squeezed and bound up with the other organs. Movement doesn't hurt me, but when I do move I hurt the others.

Peritoneum: It's exhausting: because everything is so clumped together I'm unable to move. I'd really like to face the other direction and act as protection like a tent.

The facilitator now turns some of the cards around so that the *organs* have more room and can see each other, and so the *peritoneum* and the *intestines* take on protective rolls. This gives us the following arrangement:

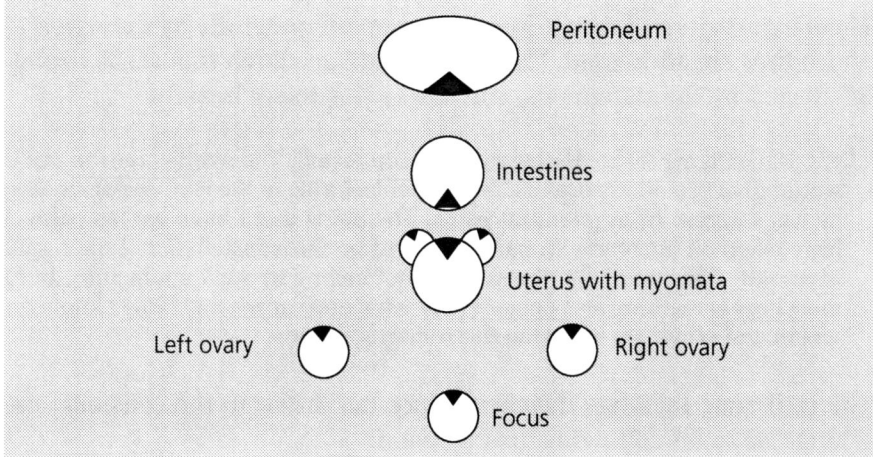

Figure 9

The facilitator now tells the *organs* to express their recognition for each other in order to improve the relationship between them. For example:

Facilitator: Now, as the *intestines*, say to the *ovaries*: 'I would like to protect you, but I'm cramping you. I'm sorry.'

The *intestines* – i.e. the client with her cataleptic finger on the symbol for the intestines – repeats this statement. The *ovaries* show that they agree.

The facilitator then instructs the intestines to say the following to the *peritoneum*:

Intestines (looking at *peritoneum*): I know we're both entangled. We both share the same fate. We live in a state of forced cohabitation.

The facilitator then tells the *focus* to express her recognition of the efforts made by the peritoneum and the left ovary with the following words:

Focus (to *peritoneum*): Thank you for protecting my organs. You have performed
your task well, about the overcrowding there is nothing you can do.
Focus (to *left ovary*): I'm happy that you are working so well and are so full of
life, even if it feels like you're inside a stocking.

The facilitator then instructs the focus to acknowledge the existence and
place of the constricted right ovary, with the following words:

Focus (to *right ovary*): I'm happy that you are still there. Even if I don't know
where you are, I will always make room for you. I thank you for your input.

These expressions of recognition are accepted gratefully by the *organs* to
which they are addressed. The client's reaction shows that she is strongly affected by the statements, and she begins to cry heavily.

Client: It's with my father that my pain is connected. The words occur to me: 'I
would give you all my organs.' My father lost a leg in the war, and since then
he has suffered from phantom pains. The pains that I have are his pains. I
have taken on his phantom pain. Even before this constellation, I often said
to myself: 'This pain, the illness, does not belong to me; I am healthy, but I
must bear something and do not know what and for whom.' Now I know for
whom and why I am suffering these stomach pains.

The facilitator then has the client place her father in the constellation,
giving rise to the following arrangement:

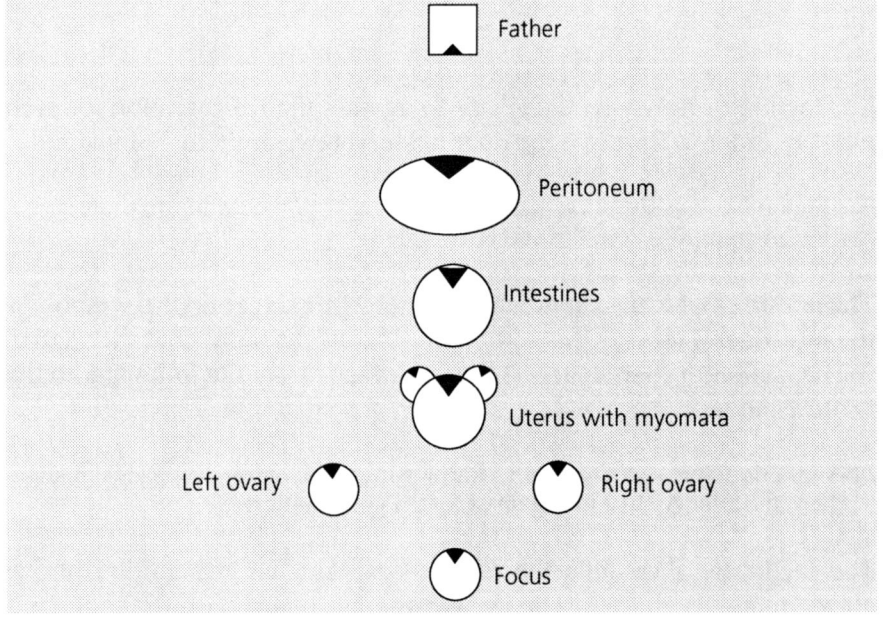

Figure 10

Facilitator: Move your hand over the constellation picture and try to feel which of the *organs* is reacting to the change.
Uterus: I feel as if I'm being squeezed.

The facilitator tells the *focus* to say the following to her *father*:

Focus: I would have given all my organs for you. I will now leave your fate in your hands and will honour you in a different way.
Client: I see an empty space where the missing leg was.

The facilitator now places the missing leg into the constellation (on the right hand side, close to the *father*) and tells the focus to say the following words to the *father*:

Focus: My organs cannot replace your leg and my pains cannot take away your phantom pains. I'm now leaving your fate entirely in your hands.
Client: I believe that *I* was my father's leg. *I* was his support.

The facilitator then adds to the constellation the father's father and mother, who died young, placing them behind the *father*.

Facilitator: Tell your *father* that from now on you are entrusting him to his own family line.
Focus: I used to think that I had to be your support. You don't need me as a support. I am entrusting you to your family line where you will find your support.
Father: This is the right way.

The facilitator then has the client perform a return ritual: she can visualise how she, together with the *organs*, place her burden at the feet of the *father*, how the *father* accepts the burden, and how she then returns to her position. The facilitator then tells the *focus* to say again:

Focus: Your support and strength comes from behind you. I am only your little daughter. Your leg and father should stay with you.
Facilitator: Now tell your *organs* that they belong only to you and are free from outside burdens.
Focus: Now you are only my organs. Now you are free, you are redeemed.
Facilitator: How is the *father's leg* feeling?
Leg: I'm feeling fine, now I can walk (away).

The *leg* is now placed further away, resulting in the following final picture:

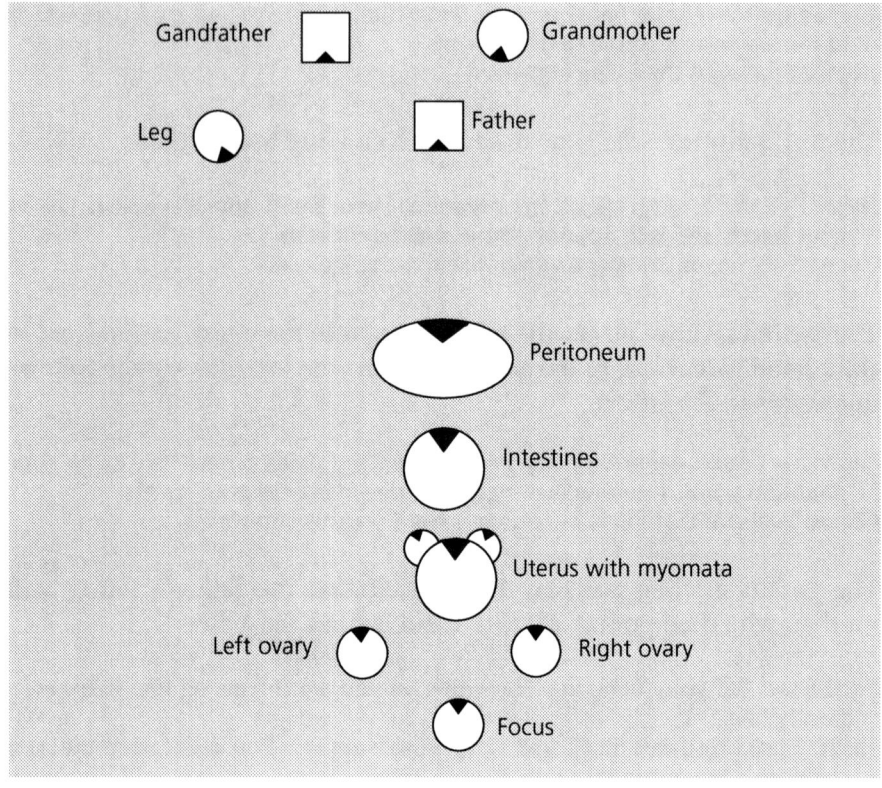

Figure 11

Facilitator: How are the *organs* feeling?
Peritoneum: Relieved.
Intestines: Freer.
Uterus with myomata: freer to move.
Left ovary: Better.
Right ovary: More connected.
Facilitator: How are the *father* and his *parents*?
Father: I am happy that she has given my burden back to me. It's much better for me. Having my *parents* behind me gives me strength.
Grandfather: I am happy to support him.
Grandmother: I am happy to have contact with him.
Facilitator: How is the *focus* feeling now?
Focus: I feel freer and more connected with my *organs*.

With her eyes and the movement of her hands (both hands leading to her heart), the facilitator asks the client to take in the final picture.

Facilitator: You will always be able to remember this picture and the return ritual. Maybe it will help you in the future if you can see you father's parents behind him.

It proved useful here to reconstruct a framework within which the client, out of love for her father, took on the phantom pain he suffered. The fact that her father had lost his leg in the war could then be understood in terms of a succession dynamic leading to his mother. Mrs I was able to see this connection some time after the constellation and she was able to view her own suffering in connection with her grandmother, who died at a very young age, and her father's phantom leg pain. After the constellation she was convinced that her pains would diminish.

Five months later, I had a follow-up conversation with Mrs I about the two constellations. This conversation ran as presented below:

Facilitator: How do you feel now? Have there been any improvements?
Client: I'm feeling really well.
Facilitator: What improvements have there been, physically?
Client: I can hardly believe my own words, but now I rarely have migraines. I hope it stays like this.
Facilitator: How often did the headaches occur before, and how often do you have them now?
Client: Before I used to have them many times in a week, now it's at the most once a month. And the intensity of the pain is also less.
Facilitator: Have your stomach pains also improved?
Client: Now I hardly need to take any pills. Before the constellation, I had to take strong pills every morning.
Facilitator: Have there been any other changes?
Client: My periods are also less painful, and overall the bleeding is less. The pain was probably coming from the endometriosis.
Facilitator: Overall, if you compare your stomach pains with before, how much would you say they have reduced?
Client: Before I constantly had really heavy pains, even after taking medication. Now, though admittedly I still feel some level of constant pain, the intensity is about 30% of what they were.
Facilitator: Has anything else changed?
Client: Yes, my obligation to my father is now less – in a positive way, that is. I can now leave him alone and don't feel constantly responsible for him. It also became clear to me that I was carrying the headaches for my mother and the stomach pains for my father.

V.2 Integrating SFT with SySt constellations

A normal therapy session usually begins with a conversation, and later a constellation is performed. In experiential groups, however, constellations are usually performed without much preliminary conversation. Indeed this is how Bert Hellinger normally works.

Contrary to Bert Hellinger's practice, however, with my clients I have found it useful to hold follow-up sessions, carry out additional constellations and, between constellations (see V.1.4), to work with methods taken from solution-focused brief therapy.

We will now look at how SFT can be integrated into constellation work through a case study of a family structural constellation. This will also help clarify the extent to which follow-up sessions boost, rather than weaken, the impulses that result from a constellation.

V.2.1 Case study 3: When burdens are assumed

The following constellation comes from a experiential group. The follow-up sessions were carried out as individual therapy.

Facilitator: What is your current problem?

Client: Since my early childhood I have always quarrelled with my mother. We don't have a normal relationship, and I'd like to straighten things out.

Facilitator: Did something happen between you?

Client: No, there's no explanation for the situation.

Facilitator: Do you have any brothers or sisters?

Client: Yes, two younger brothers.

Facilitator: Do they also have problems with you mother?

Client: No, things are ok with them.

Facilitator: Are there any excluded people in your family? You are already familiar with this question (the participant has already witnessed a number of constellations in the group).

Client: My mother's mother suffered from extreme depression and was committed to a psychiatric ward, where she died some years later. My mother never got the chance to get to know her because she was not allowed to visit her in hospital. They may even have killed her in the hospital, since it was during the Nazi period and we never found out what really happened and it was never discussed in the family.

Facilitator: What would you like to call your goal?

Client: 'Being myself' – when I'm together with my mother somehow I'm not myself.

Facilitator: Now choose someone from the group – to represent you – your equilibrium ('being myself' – the goal) – your mother and your grandmother – Then choose someone for your father – and your brother – who we'll place in the constellation later.

We call representatives that have been chosen, but not yet positioned in the constellation, **chosen representatives**. Although they are yet to be placed in the constellation, they often already show representative perception and when asked can give their reactions to the constellation events in order to clarify their perspectives.

Facilitator: Start now by positioning *yourself*, your *mother* and your *grandmother* – the *focus*, the *goal* and the *mother* can trace what changes occur when the *grandmother* is added.

The client selects representatives from the group and positions them, one after the other, resulting in the following arrangement:

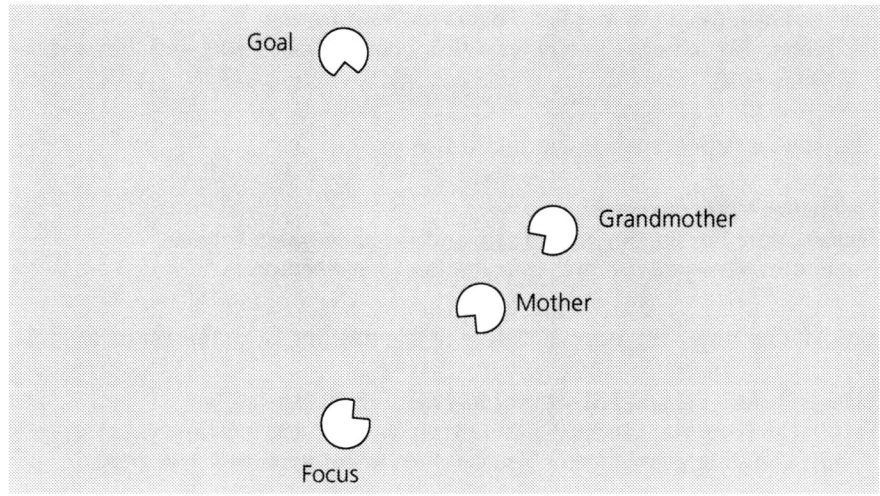

Figure 12

Facilitator: How is the *focus* feeling?
Focus: I'm standing opposite my *mother* and am furious with her. I cannot see my *goal*. When the *grandmother* came in I felt a shiver.
Facilitator: How is the *goal* feeling?
Goal: It bothers me that she is not looking at me. I get annoyed when she does that.
Facilitator (to *focus*): The *goal* is waiting for you, it's ready for you.
Facilitator (to *mother*): What changed for you?
Mother: Somehow I knew I was going to be placed in this position. I like my *daughter*. I'm not annoyed with her, but I can feel that she doesn't feel well when she looks at me. That depresses me. When my *mother* was put into the constellation I felt a chill run down my spine. I have no contact with her.
Facilitator: How is the *grandmother* feeling?
Grandmother: I also feel a cold shiver. I feel only goodwill towards my *daughter*. I'd like to be in contact with her. I can't see my *granddaughter*: I felt sad when she spoke.
Facilitator (to client): Is this picture what you expected?
Client: Yes, it's just how I know it, except what my *grandmother* said since I never got to meet her.
Facilitator (to *mother*): Turn around and look at your mother (*grandmother*).

The *mother* follows the facilitator's instructions.

Facilitator: How does that make you feel?
Mother: She is like a total stranger to me.
Facilitator: Say to her: 'You are my mother and I am your daughter.' What changes do you notice?

The *mother* repeats the facilitator's words. The *grandmother* looks at her, very pleased; the *mother* starts to cry.

Mother: I don't want to hug her. That is too hard for me.
Facilitator: Say to her: 'I'm still resentful. I really missed you, and that was too
   soon for me.'

The *mother* repeats what the facilitator said.

Facilitator: What changed?
Mother: Now I'm starting to feel sad, and the resentment is gone.
Facilitator: Now you can hug your mother (*grandmother*).

The *Mother* hugs the representative of her mother. Both then start to glow.

Mother: It does me good to see and feel her. I really missed her.
Facilitator: Now you can turn back to your *daughter* and feel how your *mother* is
   now standing behind you – You can turn to her whenever you want.

The *mother* turns back to the *daughter* and turns again, twice, to the
representative of her mother. It can be seen in her face that she is now
able to take from her mother (*grandmother*).

Facilitator: What has changed for the *focus*?
Focus: I now look at the *mother* differently. She has become much more human
   to me. When I look at the *grandmother* I still feel a chill.
Facilitator (to client): Place someone to represent the influence of the Nazi era.

The client selects someone from the group and positions that person in
the constellation, giving us the following picture:

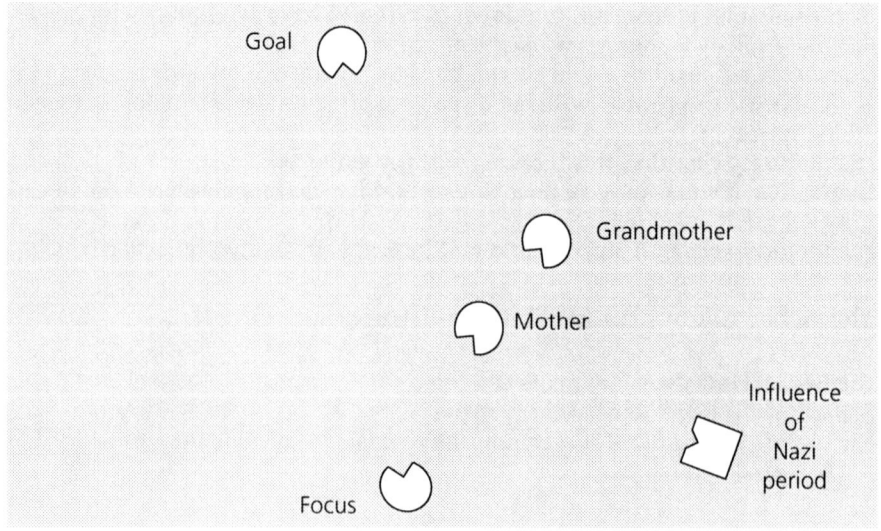

Figure 13

Facilitator: What has changed for the *focus*?
Focus: The cold shivers are getting increasingly stronger.
Facilitator: And for the *mother*?
Mother: I'm also feeling the chills as stronger.
Facilitator: And the *grandmother*?
Grandmother: I am very afraid and can feel a shaking in my body.
Facilitator: What has changed for the *goal*?
Goal: I'm no longer annoyed. Now I feel sorry for the *focus*, I'd like to protect her. The *influence of the Nazi period* is threatening.
Facilitator: How is the *influence of the Nazi period*?
Influence: I feel powerful and strong. They are all my little puppets.
Facilitator: Now we are going to perform the return ritual.

The facilitator then passes a bag to the *focus* as a symbol of a heavy burden.

Facilitator: Say the following words to your *mother*: 'Through you I have been given a heavy burden to carry. I am now giving it back to you so that it can be brought back to the place it belongs.' And then place the bag at the feet of the *mother* – Now go back to your own position and the *mother* can pick up the bag and take it (the facilitators indicates that the bag should be pressed against the upper body).

The *focus* repeats these words and places the bag at the *mother's* feet, and then goes back to her place. The *mother* lifts up the bag and holds it in front of her upper body.

Facilitator: What has changed for the *focus*?
Focus: I feel relieved, although it was not easy to give the burden back. I was able to do it because my *mother* did not hold on to it, but brought it back to its rightful place.
Facilitator: How is the *mother*?
Mother: The burden doesn't belong to me. Though maybe a part of it does.
Facilitator: Maybe you can say to your *daughter*: 'It is good that you have given the burden back to me. It doesn't belong to you.'

The *mother* says these words to her *daughter*, who nods, relieved.

Facilitator (to *mother*): Now turn yourself around and say to your mother (*grandmother*): 'I have helped you carry a lot of things – out of love – but I am only your daughter, you are the big one – I am giving back to you that which is yours – My part I will keep.' – Now place the bag at the feet of your mother (*grandmother*).

Though the representative of the mother repeats these words and follows the instructions, she is hesitant.

Facilitator: Give the bag back as if it were purely an experiment and then wait and see how if it works.

The *mother* places the bag at the feet of the representative of the mother, who picks it up.

Facilitator (to *mother*): What has changed for you?
Mother: It wasn't easy giving the burden back. I don't expect anything of her. Now I feel lighter.
Facilitator: How does the *grandmother* feel?
Grandmother: It was right that she gave the burden away. But not all of it belongs to me.
Facilitator: Then say to her: 'It is good that you returned the burden to me. I will bring it to its right place.'

The *grandmother* repeats these lines. The *mother* exhales, relieved.

Facilitator (to *mother*): Now look at the *influence of the Nazi period* and say to it: 'My part of the burden I will take – but your actions and responsibility belong to you – My family suffered a lot because of you – especially me – I am giving back to you your guilt.' – Now place the bag at the feet of the *influence* and return to your position – The *influence* can then take back the bag.

The *grandmother* repeats the facilitator's words, line by line, and then places the bag at the feet of the *influence* and returns to her position. The *influence* picks up the bag.

Facilitator: What has changed for the *grandmother*?
Grandmother: At first it felt very threatening for me to speak to the *influence*. But it worked. Now something has fallen from me; I feel more like my own self.
Facilitator: How does the *focus* feel now?
Focus: Very much better. The shivers have disappeared. Now I can also look at my *mother* and also at my *grandmother*.
Facilitator: Say to you *grandmother*: 'You are my grandmother – and I am your granddaughter – I am making a place for you in my heart – For me that is where you now belong – In the future I will honour you in a different way – by becoming more my own self.'

The *focus* repeats the facilitator's words, line by line. The *grandmother* smiles at her in a friendly manner.

Facilitator: Check that you have the blessing of your *grandmother*.
The *focus* nods.
Facilitator: How does the *goal* feel now?
Goal: For me it was an emotional rollercoaster. Now I'm completely relieved and at peace with myself.
Facilitator (to *focus*): Look now to your *goal* – What has changed for you?
Focus: I'm seeing my *goal* for the first time now. It's doing me a lot of good.

The facilitator now places the *mother* and *grandmother* behind the *focus*, and the *influence* somewhat further to the side, resulting in the following arrangement:

Goal

Focus

Mother

Influence
of
Nazi
period

Grandmother

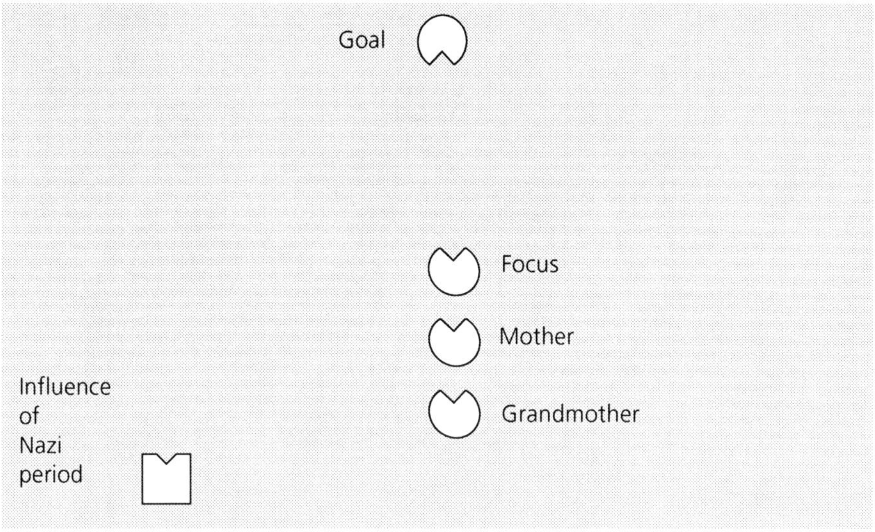

Figure 14

Facilitator: The *influence* and its symbol of burden can now sit down. Temporary influences do not last forever. When they have taken what is theirs then as a symbol that this time is passed they can sit down.

The *influence* now sits down.

Facilitator: Is that ok with the others?

The other representatives nod approval.

Facilitator: How does the *focus* feel now?
Focus: Better still, since feeling my *mother* and *grandmother* behind me.
Facilitator (to client): Now place your *brothers* to your left and your *father* to the right of your *mother*. What are your brothers called?
Client: Wilfried and Peter.
Facilitator: Then place both of them, your *brothers*, in order of their age, from right to left.

The client follows these instructions to give the following arrangement:

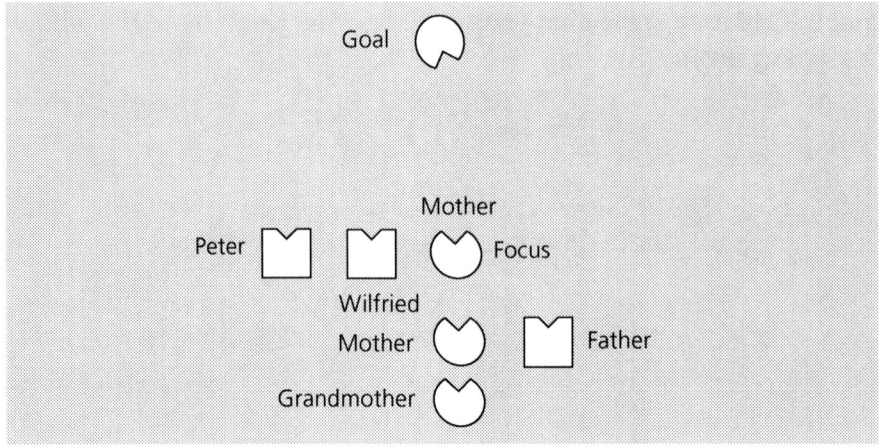

Figure 15

Facilitator: How do you feel now?
Focus: Really great.
Wilfried: During the whole constellation it felt as if I was really there already and I could feel the cold chills and the burden. Now I feel really good here. I am happy for you.
Peter: I also felt that way during the constellation, as if I had already been put into the constellation. I witnessed everything quite intensely. Now I'm very relieved.
Facilitator: How does the *father* feel?
Father: Now I feel good here, but at times during the constellation I felt very concerned for my *wife* and *daughter*.

The chosen representatives often witness the events very intensely and, as soon as they are positioned, can report on the changes they felt before entering the constellation. Just being selected as representatives changes their perception of what happens in the constellation and they experience what happens from the perspective of whom or what they are representing. It also helps to reduce the complexity of the constellation if not all representatives enter the constellation from the very beginning.

Facilitator (to client): Now you can take up the position of your *focus*.

The client does so and starts to glow.

Facilitator: Now take a look at all of them – Take your time doing this – Remind yourself of the statements that have been made – and the rituals – Let it take its effect – Now take up the picture and draw it closer to you in this way (the facilitator moves both hands towards herself and places them on her upper body) – and let it do its work – Wait and see what comes of this.

First follow-up session
Two weeks later, the client came back for an individual therapy session. Excerpts from this session are presented below:

Facilitator: What things have changed for you since the previous session?
Client: Since then I met my mother once on the street. There were no problems at all – I was no longer resentful of her. It was just like meeting a friend. I was really surprised – I used only to have bad feelings before when I saw her. This time things were ok.
Facilitator: I am pleased about that – What did you find particularly surprising?
Client: The fact that my feelings were different – I could be more myself.
Facilitator: How did you notice that?
Client: I was no longer shy – I was able to ask her things – Before I would have just reacted…
Facilitator: Hmm. (Nods).
Client: … to her unnaturalness; she would give off this overbearing air and then not say what she wanted to say – I couldn't be sure where I stood, whether she meant something like she said it, or whether she meant something completely different.
Facilitator: How did you deal with this problem this time?
Client: I took her at her word – and no longer started to think about what she actually meant – Somehow I just approached her differently –
Facilitator: Were there any other changes?
Client: … What was totally new for me was that I was able to look forward to the day. When I wake up I start to think straight away about things I might do –
Facilitator: Can you give an example?
Client: … I feel like reading something or meeting someone.

The client goes on to describe in detail who she wants to meet and the plans she makes with her friends.

Client: … Somehow I'm just happier about life. Before everything just seemed so tedious. There was nothing coming form within… I'd really retreated into myself. It's only now that I realise that.
Facilitator: Did anything else change?
Client: … Now I am better able to say what I want… I can also say no to things… That's something I used to find particularly difficult. I used to end up doing things that I didn't really want to do, but I felt obliged to do. It became quite overwhelming for me at times.
Facilitator: What do you do now when there's something you don't want to do?
Client: I say what I want to do. If someone doesn't like it, it no longer bothers me.

The client then gives details of two situations in which she was able to speak her mind and how she dealt with the anger this aroused in two of her friends: her friendship with one of the friends came to an end as a result and with the other friend she now has a clear picture of what things she would like them to do together and what not.

Facilitator: There have been a lot of changes in this short interval.

Client: Yes. Let's see if it lasts. I can't quite believe it.

Facilitator: How will you be able to have confidence in the change?

Client: Next week I'm going to visit my parents and brothers and sisters. I'll be able to see then if my relationship to my mother has really changed.

The client agrees to come back four weeks later for the next session.

Second follow-up session.

Facilitator: It's a long time now since we last saw each other. What changes have there been since then?

Client: Since last time I have visited my parents a number of times. The first time was one week later. It was difficult when we were all together. Wilfried made a scene again and bossed my mother around. It was terrible to witness how she just lets it happen. I told him off, but that just created a bad atmosphere.

Facilitator: Assuming you were able to deal with this, what would you do then?

Client: … It wouldn't bother me as much to see my mother not defending herself… I'd be better able to keep a distance… I'd be more myself… I wouldn't let myself be so dragged into things.

Facilitator: Did you also have meetings with your mother during this time when there were no problems?

Client: Yes, and we did something together. Before, we'd always have argued over it – mostly it would have been my suggestion that won in the end, but I was always aware that she didn't want to do it.

Facilitator: Was it different this time?

Client: Somehow we just understood each other better. We went shopping together, and I noticed that she was enjoying it. For example…

The client describes some situations in which she could enjoy being together with her mother.

Client: That would never have been possible before… Maybe I also used to back out a lot… I never initiated doing anything together with her… It was too difficult.

Facilitator: So it's something new that you enjoy doing things with your mother?

Client: Yes, it's something new… Maybe it was also true before, but somehow I didn't notice it.

Facilitator: Did you have any meetings with the whole family where there were no problems?

Client: Entirely free of problems, no. Something would always annoy me, but the other meetings were all better than the first one, after the session.

Facilitator: What was better?

Client: … I kept more distance.

Facilitator: How did you manage that?

Client: When something annoyed me I would talk to my father. I get on very well with him.

Facilitator: How was it after that being with your mother again?

Client: I was more myself then. It was ok.

Facilitator: Is there anything else you can do, when something annoys you, to feel more yourself?

Client: Yes, sometimes it helps when go to my room for a short while and do something I enjoy… reading, for example, or listening to music. After that I usually feel better again.

The client describes various situations in which she was angry with her mother and how it had helped to go to her room to do something she enjoys doing.

Facilitator: Is there anything else that helps you to distance yourself from the anger.

Client: … Sometimes it helps if I go into the woods. That normally helps me recover quickly.

Facilitator: Can you think of anything else that helps you?

Client: … I think that's all.

Facilitator: That's quite a lot of things you thought of that you can do!

Client: Yes, that's true… I didn't realise before that I could do something myself… Until now I always felt totally helpless.

Facilitator: Until the next time we meet, each time you get angry with your mother, you can experiment to see which things are more helpful or what changes the situation in some way – for example, standing off, going into the woods, talking to your father etc. Maybe you could also try to do some things together with your mother and then note what difference this makes the next time you meet your family.

The client nods and they agree to meet for a further session in six weeks' time.

Third follow-up session

Facilitator: OK, how are things now? Has anything changed?

Client: What we discussed in the last session has been very helpful to me. Since then I have been home many times, and on each occasion things occurred to me that I could do when I get angry.

The client describes in detail a number of situations where she was able to step back from the situation, where she would meet someone or would do something on her own, and how each time this helped her to deal with her anger.

Client: Now I no longer see visiting my family as an onerous obligation and I even look forward to it… Something fundamental has changed… And now I can deal with the situation… I also see my mother very differently. Somehow I can understand her better now.

Facilitator: It's really surprising how quickly you were able to do these things. There have been a lot of changes.

Client: Lots of my friends and fellow students have also said that I have really changed.

Facilitator: What do you notice about yourself that is different?

Client: I approach others more readily now… I'm more open, I speak my mind more… They also say I'm much more cheerful.

Facilitator: Have there been any other changes?

Client: I now feel much better about being here in Munich. Before I never used to feel at home here and used to go a lot to the countryside, but I was moving back and forth and was never settled. After a while I couldn't cope with the situation.

Facilitator: And are you now happy in Munich?

Client: Yes, all of a sudden I like it here.

Facilitator: What do you like here?

Client: I can enjoy the town… and now I know more people… It's as if a new life has begun for me here. Before I used to think that I was not a city person and everything here was so anonymous. But now there are a lot of things that I like.

The client describes an array of situations in which she now feels happy in comparison with her previous situation. It is clear that she has more contact with people. She also talks about the changes that have taken place in her student life: she is more engaged, makes more suggestions and as a result has gained more influence.

Facilitator: So a lot of things in this area have also changed significantly?

Client: Yes. Just by talking about it now, I realise how much has changed. Before I was not so aware.

Facilitator: Would you like another session?

Client: I believe I'll be able to manage on my own now. If I ever want another session, is it ok to call you?

Facilitator: Of course.

There were no further sessions and the client did not ring again. One year later, she sent me a postcard while on holiday to tell me that she now had a boyfriend and that the relationship with her mother was still working well.

Chapter VI

The nine and twelve square constellations

The twelve square constellation is an extension of the nine square constellation. In the twelve square constellation, the differences between *goal* and *miracle* are made even clearer by distinguishing between the near and distant future. Both forms grew out of a combination of solution focused brief therapy and systemic structural constellations.

It may at first seem unusual that it is possible to transform aspects of a pure conversational form, as in SFT, into the spatially arranged relationship structure of a constellation. The experiments in which I place elements of SFT in a constellation were designed to help develop theories about the differences and similarities between the two therapy forms. This made the equivalents between the two forms more visible, and therefore clarified which parts were not contained in SFT and represent a real addition to SFT. My intention was to combine the advantages of both methods in order to enhance their effectiveness further still. This resulted in the nine square, twelve square, goal approximation and solution constellations, as well as the solution geometrical interview. These different combinations have proved their value in practice, and the following examples, besides offering potentially interesting insights, also act as suggestions for practice.

The components of the nine square constellation are nine squares, a timeline and *representatives in the narrow sense*. The twelve square constellation contains three additional squares set in the future (described in detail in Chapter V1.1). The goal approximation constellation is an abridged form of the twelve square constellation. The solution constellation consists only of *representatives in the narrow sense* and is therefore closer to family constellations. Solution and family constellations both involve a timeless space in which future and past are not established. The solution geometrical interview is conducted either totally or partially using *representatives in the narrow sense*, in lieu of real conversation partners. This affords a greater importance to aspects of the constellation than to the interview, i.e. the aspects of the constellation must be dealt with first before the interview is conducted.

VI.1 Similarities between SFT and SySt in the nine and twelve square constellation

Spatial arrangement plays an important role in constellations. SFT focuses on solutions in the present, past and future. Accordingly, I have named one of the coordinate axes in the nine and twelve square table the 'time axis'. Different types of solution are represented in the individual squares of the table. If these different types of solutions are now to become the subject of a constellation, we must first clarify what these solutions correspond with, i.e. which fields they encompass. As opposed to family constellations, we are now dealing with abstract structures (solutions) whose contents we are initially unaware of. Solutions to problems can appear in the form of inner states, attitudes, situations and behaviour. These areas – i.e. states, attitudes, situations and behaviours – are entered on the second coordinate axis. We then arrive at a coordinate system described by the axes for 'time' and 'areas'.

I then split these different areas, within which the solutions appear, into internal context, external context and border. The person represents this border between internal context and external context – indeed, to an extent she creates the difference between these contexts. This separation is to be understood in the same way as George Spencer-Brown's idea of distinction (described below), whereby a distinction is made by drawing a border between the internal and external areas.

The next section may be safely skipped by first-time readers.

VI.1.1 Spencer-Brown's idea of distinction and its application in constellation work

I will now quote from Spencer-Brown's *Laws of Form* (1994) in order to explain the background to the separation into 'internal context', 'external context' and 'border':

THE FORM
We take as given the idea of distinction and the idea of indication, and that we cannot make an indication without drawing a distinction. We take, therefore, the form of distinction for the form (ibid., p.1).

The idea of distinction is introduced here as an action that is also connected with the process of indication. The form of the distinction process and the simultaneous process of indicating something is called 'the form'. The concept of form used here lies somewhere between the concept of the nature or possibility of an event, and that of a gestalt. Understood in visual terms, the form encompasses/constructs two spaces with two sides – one of which is named, the other given only as its complement – i.e. initially unnamed and with no motive, similar to the way in which we speak of the problem and the non-problem. The non-problem has no name yet and initially is only a complement to the problem, whose name/motive is discovered from the details of the miracle question.

Definition
Distinction is perfect continence.
That is to say, a distinction is drawn by arranging a boundary with separate sides so that a point on one side cannot reach the other side without crossing the boundary. For example, in a plane space a circle draws a distinction. (ibid. p.1).

In creating a distinction, two different states are generated simultaneously whose existence cannot be separated from the process of distinction. This also means that these conditions did not exist previously and first come into being simultaneously with the act of distinction. Prior to this we have only the non-distinct, the unnameable, since at that stage there existed no distinction and therefore no basis for indication and naming.

Once a distinction is drawn, the spaces, states or contents on each side of the boundary, being distinct, can be indicated.
There can be no distinction without motive, and there can be no motive unless contents are seen to differ in value.
If a content is of value, a name can be taken to indicate this value.
Thus the calling of the name can be identified with the value of the content (ibid., p.1).

What has been distinguished, the two separate spaces, states or contents can then be identified after the first act of distinction. This means that, from this point on, we are able refer to what has been distinguished.

A distinction is inseparable from a motive. The motive presupposes that what is distinguished will have different values for those performing the distinction. The value of what has been distinguished can therefore be given a name, and the calling of this name can be equated with this value.

Applied to the representation of systemic parts in constellations this would mean that the 'calling of the name' can be equated with the 'value of what has been named by the client'. Since systemic constellations use representatives to represent elements of the client's system, they perform a similar function in a constellation picture as do names in a sentence. The positioning of a representative with the name 'father' as the client's father, for example, fulfils a similar function as the use of 'father' in a sentence spoken by the client about her father.

In terms of Spencer-Brown's theory of distinction, this suffices as a basis for the elementary systems-theoretical semiotics used in systemic constellations: we are now able to equate 'the calling of the name' – i.e. positioning the representative (e.g. for the client's father) – with the 'value of the content' to the speaker or the distinguished side – i.e. with what the representative embodies for the client in the constellation process (e.g. the father as he was for her).

Interestingly, in this basic form of systems-theoretical semiotics, the distinctness of both sign and signified (e.g. the representative of the father and the father) is maintained. The equation is made , instead of presumed, while on the other hand, the precise relaying by representatives (through representative perception) of the reactions of the systemic elements represented, as an expression of the elementary identification relationship that is the basis of all logic and language and model formation, becomes comprehensible.

When we draw distinctions, therefore, these distinctions are connected with a value that one of the distinguished sides has for us. As a result, the content generated by the distinction is related to us through our intention. Therefore: distinctions are drawn on the basis of a motive, which, for us, is connected to a value. This shows that what has been distinguished is connected to an acting person and must therefore contain a subjective element.

What is distinguished is not given from the outset. What is given is the possibility to distinguish and thus to indicate something. The distinction/indication coupling is constructed by means of an action which creates the contents. Consequently, we can also see this coupling as a basis of constructivism. The following extract from *Laws of Form* clarifies this point further:

FORMS TAKEN OUT OF THE FORM
Construction

Draw a distinction.
(ibid. p.3)

Spencer-Brown calls 'drawing a distinction' a construction.

Content
   Call it the first distinction.
   Call the space in which it is drawn the space severed or cloven by the distinction.
   Call the parts of the space shaped by the severance or cleft the sides of the distinction or, alternatively, the spaces, states or contents distinguished by the distinction (ibid. p.3).

By splitting the coordinate axis 'area' in nine and twelve square constellations into 'internal context', 'external context' and 'border', we arrive, through drawing a distinction, at a separation of the room into 'internal' and 'non-internal=external context'. The border refers to the person who draws the distinction. We ourselves are thus defined by the possibility of distinguishing by actions – in other words, our existence shows itself by our drawing distinctions. What we distinguish is generated by our drawing distinctions. And by drawing distinctions we as a border become clearer. This corresponds to the process of individuation and distinction.

Unwritten cross
Suppose any s_0 to be surrounded by an unwritten cross.
Call the crosses standing under any cross c, written or unwritten, the crosses pervaded by the shallowest space in c (ibid. p.7)

The term *cross* as Matthias Varga von Kibéd views it is both a request and a description. It is a noun, as in 'a cross', and a verb in the imperative, as in 'Cross!' The somewhat secretive *unwritten cross* in the *Laws of Form* gives, according to his interpretation, an indication of the implicit context.
   The framework within which we draw distinctions corresponds to the implicit context indicated by the *unwritten cross*. Where we experience the whole, we draw nearer to this context. In the moment that we name the experience, however, we lose this area, since the naming separates us from what is named, and we again become the border between what is named (the external context) and our experience (the internal context). Moving closer to the implicit context corresponds to the process of expansion and dissolution of the subject.

VI.1.2 The coordinates and squares of the nine and twelve square table

The nine and twelve square table is described by two coordinates, the time axis and the axis for the areas. Because SFT differentiates between 'that which is good and should remain so', the exceptions and the appearance of the *miracle*, I have divided the time axis for the nine square table into three discrete parts:

-   past
-   present
-   future

In the twelve square table, the 'future' area is further divided into 'near future' and 'distant future'.

Similarly, the axis for the different areas is split into three discrete parts:

-   internal context
-   border
-   external context

This gives us nine squares, as shown in the following schema:

Schema for the nine square table			
Future	1	2	3
Present	4	5	6
Past	7	8	9
Time / Area	Internal context	Border	External context

Figure 16

The individual solutions are entered in the squares. The squares for solutions in the present (4 to 6) refer to the question: 'What is working at present?' The squares for solutions in the past (7 to 9) refer to the question: 'What solutions were successful in the past?' We also find exceptions to the problem, and the squares for future solutions refer to the question: 'From what will I recognise that the problem is solved?' The following table gives an overview of the different questions for each time period.

Questions relating to the different time periods:

Future	From what will I recognise that the problem is solved?
Present	What is working at present?
Past	What solutions were successful in the past?

In the twelve square table, the future area is further divided into near future (the field of the goal) and the distant future (the field of the miracle), giving a total of twelve squares. The lines of division between each of the time periods and the different contexts create static borders. When working with both the twelve and nine square table these can be marked on the floor or shown using a rope. This gives us the following schema:

Schema for the twelve square table

Time / Area	Internal context	Border	External context
Distant future			
Near future			
Present			
Past			

Figure 17

The time axis, which is initially split into three distinct areas, can also be understood as continuous, i.e. there is a continuous timeline running through the areas. This corresponds to the scaling found in SFT. We now have a discrete and a continuous division of time, on which continuous and discontinuous processes of change can be projected. This upholds the **principle of transcontinuity**.

This principle, introduced by Luc Isebaert and Louis Cauffman of the SFT school in Bruges (Korzybski-Instituut in Bruges) at the 1997 EBTA conference, shows how it is essential for therapeutic processes that processes of gradual and sudden change are interlaced reflexively. Processes of sudden change are often encouraging, but sometimes also frighten by unsettling stable, familiar situations. They are often experienced as if they were outside one's own control. Processes of gradual change, on the other hand, while more controllable, are also slow and require greater patience.

SFT aids processes of gradual change by using scales and assigning exercises, and processes of sudden change by the use of the miracle question. Constellations are initially designed for sudden change. The following direction, used at the end of a successful constellation, facilitates a subsequent process of gradual change:

'Take this picture in and follow the impulses for action that arise from it!'

The twelve squares and the timeline are marked on the floor. They represent *non-personal locations* and are established before the constellation begins. This can be done by the facilitator, or by the client, who, using her intuition, draws the timeline on which the coordinate system will be based. In the client's internal picture, the timeline may be bent. Where this is the case, the coordinate system will also be bent accordingly, with the point of inflexion often falling at the transition from present to future, which we call the *Point of Decision*.

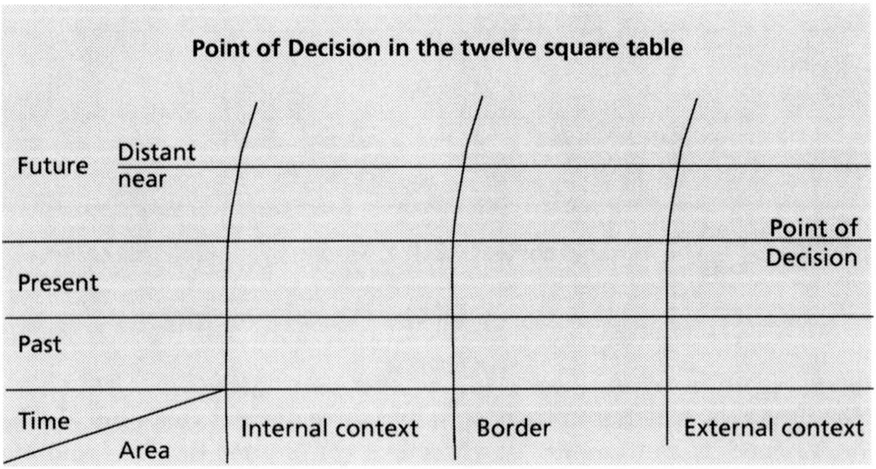

Figure 18

The twelve squares determined by the two coordinates represent solutions in the present, past and future for the internal and external context and the border. In some cases, the *solutions* act as if they were obstacles. Where this is true, using positional and process work, the representatives acting like obstacles can find a position in which their qualities as solutions become clear.

The border in this case represents a person, who finds herself on the border between an internal and external context. To an extent, it is the area between the internal and external that makes us what we are. By internal context I mean all internal variables, such as cognition, emotions, physical sensations, bodily functions etc.; by external context I mean people, situations, contextual areas etc.

VI.1.2 The symbols of the nine and twelve square constellation

Apart from the twelve squares and the timeline, twelve square constellations also use *representatives in the narrow sense*. These represent the different features in the solution focused interview: the *focus* (for the client), the *goal*, the *miracle* and sometimes also the *context of the miracle* (a representative for the reactions of others to the changes in the client). *Goal* and *miracle* are normally positioned by the client in the *future/border* area, while the *miracle* stands at a greater distance from the *focus* than the *goal* – i.e. the *miracle* stands in the distant future, the *goal* in the near future. Since the *miracle* plays a central role in SFT, I extended the nine square constellation to twelve squares by adding the distant future – the area of the *miracle*.

Sometimes clients also position *goal* and *miracle* in a different square, and this should be taken into account during interpretation. If the *miracle* is placed in the *future/internal context* area, this indicates that the *miracle* exists more in the imagination. To become reality, it needs to be placed in the *future/border* area and be able to remain there comfortably for the duration of the constellation (without being affected by or disturbing other representatives). If the *miracle* is placed in the past, this can often indicate the existence of an entanglement. In this situation, the *context of the miracle* outweighs the *miracle* itself, and it is advisable to divide the *miracle* into two parts: the *miracle* and the *context of the miracle*. This allows us to obtain differentiated answers from the representatives, instead of mixed perceptions, for the *miracle* and the *context of the miracle*.

The following diagram shows the different symbols used in twelve square constellations. The representatives are shown in what are frequently occurring positions.

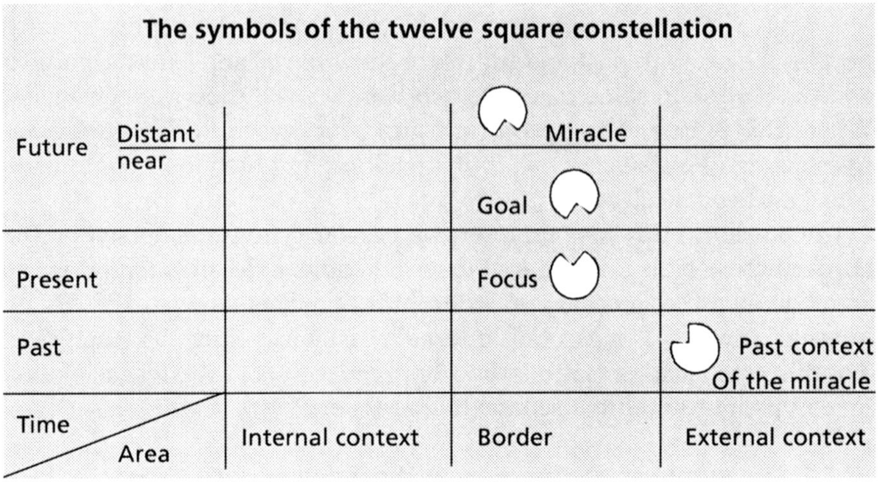

The symbols of the twelve square constellation

Time Area	Internal context	Border	External context

Figure 19.

VI.1.4 The SFT feature twelve square table

The following diagram shows how the information gained from an interview is allocated, prototypically, to the squares of the nine and twelve square table.

The exercises cover the entire area of the *future*, and the miracle question the entire area of the *distant future*, since both include the *internal* and the *external context* and the *border*. The area of the *external context* belongs to the *context of the miracle*, since both future reactions as well as loyalties to people from the past can be accounted for by the miracle question. The exceptions cover all three areas of the squares for the *past*. The use of previously useful belief statements also represents an exception situation (in which the problem was absent). Some of the physical indicators of the solution may of course also already feature in the *present/internal context* area, since signs of the solution can also appear in the present.

VI.1.5 Differences between the nine square table in NLP and the nine and twelve square constellation

In the practice of NLP, Robert Dilts has already developed timeline procedures, and, together with Robert McDonald, used nine square tables containing a coordinate, besides that for time, with a division between *higher self*, *self* and *other people* (Isert 2000). This approach was further developed by Tad James and Wyatt Woodsmall (1992), though their model is relatively mechanistic. They used timeline work to replace negative memories with positive ones, to create goal expectancy, dissolve belief and value conflicts, and change personality. There are some fundamental differences between working in this way (in NLP)

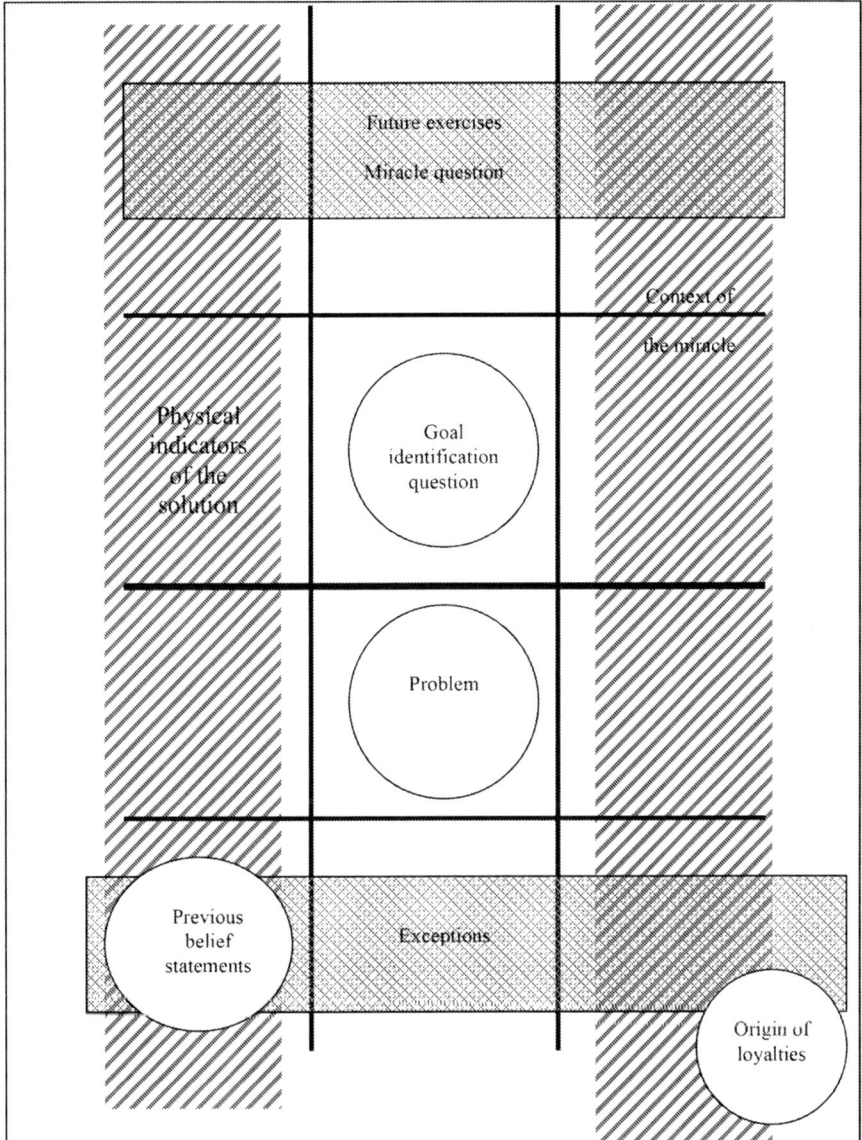

Figure 20

and the twelve square constellation as we use it here. These differences are described below.

1. We use the twelve square table in a solution focused way, i.e. we don't look for past traumas and their solutions, as in timeline work. We look instead exclusively for past resources. Where representatives do not act as resources in the first constellation

picture, as may occur, they are not positioned in the constellation as 'obstacles'.

2. Instead of working directly with the client, we work with representatives. This allows the client to adopt a meta-position for the total duration of the constellation.

3. The precise spatial arrangement of elements in relation to each other plays a more important role. Angle, distance, lines of sight act as distinguishing features.

4. For the future area we differentiate between two zones: that of the goal, and that of the miracle. The zone of the miracle itself opens up a new area: the client's new way of life including all reactions from her environment. This is not a separate area, but one subject to continual change.

5. The zones of the horizontal coordinates are understood more generally in our twelve square table and do not presuppose a personality model for the self and higher self. Our division is based on George Spencer Brown's concept of distinction.

6. In Robert Dilts' timeline work the client searches for resources that her parents lack and then passes them on to them so that the parents can behave, retroactively, as if the trauma had not occurred. This retroactive changing of an individual past is still very cause-oriented. It implies that something different first needs to happen before a solution can occur. In the solution focused approach, however, the amazing thing is that nothing need change and the solution can happen suddenly, like a miracle.

When we place family members in the constellation, they represent resources for us. If loyalties to excluded people hinder steps taken towards the future goal, we do not change the excluded people but our relationship to them: instead of suffering with them, we transform the loyalty into a shared pleasure in the fact that things will improve. To think that the excluded person would begrudge us success, or wish that we suffer with them equally, is to confuse the reaction of a person in a negative situation hindering them with that person's true essence. SFT trusts that, essentially, we will act 'correctly', and will know our own way, otherwise we cannot trust the answers to the miracle question.

VI.1.6 Applying nine and twelve square constellations

The type of constellation we use depends on the client's problem. The twelve square constellation is a very general schema and therefore it can also be used as a meta-constellation for family or organisation constellations. How the twelve square constellation, used as a meta-constellation, can be combined with other types of constellation will be shown in Chapter VI.4. *Twelve square constellations* make use of dynamic aspects and represent solutions in the constellation as sources of energy.

The *twelve square constellation* (and the *nine square constellation*) can be used in the following different ways:

1. By performing the interview on the twelve square table. This is particularly helpful when the client experiences difficulties imagining something. The spatial arrangement can open up a different channel of experience.
2. In using the twelve square table as an array of resources. This form can be used where there is a need to support what is already working for the client with resources.
3. In applying the *twelve square constellation* as a meta-constellation. In this form the twelve square table acts as a matrix for form 2. For example, a family constellation can be implemented within the framework of a twelve square constellation. This uses the solution focused framework of the twelve square constellation as a source of energy in order to balance out the weight and intensity of the family constellation so that the client does not relapse into her problem consciousness.

These three forms will be explained in the following sections through examples.

VI.2 The interview in the twelve square table

For clients who want to see more action during the therapy, the nine and twelve square constellation offers a good alternative to the conversational form of the interview. It can be difficult for some clients to discover or experience solutions during a conversation, a process that can be facilitated by a constellation. The twelve square table offers the client the additional opportunity to position herself in the *future/border* area and to experience how a future state feels without being able to name it. The squares in the twelve square table act as non-personal representatives for the areas of intersection of the coordinate axes. This allows the corresponding feelings to be felt directly in the individual squares, i.e. the twelve square constellation allows *visitors* (in the SFT sense, see Chapter II) to develop ideas for goals out of the 'future' experiences relayed to them.

The following experiment can be used to put the twelve square constellation to the test with a problem of your own.

VI.2.1 Experiment 7

1. Think about a problem you would like to work on.
2. Walk around in the room, and find the place where you feel most comfortable.
3. Stand on this place.
4. From this position, see where you perceive the future and the past to be.
5. Mark your position with a marker (e.g. a shoe) which will then represent your *focus*. This position is in the *present/border* square.
6. Using string or a tape measure, mark the remaining eleven squares starting from your position so that a twelve square table is created on the floor.
7. Take up the position of your *focus*, and ask the following questions:
   - What is your goal?
   - When you achieve your goal, what exists instead of your problem?
   - From what can tell that you have taken a first step towards your goal?
8. Chose another position marker (e.g. a shoe, cushions or tiles) for your *goal* and walk around the room with it until you find a place for it that feels right to you.
9. Place the symbol for your *goal* on the floor.
10. Now move into the position of your *focus*.
11. Answer the following questions or follow the instructions accordingly:
    - What has changed for you now you can see your *goal*?
    - Are you able to make contact with your *goal*?
    - Take a small step towards your *goal* and observe what difference this makes to you.
    - If this was too much for you, you can take a step back again.
    - If this was a pleasant experience for you, you can take another small step forwards.
    - What difference does this step make for you?
12. Put the position marker back in the position of the *focus*.
13. Now move into the position of your *goal*.
    - How do your sensations change in this position?
    - What suggestion would you like to make to the focus from the position of your *goal*?
14. Mark the position of your *goal* again with the symbol.
15. Go back to the position of the *focus*.
    - What changes for you when you hear the proposal made by your *goal*?
16. Now walk around the twelve square table to the *distant future/border* square and on the way ask yourself the miracle question:

Assuming – after this constellation – you go about your work – and in the evening you eat together with your family or friends – and at some point you become tired – and go to bed – and assuming – during this night a miracle occurred – and your problem was solved in one fell swoop – just like that – How would you notice this the next morning? – What would then be different?

After you have answered this question, turn around and look in the direction of the *focus*.

Would anyone apart from you notice the miracle?

17. When a person appears, move into the corresponding square, probably *external context/distant future*, and mark the spot with a place marker.
18. Move into the position of this person, and sense how this person will react when the miracle happens for you.
19. Move back to the position of the miracle, and check the effect on you in this position.
20. In the position of the *miracle* you can ask yourself the following questions:
    - Who would notice it and from what?
    - How would others react to it?
    - How do you react to the reactions of the others?

    While doing this, for each person that appears, look for places in the *external context* square and then answer the questions from each position. Every time you change places, it is important to put down a place marker straight away. You will feel your reactions (in the future, when the miracle has occurred) when you move to the position of the *miracle*.
21. If, when you are in squares belonging to the border, thoughts, emotions or physical sensations occur, then move over to the square to your left (*internal context/future* or *present*) and place symbols on the corresponding positions.
22. Here you can again conduct a dialogue with your internal parts, in each case changing places and using place markers.
    - What difference do you feel in the position of the *miracle* in comparison with what you felt in the position of the *goal*?
    - Turn around to your *focus*. What would you want to say to it from this position?
23. Mark the position of the *miracle* again with the place marker, and go back to the position of your *focus*.
    - What has changed for you in the meantime?
    - Take a step forward again and check if it feels easier?
24. Go slowly back to the past, and, while doing so, ask yourself the following question:
    - Were there situations in the past that contained parts of the miracle?
25. Stop when you remember a situation of this kind. If a helpful person appears, move into the square to your right, the external context, and stand in the place of that person.
    - What would this person say to you?
26. Mark this position for the unknown person, and move back to your position in the past.
    - How do you feel when you hear the words of the *helpful person*?
    - What difference does this make to you?
27. You can also ask the *helpful person* a question. Afterwards move into the position of the *helpful person* and answer, and then see what effect the answer has on you when you are back in the position of the *focus*. With each change of position, move the place marker to the new position.
28. You can go back further into the past and see what helpful situations arise.
29. If other people are involved, place a position marker for them and see what this person would say or advise. Afterwards go back to your position and check the effect of the words.
30. If you remember situations in which helpful thoughts or emotions arise, you can then move to the *adjacent* square to your left (*internal context/past*) and put down a place marker for the thought or emotion.

31. Stand in the position of the *thought* or the *emotion* and, from there speak to the *focus*. Change places again and check how what was said affects you.
32. You can also ask questions of the *thought* or *emotion* and get an answer by moving into their position. This way you can enter into a dialogue with people from the past and helpful thoughts and emotions. As opposed to a visualised dialogue, it is also possible for you to obtain information about representative experience, based on the assumption that is possible to experience alien psychic states in this way.
33. To finish, go back again to the position of the *focus*.
    • What has changed for you through this?
    • What new perspectives have opened up?
    • Which dialogues were helpful to you?
    • Which advice would you like to act on?
    • How can you achieve that?
    • Are there any people that are helpful to your goal that you could call on?
    • Which helpful thoughts and emotions would you like to draw on more frequently in the future?
34. Make some notes on these ideas and behavioural insights, and try to integrate these into your daily life, step by step. As before: a little is better than too much.

VI.2.2 Applying the twelve square constellation for an organisation

Twelve square constellations have also more than proved their worth in working with organisations and institutions. Below I provide some examples of useful questions that can be asked when implementing a twelve square constellation in an organisational context.

When we perform a constellation for an organisational group, it is recommended initially that someone (a spokesperson) is chosen by the group to select the focus and the other representatives. In an organisational context, therefore, we are dealing with a three-stage operation:

• The team or department, which chooses
• a spokesperson for the group, who then chooses
• the focus and the representatives of the systemic parts

We call this a **multi-stage organisational structural constellation**. Where gender roles feature as part of the problem, we have found it useful to select two spokespeople, who then select the representatives together. Where other divisive factors come into play, it is important to choose a spokesperson from each party, who again select the representatives together.

When working with organisations as teams, it is particularly important to ensure that everyone is able to save face. Organisational structural constellations are particularly suited to this field, since they allow for **hidden work**. In a twelve square constellation, for example, the *focus*, *goal* and *miracle* can all be positioned, with no need to reveal any of their content. The client answers the solution focused questions quietly for himself so only he knows what the goal and miracle mean to him.

If the team is very small, symbols as place markers on the floor can be used instead of people. To prevent the client from continually looking down at the floor when he moves to a place marker and is looking towards other markers, the facilitator may hold a cataleptic hand over the marker that the client is looking towards, and the client can then look at the hand instead. This technique is also particularly useful in coaching, which normally only involves one person.

The twelve square constellation starts with the chosen spokesperson for all those belonging to the group choosing the representatives for the systemic elements and positioning them in the room. When the spokesperson has positioned the *focus*, he is asked to stand behind him briefly and to indicate in which direction his future lies and where it begins. This area is then marked on the floor or indicated using string. Similarly, the spokesperson is then asked to indicate in which direction he sees the past and where it starts, with the area marked as before. It is also possible not to mark the time zones, but instead to remember the areas and identify them by their position in the room – for instance, the future is by the window. The squares are said to be 'positioned' at this moment, i.e. their effects start the moment they are named.

The *focus* can also be asked where, for him, the time zones are located. Generally his answers tend to agree with what the group spokesperson says. The *internal context* and *external context* areas are explained briefly by the facilitator and marked besides the column for the *border* that has been marked in-between. The coordinate system for the nine square table is positioned in this way, and can then be extended to the twelve square table by asking the *focus* to move into the future until he senses a change, where the border to the *distant future* is drawn.

Another option is for the facilitator to draw the twelve square table on the floor, and then to ask the chosen spokesperson for the team or department to find a suitable place for the *focus* within the twelve square table. The advantage of the former method is that the coordinate system is established in a more personal way and may be experienced as more appropriate

The positioning of the *focus* in the twelve square table says something about how far away the team (or department) is from its goal with respect to the problem, whether there is any eye contact at all, and whether the *goal* and the *focus* are able to see each other. If the *focus* is not in the *border* area, however, this can be interpreted with the help of the coordinate system, for example:

- If the *focus* is standing in the *internal context* area, he may be living more in his imagination
- If the *focus* is in the *past*, then a past event may hinder progress or the *focus* may be focused on the past
- If the *focus* is in the *external context*, possibly a member of the team (or department) inadvertently represents an excluded person

These indications can be used as ideas for rituals and rearrangements, but should not be used as interpretations in any diagnostic capacity.

Normally, the spokesperson chosen for the team (or department) places the *focus* in the middle square, i.e. *present/past*. Assuming this to be the case, we can start with the following questions:

'What is the team's current problem?'
'What does the present situation look like?'
'What needs to change for you all here?'
'After you achieve your goal, what will there be instead of the problem?'
'What would you like to call your goal?'

The spokesperson can now select a representative for the *goal* and position them. The facilitator can then ask the *focus* the following:

'How is your connection with the *goal*?'
'Is it possible for the team to take a further step towards the goal?'

The spokesperson may be asked the following in connection with the *external context* (three squares):

'Which customers are satisfied?'
'What are they satisfied with?'
'Who is a trustworthy partner or consultant?'
'What out-sourcing is proving useful at the moment?'
'What type of market orientation would be successful in this situation?'

Afterwards he can again select and position representatives for the respective customers, partners or consultants, and actions. The representatives can then be asked in turn what they found helpful and what is going well at the moment. The *focus* may also question the representatives who might find that they are able to answer. This may sound extraordinary, but this answering of questions happens in the same way as the experiencing of physical sensations that actually belong to an alien system. The representatives do not think about what answers to give, rather they listen for the answers that arise within them or the words that enter their minds. This is similar to representative perception.

The questions asked of the spokesperson in respect of the *internal context* (three squares) would be as follows:

'Which structures, measures, colleagues are performing well at the moment?'
'Given what is currently happening in the organisation, what is useful in addressing the problem?'

Again, the corresponding people and measures can be positioned and enter into dialogue with the *focus*.

The following more specific questions can be asked of the spokesperson about the entire *past* area (three squares):

'When was work going well?'
'When was a similar problem in the organisation previously overcome successfully?'

Similarly, the following more specific questions can be asked in respect of the *past external context*:

'Which consultants (partners etc.) were helpful?'
'At what times were customers satisfied?'
'What were they satisfied with?'
'For what was the organisation valued?'

And again with the *past internal context*:

'Which measures, rituals, restructuring within the organisation were helpful?'
'Which company culture has been shown to be successful?'

Again, the named systemic elements (people, groups of people, influences etc.) can be represented by group members, positioned and asked questions by the *focus*.

If the questions listed above are put to the *focus* of the constellation, and not the spokesperson, the form of constellation will be similar to the **solution geometrical interview**, in which the solution focused conversation uses representatives instead of real conversation partners (described in more detail in Chapter IX).

If the *twelve square constellation* takes place as part of individual coaching, the client then moves on her own into the position of each of the symbols. From the position of the *focus* she is able to ask all the questions relating to the *internal* and *external* context of those representatives (symbolised with place markers) whose answers she is interested in. Afterwards, she puts herself in the position of each place marker in turn and checks to see what answers come to her spontaneously. By moving into the different positions and changing location each time, the client can experience the different perspectives of the other systemic parts. This marks a difference from the solution focused conversation, in which a change of perspective only takes place in the imagination. The solution focused interview, and in particular the miracle question, can be performed in your head, but a physical change of location will normally increase the intensity of the experience.

The following questions can be put to the spokesperson with regard to the *distant future areas*:

'What visions do you have?
'From what would you notice that all your problems were solved?'

The organisational idea of business re-engineering, for example, is also a method that leads to this area in one step.

Some questions that could be asked of the spokesperson about the *distant future/external context* square would be as follows:

'What additional customers, consultants or partners will there be when the problem is solved?'
'What new market orientation do we need to consider?'

Questions asked of the spokesperson about the *near* and *distant future internal context* (two squares) could be as follows:

'What changes will be possible in the organisation then?'
'What increases the employees' readiness to act?'

In answering the questions relating to the areas of the *near* and *distant future/border*, the *focus* can step into this area and experience the solution directly. The same people and influences mentioned can be positioned again and enter into dialogue with the *focus*.

In coaching, for example, when the client places himself in the *distant future/border* square, it would also be possible for him, from this perspective, to give himself (represented by a place marker) advice or to say something to himself in the present that could help him move towards his *goal*. The twelve square constellation allows the client to solve problems himself by moving to the relevant squares. These experiences sometimes enable a different kind of action than that seen when the whole process takes place through conversation. In my opinion, the twelve square constellation is a very effective instrument for use in coaching and, with guidance, self-coaching.

VI.3 The nine and twelve square table as an array of resources

When the nine and twelve square table is used as an array of resources, it is first marked on the floor (alternatively, the client senses where it is and how far, for her, the *present* stretches, when, for her, the *near* and *distant future* begin, and where, for her, the *past* lies). Afterwards the client positions her *goal* and then places herself in the *present/border* square.

From this position she is able to cast her view over all the squares to check whether something appears to her in any of the squares. When this happens, the facilitator can hold a cataleptic hand over the position where someone or something appeared. The client can then check whether she knows the person or thing and say what changes when she looks at the palm of the cataleptic hand (held at eye level). After this she can move to the position marked by the cataleptic hand and, from there, sense what supportive words could be spoken to the *focus*. She can then check the effect of these words herself from the position of the *focus*. As soon as the client changes her position, a place marker should be put in the vacated position.

This process can be continued until the resources stop appearing. During this, the client checks the positions in which new resources appear and enters into dialogue with them. This gives the client the possibility of having a multi-perspective experience, and while doing so, she can check if she is able to take a step towards her *goal*.

This type of twelve square constellation can also be combined with a Virginia Satir integration exercise. At the end of the constellation, each individual resource can say one of the following to the client:

'I am your ability to …'
'I will support you by …'

While saying this, they can pass something on or send 'energy' to the client using their eyes. The client can then absorb this final picture.

In the example given below we will use only a nine square constellation since the client's goal is clearly defined to rediscover resources.

VI.3.1 Case study 1: Transformation of a traumatic situation

Mrs L. came to one of my experiential groups with the desire to become more self-confident. The preliminary interview and subsequent constellation was as follows:

Facilitator: What is your current problem?
Client: I often feel so lacking in self-confidence that I don't do things that I am actually capable of doing. I often hold myself back… at work I also hold myself back a lot.

Facilitator: When you no longer lack self-confidence, how would you be instead?

Client: I'd do the things that I'd like to do.

Facilitator: What would that be?

Client: Actually I always wanted to go freelance in organisational consulting, but never had the courage to take this step. And the work I do in my job is not stimulating enough for me in the long run. I'm often bored.

Facilitator: If you were more self-confident, what's the first thing you'd do in order to go freelance?

Client: ... I'd offer consultancy and courses and promote more.

Facilitator: How would you do that?

Client: I know people from when I was studying with whom I could collaborate and through whom I could build up contacts. I only need the courage.

Facilitator: If you were behaving more self-confidently, how would others notice this?

Client: I'd talk more to them ... I'd express my opinion from time to time ... and I'd participate in more things.

Facilitator: How would others react if you were suddenly to behave so differently?

Client: ... They'd be amazed ... Most would be happy ... There'd naturally be one or two who would begrudge it me.

Facilitator: How would you deal with those people if you were more self-confident?

Client: ... I'd get on with my things despite them.

Facilitator: How would they react to that?

Client: Some would be angry ... and some would show me more respect.

Facilitator: How would you deal with the anger that some of them would show if you were more self-confident?

Client: ... I'd stay the same ... and I'd remain calm and speak to them in a very normal way. I'd no longer be frantic and irritable.

Facilitator: How would you be instead?

Client: I'd be relaxed. Yes, that's it. I'd be able to stay relaxed.

Facilitator: Would there be anything else that would also change?

Client: Yes, I'd go out more and meet friends. I've very often been quite withdrawn

Facilitator: How would friends react to this?

Client: They'd say: 'At last!'

Facilitator: Is there someone in your family who was denied success due to certain circumstances?

Client: ... Not that I know of.

Facilitator: Or is there someone who was excluded? You know this question already.

Client (laughing): ... I cousin of mine had an accident, but otherwise I can't think of anything.

Facilitator: Then we can move to the constellation now ... Choose someone from the group for you and someone for your goal ... What do you want to call your goal?

Client: 'Self-confidence'.

Facilitator: First of all, position only your *focus*.

Facilitator (to *focus*): In which direction do you feel the future? ... And the past? ... And up to what point does the present stretch?

The *focus* points in front of herself and behind herself, and indicates the borders for the *present/border* square. The facilitator then draws the coordinate system of the nine square constellation.

Facilitator: Here to the right is everything to do with external influences (points to the squares for the *external context*)... Here to the left is the inner area, your thoughts, emotions, physical reactions etc.

The *focus* nods. The client has in the meantime gone back to her seat.
Facilitator: Next position your *goal*, the self-confidence.

The client then positions the representative, and we arrive at the following picture:

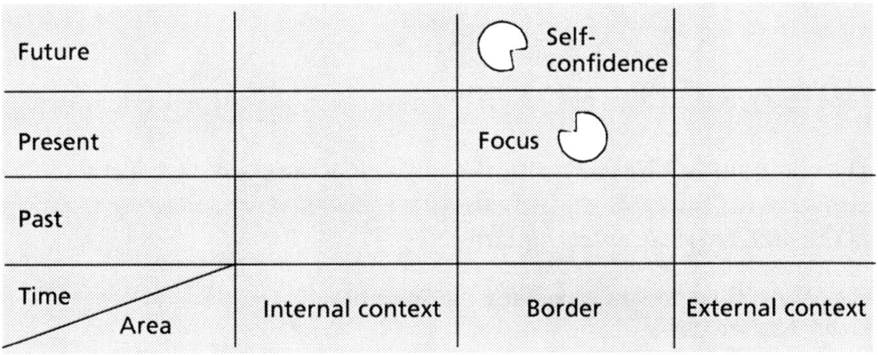

Time Area	Internal context	Border	External context
Future		Self-confidence	
Present		Focus	
Past			

Figure 21

Both representatives are asked about their condition.

Focus: I can see my *goal*, but am a little afraid.
Goal: I feel quite stable here but feel little contact with the *focus*.
Facilitator to the client: Does the picture seem right to you?
Client: Yes, completely.
Facilitator (to *focus*): Now turn around once in a circle and see if a resource appears to you in any of the squares.

The *focus* turns around slowly in a circle.

Focus: Yes, there (points to the *past/external context* square).

The facilitator holds a cataleptic hand over the square indicated and asks the *focus* to indicate more precisely where she senses the resource. The *focus* indicates the position by saying 'there'.

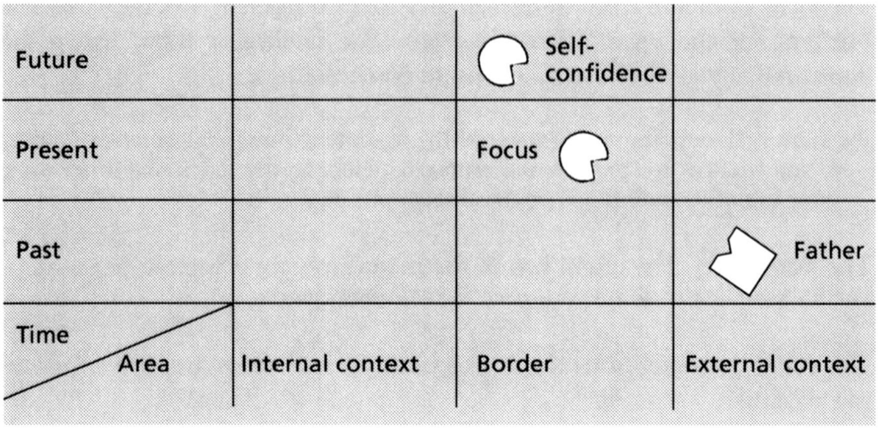

Time Area	Internal context	Border	External context
Future		Self-confidence	
Present		Focus	
Past			Father

Figure 22

Focus (surprised): That's my father! I've never seen him as a resource before.

The client nods. The facilitator then instructs the client to select a representative for her father, which she places in the corresponding position in the *past/external context* square.

Facilitator: How do you experience the *father* now?
Focus: As a support.
Facilitator: Have another look around, where do you find the next resource?
Focus: There (points to *past/internal context* square)

The facilitator again holds a cataleptic hand over the corresponding position.

Focus: It does me good, but I am a little afraid to look in that direction
Facilitator (to client): Select someone from the group for 'that which appears to the focus'.

The client chooses a representative and positions her.

Facilitator (to *focus*): What has changed for you?
Focus (tearful and with child's voice): I feel very strange.
Facilitator (to *focus*): Choose a number.
Focus: Five.

The *focus* has now become an *evolutionary representative*. She initially represented the adult client and now, for a short period, represents the five-year-old client. *Evolutionary representatives* can experience more than one state simultaneously, as in this example: the client's adult state and the five-year-old state. Given their ability to represent different stages of life at the same time, *evolutionary representatives* belong to the general form of **ambiguous representatives** (see also Chapter III.1.2.3.4). *Evolutionary representatives* help gain access to traumatic situations.

Facilitator (to client): What happened when you were five years old?
Client: ... We were visiting friends of my parents, I knocked over a vase and the whole table was made wet. The man became extremely angry and hit me, and my parents did nothing to protect me. That was big shock for me.
Facilitator (to client): Select someone else from the group as a representative for this situation.

The client chooses and positions a representative. We arrive at the following picture:

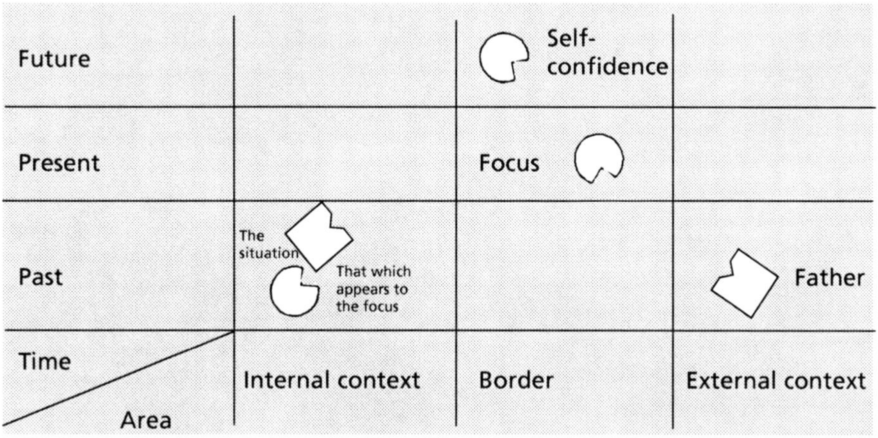

Future		Self-confidence	
Present		Focus	
Past	The situation / That which appears to the focus		Father
Time / Area	Internal context	Border	External context

Figure 23

Facilitator: How is the *focus* now?
Focus (crying): My knees are shaking, I am terribly afraid.
Facilitator: How is the *situation*?
Situation: I feel very powerful here.
Facilitator (to *situation*): Walk slowly over to your left and go behind the circle (of observing group members), release yourself from your role, and then sit down.

The *situation* follows the facilitator's instructions. The *focus* and '*that which appears to the focus*' breathe out.

Facilitator: What has changed for the *focus*?
Focus: A heavy burden was been removed from my shoulders
Facilitator: Situations pass, and we also need to let them pass, we shouldn't hold on to them. '*That which appears to the focus*', are you five years old? (To the *focus*) Go to her now, console her, as one consoles a child. Who else does she have today?

'*That which appears to the focus*' is now renamed as the *five-year-old*. This is followed by an application of the **alter ego method**: the *focus* is instructed to console her alter ego: the *five-year-old*. This technique is useful when it is suspected that the adult is finding it hard to connect with one of her earlier states due to traumatic events. This method re-establishes this contact (see also Chapter V.1.3).

The *focus* moves to the *five-year-old* and puts her arms around the representative, who nestles in the embrace. Both cry for a while, then straighten up. The therapist leads them both back to the *focus's* previous position. The client, also crying, observes the scene eagerly.

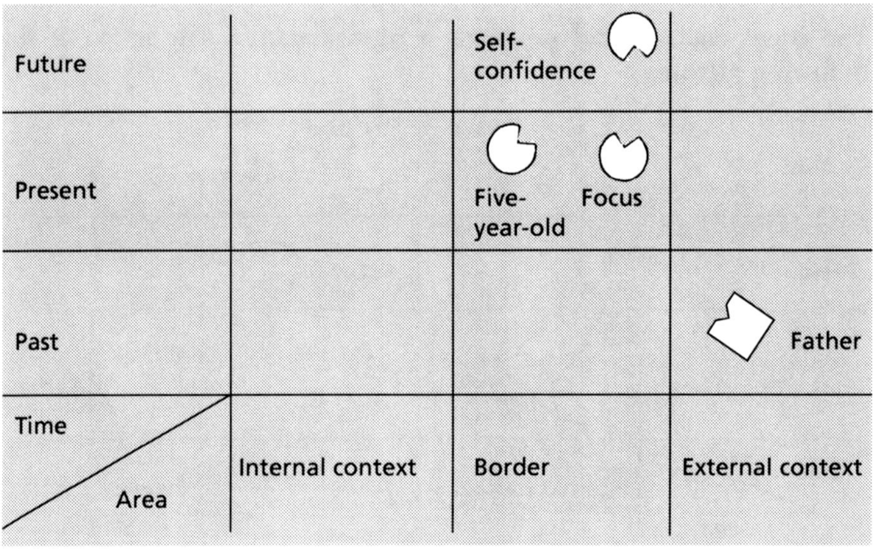

Time \ Area		Internal context	Border	External context
Future			Self-confidence	
Present			Five-year-old Focus	
Past				Father

Figure 24

Facilitator: How is the *focus* now?
Focus: Now I can see my *goal* much more clearly and feel attracted by it. I could also take a step towards it.
Facilitator: Then do so together with the *five-year-old*.

The *focus* slowly moves three steps towards the *goal* together with the *five-year-old*.

Focus: This is far enough for the moment … I can also feel the support of my father.
Facilitator: And how is the *goal* now?
Goal: I've made contact with the *focus*. It's good that the *focus* has the *five-year-old* so close to her. I'd like so much to give the *focus* more.
Facilitator (to client): Now you can release your representative and take her position.

The client swaps places with the *focus*.

Facilitator: Look behind you and feel the support of your father … Now look at
   your *goal* The *goal* can make eye contact and start to 'give' using its eyes. (To
   client) And you can take from it as much as you need.

The client follows the instructions.

Facilitator: Now take the *five-year-old* by the hand and take a step forwards
   together with her. How do you feel now?
Client: I can hardly believe it. I'm getting so much energy from my *goal* and
   would like to move closer to it.
Facilitator: Then do so.

The client moves towards her *goal* together with the *five-year-old*. The
representative for the *self-confidence (the goal)* opens her arms, and they
grasp each other by the hand. The client is deeply moved.

Facilitator: Absorb this picture and let it continue to work. You will always be
   able to return to this image.

Some time later I received a postcard form the client. She wrote of how
a lot of things had changed in her life, and that she had taken the first
steps towards going freelance. She said the constellation had given her
great self-confidence.

   Since **situations as events** are only transitory, their removal from the
constellation picture symbolises the fact that they have passed and no
longer belong to the present system. As opposed to systemic elements –
e.g. family members, resources, goals – situations are external influences on a system. In our example, after the 'dismissal' of the situation,
the *five-year-old* can again be the *five-year-old* to the full, and without
being continually reminded of the situation. When the *focus* takes the
five-year-old into her arms, she integrates this aspect into herself. By
treating external influences and events like systemic members, we
appropriate them and find it difficult to part from them later on; we
adhere to them and remain under their influence. A constellation is a
good means of saying goodbye to situations that have mistakenly
become systemic elements in this way.

VI.3.2 Experiment 8
Think of a problem in which it would be useful to discover some additional resources. Mark out a nine square table on the floor, choose
something to represent yourself and something for your goal, and position both in the nine square table. Look at the squares marked on the

floor and check to see in which square a resource might first appear. Lay down a place marker for this resource and enter into a dialogue with it, changing places with it as you do so. Afterwards, check if other resources appear, and repeat the process.

When performing these exercises on your own, you may often become wrapped up and absorbed in the individual 'roles'. In a therapeutic situation, the therapist, as an outsider, will be able to help if this occurs. It is important during this experiment, therefore, that you always adopt a meta-position, which can be achieved by de-roling entirely after assuming each position and viewing the picture from the outside. Go as far as you can with this experiment. Even the smallest step forward represents progress. A small fragment of a constellation may still give rise to important changes.

VI.4 Nine and twelve square constellations as meta-constellations

A constellation becomes a meta-constellation when it serves as the framework for another constellation. Naturally not all forms of constellation are suited to this. The most suitable forms are those that have more general structures and allow for extension – e.g. the *belief polarity constellation, the goal approximation constellation* and *the tetralemma constellation.*

The *tetralemma constellation* (see also Chapter III.1.1.2.3.1), for example, allows a structural level change to a family structural constellation while still retaining the framework of the tetralemma throughout. The family constellation thus takes places within the structure of the tetralemma.

The advantage of this approach is that when the client has, for example, a decision issue, this can be positioned in the constellation directly and relevant family issues are allowed to show themselves. The client's issue need not be stated as a family issue and reformulated. Instead the facilitator can work with the issue on the structural level at which it shows itself. In a meta-constellation, if a family issue arises within the constellation, the corresponding people can be placed in the constellation and the family issues dealt with from within the meta-constellation, with the meta-constellation acting as a protective framework for the family constellation. The positions of the tetralemma as *locations* can, in many cases, act as sources of energy whose presence can reduce the intensity of the family constellation. The framework of the dilemma in the tetralemma constellation determines which part of a family constellation, say, is relevant to the problem. This can then be worked on, and subsequently the decision issue can be further dealt with in the meta-constellation.

The *belief polarity constellation* is also very suitable for use as a meta-constellation. In the belief polarity constellation, *knowledge* (cognition, clarity), *love* (trust, compassion) and *order* (duty, action) are positioned as the *locations* arranged in a triangle, with *wisdom* as a free element and the *focus* as the representative of the client. Within the framework of these energy sources, a family, organisation or political constellation can be performed. In all of these cases, the constellation within the constellation is strengthened by the energy sources, and particularly intense issues are reduced to a more tolerable level.

Both the *nine* and *twelve square constellation* and the *goal approximation constellation*, through their solution focused framework – i.e. the positioning of the *goal* and the *miracle* – provide a context in which it is easier to find a direction when resolving entanglements. Because the constellation also includes *that which becomes available*, after the problem is solved, i.e. in lieu of the suffering, entanglements or trauma etc., the client is then less likely to fall into a 'hole' when a burden is removed but there is still nothing in sight to replace it. Though the disappearance of a burden brings relief, it does not yet indicate a new direction. The *goal* and the *miracle*, on the other hand, represent what will exist after the entanglement has been released. The client gets a new orientation and begins to act accordingly. This is why clarifying what will be there when the suffering is gone represents such an important part of the preliminary interview.

An example of the *twelve square constellation* as a meta-constellation is given below using the second part of the preliminary interview from Chapter V.2.

VI.4.1 Case study 2: Combining the nine square constellation with a family constellation: where loyalty to the parents hinders professional advancement

Ms S. came to me for help in revising for her technical baccalaureate diploma examination, which she was re-sitting after having failed once and missed the examination another time because of illness.

In the initial interview she told me that her mother had very much wanted to be a teacher, but was unable to go to university after becoming pregnant with the client.

The constellation performed after the interview is given below. (The names of the representatives are shown in italics.)

Facilitator: I suggest that we do a constellation for your problem. This means that first you need to choose a symbol for yourself, and place it in a position that feels right to you. In the same way choose symbols for your exam and for 'what will happen afterwards', and place them so that it feels to you how they stand together. This will create a picture in the room of your internal view of the exam situation. Start by choosing the symbol for yourself.

The client nods and chooses a cushion.

Facilitator: Take the cushion in your hands and walk around the room until you feel you've found the right place, and then place the cushion on the floor.

The client goes around the room and then places the cushion on the floor.

Facilitator: What direction are you looking in from this position?

The client indicates a direction.

Facilitator: Now move to the position of the cushion and say in which direction you feel your future and your past lie.

The client indicates the direction of the *future* in front of her, and the *past* behind her. The facilitator marks the nine square table on the floor.

Facilitator: Where does the *distant future* start for you after the *exam*?

The client points to a position, which is then marked by the facilitator who explains the schema again:

Facilitator: This is your *present* ... this your *past* ... and here is the *near* and *distant future*. Imagine that to your right is everything that you experience externally: people, situations, events etc ... here in the present ... here in the past ... and here in the future. Imagine that to your left is everything that is inside you: your thoughts, emotions, physical processes and your perceptions, imagination etc ... here in the present ... here in the past ... and there in the future.

The client nods in agreement.

Facilitator: Now choose another cushion for your *goal* and put it in the place that feels right to you ... and indicate the direction in which the *goal* is looking.

The client follows these instructions. In the same way, the therapist instructs the client to position her exam, her studies and goldsmithery. This gives the following the picture:

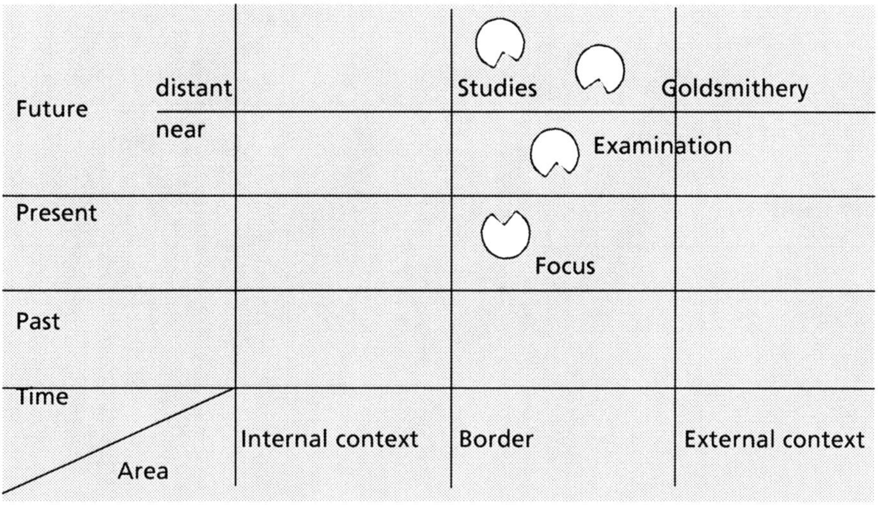

		Internal context	Border	External context

Figure 25

Facilitator: Now stand in your place, and see how you feel there. What are your bodily sensations?

Client: I feel my knees shaking, the *exam* frightens me, it's pressuring me, I don't like looking at it. I can't see the *studies* or the *goldsmithery*.

I decided to experiment with the theory that one part of her fear was caused by the proximity to the examination, and the other part by the fact that the client was unable to see what would follow. Based on this analysis, I first repositioned *examination, studies* and *goldsmithery*, resulting in the following picture:

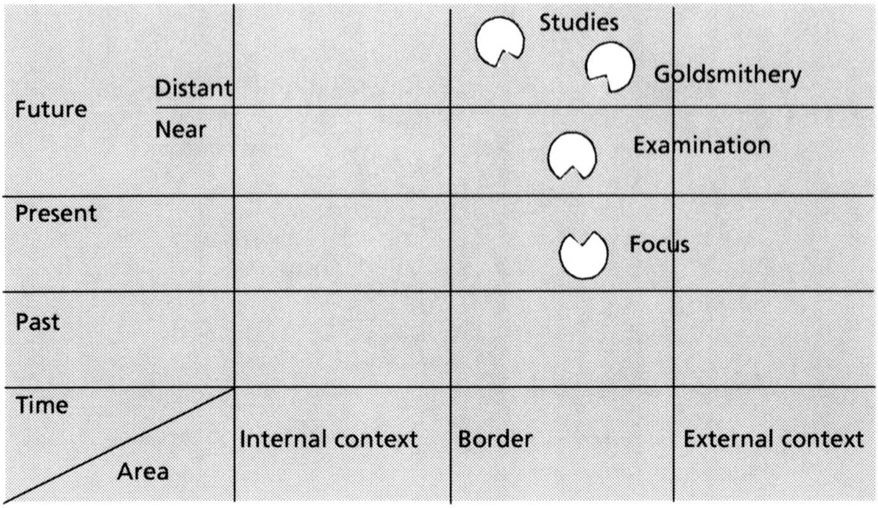

Time / Area	Internal context	Border	External context

Figure 26

Facilitator: What has changed for you?

Client: It feels good to see the *studies* and *goldsmithery*, it makes more sense, and from this position I can see the *exam* better.

Facilitator: Choose a symbol for your mother and again walk around the room with it. Find its right place is and indicate its line of sight.

The client walks around the room and eventually puts the symbol down, and we arrive at the following picture:

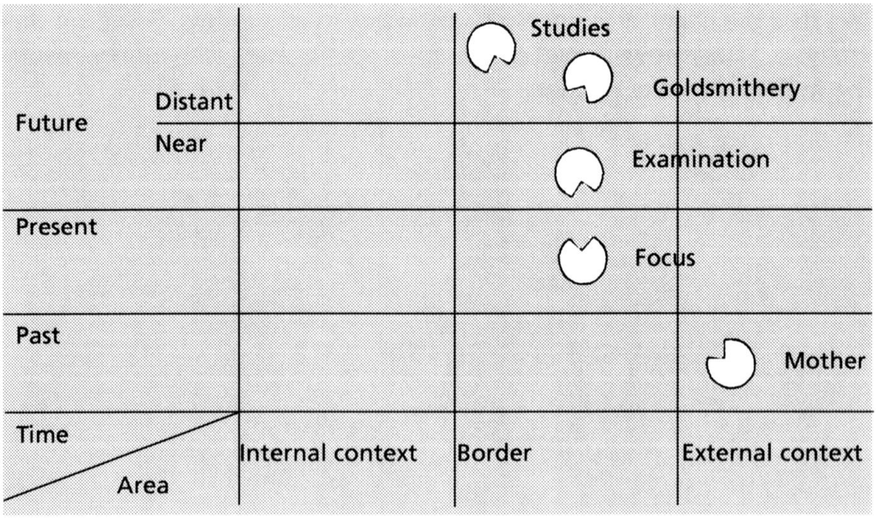

Figure 27

Facilitator: Now go back to your position, and see what has changed in the meantime.

Client: I feel someone behind me... a kind of pressure.

The client is now repositioned so that she makes eye contact with her *mother*.

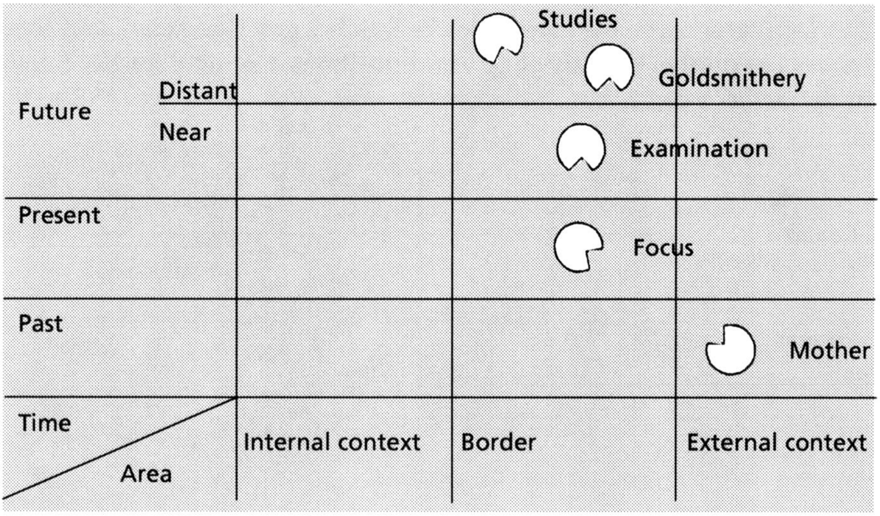

Figure 28

Facilitator: What has changed for you now?
Client: Now I can see my *mother*:
Facilitator: Say to your *mother*: 'Dear mother, even though you were unable to learn a profession, I am going to take this step now.'
The facilitator holds a cataleptic hand up to the *mother's* eyes level.

The client begins to cry and is finding it difficult to say the words.

Facilitator: 'Dear mother, even though you were unable to learn a profession, I am going to take this step now.'

The client repeats the words, crying.

Client: Now it's getting easier. But I'm afraid it will be too much for my mother.
Facilitator: Then move into your *mother's* position and see how she feels.

The client moves to the place of the *mother*, and the facilitator holds the cataleptic hand up at the position of the *focus*.

Client: From here it's OK. I can also see how my professional goals look to her.
Facilitator: Say to your *daughter*: 'It makes me very happy that you will do what I did not manage to do. You have my blessing.'

The client repeats the statement.

Facilitator: Change places again and take up your own position. How do you feel now?

Client: Much better. Now I believe that my mother is pleased. I couldn't imagine it before.

The facilitator turns the client back to face her *goal* (the *exam*), and then moves the mother slightly closer, and positions a symbol for her father to the *mother's* right.

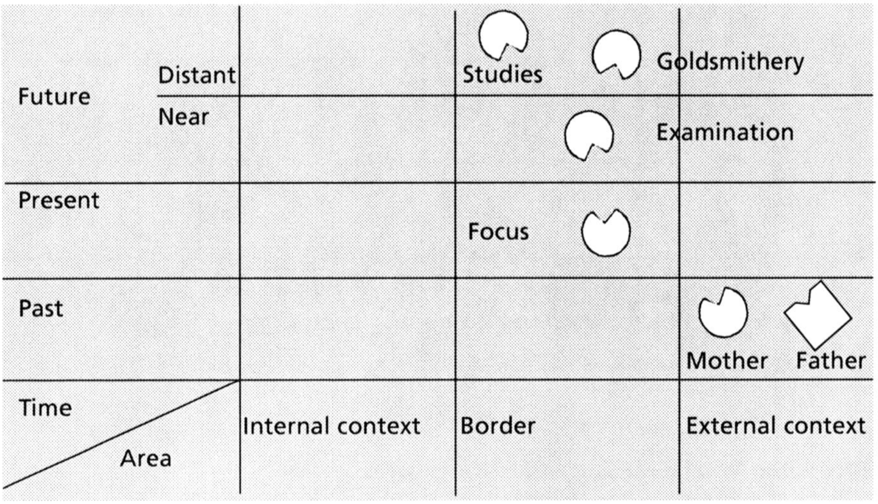

Time Area		Internal context	Border	External context
Future	Distant		Studies ◠	Goldsmithery
	Near			◠ Examination
Present			Focus ◡	
Past				◡ ◇ Mother Father

Figure 29

Facilitator: Now take another look behind you. Do you see how your *mother* and your *father* are supporting you?

The facilitator holds two cataleptic hands up to the parents' respective eye levels. The client nods.

Facilitator: Now again look towards your *exam*. What has changed?

Client: The *exam* is no longer threatening. I can look forward to my *studies*, and the *goldsmithery* also seems attractive. Now I again feel *hope* that I will pass the exam. I feel strengthened strongly from behind.

When the client speaks about *exam* and *studies*, she looks towards each of the representatives, and her unconscious will relate her statements to the real exam and her real studies. This induces the desired hypnotherapeutic effect. The continual switching between representatives and the represented works hypnotically, as if only the represented were being dealt with.

Facilitator: You can absorb this picture, and be open to the changes… and follow the impulses that arise as a result.

The client passed her exam and decided to pursue her studies.

VI.5 Using what has been for what is to come

Constellation work is based on the transmission of experiences. The constellation method can be used to bring back to the present and again make available experiences from the past in which the current goal had already been achieved – i.e. the exceptions to the problem. Though these 'solutions in the past' (see Chapter II.1.6) can be discovered in the solution focused interview, the intensity of the experience is much greater in constellation work.

A further opportunity is given by working with the timeline.

When the focus is taken back into the past on the timeline, long forgotten 'solutions in the past' may appear that the client did not remember during the interview. The combination of the solution focused interview and systemic structural constellations expands the chances of finding solutions in the past. This is demonstrated in the following nine square constellation.

VI.5.1 Case study 3: Fear of changes in the future

The following constellation was performed as part of a further education seminar.

Facilitator: What is your current problem?

S.: I'm finding it hard to make progress towards what I'd really like to achieve. Mostly I just make half-hearted efforts, or, like before, after a while it becomes all talk and no action. As soon as I come close to my goal I feel afraid.

Facilitator: What goal are you aiming for at the moment?

S.: I'd like to go freelance in my job.

Facilitator: What would this mean for you specifically?

S.: I'd have to give up the security of my current position or only work part time at most. And I'd have to find my own clients. I know that I'd find it much more fun doing freelance work and I know I'm capable of working more independently, but it still feels initially like jumping in at the deep end.

Facilitator: Have there been times in the past when were able to achieve your goals?

S.: Yes, but that was a long time ago.

Facilitator: I propose we perform a nine square constellation. For this you must first choose someone from the group to be your representative and then place that person in the room.

The client follows the facilitator's instructions and positions a representative.

Facilitator: Stand behind your representative, touch her on the shoulders, and see where you feel the future lies for you.

The participant points in the same direction as given by the line of sight of her representative.

Facilitator: Now feel where the past lies.

The participant points in the opposite direction.

Facilitator: In front of you lies the area of the *future*, and behind you the area of the *past*. Picture a timeline on which your representative is standing in the *present*. Imagine now that on your right-hand side, in a strip parallel to the timeline, lies everything that is external to you, e.g. other people, or areas like work or another country. On your left-hand side is everything that lies within you, e.g. sensations, thought, inner dialogues, belief statements, bodily reactions etc.

The participant nods.

Facilitator: Now choose someone from the group for your current goal, and then position it.

The participant chooses a representative for her goal and positions it in the constellation, resulting in the following picture:

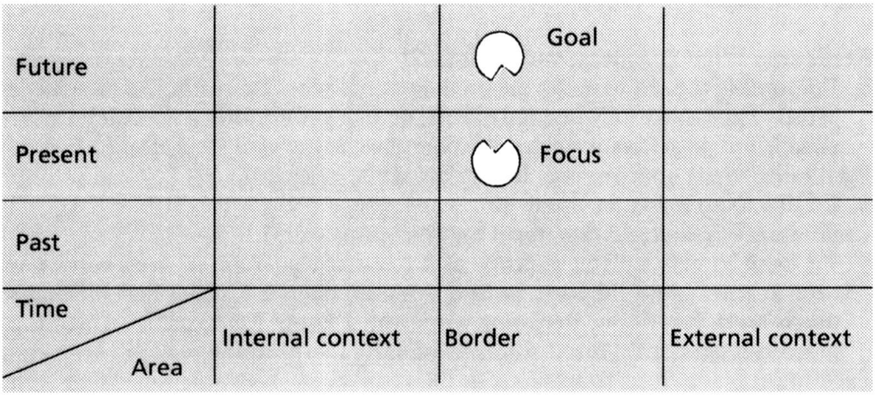

Time / Area	Internal context	Border	External context
Future		⌢ Goal	
Present		⌣ Focus	
Past			

Figure 30

Facilitator (to *focus*): How do you feel?
Focus: I see the *goal*, but I don't feel balanced.
Facilitator: Take a step towards the *goal*. What changes for you?
Focus: I feel unsettled and afraid. I don't know what is going to happen.
Facilitator (to S.): Does that correspond with how you feel?

S.: Yes, exactly. I don't know how things will change when I reach this *goal*, and that frightens me.

Facilitator: Assuming, you'd already achieved this *goal*, how would you notice this?

S.: I'd have the feeling I could finally take decisions on my own, and that I'd have enough customers.

Facilitator: And if it happened that there were fewer customers although the problem had already been solved, what would you do then?

S.: I'd probably do some advertising, send out brochures, and then I'd probably wait and see ... That's what I'm afraid of, that I won't find enough customers.

Facilitator: And if your problem were now solved, how would you deal with things then?

S.: I don't know.

Facilitator: (nods and remains silent)

S. (shaking head): Nothing occurs to me... I've no idea.

Facilitator: (nods and remains silent)

S.: (continues to shake head)

Facilitator: Place that in the constellation as well, the thing that will be your new task afterwards.

The seminar participant chooses and positions another representative from the group, resulting in the following picture:

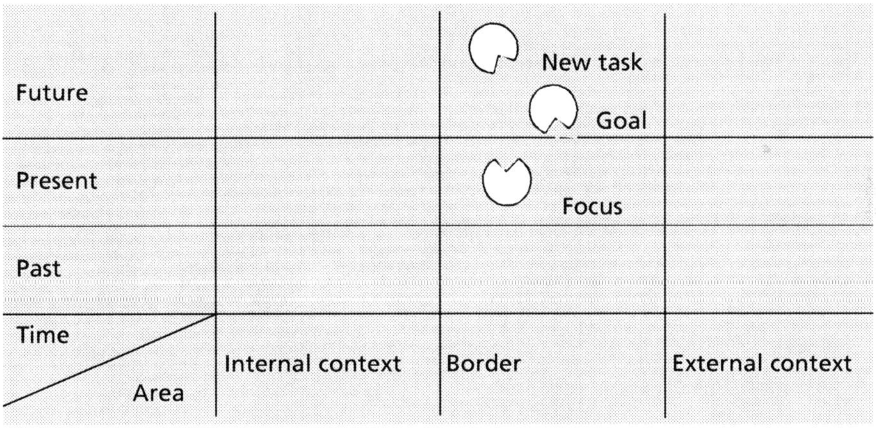

Time / Area		Internal context	Border	External context
Future			New task, Goal	
Present			Focus	
Past				

Figure 31

Facilitator: What has changed for the *focus*?
Focus: It feels good when something else appears behind the *goal*, but the *new task* frightens me.
Facilitator: Take another step towards your *goal*. What changes?
Focus: The fear increases.
Facilitator: How does the *new task* feel?
Task: My view of the *focus* is foggy.
Facilitator: Go a few steps back into the *past* and stop when you reach the situation where you can approach the future, even though you didn't know what it looks like.

The *focus* moves backwards, step by step and eyes closed, and then comes to a halt.

Focus: From here I can see easily towards the *goal*, as if there existed nothing else for me.
Facilitator: (to S.): Can you remember this situation?
S.: It occurs to me now that I used to tell myself: 'The goal is the solution.' Later I had experiences in which things were very different. I saw that when I reached the goal, that wasn't the final solution and new problems could arise. Before I used to think, when I reach that stage everything will be OK. Now I know that solutions are usually very limited.
Facilitator: Choose and place another representative for the statement: 'The goal is the solution'.

The participant follows these instructions, and we arrive at the following picture:

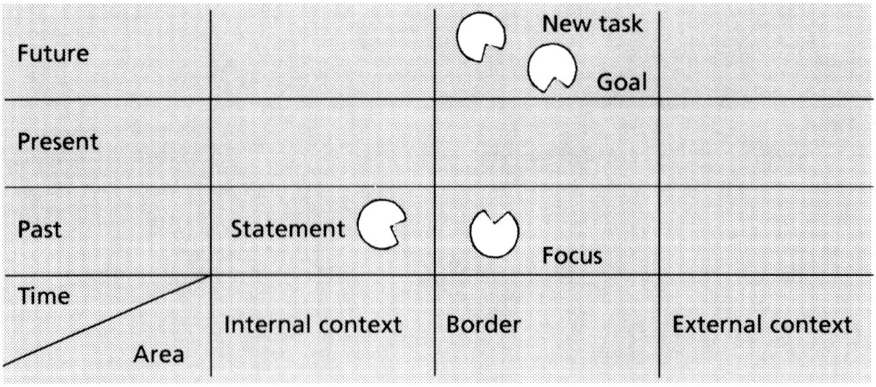

Time / Area	Internal context	Border	External context
Future		New task / Goal	
Present			
Past	Statement	Focus	

Figure 32

Facilitator: What has changed for the focus?

Focus: I can hardly feel the *statement*.

Facilitator: Say to the *statement*: 'You have given me much energy. You helped me take steps towards my goal.'

The *focus* looks towards the *statement* and repeats the words.

Facilitator (to *focus*): What has changed for you?

Focus: I have more energy and can see the *goal* better.

Facilitator: Take a step towards the *goal*.

Focus: That's easier now, and I can also see towards the *new task* … My fear is gone.

Facilitator (to S.): You can now take the position of your representative, and your representative can sit down. Look around, and feel how far you can move towards your *goal*.

The representative and S. change places. S. moves slowly towards her *goal*.

Facilitator: The *statement* can also turn round now look towards the *goal* together with the focus. (To S.) You can always look around to your *statement* and then turn back to your *goal*… How do you feel now?

S.: I began to feel a comforting warmth when I moved towards my *goal*. This is now a good place for me. I can see my *goal* clearly as an orientation, and the *new task* behind it gives me strength. I can feel the positive effects of the *statement* from behind, but the *new task* is becoming more important for me.

Facilitator: Take this picture and absorb it, place your hands over your heart as a sign that you have received the picture. Everything else can occur in the outside world.

Following the constellation the participant reported finding it easier to approach new ideas and perform tasks.

Chapter VII

The goal approximation constellation

The goal approximation constellation is an abridged version of the nine square constellation. It can be supplemented to create a nine square constellation. Being simpler than the nine square constellation, it is often easier for the client to follow.

VII.1 The components of the goal approximation constellation

The goal approximation is made up of the following parts:

- the focus (representative)
- a timeline (non-personal location)
- the goal (representative)
- the miracle (representative)
- the context of the miracle, e.g. excluded people (representatives)

The first three parts feature in all goal approximation constellations. Since every constellation is conducted from a given perspective – i.e. the perspective of the client – it is important to include the *focus* as the representative of the client, as well as the parts specific to the particular type of constellation in use.

A constellation, therefore, does not show reality in itself, but reality as seen from the perspective of the person beholding it. A constellation thus says something about the view of the client, and nothing about any general reality. Of course, the client's view may happen to coincide with the perspectives that arise during a constellation, but this is not inevitable.

VII.1.1 The perspectives of the constellation

Constellations are not objective in terms of their levels of interpretation and symbolism; they are performed from the client's perspective, as determined by her problem. Initially, we are dealing with the perspective of:

1. the client vis-à-vis her problem

This is followed by the further internal perspectives of:

2. the client's representative or 'protagonist' (i.e.the focus)
3. the other representatives
4. actual system members who may also be present
5. present participating observers
6. present scientifically interested observers
7. present hostile observers

The protagonist adopts a special attitude, since it is in the solution picture of the constellation that solutions to the conflict must appear – while the remaining representatives need receive only indications of which processes still need to be performed. The representatives should still be able to voice their reactions, but these can be put to one side with the comment, 'This is now relevant to so and so … but not to the current context.' The protagonist's wishes thus receive more attention than those of the other representatives.

Any system members present are relevant in so far as the client is not able to be quite as free in front of, say, family members, as compared with being alone, due to expected consequences. Participating and particularly any hostile observers will also influence the constellation to the extent that the client may withhold some of the more intimate aspects of her present situation, and the facilitator must also consider the client's need for protection in what she says.

Besides these internal influences, other external influences on the constellation must also be allowed for, for example:

8. absent family members
9. absent hostile or critical third parties
10. absent referring agent
11. absent and intended recipients of reports

Not only present observers, but also absent observers, who have been told about the constellation, or will be able to observe change in the client's behaviour, or read reports of the constellation, are relevant for the constellation.

The reactions of these groups to the results of the constellation may affect the client retroactively. If these five perspectives are not taken into account, the client may suffer from the reactions of these absent parties, so that the positive effects of the constellation are endangered. If the reactions of absent referring agents – e.g. doctors or parents – are not taken into consideration, the client may become frustrated by their potentially hostile reactions, and again the effects of the constellation may fade into the background. If, on the other hand, these potentially negative reactions are included, the client is then able to prepare for them in advance.

Absent affected people, such as colleagues and the client's children, who will directly experience a change in the client's behaviour, may react in a surprised, hostile or pleased manner. It is again important that the client thinks carefully about whom she discusses the constellation with. For example, she should refrain from discussing the pros and cons of constellations in general with people who are critical of them , so as to avoid losing contact with her own experience.

VII.1.2 Establishing the timeline

The timeline, similar to the nine square constellation, can be established in different ways, such as:

- the therapist/facilitator marks out the timeline on the floor
- the client detects which position in the room feels right for her and then senses where future and past lie
- the client positions her representative (the *focus*) first, who then states where future and past lie.

In the first case, the timeline provided acts as a grid along which the representatives can be placed and to which their unconscious (and conscious) reactions may be aligned. In the second case, we learn some-thing about the topography of the client's internal temporal structure. In the third case, instead of the client, the *focus* is asked to provide the timeline. However, my experience is that the format of the timeline given by the client and the *focus* is nearly always the same.

The areas '*present*', '*future*' and '*past*' are marked on the timeline , all three questions being asked separately (i.e. independently of each other in their outcome) by the client or the *focus*. We call this a **three-part coding of the timeline**.

VII.1.3 Introducing the goal and the miracle

Before introducing the goal to the constellation, it is important to find out what exists instead of the problem. The goal needs to be formulated positively, be divisible in small steps and realistic. It should also be remembered that it is the client's goal that is important, and not that of the referring agent or family members (see Chapter II.1.5.1).

A representative for the miracle may also be added, especially where the goal is too short-term. The miracle will then provide a longer-term perspective.

When the *miracle* enters the constellation it may initially be very weak. This is particularly the case where the context of the miracle is very burdensome, as, for example, when a person's return to health, with the energy and professional activity this implies, is greeted by rivalry and envy. In this case, it is advisable to split the miracle into '*miracle*' and '*context of the miracle*'. This allows the power of the miracle to reassert itself fully through the '*miracle*'.

VII.1.4 Extending the constellation to include excluded people

The context of the miracle includes all the people who react to the change in the client, as well as all those who belong to the client's past context, such as excluded people. A constellation should also always include those who react negatively.

Sometimes the dynamic of a problem only becomes clear when excluded people are brought into the constellation. We can then feel what effect they have on the *goal*, and if they do not affect the *goal*, this can be taken as an indication that they no longer play a role in the problem, or have already been integrated by different means. Verifying whether the addition of excluded people affects the *goal* demonstrates to the client that the process being followed is not theory-based, but that a particular emphasis is placed on testing hypotheses. The constellation corrects our mistakes in different ways and opening up new hypothetical avenues.

If many excluded people are added, a de facto family constellation will take place within the *goal approximation constellation*. This 'family constellation' has undergone a change to its grammar and now contains a *timeline*. We call this a *family structural constellation* so as to distinguish it from the standard family constellation.

If a *family structural constellation* takes place within a *goal approximation constellation*, we describe this goal approximation structure as a *meta-constellation* for the *family structural constellation*. The difference between this and the standard family constellation is defined by the addition of at least one *timeline* and the *goal*. This emphasises the new direction already hinted at by the *goal*.

The goal need not necessarily be specified clearly at this stage. This gives an advantage over the solution focused interview, because we are still able to move towards a goal, even when the client is unable to describe her goal. In terms of visitor-type interaction between client and therapist, this form of the *goal approximation constellation* also offers an opportunity to become acquainted with a new direction or goal. The *timeline* then helps the client pursue her desire to move towards to her goal with more certainty.

Different aspects of the *goal approximation constellation* will now be demonstrated below using various different case studies.

VII.2 Case study 1: What the miracle needs to become reality

This case comes from a higher education seminar. It provides an informative example of the role of the miracle in the *goal approximation constellation*. The miracle in a constellation has the function of guiding the client beyond her narrow goals. The participant in this particular case was finding it difficult to give a precise answer to the miracle question. I therefore recommended a constellation using two parts, the *focus* and the *miracle*. The participant selected two representatives from the group and positioned them as shown below.

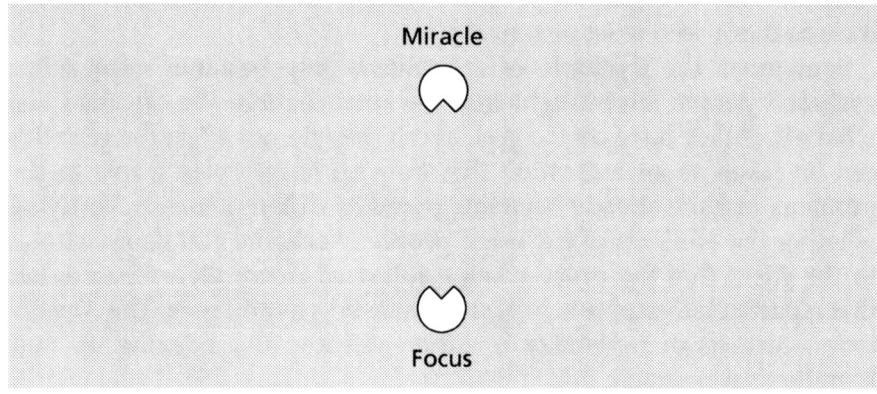

Figure 33

Facilitator: How is the *focus* feeling?
Focus: I have to keep looking at the floor. I can't feel the *miracle*.
Facilitator: How is the *miracle*?
Miracle: I also have no contact with the *focus*.
Facilitator (to *focus*): Try and look at the *miracle*!

The constellation starts with process work, since the positioning of the two representatives is already suitable for this.

Focus: Even when I look towards it, there's no contact.
Facilitator: Try and take a small step in the direction of the *miracle*.
Focus: That's very, very hard. I don't consider the *miracle* realistic.
Miracle: I'm still not present. I need to be believed in to come into existence.

It can be surprising what philosophical statements we hear from representatives and how clearly they are able to describe processes! This demonstrates that constellations are always an interesting activity.

Facilitator (to *focus*): How did you feel when the *miracle* said that?
Focus: It's true, I'm not able to believe in the *miracle*.
Facilitator (to *focus*): Say that to the *miracle*.
Focus: I'm not yet able to believe in you.
Facilitator: What changes for the *focus*?
Focus: It's a bit clearer to me now.
Facilitator: What changes for the *miracle*?
Miracle: It feels good when the *focus* admits to her lack of trust. It makes things clearer.
Facilitator (to *focus*): Take another step towards the *miracle*.
Focus: It's a little easier now… But then I have to move back.
Facilitator: Yes, take a step back again. Sometimes we have to go back and forth to be able to move closer.

Here the facilitator sows the idea that the client can in the future take a step back, provided the orientation is maintained.

Focus: (takes a step back): Now I feel better.
Facilitator: What's different in this position now compared with before?
Focus: Now I'm able to look at the *miracle*, even if it's still far away.
Facilitator: What has changed for the *miracle*?
Miracle: I'm slowly coming into being. I'm finding my feet.
Facilitator: How does the *focus* feel when he hears that?
Focus: I also feel more stable. It feels good to see the *miracle*.
Miracle: I'm feeling more grounded.
Facilitator (to *focus*): Take another step forward and afterwards take a small step back. How does that feel?
  Focus: It feels good to able to take a step back again.
Facilitator: It's perfectly OK to move back and forth. Everyone needs their own time and their own way of moving closer.

Here the facilitator again points out that it's quite normal to take a step backwards. This conveys the idea indirectly to the client that what she is doing is correct and she can lose her self-doubt.

Facilitator: How is the *miracle* feeling now?
Miracle: I think the distance is right now. I've got my feet firmly on the ground.
Facilitator: We can check this. (To *focus*) Take another small step forwards.

The *focus* follows the instruction. The *miracle* gestures that this is too close.

Facilitator (to *focus*): Go back to your previous position. We can't go any further here. (To *focus*) How do you feel now?

Focus: This position is good. I can see the *miracle* now and have contact to it.
Facilitator (to client): Now take the place of your *focus*.

The *focus* de-roles, and the client takes her place.

Facilitator: How do you feel there?
Client: Good. I feel much lighter than before. It's very new for me to be able to look at the *miracle*. (Starts to cry)
Facilitator: Say to the *miracle*: 'I see you now for the first time. You are very new to me.'

The client repeats the words, beaming and clearly moved.

Facilitator: You can take this picture now and let its effects continue to work on you in your heart. Follow the impulses it gives rise to.

This constellation demonstrates clearly how approximation processes can be performed directly. The timeline makes the dynamic of the process clearer. The constellation was performed in the form of a conversation, in which approach and doubt alternated, and the reactions of the *focus* were dealt with on each occasion with positional changes or ritual statements.

Besides demonstrating the client's individual nature, the constellation also showed what the miracle required in order to become reality: it needed to be seen and accepted as true to become reality. The approximation process in this constellation is also a metaphor for the realisation of miracles.

VII.3 Case study 2: Different constellations in one course of therapy

The following case took place over four therapy sessions, performed in different groups and in different locations. This might seem an unusual arrangement, but since many of my clients must travel long distances, and since I also travel a lot due to my frequent seminar work, it is possible to combine both. I set the frequency of therapy sessions according to the client's needs, and larger intervals are common. The four sessions described below all took place within the space of one year. The problem dealt with was heavy abdominal pains and premenstrual syndrome (PMS) which the client had been suffering from for around ten years. Repeated surgical intervention had only brought short-term relief, and the client was therefore very keen to try other solutions. She was also faced with the dilemma of whether to accept a new employment position she had been offered, which she found attractive, but her fear was that she would be hampered by her constant pains.

This was the main topic of the first session, while the following three sessions dealt with relationship problems. (The names of the representatives are again shown in italics.)

First session
Facilitator: What is your current problem?
Client: I've been suffering extremely heavy pains for some years, especially during my period, but also at other times. This limits me, and I find it very hard to plan anything in advance. The pain can always get in the way.
Facilitator: What did the doctors have to say?
Client: Well, I have adhesions, due to the many operations I've had, and I have a tendency to form cysts. Some of these were operated on, after which I would feel better, but only for a short while.
Facilitator: I'm going ask you now what is perhaps a difficult question: When you go back home tomorrow and tell your boyfriend about the constellation group, and perhaps you then do something nice together … and finally in the evening you feel tired and go to bed … and assuming during the night a miracle occurs … and in one fell swoop the problem that brought you here was solved … and that really would be a miracle, wouldn't it? … And then you wake up the next morning … and no one tells you that this miracle has occurred, how would you notice it when you wake up in the morning?
Client: … I'd get up feeling full of energy and would no longer feel the pain.
Facilitator: What would be there instead of the pain?
Client: I'd feel strong and healthy, I'd be more adventurous. I'd let myself be, I'd be more myself. I'd also approach Peter more.
Facilitator: How would he react to this?
Client: He'd be pleased. That's something he really wishes for.
Facilitator: What else would be different?
Client: I'd feel confident of having a child, something Peter would want as well.
Facilitator: And apart from that, is there anything else that would change?
Client: I was recently offered a new position that I'd very much like to accept. But as long as I have these pains that won't be possible. However, it is a good opportunity for me.
Facilitator: And anything else?
Client: I'd generally let myself be more, I'd be more approachable.
Facilitator: How would friends, colleagues and people you know react to this?
Client: They'd be pleasantly surprised. They often find it difficult when I retreat into myself.

In terms of the consequences of the miracle, the client only mentions positive reactions. This may indicate the existence of an entanglement.

Facilitator: Is there someone in your family who died very young or in tragic circumstances?
Client: … I can't think of anyone.
Facilitator: I propose that we perform a **constellation of the excluded topic** for you. Choose someone from the group for you…and someone for the official topic, your pain. You spoke about your pain. We will take for the official topic your body part where the pain is: for warmth. Now also choose someone for the defocused topic. In your case, this will be *the subject of the pain*.

Client: I want to also constellate Peter.
Facilitator: Choose a representative for Peter. This topic is important for both of you. Now constellate the representative.

The client chooses the representatives from the group and places them one by one in the constellation. This results in the following initial picture (again the ⌐ symbol stands for male representatives and the ◯ symbol for female representatives):

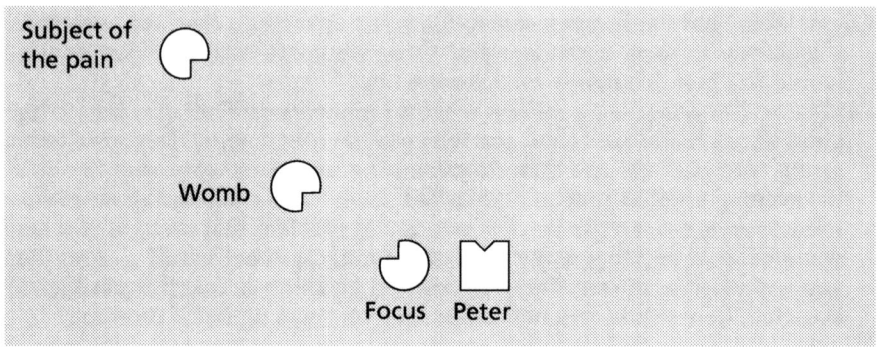

Figure 34

Facilitator: How does the *focus* feel?
Focus: I feel cramped, crowded and threatened. I don't want to look in front of me at all.
Facilitator: How is *Peter*?
Peter: I am happy to support her (the client).
Facilitator: How is *the subject of the pain*?
Subject of the pain: I feel strong and would very much like to see more of the *focus*.
Facilitator: How is the *womb*?
Womb: I feel very cramped here, I feel very bad.

Since the *womb* is covering *the subject of the pain*, I now rearrange the representatives so the focus can see past the *womb* (on its left-hand side) to *the subject of the pain* and so the *womb* is looking in the same direction as focus.

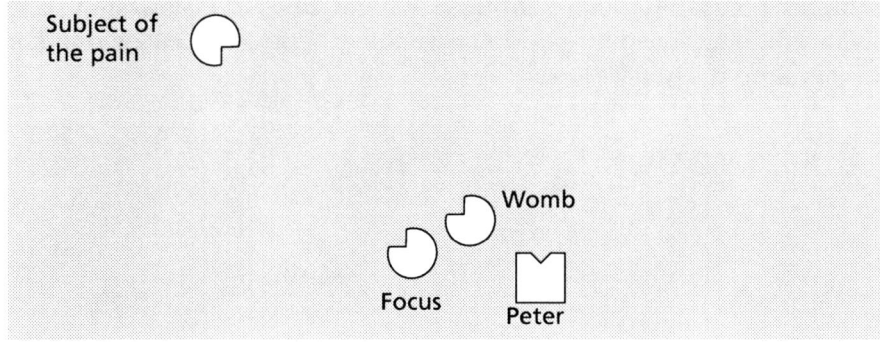

Figure 35

Facilitator: What has changed for the *focus*?
Focus: I feel threatened in this position (looking at *the subject of the pain*).
Facilitator: How is the *womb*?
Womb: A little better. It's good to no longer have *the subject of the pain* behind me. It's better to be able to see it.
Facilitator: How is *Peter*?
Peter: I'd like to have her closer to me. I feel uneasy about the others.
Facilitator: How is *the subject of the pain*?
Subject of the pain: I feel very affectionate towards the *focus*.
Facilitator (to *focus*): Change places with *the subject of the pain*.

The *focus* and *the subject of the pain* change places.

Facilitator: How do you feel there?
Focus: Much better.
Facilitator: Then switch places again.

This successful testing for partial pattern representation was then followed by a ritual to disrupt it: the *focus* walks very slowly towards *the subject of the pain* until she is placed by the therapist next to *the subject of the pain*.

Facilitator: What has changed now?
Focus: I feel clearer.
Facilitator: Now go back to your original positions. (To *focus*) How do you feel now?
Focus: The threat is now gone.
Facilitator (to client): Can you think who this could be (*the subject of the pain*)?
Client: ... My great grandmother died shortly after giving birth to her sixth child at the age of 35.
Facilitator: That's relevant. We'll now rename *the subject of the pain* as the *great grandmother*.

Here we have an **explicit structural level change** to a **partial family**

structural constellation combined with a body constellation. The focus is strengthened by positioning another representative behind her to represent the female line.

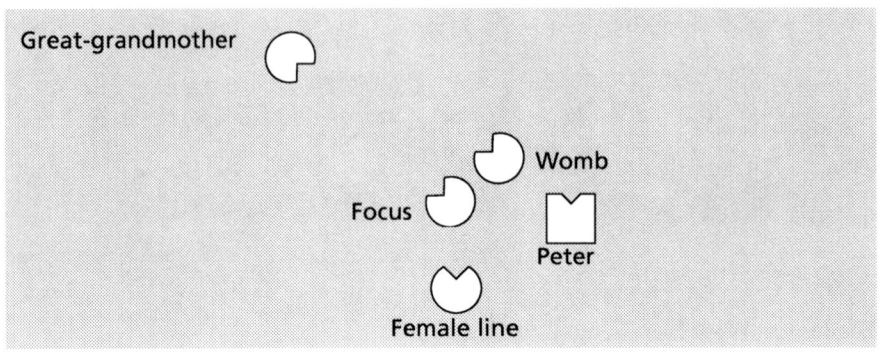

Figure 36

Facilitator: (to *focus*): Say to your *great grandmother*: 'You are my great grand-mother, and I'm your great granddaughter. A lot of your difficult fate has reached me. It has affected me strongly, and I have suffered a lot. This that I received from you, I will now leave with you – all of it. I will honour you from now on in a different way, by making room for you in my heart and letting myself feel better from now on. You can be pleased for me and for my success.'

The *focus* repeats these words. The representative and the client both begin to cry.

Facilitator: How is the *great grandmother*?
Great grandmother: I like my *great granddaughter a lot*. I wish her great success.
Facilitator (to *focus*): How do you feel now?
Focus: I'm very relieved. It touches me to see my *great granddaughter*.
Facilitator: How is the *womb*?
Womb: Very much better, freer, relieved. I feel at ease with the *focus*.
Facilitator: How does the *female line* feel?
Female line: I'm happy here supporting the *focus*.

The facilitator instructs the client to move into the position of the *focus*.

Facilitator: Look at your *great grandmother*, and see how she is well disposed towards you. Maybe you can put up a picture of her. Look at your *womb*: it feels at ease with you. Look at *Peter*: he supports you. Now absorb this picture as it is, and let it take effect.

Second session
The second session took place four months later.

Facilitator: What has improved since we met saw each other?
Client: I already felt an enormous sense of relief during the train journey home.
  My hopes were raised that I'd be able to get well again. The doctors' prog-
  noses were always so bad, and I'd given up all hope of it getting better. The
  pain has decreased with time: it's less intense and less frequent. For
  example, I can now sit down for longer without the pain starting. My confidence in my own body has increased. The contact with my great
  grandmother makes me stronger. I put up a picture of her and, without my
  telling her about the constellation, my mother also put up a picture of the
  same great grandmother. I also accepted the new employment position, and
  I'm really enjoying it. I'm more active now. To remember the constellation, I
  often place my hands on my stomach, in the position where the representative for the great grandmother touched me. That always helps soothe me.
Facilitator: What's your problem today?
Client: I want clarity. I want to stand with my feet firmly on the floor. I want to
  be clearer in my relationship with Peter, and not to be always darting off
  here and there.
Facilitator: Assuming you already had clarity, how would you notice this?
Client: I'd be able to say: 'I want this, and I don't want that.' I could set limits
  and talk about myself and be enthusiastic, and not just drift along with the
  stream.
Facilitator: Were there times in the past when things between you and Peter
  were clear?
Client: Yes, when I was spontaneously happy and I let myself go.
Facilitator: Any other times?
Client: No, not without a great deal of effort and hard work. Getting involved
  in a relationship is very stressful for me.
Facilitator: And how do you feel when you do?
Client: Sometimes it's a relief, but usually I'm just stressed by having to show
  myself.
Facilitator: Is there any other relationship in which you have clarity?
Client: Yes, with my friend Constance, and with my brother. Those relation-
  ships are defined. It's very easy and makes me feel good. I don't feel stressed
  that I have to show myself, I'm in tune with it.
Facilitator: And what's different with the friend?
Client: Maybe it's because she lives a long way away and I don't see her daily,
  and because she herself has a lot of clarity.
Facilitator: Do you remember the miracle question, that happened over night?
  (Client nods) ... How would you notice that the problems that brought you
  here were solved?
Client: I'd feel it in my body. It would be more solid, more integrated. I'd be
  able to feel it in a more integral way.
Facilitator: How would Peter notice that the miracle had happened?
Client: From my look: I'd look at him more directly, and from my voice, which
  would be fuller and deeper... and my body, my posture would be more
  upright.
Facilitator: What else?

Client: I'd be keener to tell him about my things, the things that belong to me. I'd have a clearer conscience.

Facilitator: Would anyone else notice?

Client: Yes, my colleagues at work.

Facilitator: What would they notice?

Client: My clear-cut manner. I'd make fewer jokes, would cooperate more and have a more open view. I'd show myself more.

Facilitator: How would your colleagues react to this?

Client: Most would be pleased, but some would be envious and there could be some misunderstandings.

Facilitator: How would you deal with this?

Client: I'd wait and see what happens first, and then decide with whom I wanted to have more contact and who not.

Facilitator: Now I want to ask you a completely different question: Did either you or Peter have any previous relationships?

Client: I was engaged once. He left me, though I gave him no reason to. After the separation I felt down for a long time. Peter had two previous relationships, both of which ended on good terms. We keep in contact with both of his previous girlfriends.

Facilitator: Good, I'll keep that in mind. I propose now to perform a **goal approximation constellation**. What do you want to call your goal?

Client: 'Clarity, directness and clear conscience.'

Facilitator: Choose someone to be your representative and someone to be your goal, and then place them in the constellation.

The client chooses the representatives and places them in the constellation, giving the first picture:

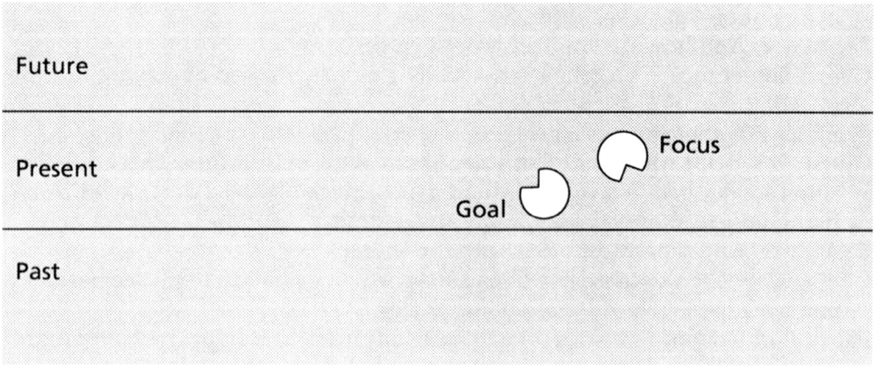

Figure 37

Facilitator (to *focus*): Where for you is your future?

Focus: (Points behind her).

Facilitator (to *focus*): And the past?

Focus: (Indicates the direction in front of her).

By no means do timelines always follow a straight line. Sometimes the client's timeline can be bent, and the positioning of the other representatives in the constellation need to be interpreted accordingly.

Facilitator: How is the *focus*?
Focus: I used to have autonomy, but that's lost now. Ever since the *goal* has been there I can feel a chill in my jaw and in my right shoulder.
Facilitator: How does the *goal* feel?
Goal: I have no orientation. I can't see upwards.
Focus: When the *goal* speaks it sounds like its coming from offstage.

The facilitator places the *goal* in the *future* and tells the client to introduce her *great grandmother* and *great great grandmother* in order to check that the great grandmother, who died shortly after giving birth, has been fully integrated into the client's internal picture.

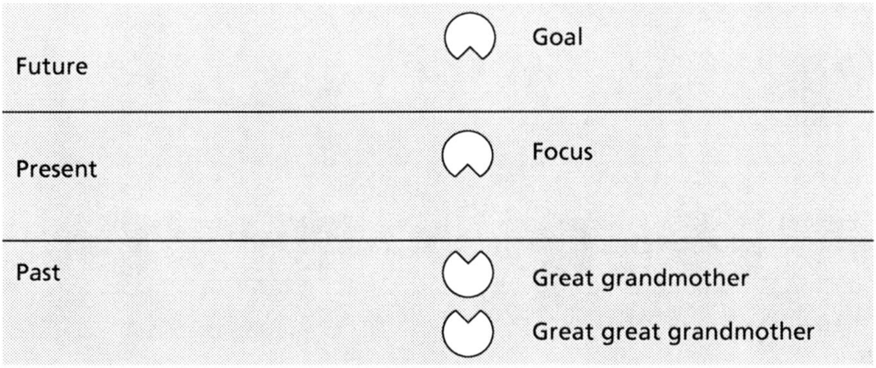

Figure 38

Facilitator: What has changed for the *focus*?
Focus: I feel comfortable, as if I'm in a trance the whole time.
Facilitator: How is the *great grandmother* and her mother?
Great grandmother: I'm also in trance. I like her (the *focus*).
Great great grandmother: I'm far away.
Goal: I'm getting angry now.

The facilitator turns the *focus* around to face the *goal*.

Focus: This is very new. She (the *goal*) has a posture (hands on hips) that I'm unfamiliar with. I'm confused.
Goal: I want to seduce her to life: like a young lover, I want to show her how beautiful life is – how vital and exciting. (To *focus*) I'm a part of you, I'm well-meaning and have strength for you. My appearance is so that you can take control of your own life.
Focus: I'm still waking up.

The *focus* looks around to the *great grandmother* and the *great great grand-mother*. The facilitator instructs the *focus* to say to them: 'Please look kindly on me, when I now turn towards my own direction.'

Focus: Please look kindly on me when I now turn in my direction.

The *great grandmother* and the *great great grandmother* nod in agreement.

Great grandmother: What you found in me in the past you will also find in the future in your goal.
Great great grandmother: It's good that you have strength and are moving into the future, that you're moving forwards.
Focus: That's nice, but I don't know if I want to.
Goal: I am ready to give her everything she needs to come (into the future).
Focus: I need support.

The facilitator instructs the client to introduce *Peter*.

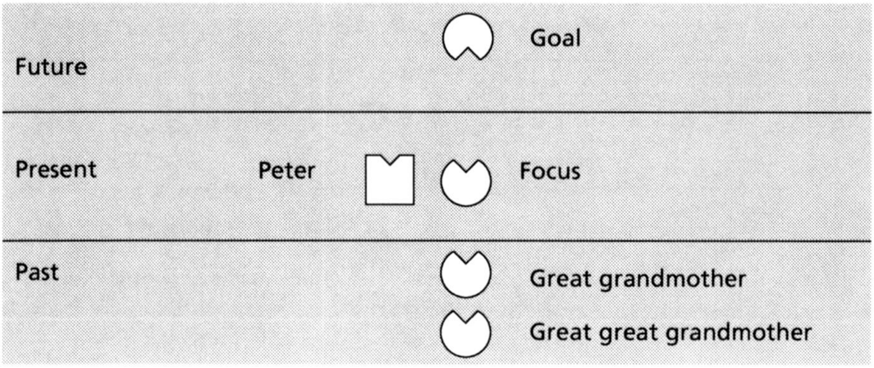

Figure 39

Facilitator: How does *Peter* feel?
Peter: I'm focused on her (the *focus*).
Facilitator: Did anyone feel a change when *Peter* was added?
Focus: It's OK to have *Peter* next to me, the *goal* is now interesting.

The facilitator moves *Peter* over to the right-hand side of the *focus*.

Facilitator: Is there any improvement?
Focus: I feel a sharp pain, this is risky.
Goal: I don't want the *focus* only to align herself to *Peter*.

The *focus* and *Peter* look at each other. The facilitator instructs both of them to move towards the *goal*. However, the representatives announce that they are unable to do this. The facilitator then asks the client to position a *goal* for *Peter* opposite to him. This changes the constellation into a **multi-focal constellation** with an absent second client. We are now working with two systems, and in order to ensure their smooth interaction, it is important that neither system receives appreciably more attention than the other. It is therefore recommended, as in this example, to introduce the goal and, where appropriate, the family line for the second system.

Facilitator: It can be helpful if each is able to move towards his own *goal*.

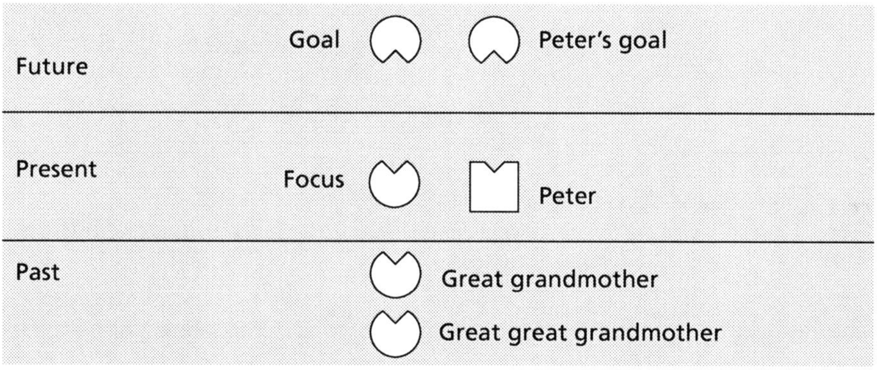

Figure 40

Peter: Now I feel stronger.
Focus: I'm happy that his *goal* is looking towards him, and mine towards me.
Goal: I'll look after her well, whatever happens.

The facilitator tells the client to take the position of her representative.

Goal: I feel incredibly strong, I can start to give myself.
Client: I have the feeling that Peter thinks I am going to let him down or even leave him when I start to move (towards the *goal*).
Facilitator (to client): Say to him: 'Even when I move towards my goal, I will still be with you.'

The client says these words to *Peter*. The facilitator then asks *Peter* to say how he feels on hearing these words.

Peter: I feel rather neutral. I have nothing against the *goal*, I don't mind if she goes.
Client: I don't believe him. When I look at him I start to cry.

The facilitator asks the client's representative (the *focus*) to return to the position occupied by the client and asks the client to add a representative for her former fiancé.

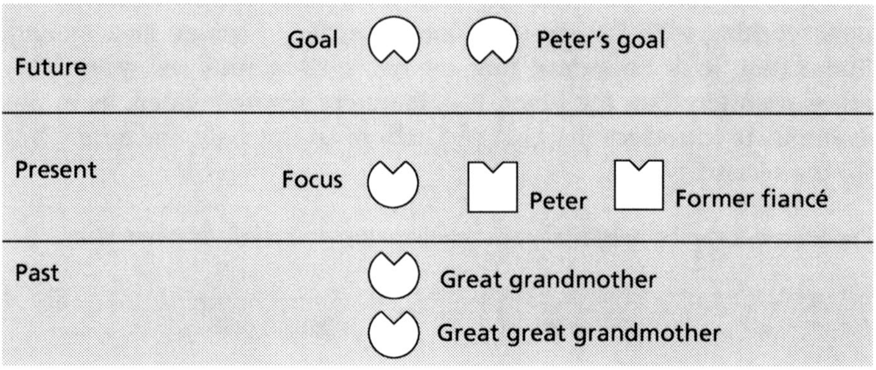

Figure 41

Facilitator: Who feels a change?
Focus: I feel depressed by my *former fiancé*. But I only have contact with *Peter*.
Peter: It feels as if I had done something.

The facilitator tells the focus to say to her *fiancé*, 'You were very important to me, you remain my "first",' and, to *Peter*, 'He came before you, and you came after.'

Focus to *fiancé*: You were very important to me, you remain my first.
The *fiancé* nods, pleased.
Focus to *Peter*: He was before you, and you came afterwards.
Peter (nodding): That is clear to me.

The facilitator tells *Peter* to say to the *fiancé*: 'You were before me, and I only came after you.'

Peter: You were before me, and I only came afterwards.
Facilitator: Has anything changed for anyone?
Focus: I feel relieved that he (the *former fiancé*) is no longer angry with me. I feel stronger and am able to move towards my *goal* now.
Peter: Things are clear like this, more complete.
Fiancé: I feel I've been seen and respected.

The facilitator tells the client to say to her *former fiancé*: 'Please, look kindly on me, when I move towards my goal.' The client repeats the statement.

Great grandmother: I'm pleased about this step.
Facilitator (to client): Now, together with *Peter*, take a step towards your *goal*.

The client and *Peter* do as instructed. The client is strongly moved and starts to cry.

Facilitator (to client): Absorb this picture as it is and then take a further step together with *Peter* into the *future*. Your *great grandmother* and her mother will give you the necessary strength from the female line, and your next steps will take place in the outside world.

Third session
Two months later the client came back for a third, and this time individual, session.

Facilitator: What has improved since we last met?
Client: Things are going very well in my new position. I'm coping well with the work and the contact with the others is very good: for example, recently …

The client then listed a number of situations in which she was able to act more self-confidently than before.

Facilitator: What else has improved since the last constellation?
Client: It was very good that my great grandmother was introduced again to the constellation last time. I felt really good to feel her presence behind me and to feel how the female line is supporting me. I'm now more able to be myself, and I'm more involved in groups.
Facilitator: Has anything else improved?
Client: Yes, I can look after myself and limit myself better now. I no longer like doing a bit of this and a bit of that: I've become considerably more goal-oriented. I can also feel that my abdomen is more relaxed. The feeling I get is somehow different. It feels more as if it belongs to me.
Facilitator: Has anything changed in your relationship with Peter?
Client: I'm able to talk to him better, to tell him more things … and I feel more confident about following my own goal. My voice has grown fuller and deeper and my posture more upright. However, there's something that happened that's really bothering me.
Facilitator: (nods)
Client: I met a woman that I find very attractive. I don't want this at all. I want to stay close to Peter, but I don't know how to handle it. I don't know what it means, maybe I'm lesbian, I am a bit confused.
Facilitator: Does Peter know?
Client: I haven't spoken to him about it yet, it's still so unclear to me. I only want to talk to him about it when I myself have more clarity.
Facilitator: How does he react to your lack of clarity?
Client: Of course he notices that something's not right, but he interprets it differently: he thinks I'm holding back like before. He asks what he can do to make things like they were before.
Facilitator: Remember the miracle … if it happened in the coming night … and this problem was solved … How would you notice this?
Client: I'd be relieved.
Facilitator: In what would you see this?

Client: The pressure would be gone from my chest ... I'd have even more energy ... I'd be myself again ... I could think better, do something for myself.

Facilitator: What would you do for yourself again?

Client: I'd start reading again, for example ... devote myself more to my new position ... I'd meet friends again ... and could be more open with Peter again.

Facilitator: How would Peter notice this?

Client: I'd talk to him more ... involve him more, do more things together with him.

Facilitator: How would he explain this?

Client: He'd think: 'Now she re-emerging form her hole, it's good that this setback has been overcome.'

Facilitator: How else would you notice that the miracle had happened?

Client: I would separate from my friend ... though that would be difficult because I will still see her at the evening course I'm doing. I don't really know how I'd be able to manage it.

Facilitator: (remains silent and waits)

Client: ... I'd have to tell her that it really can't continue ... But I dream of her at night ... What am I to do?

Facilitator: Yes, that really is difficult. What are you going to do?

Client: It would be hard ... somehow I'd have to pull through ... But I'm still not that sure.

Facilitator: How would you notice that you were surer about it?

Client: ... I'd be clearer, I'd know what I wanted.

Facilitator: And what would you do then?

Client: ... Well, I'd separate (from her). I'd deal with the difficulties.

Facilitator: How would you react to the difficulties that would arise?

Client: ... I think I'd be very open with my friend, would explain my situation clearly to her ... Actually until now I've been protecting her ... not telling her how much I'm also suffering ...

Facilitator: How will your friend react when you explain your situation so clearly to her?

Client: I don't think she would understand me. She'd be incredibly disappointed ... feel deserted ... (Client falls back into her 'problem-physiology'.)

Facilitator: If the miracle happened now, how would you react?

Client: Well ... then I'd be more accepting of my own needs, would stand by myself more ... But I don't want to disappoint her.

At this stage it is usual to see a change in the client's physiology: from problem-physiology (crooked posture, paleness, strained facial expression) to solution-physiology (upright posture, glint in the eye, gentle redness of the cheeks).

Facilitator: Can you imagine a situation in which she wasn't disappointed?

Client: No, I can't.

Facilitator: What do think you are going to do?

Client: I will have to disappoint her, if I'm honest with myself ... And if the miracle happened I'd have the strength to do it.

Facilitator: How would your friend react when she sees that you're serious about looking after yourself more?

Client: She'd be angry with me for a while and try to win me back … and then she'd keep a distance.
Facilitator: Would others in your evening course notice this?
Client: Yes, they'd sense that something had changed between us.
Facilitator: How would they react to this?
Client: … They'd stay out of it … maybe they'd try and avoid seeing us together.
Facilitator: How would that be for you?
Client: Well, I'd have to accept it.
Facilitator: Would anything else change for you?
Client: … I'd enjoy the course less, it'd become a burden to me.
Facilitator: Who or what could be of help to you in this situation?
Client: … I'd have to concentrate more on myself again … and otherwise … I don't know.
Facilitator: I suggest we perform another constellation with the resources.
Client: Yes, I need that.
Facilitator: Choose one of the cushions to be a symbol for you, and move around the room with it until you find a suitable place … and then mark the spot with the cushion … In which direction is the future for you? … And the past?

The client follows the facilitator's instructions, positioning the cushion and indicating the directions for the future and the past. The facilitator draws out a nine square table (as described in VI.1.2) on the floor using string.

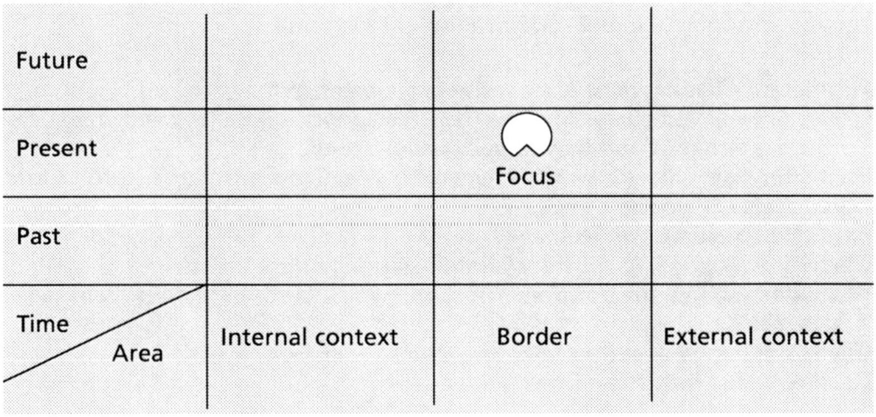

Figure 42

Facilitator: Everything that lies before you is the future. Everything that lies behind you is the past. Here on this line to your right is everything that is outside of you, e.g. Peter, your colleagues, friends, relatives and also events and situations, here in the past. Here on this line to your left is everything that happens inside you, i.e. your thoughts, emotions, physical reactions… Here in the future, there in the past… that is, the inner pictures or statements

that have been helpful to you in the past. Is everything clear so far?
Client: (nods)
Facilitator: What would you like to call your goal?
Client: Having strength.
Facilitator: Good, let's call it 'Strength' for short, and you will know what is meant by that... Choose a cushion for strength and position it somewhere in the table.

The client chooses a second cushion and, having placed the *focus* in the *present/border* square, she places her *goal* (*strength*) in the *future/border* square.

Facilitator: Stand in the position of the *focus*. How do you feel there?
Client: I can see the *goal*, but I have no contact with it.
Facilitator: Release yourself from this role now. You can do this by shaking out your arms and legs and saying your name to yourself. Every time you move into the position of another representative symbol, it's important to de-role beforehand to avoid becoming confused... Now move into the position of your *strength*... How do you feel there?
Strength: It's the same. I can see the *focus*, but have no contact with it.
Facilitator: Go back to your *focus's* position now. Look around. These are the squares in which your resources are located. Which square do you want to begin with?
Client: (points to the *past/internal context* square)

The facilitator holds her cataleptic hand over the *past/internal context* square and instructs the client to look at her hand.

Facilitator: What happens to you when you look here?
Client: A statement comes to mind that was always helpful to me before: 'Stay true to yourself, don't let yourself be distracted.'
Facilitator: Say to the *statement*: 'I remember you, you were often helpful to me.'
Client: (repeats words)
Facilitator: How do you feel now?
Client: It feels good, to see this *statement* like this in front of me.
Facilitator: Go into the position of the *statement*... How do you feel here as the *statement*?
Client: I'm happy to support her (the *focus*).
Facilitator: Say this to the *focus*.

The client repeats the sentence and then returns to the position of the *focus*.

Facilitator: Look again at the squares. Where do you see another resource appearing for you?

The client points to the *past/external context* square. The facilitator again holds her cataleptic hand over this square and asks the client to indicate the precise spot where something appears.

Facilitator: Who appears for you here?
Client: My grandmother. She always supported me when I was a child. She always stood by me, even when I did something wrong… Also since my first constellation my great grandmother is a support for me. I put up a picture of her. I have a warm feeling for her.
Facilitator: Good. Now choose a symbol for your grandmother and one for your great grandmother and place them.

The client chooses the cushions and places them in the constellation, then moves back towards the position of the *focus*. This results in the following picture:

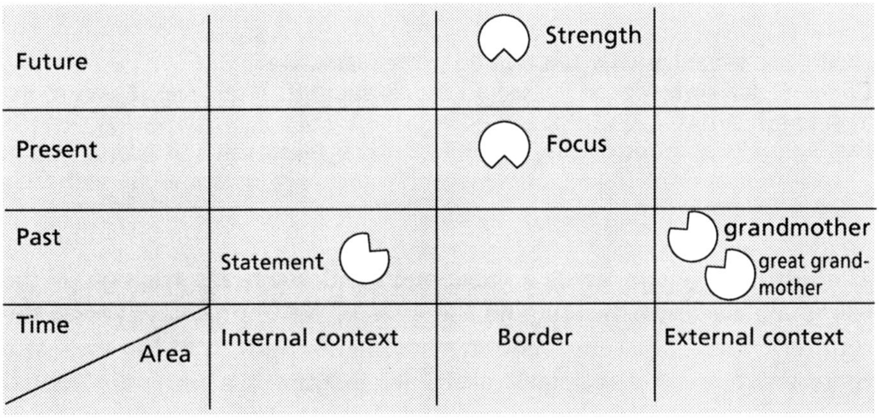

Time / Area	Internal context	Border	External context
Future		Strength	
Present		Focus	
Past	Statement		grandmother / great grand-mother

Figure 43

Facilitator: How do you feel now?
Client: I feel supported and no longer so alone. But I'd like to add Peter and a school friend to the picture. I was always supported by them.
Facilitator: OK, go ahead.

The client places cushions for Peter and her school friend and then returns to her own position.

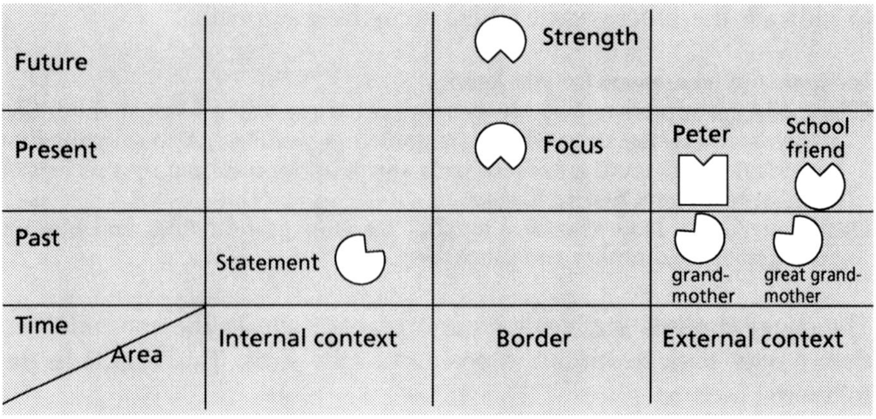

Figure 44

Facilitator: What has changed for you in the meantime?

Client: It feels very good to see so much support. I can feel it giving me strength.

Facilitator: Turn around again to the individual resources, and take a look at each. You can look them in the eye, and let them give you strength with their eyes.

The facilitator again holds a cataleptic hand over each cushion so the client can more easily imagine the eyes of the representatives at the right eye level. This intervention – taking strength from the eyes of a representative – is particularly useful where there has been only limited previous contact with the represented element. This ritual strengthens the represented element as a source of energy and a resource.

Facilitator: Look now at your *goal*. Has anything changed?

The facilitator again holds her cataleptic hand over the place marker.

Client: Yes, now I have contact with my *strength*. I feel it, and I can see my *goal* more clearly.

Facilitator: Feel how your supporting *statement* gives you strength from behind and to your left. Remember the many ways your *great grandmother* helped you, feel the warmth and good wishes from her. Feel *Peter*, who is standing, helpfully, at your side. And remember the support of your *school friend*. Absorb all of them, and move towards your *goal*.

The client takes three steps forwards and stretches out her hands towards the *goal*. After a long silence, the facilitator asks:

Facilitator: How do you feel now?

Client: Very good. I feel brave again.

Fourth session

Three months later the client took part in a group, in which the topic was again her relationship with her friend.

This time I tried a somewhat unusual type of constellation, a **conflict constellation,** used to dissolve an **accidental constellation.** The concept of the *accidental constellation* (see Varga von Kibéd and Sparrer 2000) is based on the observation that under certain circumstances processes similar to constellations can occur in everyday life. Every constellation presupposes that someone adopts the perspective of the client. In some day-to-day situations this happens when a person becomes the centre of attention in a group. This can happen, for example, during family celebrations or at other group events. As in a constellation, all the people involved are orientated towards one person – for example, the organiser or the speaker. A constellation for the person in the central focus may then take place accidentally, i.e. without any formal positioning. Those present slip into representations within the family system where there are pre-existing entanglements. In other words we all carry our family system around with us, and the positions of any excluded family members, being vacant, may attract strangers, who, without doing anything themselves, slide into and occupy these positions.

By applying this concept to groups, we can understand better incidents that would otherwise be considered incomprehensible. During group events, for example, for no apparent reason, someone may start to behave in a way that is not at all 'normal' for them, and thus has begun to represent a person from the family system of the central person. Group participants are often appalled with this behaviour and arguments often ensue with no one really knowing what it is all about. Situations that slide out of control, appear incomprehensible at the time, which seem to be 'haunted' and in which the actors themselves do not understand their own actions, may be seen as *accidental constellations*, or can be reconstructed as such. *Accidental constellations* like this are probably occurring all the time. In general, however, different constellations will cancel each other out, in a similar way to the process of noise reduction. It is more noticeable in situations in which a single person takes centre stage and everything is directed towards one single person. Because things are experienced from this person's perspective, the space around her is, in a manner of speaking, 'primed' for the occurrence of an *accidental constellation*. The process of an *accidental constellation* is different from the process of **transference** in a number of ways:

- In *accidental constellations* other people slip into a family system and become representatives of excluded family members, whereas in transference the main person sees family members in other people.

- The process of the **accidental constellation** occurs passively, while in transference the main person actively projects onto others.
- In **accidental constellations**, a person begins to represent an excluded person from an alien system, while in transference another person is projected 'into' the affected person, without that person's behaviour changing (as in accidental constellations). In accidental constellations the person changes her behaviour. This is more like counter-transference than projection.

Th effects of an **accidental constellation** can be dissolved by positioning the conflict that has occurred in a constellation, i.e. the people involved in the conflict are introduced retroactively to the constellation. It then becomes clear in the constellation whether someone has represented another person, or whether the conflict situation can be reconstructed so that it reaches a solution. Conflicts that appear to be unintelligible or absurd are often **accidental constellations**. This hypothesis should therefore be tested frequently using a **conflict constellation**.

Our case study suggests two hypotheses: the client may have slipped into her friend's system and represent one of the friend's family members (the feelings she has for her friend would then be feelings that do not in fact belong to her, but belong instead to the person she represents in the friend's system); equally, the friend may have slipped into the client's system and be representing an excluded person for the client. I used a **conflict constellation** to test these hypotheses.

Facilitator: What things have changed for you since we last saw each other?
Client: At first it gave me a lot of strength. I was able to speak to my friend in plain language. What I'm finding hard now is that we don't see each other any more: we avoid each other.
Facilitator: That's not so unusual after a separation.
Client: Yes, but somehow I have the feeling something is still not clear, otherwise we'd be able to talk to each other again, we'd no longer avoid each other.
Facilitator: If everything was clear, what would be different?
Client: We'd be able to greet each other again. I'd not longer avoid her, we'd be able to talk to each other normally again.
Facilitator: Let's have a look at what's remained unclear between you. We are going to do a conflict constellation. Were just the two of your involved in the conflict?
Client: Yes.
Facilitator: Then choose someone from the group to represent you and then someone for your friend, and position them both.

The client chooses two participants from the group and places them accordingly. This gives rise to the following picture:

Figure 45

Facilitator: How does the *focus* feel?
Focus: I feel affected by the *friend*. She's drawing me in somehow, but I don't want to go to her. There's something between us.
Facilitator: How is the *friend*?
Friend: I feel she's not giving me any attention, I feel somehow deserted... I'm angry with her.
Facilitator (to client): Is this how you see things?
Client: Yes, it's just like that.

To test the hypothesis that the friend is representing a person for the *focus*, the facilitator holds a cataleptic hand behind the *friend's* head and asks the *focus* to observe whether something changes when the cataleptic hand becomes visible to her. The facilitator then tells the *friend* to move slowly to the left so that the cataleptic hand becomes visible.

Facilitator: Does anything change for you when the *hand* becomes visible?
Focus: The *hand* is more important to me than the *friend*.
Facilitator (to client): Choose someone to represent *that which appears to the focus*, and position that person in the position of the *cataleptic hand*.

The client follows the instructions, choosing a representative and positioning her accordingly. We arrive at the following picture:

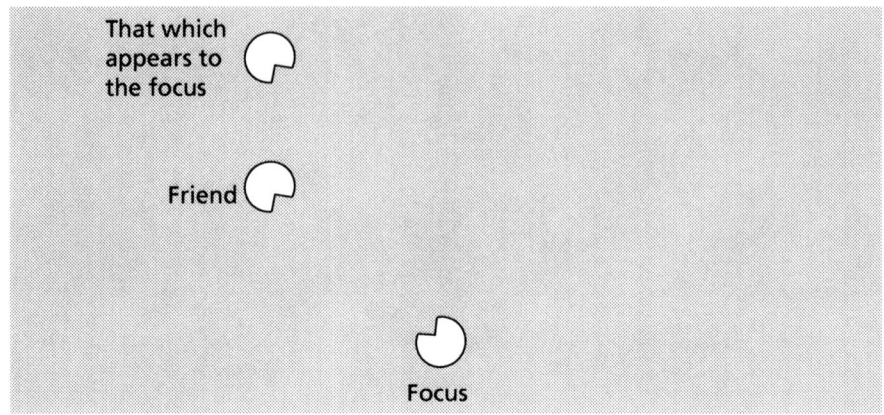

Figure 46.

Facilitator (to focus): Say to *that which appears to the focus*: 'You belong to me, even if I don't know who you are. I respect you and you have a place in my heart.'

The *focus* repeats this statement word for word.

Facilitator: What has changed for you?
Focus: It feels good to see her. I have a lot of sympathy for her.

The facilitator puts a cushion into the hand of the *focus* and asks her to say, 'I have carried this for you ... out of love ... and although it is hard for me, I'm giving it back to you because it does not belong to me.' Afterwards the *focus* is told to lay down the cushion at the feet of *that which appears to the focus*. The *focus* repeats the statements and places the cushion at the feet of *that which appears to the focus*.

Facilitator: What has changed for you?
Focus: I feel much better. I can now look towards the *friend*.
Facilitator: How is *that which appears to the focus*?
That which appears to the focus: This burden does not belong to me either.
Facilitator: Then say to the *focus*: 'This belongs neither to you nor to me. I will take it to its right place.' Then turn around and place the cushion where it feels right to you.

That which appears to the focus repeats the statement to the *focus*, and then lays down the cushion behind her and to her right. The representative then returns to her position and smiles, relaxed.

Facilitator: How is the *focus* now?
Focus: That's good for me.

We now test to see whether the client also has also been representing someone to the friend. The facilitator holds her cataleptic hand behind the *focus* and asks the representative of the *friend* to observe whether anything changes for her when the cataleptic hand becomes visible again. The facilitator then asks the *focus* to move slowly to the left so that the cataleptic hand becomes visible to the *friend*. In this way, the *focus* and the person she represents are represented by two representatives: the *focus* and the *cataleptic hand*.

Facilitator: Does anything change when the hand becomes visible?
Friend: I feel attracted to her as if by magic. I'm less and less interested in the *focus*.

The facilitator chooses a representative from the group for *that which appears behind the focus* and places her in the position of the *cataleptic hand*.

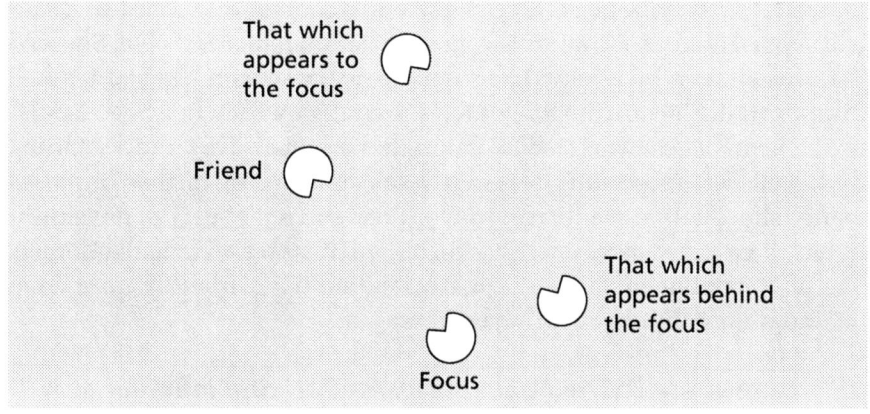

Figure 47

Facilitator (to client): It seems as if you have been representing someone to your friend from her system – as if you had slipped into her family system.
Facilitator (to *focus*): What has changed for you?
Focus: I feel liberated, like a burden that falls away. It's now much easier to look at the *friend*, the attraction is gone.
Facilitator (to *friend*): How do you feel now?
Friend: I'm interested in *that which appears behind the focus*. The *focus* is no longer so important to me… The resentment is not as strong now.
Facilitator (to client): Now go to the position of the *focus*.

The *focus* releases herself from her role, and the client takes her place.

Facilitator: How do you feel now?

Client: Relieved … It's as if a something had been taken away from me. I can look at the *friend* now with fresh eyes, it feels good. There's a lot of goodwill coming from there.

Facilitator: Say to the *friend*: 'You have confused me with someone else. I'm sorry that I hurt you, but I was seeing someone else in you. Maybe we can face each other in a new way now.'

The client repeats the words to the *friend*.

Facilitator: How is the *friend* now?

Friend: It feels good that she said that. But I will need more time before I can face her again.

Facilitator (to client): Take this picture and entrust it to your unconscious, and then be open to what change will come.

The client starts to cry as she absorbs the picture. Three weeks later she telephoned to say that she was now able to separate from her friend. However, her friend had not been able to separate from her. She believed that she had been representing the friend's mother and that her friend had represented an important woman in her own mother's life. She said the constellation had helped her; that the inner scream she had felt had disappeared. She now no longer felt the conflict within her. She also did not believe that she was lesbian, but rather bisexual. This understanding dissolved her uncertainty towards Peter. In terms of further improvements, she said that her increased workload did not affect her physically. In fact, it gave her more energy, which she felt above all in her abdomen. She also mentioned that her great grandmother's friendly gaze from behind was continuing to bring her strength.

VII.4 Case study 3: The goal approximation constellation as a meta-constellation – 'the importance of what is there instead'

The following constellation uses the *goal approximation constellation* as a meta-constellation, i.e. the structure of the *goal approximation constellation* is used to support another type of constellation. This second type of constellation uses the coordinates of the first to help symbolise the client's real goal. The framework of the *goal approximation constellation* aids focusing on the solution as well as the process of goal approximation. This is best combined with a more problem-orientated type of constellation, since this allows the advantages of the solution focused and problem-oriented approaches to coincide. In the following we use a combination of a goal approximation and a family constellation, the benefits of which are made very clear in this example. (The names of the representatives are again shown in italics.)

Facilitator: What is your current problem?

Client: I'm feeling much better, but I'm still finding it hard to do things that do me good. Although I'm often aware of what I should do to feel better, I don't do it. I find this hard to understand myself.

Facilitator: What would be different if you did what was good for you?

Client: I'd be happier and more successful. I'd simply feel good.

Facilitator: How would others react to the change?

Client: They'd say: 'At last! We knew you had it in you!'

Facilitator: Is there anyone who would react negatively?

Client: No, not yet. I've already taken a first step in this direction.

Facilitator: Does guilt play a role in your family?

Client: … Yes, my grandfather was in the SS.

Facilitator: Now choose someone for you and your goal. What would you like to call your goal?

Client: Happiness.

Facilitator: And choose someone for your grandfather, and position them all.

The client chooses three people from the group.

Facilitator: Start with yourself. Touch your representative on the back using both your hands, breath deeply, and feel how your feet touch the floor. Let yourself be led by your hands, and follow the movement that arises.

The client positions his own representative first.

Facilitator (to client): In which direction does the future lie? And the past? And the present?

The client points behind himself for the future, and in front of himself for the past, and then points to his current position for the present.

Facilitator: Now position your *goal* and your *grandfather*.

The client positions both as instructed, and we arrive at the following picture:

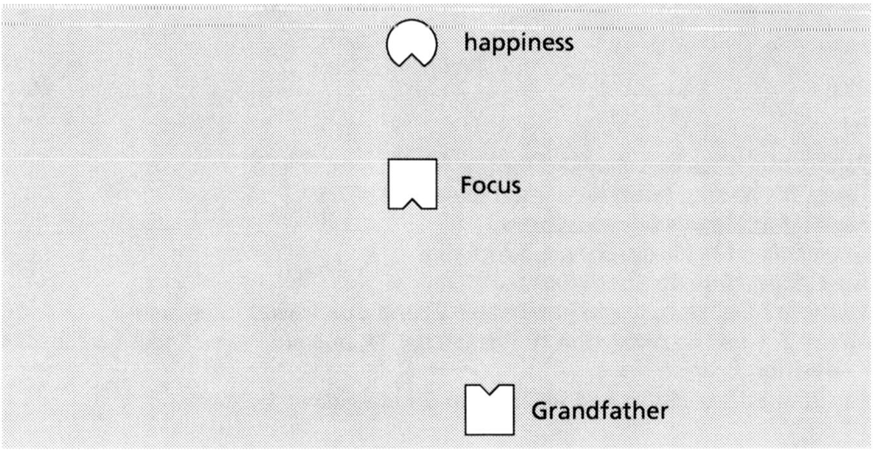

Figure 48

The picture shows that the client is facing the past and as a result cannot see his goal at all. This explains why he is unable to do what is good for him: the past prevents him.

Facilitator (to client): No wonder you find it hard to pursue your goal.
Facilitator (to *focus*): How do you feel?
Focus: Not good. I feel very heavy and feel a coldness.
Facilitator: How is the *happiness*?
Happiness: I feel totally uninvolved.
Facilitator: How's the *grandfather*?
Grandfather: I feel strong.
Facilitator (to client): Choose two more representatives for the victims, and position them.

The client follows the facilitator's instructions. When he sees the two *victims* in their positions he begins to cry.

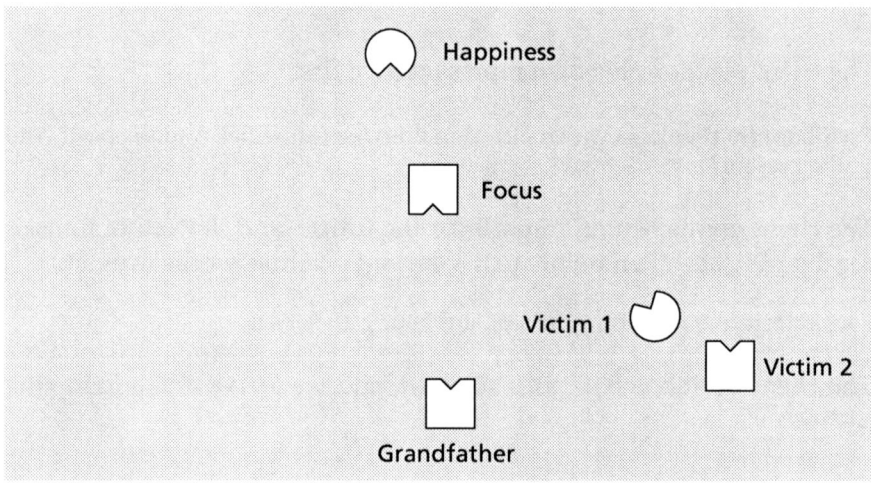

Figure 49

Facilitator: What has changed for the *focus*?
Focus: It's harder, but it feels good to see the *victims*.
Facilitator: How is the *grandfather*?
Grandfather: It's harder for me, I feel stiff.
Facilitator: How do the *victims* feel?
Victim 1: I feel attracted to him (*victim 2*) and don't want to be here.
Victim 2: I feel a connection to her (*victim 1*), but otherwise I feel bad in this position.
Facilitator: *Grandfather* and *victims* should now leave the room.

The *grandfather* and the *victims* leave the room.

Facilitator: What has changed?
Focus: It's a little easier, but there's a hole here now.
Happiness: I can breathe out.

The facilitator brings the *grandfather* and the *victims* back into the room. The client follows the scene as if spellbound. He is strongly moved.

Facilitator: How did you feel outside?
Grandfather: Better.
Victim 1: Also better.
Victim 2: The same, better.

The facilitator asks the *grandfather* and the *victims* to lie down next to each other on a blanket. The client begins to cry.

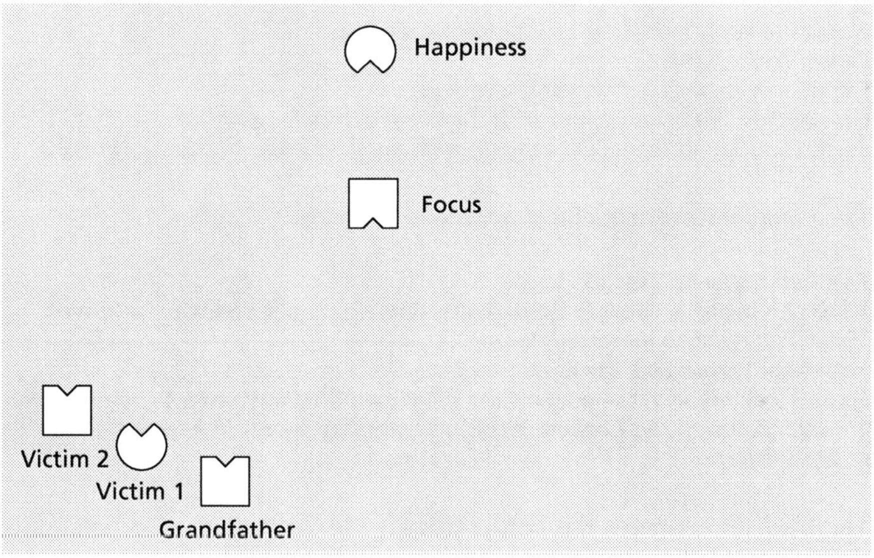

Figure 50

Facilitator: How is the *grandfather* now?
Grandfather: I feel at ease lying here.
Facilitator: How are the *victims*?
Victim 1: It feels very friendly here.
Victim 2: For me too.
Facilitator: How does the *focus* feel when he sees that?
Focus: It comforts me a lot, it makes me feel calmer.
Facilitator: Take this cushion as a symbol of the burden you received from your grandfather, and give the cushion back to him, first saying: 'You are my grandfather, and through you I am connected to my family line.'

The *focus* repeats these words.

Facilitator: 'I received this burden from you. It belongs entirely to you. I have nothing to do with it. I'm giving what is yours back to you now – all of it.'

Again, the *focus* repeats these words and places the cushion on the *grandfather* (lying on blanket), and then returns to his position.

Facilitator: Say now to the *victims*: 'I have shared in your suffering and have denied myself things in my life as a result – for example, happiness. But now I'm also leaving you to your fate and will respect you from now on by different means, namely by allowing myself to feel good and doing something with my life. And I will dedicate something to you.'

The *focus* repeats these words and is strongly moved. The client's eyes also fill with tears.

Facilitator (to *focus*): How do you feel now?
Focus: Very relieved.
Facilitator: How does the *grandfather* feel?
Grandfather: That was correct with the burden. It belongs to me.
Facilitator: Say to the *focus*: 'Leave it with me, and go and follow your path.'

The *grandfather* repeats these words to the *focus*.

Facilitator: How do the *victims* feel?
Victim 1: He has nothing to do with our fate, he should no longer interfere.
Victim 2: It's not so important to me.
Facilitator (to *focus*): How do you feel now?
Focus: I feel relieved, but now it's as if I have nothing anymore: somehow it was easier to carry the burden. No I have nothing at all. In a way I'd like the burden back.

The facilitator rotates the *focus* through 180 degrees so that he is now looking towards his *goal*.

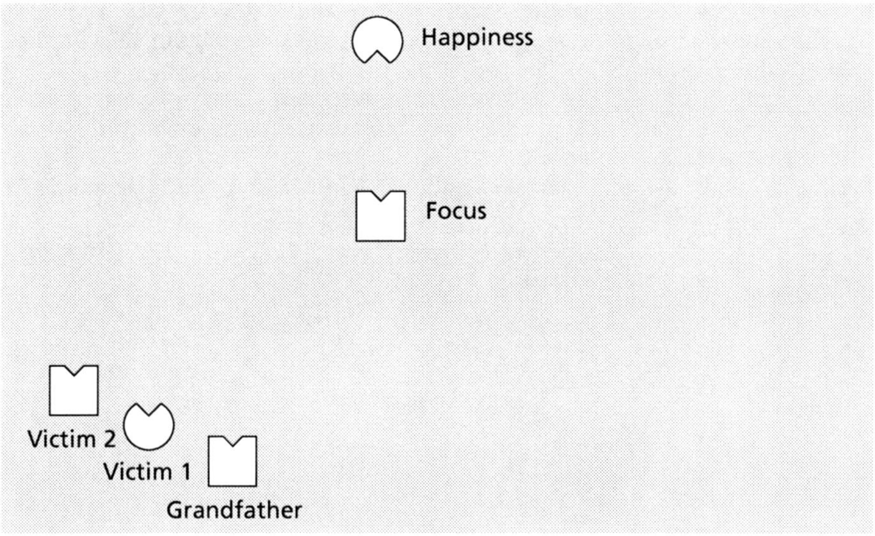

Figure 51

Focus: Yes, that's getting better now. That is something.
Facilitator: Take a step towards your *goal*.
Focus: I can only move in an arc.
Facilitator: That's OK. We don't always take the direct route.

The *focus* takes a number of steps towards the *goal*. The facilitator takes someone from the group and introduces her as the *miracle*.

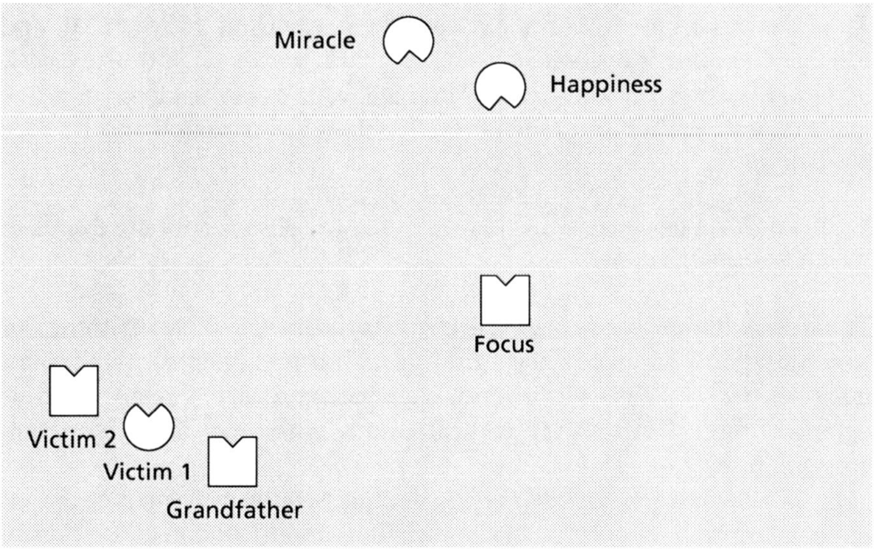

Figure 52

Facilitator: This is the *miracle*. When you've reached your *goal* and have achieved your happiness and your success, and everything this implies, that's the miracle.

Focus: That's really incredible. I suddenly feel energy and a certain joie de vivre. This is totally new to me. Now I can move directly towards the *goal*. I don't need to move in an arc.

Facilitator: Move towards your *goal*, and take a look at the *miracle* as you do so.

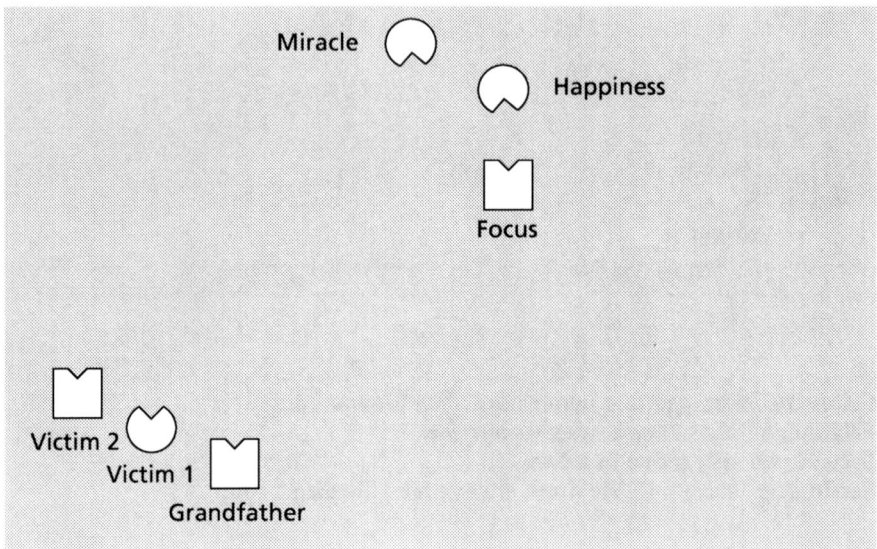

Figure 53

The *focus* moves towards the *goal* until he is standing in front of it, and touches the *miracle* by holding out his arm towards it. Both the *focus's* and client's eyes fill with tears. The facilitator asks the client to move into his position in the constellation. He does as instructed and his face starts to glow.

Facilitator: Take this picture and absorb it. You can always return to this place and take energy from it.

This constellation made very clear the importance of the existence of something new instead of the suffering or burden; otherwise, the client may fall back into his old pattern. As a consequence, I nearly always combine family structural constellations with goal approximation constellations.

It also becomes clear how, when dealing with family members that have committed an offence, both restriction and inclusion of the family line is important. I have seen family constellations which emphasised only the possibility of the offender's leaving and the client subsequently lost the connection to her ancestral line. Inclusion using the words 'Through you I maintain the link to my ancestors' indicates the existence of certain facts that cannot be denied. The kin relationship also remains intact. 'Leaving' does *not* mean 'From now on you are no longer my father, daughter etc...'

Constellations always point us in the direction of the things we need to pursue. The consequences of the constellation will show us if we have forgotten something, which can be added later on. Seen from this perspective, it makes sense, as a facilitator, to find out what happens after a constellation: therefore the necessity of further work cannot be ruled out from the start.

Chapter VIII

The solution constellation

I developed the **solution constellation** to facilitate a direct translation from SFT to constellation work. It allows us to see which qualitative aspect is added to the solution focused interview when solutions in the present, past and future are positioned in the constellation. Before performing this kind of constellation, it is worth conducting a solution focused interview, because, firstly, the client will then know what to expect from the individual parts, and, secondly, this will make the complementary aspect of the constellation clearer.

Excluded people who did not appear in the preliminary interview may appear during the constellation. They are often only remembered by the client during the constellation process, while sometimes it is the representatives who indicate the existence of excluded people after sensing an absence or feeling a cold chill. The act of remembering excluded people often is only made possible by performing a constellation.

Whether we need to include an excluded person in order to solve the problem, however, remains an open question. Based on a high number of experiments and practical applications in therapeutic situations, I have come to assume that constellations can facilitate and accelerate the finding of a solution. Performing exercises and daily practice routines help the client to maintain the goal-orientation. Indeed, the energy required by the goal-orientation is won through action and practice. The constellation supports the process of goal achievement by means of a change of attitude. Of course, we also see a change of attitude in SFT in the answering of the miracle question: an answer to the miracle question is only possible if the client changes her problem-oriented attitude into one of hope and gratitude. The constellation experience, however, is usually more intense than that of imagining the miracle.

In previous chapters, I presented the different types of solution focused systemic structural constellations, from the most complex down to the simplest. Looking in the other direction, we see that the *solution constellation* does not contain a timeline; rather it moves in a timeless space (as with family constellations). Of course, implicitly it still contains a timeline: when, at the end of a constellation, we ask the *focus* to move towards the *goal*, we act as if there were a timeline drawn between the *focus* and the *goal*. By issuing the instruction to walk towards the *goal*, we install a timeline implicitly and there is a natural structural level change to a *goal approximation constellation*.

A natural change can also take place from a *goal approximation constellation* to a *nine square constellation*. To the left and the right of the timeline in the *nine square constellation* we often already find the external and internal contexts, which can be installed as soon as they are named.

VIII.1 The components of the solution constellation

The *solution constellation* is made up from parts of the solution focused interview. As opposed to the *goal approximation constellation* and the *nine square constellation*, it does not contain a timeline, and, as such, lacks a temporal and dynamic aspect. A synchronous picture is constructed, which, at the most, relates to the sequence of events in the system. In this respect, the *solution constellation* is similar to the *family structural constellation*, since we also position elements from the present-day family and family of origin, the dead, the living and sometimes even previous partners.

A *solution constellation* is made up of the followings parts:

- the focus (the representative of the client)
- the goal
- the exceptions
- the miracle
- the context of the miracle

These five parts are all *representatives in the narrow sense*. They can be understood as the coordinates at which the problem reveals itself. We recognise the relationship structure between the *focus*, the *goal*, the *exceptions*, the *miracle* and its *context* in the way each is aligned with respect to the others. In cannot be said in advance which part of the problem is mapped onto which parts of the *solution constellation*, and the *solution constellation* is therefore not canonical – there is no mechanical translation.

As with *goal approximation* and *nine square constellations*, the *solution constellation* starts with the *focus* and the *goal*. Given the lack of a timeline, the place in which the *goal* is positioned tells us nothing about whether the client's goal is seen to be in the future or the past.

The *context of the miracle* should be added in addition to the *miracle*, because otherwise the content of the miracle and the reactions to the miracle from the environment will become confused. In order to highlight the specific quality of the miracle, we need to distinguish between miracle and context. It is in the *context of the miracle* that obstacles to goal achievement, or the advantages that come from not solving the problem, appear.

In the exceptions we sometimes come across traumatic events. Representatives of the exceptions may have ideas or thoughts that remind the client of a specific situation. These *evolutionary representatives* (described in detail in Chapter III.1.1.2.3) are able to go back in time to an age at which a traumatic situation occurred for the client. They then represent for the client both the adult age and the corresponding childhood age, and thus belong to the group of *ambiguous representatives* (see Chapter III.1.1.2.3). However, the exceptions often also represent resources (as in the case study below).

In SySt constellations, the abstract parts of, say, 'goal' and 'exceptions' are also given additional, precise names, such as 'Success' or 'Work situation'. This makes it easier for the client to translate the constellation to her real-life situation.

Although *solution constellations* feature solutions in the first constellation picture, this does not mean that the solution is already there from the beginning. Instead, the solutions are positioned in the first picture in a version that has been distorted by the problem. We first need to perform rearrangements and rituals before we arrive at a solution.

Again, from the type of constellation, we do not know in which of the five parts of the *solution constellation* excluded people might appear – they may appear in different parts from one constellation to the next. The following examples demonstrate some different forms of the *solution constellation* and are not prototypical. *Solution constellations* are often very different from one another. Rearrangements are usually made by using the grammar of other systemic structural constellations, e.g. *problem constellations, goal approximation constellations* and *belief polarity constellations*. I developed *solution constellations* to facilitate easier and more fruitful comparability between SFT and constellation work, and not, initially, as a new type of systemic structural constellation. The *solution constellation* can be a useful short and concise form of constellation.

VIII.2 The solution constellation as an array of resources

VIII.2.1 Similarities and differences between problem and solution constellations

In the following case study we find resources in the exceptions to the problem. The answer to the miracle question has some similarities with the 'future exercise' in *problem constellations*. These parallels with *problem constellations* can help when looking for ideas for interventions as they give us a heuristic structural analogy schema for the development of interventions.

One way in which the two constellation forms differ is that, in comparison with *problem constellations*, the procedure followed in *solution constellations* corresponds more clearly with the solution focused attitude, while obstacles, at least initially, are not mentioned at all. Obstacles can appear in the relationship structure of the *solution constellation* and as such are not systemic elements of the solution structure; rather, they appear within the structure, i.e. they appear or disappear during the process of change as structural aspects of the constellation picture and are not systemic elements of the constellation. The *problem constellation*, on the other hand, is close to the language of the client, something that can also be an advantage.

Because *solution constellations* do not presuppose obstacles as systemic elements, they need fewer premises to be fulfilled as to be applicable than *problem constellations*. This is conducive to a direct approach to the goal. The advantage of *problem constellations* is that the client can learn that what she thinks is an obstacle can be transformed into a resource, or an as-yet-unseen aid. *Solution constellations* do not offer this insight into the transformation process in such a detailed way.

VIII.2.2 Case study 1: More success at work (part 1)

Mr P took part in one of my constellations groups. He had set up a small business the previous year, which so far had been only moderately successful. He explained how he was brooding a lot and getting in the way of his own success. He wanted to find out how he could improve the turnover of his business using a constellation. The preliminary interview is given below, followed by the constellation. (The names of the representatives are again shown in italics.)

Facilitator: What is your current problem?
Mr P: I would like to be more successful. About a year ago I opened my own business, but it's not running particularly well.
Facilitator: What do others say about it? Do they also think that your business ought to be doing better?

Mr P: Yes, with the location I have I ought to be doing better. I helped a friend build up his business before, so I am able to make a comparison. In terms of success, I'd say I'm in the bottom third.

Facilitator: Hmm.

Mr P: I also have the impression that I am somehow holding myself back, and I'd like to look at this in a constellation.

Facilitator: Are there any exceptions to this situation? Are there times when your business runs better than others?

Mr P: Yes, on some days I clearly have more customers.

Facilitator: What do you do differently on these days?

Mr P: ... I'm not so lost in my thoughts ... I have more energy and am somehow faster ... I'm also not as tired as otherwise.

Facilitator: And what is there instead of the tiredness?

Mr P: I feel well rested ... clear and ... awake.

Facilitator: Is there something else you do on these days?

Mr P: Yes, I go out into nature from time to time. My business is in a very beautiful area ... In fact, I ought to enjoy it more often, but somehow I forget.

Facilitator: What changes for you when you go out into nature?

Mr P: I think about different things ... I don't think continually about all the things I need to do ... I relax and am more myself.

Facilitator: And what else changes then?

Mr P: I get more done then ... I'm not being distracted all the time ... I'm more relaxed but also more efficient.

Facilitator: And what do you do with the time you save?

Mr P: Well, more customers come, and I'm busy. When I gather momentum, things run on their own. It's as if the success sets the ball rolling.

Facilitator: Are there any other situations in which your work went so well?

Mr P: ... Yes, when I was aware of how good I have things ... I mean, how the beautiful countryside is so close ... and that I'm actually doing what I really like. When I think about it I have some inner peace. Sometimes I realise it all of a sudden, in a sort of 'Aha!' experience, and then work goes well.

Facilitator: Can you think of any other situations in which your work went so well?

Mr P: ... No, I think basically that's it.

Facilitator: Is there someone in your family who wasn't able to be successful?

Mr P: ... No, I can't think of anyone.

Facilitator: Good, now we can start with the constellation. First choose someone from the group to represent you ... Stand up and look around the circle. Sometimes it's easier when you stand up.

Mr P chooses a representative for himself.

Facilitator: Now choose someone to be your goal. What do you want to call it?

Mr P: 'Success'.

Facilitator: So choose someone for 'success'

Mr P looks around in a circle and chooses a representative for his *success*.

Facilitator: Next choose representatives for the exceptional situations, in which you were already successful. What would you like to call the first one?

Mr P: 'Sufficient sleep'. Facilitator: We'll call that '*sleep*' for short, and you will know what it means to you. Now select a representative for '*Sleep*' ... What name do you want to give to the second exceptional situation?

Mr P: 'Nature'.

Facilitator: Good. And what do you want to call the third?

Mr P: 'Remembrance'.

Facilitator: What does 'remembrance' mean to you?

Mr P: It's when I suddenly realise how good I have it, or I find my feet again. That's like an 'Aha!' experience to me.

Facilitator: Good, then now choose someone for '*Nature*' and someone for '*Remembrance*', and then position all the representatives ... Start with the *focus* (the representative for Mr P). Stand behind your representative ... touch him with your hands on his back ... Pay attention to your breathing and feel your contact with the floor with your feet ... take a step forwards and follow the movement that arises.

Mr P selects his representatives and positions them, one by one, in the constellation. We obtain the following picture:

Figure 54

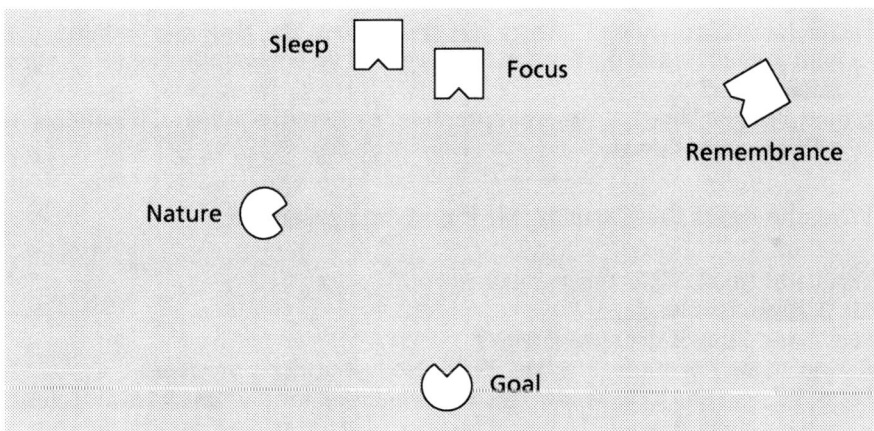

Facilitator: How do you feel when you see the picture from the outside?

Mr P: I'm surprised how close the *goal* is and how visible it is.

Facilitator: Sometimes the *goal* is closer than we think ... How does the *focus* feel?

Focus: I can see the *goal* and am surprised at how close it is. I feel support on my right from the *sleep*: it might be able to come a bit closer.

The *sleep* moves slightly closer to the *focus*. With a friendly nod, both show that this feels better.

Facilitator: How does the *sleep* feel?

Sleep: I'm happy to be close to the *focus*. But he's not giving me much attention. By the way, it's not a matter of how much sleep: I only need it to be deep and short. But he (the *focus*) is not giving me enough attention. He should appreciate me more.

Facilitator (to Mr P): Is this true?

Mr P: Yes, that's exactly how my relationship to sleep is. (Mr P smiles in agreement.)

Facilitator (to *focus*): Look around to the *sleep*, establish eye contact, and take strength from him through his eyes.

The *focus* turns around to the *sleep* and looks into his eyes. They look at each other for a long time. The *focus* shows that he feels moved.

We often use this ritual in SySt constellations to establish contact between systemic elements or to allow energy to flow from one part to another – usually one that is hierarchically lower. This ritual may also be used for 'taking energy from the family line' – i.e. in family constellations when the *mother* or *grandmother* (or *father* or *grandfather*) is placed behind the *daughter* (or *son*).

Facilitator: When enough energy has been taken, the *focus* can indicate this with a small nod of the head to the *sleep*, and then turn round again … How is the *nature*?

Nature: I'm just here … I feel unappreciated by him (the *focus*) … it's almost as if I were superfluous.

When he hears these words, Mr P nods in agreement.

Facilitator (to Mr P): Is this familiar to you?

Mr P: Hmm (smiling)

Facilitator: How is the *remembrance*?

Remembrance: I'm not feeling bad. But I also feel underappreciated.

Focus: I'd also like to have him (the representative for the 'remembrance') closer to me. I think it would be best if he were to stand behind me like the *sleep*.

Facilitator: If this is OK with the *remembrance*, it can change its position accordingly.

The *remembrance* moves next to the *sleep*. The *focus*, *remembrance* and *sleep* exchange friendly smiles, indicating their agreement with the change.

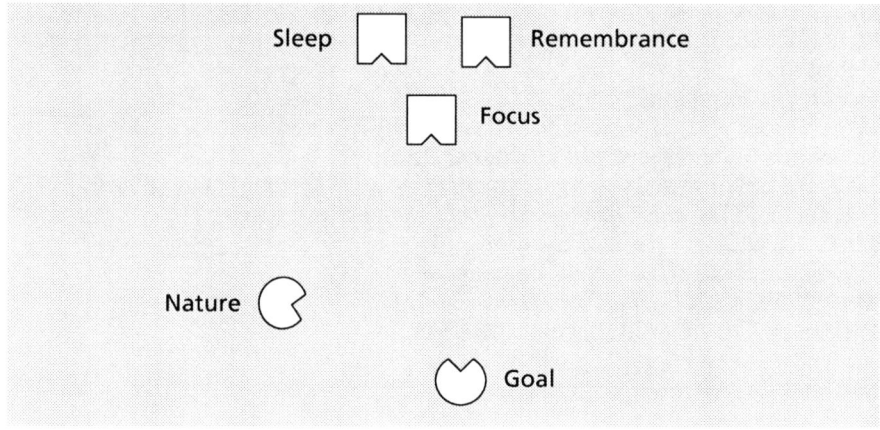

Figure 55

Facilitator: How does the *goal* feel?
Goal: I can see the *focus* very clearly, and have contact to him. But I'm not complete, there's something else missing....something that stands for how it is after the goal is achieved… something like the family.

VIII.2.2.1 Note on the natural occurrence of solution focused forms of intervention in SySt constellation work

In this case study, we learn that the constellation is still not complete for the *goal*. At this stage, the miracle question is yet to be posed because I immediately wanted to transform the information from the preliminary interview into a constellation. My aim in this was to let conversation and constellation flow into each other, so that verbal and nonverbal communication could melt into a new whole and both approaches become simultaneously useable.

It now becomes clear that the (as yet unasked) miracle question forms part of the solution process that arises, entirely naturally, out of the constellation. This shows that the miracle question is not an artificial method, but a question that poses itself of its own during the solution process.

VIII.2.2.2 Continuation of case study 1: More success at work (part 2)

Facilitator (to Mr P): Assuming … the constellation is successful … and when you arrive home this evening … you see your family … and eventually go to bed… and then assuming … the full effect of the miracle would unfold during this night … and everything that brought you here were to be solved in one fell swoop … how would you notice this in the morning?
Mr P: Well, I'd wake up different … I'd be calmer … more myself.
Facilitator: And what else would be different?
Mr P: I'd no longer worry as much.

Facilitator: And what would you do with the extra time available to you?

Mr P: I'd concentrate more on my work, I'd be more active… I'd delegate more tasks.

Facilitator: To whom?

Mr P: I hired a saleswoman, but I'd definitely hire someone new as well.

Facilitator: What else would be different?

Mr P: I'd have more drive and more energy… I'd be completely myself.

Facilitator: Who, apart from you, would notice this change?

Mr P: My wife and my two children.

Facilitator: From what would they notice it?

Mr P: I'd have more time for them.

Facilitator: How would they react to this?

Mr P: They'd be happy.

Facilitator: And how would that be for you?

Mr P: Wonderful.

Facilitator: Would other people also notice the change?

Mr P: Yes, of course: my customers. That would be good for them.

Facilitator: Anyone else?

Mr P: Yes, my friends.

Facilitator: How would they react?

Mr P: They'd say: 'At last! We always knew you could do it.'

Facilitator: OK, now choose someone form the group for 'what comes after the goal', and position this representative.

Mr P chooses another representative and places her in the constellation, giving us the following picture:

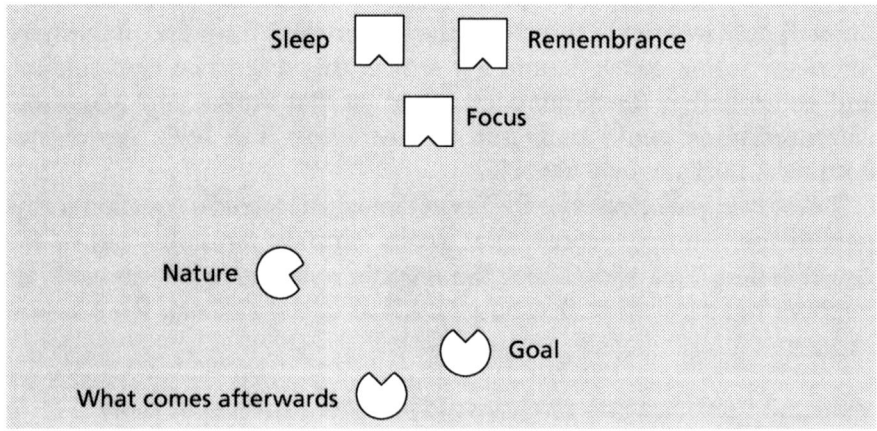

Figure 56

Facilitator: What has changed for the *focus*?

Focus: The *goal* is now more attractive and has moved closer. Now I also feel strong support coming from the *sleep* and the *remembrance*. Only *nature* is not yet right in the right place for me.

Facilitator: What has changed for the *nature*?

Nature: I'm still not getting enough attention and can't be effective yet.
Facilitator: Place yourself behind *sleep* and *remembrance*. Do you feel better
    there?

The *nature* moves behind the *sleep* and *remembrance*.

Nature: Much better.
Focus: Now I can also feel the strength of the *nature* behind me.

Both *sleep* and *remembrance* nod to show their agreement.

Facilitator: What has changed for the *goal*?
Goal: I feel much better. Somehow the picture is now more complete. It would
    be good for me if the family were also added. I feel that it's an important
    source of energy. It would open up an entirely new dimension.
Facilitator (to Mr P): Then choose someone to be your family and add them to
    the constellation.

The family is represented by a single person, as in this situation it is the
family – in contrast to the work situation – that is of more interest to us
rather than the individual reactions of family members. If we were to
add all the family members in this situation, this might bring about a
structural level change to a family constellation, and this would compli-
cate the constellation unnecessarily as well as be tiring for the
representatives due to the increased duration. The rule of thumb in use
here is 'better short and therefore concise, than long and complex'.
Consequently, in SySt constellations it is important to find an **appropriate level of complexity reduction**.

Mr P selects a representative and places her on the left-hand side of
the *focus*. The other representatives nod and smile in agreement with
the change, and we obtain the following picture:

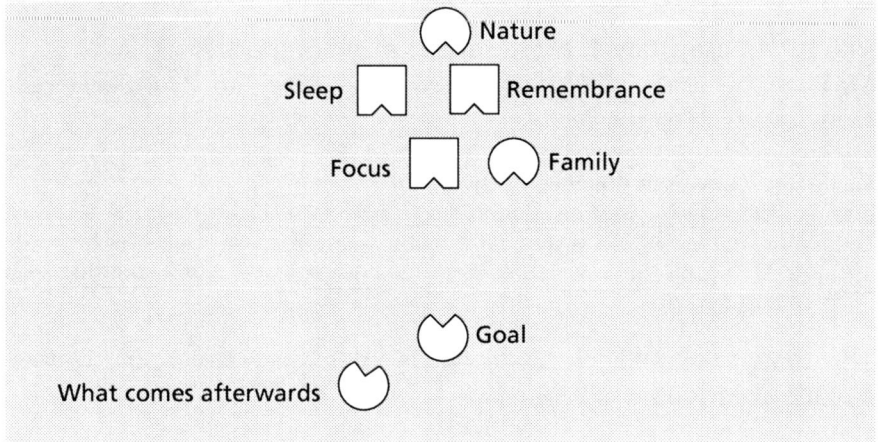

Figure 57

Facilitator: What has changed for the *focus*?

Focus: I feel even more support now. This position gives me a lot of strength, and the *goal* was become considerably clearer to me. Now I know better what I really want.

Facilitator (to Mr P): Now you can move into the position of the *focus*, and the *focus* can de-role and sit down.

The focus and Mr P follow these instructions. Mr P's eyes begin to glisten, and he looks at each of the representatives in turn.

Facilitator: You (Mr P), together with your *family*, can take a step towards the *goal*. While doing so, and notice how this feels, and take this picture to be a new beginning.

VIII.2.2.3 Note on implicit and explicit timelines

The instruction to take a step towards the *goal* indirectly introduces a timeline. This changes the *solution constellation* into a *goal approximation constellation*, which in this case has the advantage letting us test out some initial steps in the direction of a suitably modified future.

Constellations do not normally have an *explicit timeline*. Normally, they encompass a timeless space in which the dead and the living, for example, are both present. However, we do have the option of introducing a timeline. In Bert Hellinger's classic family constellations, parents are found next to each other in the solution picture, as are children. We usually also find the grandparents, positioned behind each parent accordingly. The moment the therapist asks the children to turn to face their future, an unambiguous time axis is felt in what was initially a timeless solution picture based around a parent and grandparent arrangement. We also call this process the induction of an *implicit timeline*.

VIII. 2.2.4 Case study 1: More success at work (part 3)

Mr P and his *family* take a step forwards. The step Mr P takes is larger than that taken by the *family*.

Facilitator: How does this feel for the *family*?

Family: I'm not going that far. I'm holding back.

Facilitator (to Mr P): Take a step back again ... and then another step forwards ... (to Mr P) but make sure that this time your *family* is really standing next to you afterwards.

This time, Mr P and his *family* slowly take a step forwards together, looking at each other all the while.

Facilitator: How does the *family* feel now?

Family: This feels good.

Facilitator (to Mr P): How do you feel now?

Mr P: This is exhausting and unfamiliar to me... but it's making me feeling better.

Facilitator: Take another step forwards in the same way!

Cautiously, maintaining eye contact and smiling at each other, Mr P and his *family* taken another step forwards.

Facilitator (to Mr P): Turn around again to your resources.

Mr P looks around, beaming. The *resources* nod in agreement.

Facilitator: How does the *goal* feel?
Goal: It's very important for me that the *family* receives this attention and that *what comes afterwards* is standing next to me.
Facilitator: How is *what comes afterwards*?
What comes afterwards: I feel very good. The contact with the *goal* is very good for me. I'm in complete agreement.
Facilitator (to Mr P): You can absorb this picture using this movement (moves both hands towards her heart) and be open to what it leads you on to ... because a constellation always ends with the start of something new. As you do so, take another step forwards together with your *family.*

Mr P follows these instructions.

Half a year later, Mr P told me that he had much more energy and was feeling much better. He was still sleeping too little at times, but the constellation was helping him to be more aware of his body. He had developed some new ideas in his work and things had improved financially. He expected there to be further changes in the future, which he was already looking forward to.

VIII.3 The solution constellation with a change of structural level

Changes of structural level can also occur in a *solution constellation*, especially a change to a family constellation. If, before starting the constellation, the client confirms that a family member had previously been unable to achieve the goal that he or she had set themselves, this will of course lead to an initially implicit change of structural level or the induction of a systemically ambiguous constellation. The first constellation described below shows how this change may also occur spontaneously.

The following constellation is performed in hidden form. This is of particular interest, as, in general, clients don´t have many associations for 'exceptions', 'miracle' and 'context of the miracle' – in contrast to elements of other systemic structural constellations, e.g. 'obstacle', 'defocused topic' or 'knowledge'. Although the individual parts of the *solution constellation* are introduced with short questions, they cannot be specified in detail through further questioning because the answers remain hidden. Thus the client also only receives an indication as to the content of the individual parts of the constellation. However, the process of these constellations shows that this does not compromise or influence in any appreciable way the work performed.

VIII.3.1 Case study 2: Hidden work: The context of the miracle as an obstacle

The following constellation took place as part of a further education seminar and was performed by the author together with Matthias Varga von Kibéd. At the client's request, the constellation was performed in hidden form. Some situations call for a particular level of discretion, which can be achieved using hidden work that is available in SySt constellations. It is therefore particularly suited to work with organisations.

The following example shows well how, even with no knowledge of family background, excluded family members can also be incorporated into the 'context of the miracle' and may appear spontaneously in the bodily sensations of the representative for that systemic part. (The names of the representatives are again shown in italics.)

Facilitator: You can all answer the following questions for yourself, without saying the answers out loud. First formulate your problem to yourself.
Client: (nods)
Facilitator: What do you call your goal? … What is there instead of your problem? … Is this clear to you?
Client: (nods)
Facilitator: Was there a time in the past when your problem was solved?
Client: (shakes head)
Facilitator: Maybe just for a short while?
Client: (thinks about it for a while then shakes head again)
Facilitator: Now I will ask a difficult question: … Assuming … we had performed the constellation successfully, and you do something else afterwards … and some time during the evening you go to bed … Assuming … during the night a miracle occurred … and your problem is solved in one fell swoop … and that really would be a miracle … and then you wake up in the morning … and no one tells you that this miracle has occurred … how would you notice that it had occurred?
Client: (thinks then nods)
Facilitator: What would be the first thing you'd see it in? … Take your time … and think through the next day … What would be different for you then? … What would you do differently? … What different thoughts would you

have? ... Is there anything else that would make a difference?
Client: (thinks, nodding occasionally)
Facilitator: If your miracle had happened, who, apart from you, would notice it? What is his or her reaction?
Client: (thinks a while, then nods)
Facilitator: Is there anyone else that would notice it? ... Is there anyone that would react negatively?
Client: Yes, basically there's just one person that would react negatively to it.
Facilitator: We will call the people who react to your miracle, that is, essentially just this one person, the 'context of the miracle', or just 'context' for short.
Client: (nods)
Facilitator: Is there someone in your family who was unable to achieve your goal?
Client: Yes, my mother.
Facilitator: We will include her in the constellation. Now we have all the parts of the constellation. Now choose someone from the group for you ... for your goal ... for the miracle ... for the context of the miracle and for your mother, and position them in the constellation... Stand behind your representative ... breathe deeply ... touch him with both hands on the back ... take a step forwards ... and follow the movement that arises.

The client positions the representatives, one after the other, and we obtain the following picture:

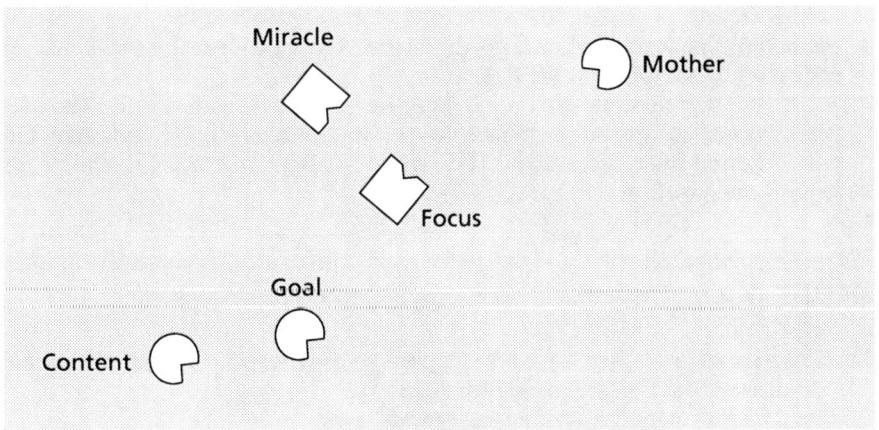

Figure 58

The facilitator now asks each part how they feel.

Focus: As I was being led around, I was thinking, 'Where is this going?' It was like ... as though things kept banging into me. Finally, around this spot, there was this circular movement, and I felt that I was being guided. I nearly fell over backwards. I was surprised that the *goal* bumped into me. Afterwards, the *miracle* came up to me like a sniffling thing. My basic idea was to keep my eyes closed. When the *mother* was added, I felt a chill: I stopped breathing for a moment, my neck stiffened; I still feel stiff, it's like I'm surrounded. I wouldn't wish this even on my enemies.

Goal: I'm fixated, looking up at where the beams enter the wall. My left shoulder hurts. It unsettled me when I bumped into the *focus*. It got better when I spoke with the *focus*. Behind me it's too cramped. Otherwise, nothing occurs to me.

The chill felt by the *focus*, when the *mother* appeared, and the fixation of the *goal* on a particular spot on the ceiling could be an initial indication that there is an exclusion connected with a tragic episode of fate.

Miracle: I was led in an erratic way. For the last few metres I had to breathe out rapidly, it was like being in a sluice gate. I needed guiding to get to this place. The block is in me myself. I regret that I can't see the *goal*. It was comforting when the *mother* came in.

This shows that it is important for the *miracle* that the *mother* was added.

Context: It felt good while I was being guided. I was confused before as the representatives were being guided. It was like at the train station, where people are continually coming and going. When the *goal* spoke, my heart began to beat faster, and I was starting to be really agitated.

Mother: I didn't want to get so close to the *focus*, he's as big as I am. I was staggering around in circles. My left arm was shaking. When the *focus* spoke, it got better. I'm sorry that he feels threatened by me. When the *goal* spoke, it got better. I'm fixated on the *focus*.

Focus: As the *miracle* spoke just now, it got easier, I can breathe better. The *goal* is no longer so important. Since the *mother* spoke, it again feels like I'm nearly falling over backwards. The *mother* has been miscast. The mother is behind me (points to *context*).

Here we see that there is a strange form of confusion between the *mother* and the *context of the miracle* that requires some process work.

Goal: I was annoyed when the *mother* (points to the *context of the miracle*) spoke. I'm pleased that the *context* is interested.

Mother: I was also annoyed when the *context* spoke.

Context: Since the *mother* has become the topic, my knee has become wobbly.

Here we receive further indications that the *context of the miracle* has been representing the *mother* in one form or another.

Facilitator (to client): Does what they say fit for you?

The client nods in agreement. The facilitator rearranges the representatives so they can see each other better, and so each has more space. We arrive at the following picture:

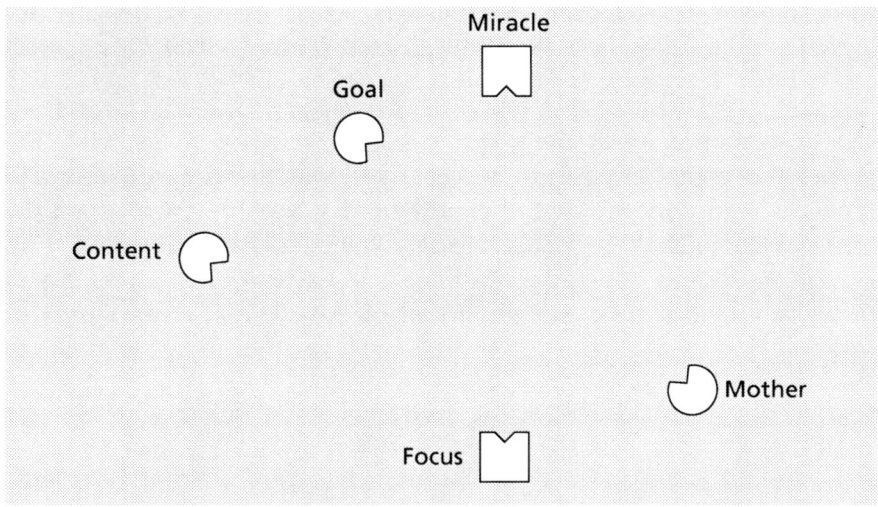

Figure 59

Facilitator: How does the *focus* feel now, what has changed?

Focus: I'm looking at who they all are. They are all strangers to me, including the woman there (points to the *mother*). My left leg is very wobbly. It's an effort to realise that they are there.

Since the *focus* is finding it hard to stand in his position, the facilitator positions behind him three representatives for the male family line, starting with the grandfather.

Facilitator: If you turn around you will see your *male line* behind you ... starting with the *grandfather* ... behind him is the *great grandfather* ... and behind him the *great great grandfather* etc ... Now imagine a long line behind you ... and take energy from it.

The *focus* leans on his *grandfather* and starts to cry. He then closes his eyes, breathes deeply, and opens his eyes again.

Focus: The *context* and the *goal* are now less important. I can see the *miracle* better now. I don't know the *mother*.

That the *miracle* is now becoming more important than the *goal* indicates that the *goal* may still have the form of the 'absence of the problem'. And that the addition of the ancestral line has had such a large influence could indicate that – by not having featured in the client's picture before – this had to some extent been missing for him, an excluded element. Consequently, the facilitator then asks the client to move into the position of the *focus* and to feel the long ancestral line behind him for himself.

Client: But I don't know them (confirmation of the suspicion of a partial exclusion). I don't remember my mother either. I was brought up by foster parents.

This information from the client explains, retrospectively, why the *mother* was experienced as a 'miscast', and was therefore unknown to the *focus*, and why the *context* experienced a 'wobbly knee' when the *mother* became the topic. This strongly suggests that the *context of the miracle* represents the foster mother. The exclusion indicated many times so far now turns out to be that of the client's whole family of origin.

Facilitator: As their descendant, you have a right to be with them. Come now and join their line, and notice how that feels.

The client follows this instruction and leans against his *ancestors*.

Mother: I felt a really strong tug to the left and was totally relieved when the *ancestors* came. Now I can stand up straight again.
Client (to *mother*): It feels incredibly good to hear that.
Facilitator: You can now stand to the left of the *ancestors*, and see if that's better for you.
Mother: Yes, I feel better here.
Miracle: It did me a lot of good when the *focus* looked behind. It was nice to see how he made contact. I don't know what the *goal* wants from me. I can't see the *context* any more from here.
The *focus* is asked to return to his position, and the client takes his seat again.
Context: It did me good when the *ancestors* came and now the *mother* is standing further back.
Facilitator (to *context*): Say to the *mother*: 'It is better for me that this is your place … and I am me … and you are you … and no one can replace you as the mother.' … and then add: 'I took on something for you … and it did not work.' … and then say to the *focus*: 'I am only your foster mother … this is your real mother.'

The *context of the miracle* is explicitly changed (renamed) as the *foster mother* and thereby an explicit change of structural level to a *family structural constellation*.

The *context* repeats these statements to *mother* and *focus*, respectively. The *focus* then answers:

Focus: Now there is no longer a miscast, now she is my mother.

In the meantime we have the following constellation picture:

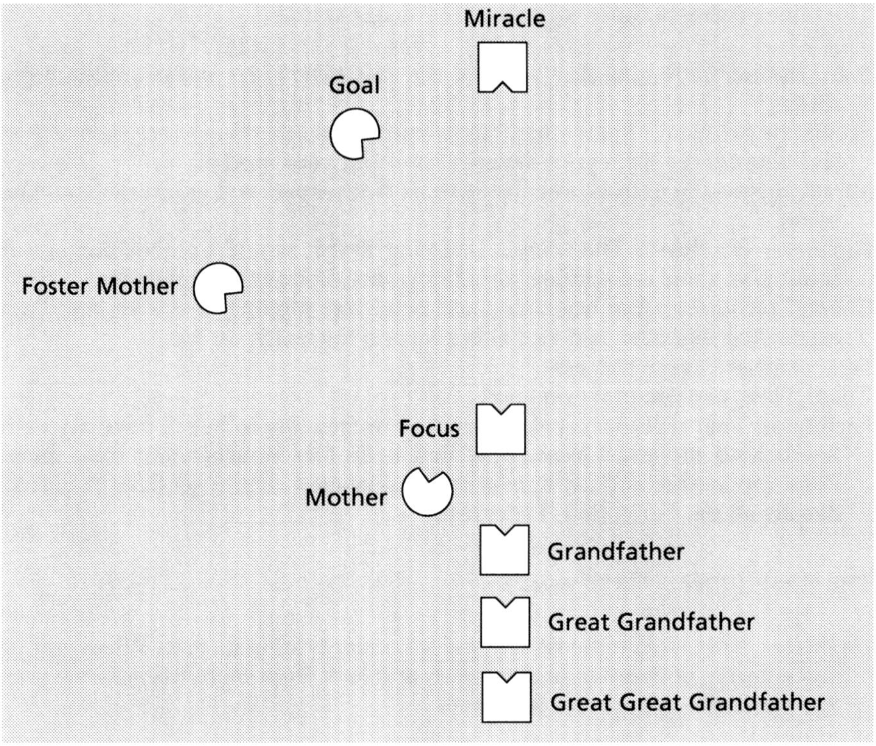

Figure 60

The facilitator asks the client again to take the position of his *focus*. Client and *focus* change places.

Facilitator: Now see how you feel here. If you like, you may also ask the representatives questions – the representatives can say whatever occurs to them or just wait.
Client (to *foster mother*): Why didn't you take care of me?
Foster mother: I didn't have the miracle. It's good that the *miracle* is there. It's like cooling water in which I can swim
Client: Are you ready to do things better?
Foster mother: With the help of the others, yes.
Client: I need something else from you.
Facilitator: Turn around to your *mother*, and take strength from her eyes.

The client does as instructed: looks at his *mother* and takes energy from her through eye contact.

Facilitator: Now turn back round again and say to the *foster mother*: 'When I need something, I will take it from her (the mother). She can give me what I need.'

The client repeats these words to the *foster mother*.

Foster mother: Only now do I begin to see you. (The *foster mother* smiles at the
   client.)
Facilitator (to client): Remember that in future you can always look behind you
   and take energy from your ancestral line and your mother.
Miracle: Instead of reproaching the *foster mother*, respect and gratitude would be
   better.
Facilitator (to client): The *miracle* is saying that it would be good for you if
   could give some recognition for what your foster mother gave you.
Client: I recognise what was there, and what was missing, was a lot, and I am
   expressing this now, and that was a lot and too much for me.
Foster mother: I know this now.
Client: Now you can make amends.
Facilitator: That will make you dependent on her. Say to her: 'I have my own
   line behind me and I know now that I can take nourishment from there.
   What my mother and my ancestors can give me I cannot get from you. And
   despite all the difficulties, I survived.'

The client repeats these words.

Facilitator: Now look at the *miracle* and take energy from its eyes. When you've
   had enough, bow down in front of it, and look from there towards the *goal*.
   You can make this into a good habit.

The client follows these instructions.

Goal: I feel very good when you refuel from the *miracle*. This energy is good for
   the both of us.
Foster mother (to client): I'm very happy that you went to the *miracle*. Maybe
   there's something there that we can both see something beautiful in.
Client: That would be nice.
Facilitator: Look back round at the *miracle*, and take energy form there with the
   knowledge that you are being supported form behind. This is how things
   will be from now on. Now absorb this picture completely, and be open to
   what your heart does with it… because a constellation always ends with the
   start of something new.

Chapter IX

The solution geometric interview

In the **solution geometric interview**, the constellations experience and the solution focused procedure are combined interactively. The *solution geometric interview* offers the most surprising opportunities to perform a solution focused interview partially or entirely using representatives in lieu of the actual people. The verbal language then becomes part of the representatives' perception and is thus understood more receptively than actively. In the solution geometric interview, it is recommended that excluded members be introduced from the start or in any case as early as possible. It is also recommended to do as much rearrangement as necessary at the start until temporal order (e.g. in a team or a sibling line) has been respected and the individual representatives establish eye contact with each other, thereby allowing dialogue to be established. That is to say that the constellation criteria should be met before the interview can start.

If the interview is begun without first respecting the constellation criteria, however, topics such as excluded people and the finding of a suitable arrangement for the participants will come to dominate proceedings. This can give rise to intense experiences for the representatives, which can be managed far more easily through positional re-arrangements than during the conversation. On the other hand, it can also be useful to respond to this representative perception during the conversation and then introduce changes using scaled questions, thereby obtaining indications for re-arrangements.

If, during the *solution geometric interview*, other relevant people are mentioned, these can then be brought into the constellation using representatives. This allows them to be integrated and contribute to the conversation as people present through representation.

The advantage of combining the constellations experience with solution focused procedures lies in the ability to add absent people to the constellation and talk with them. We are therefore able to perform interviews with absent people during therapy, organisational consulting and mediation. The many fields of application for the **constellation of absent people** will be presented below.

IX.1 Application: Teams – The constellation of the absent team

With large teams in clinics or consultancy institutes it is not uncommon for only a part of a team to be present for a given session. Generally speaking, those that come to a session are those who happen not have any meetings and those interested in change (the latter are usually the 'customers' in the SFT sense). However, it is still important to take into consideration the perspective of those not present. This can be done using the *Constellation of the absent team*.

IX.1.1 The constellation dominates the conversation

Where exclusion and succession tendencies have become an issue for a given team, the constellation method can provided a suitable way of reintroducing the absent people and breaking up this dynamic. The constellation can be particularly useful where tendencies come to the fore in a team that make no sense in the context of those present. On the other hand, when trying to dissolve current conflicts or change the time structure, the formation of the team or an organisational structure, the solution focused interview can help develop the relevant steps. It is then easier to implement the results of the interview precisely using the exercises.

The solution focused approach is accepted more readily by organisations than in a therapeutic context, since companies are task-orientated systems and more attuned to goal achievement. Families, on the other hand, are more development and propagation-oriented, placing emphasis more on relationships and bonded connections. Nonetheless, situations also arise in organisations and their subsystems where bonded connections are much stronger and ignoring the systems theory basic principles can have dire consequences. The following case study is one such example.

IX.1.1.1 Case study 1: Succession tendencies in a team

Mr M participated in a personal development group. He had just been appointed project manager of a team that had been in existence for a long time. His predecessor, who had been well-liked, had died suddenly of a heart attack. Mr M had recently been involved in ten near-fatal accidents. Through a constellation, he wanted to see if this tendency could be changed. (The names of the representatives are again shown in italics.)

Facilitator: What is your current problem?
Mr M: Recently I've suffered a whole range of near-fatal accidents, and this disconcerts me a lot.

Facilitator: After you had the first near-fatal accident, what was then different from before?

Mr M: I've had a new job for four months, and I have to drive for around an hour to get there from my home. During these journeys, there's been around six occasions when I nearly hit or drove into another car. I was alright each time, but I'm considering switching to the train. In addition, I've nearly been run over by a car on three separate occasions, despite having looked around well beforehand.

Facilitator: Is there something special about your new job?

Mr M: My predecessor died suddenly of a heart attack and they needed a replacement urgently because the existing project was coming to an end and the deadlines would be missed otherwise. One of my colleagues (Mr K) suffers from frequent tachycardia and has been off work a lot recently.

Facilitator: Were there periods before when you suffered frequent accidents?

Mr M: No.

Facilitator: I suggest we do a constellation of you and your colleagues. How many are there of you working on this project?

Mr M: There's six of us, four men and two women.

Facilitator: In what order did the people join the team?

Mr M: Mr N, Mr K, Mr E and Mrs S all joined the team at the same time. After them came Mrs F and then finally me.

Facilitator: OK, choose someone from the group to represent you… someone for Mr N … for Mr K … for Mr E … Mrs S … Mrs F… and someone for your predecessor, the previous project manager … and place them, one after the other. First, stand behind your representative, touch him on the shoulders, feel your hands, feel the soles of your feet on the floor, and take a step forwards following the direction that arises.

Mr M places all the representatives in the constellation, one after the other. We then obtain the following picture (the *focus* stands for the representative of Mr M).

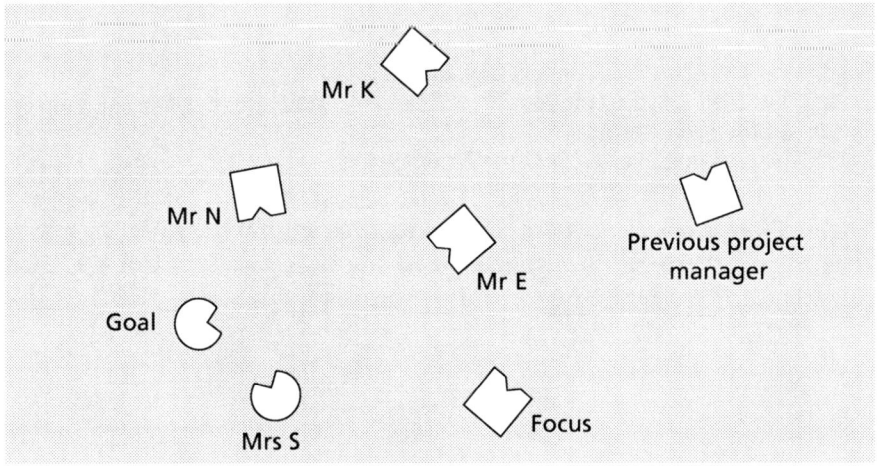

Figure 61

The facilitator now asks each representative about the sensations they experience in their respective positions.

Focus: I can see the *previous project manager*. I find this direction interesting. It draws me towards him. Otherwise I feel I don't really belong and feel weak.

Previous project manager: I'm looking backwards. That's all that interests me. I no longer have anything to do with what is behind me.

Mr K: It's as if my heart were vibrating. This bothers me. I'm very weak and exhausted. I can only see the *project manager* (points to the *previous project manager*).

Mr N: Somehow the four of us belong together (points to *Mr E, Mrs F, Mrs S*). I feel the others less strongly. I feel cramped in the circle. I can't see the *focus*.

Mr E: I also only see us four. I'm bothered by what's happening behind me. I'd like to turn around.

Mrs S: I can only see the four of us. However, we're standing far too close to each other. I feel very cramped.

Mrs F: I'm a little confused. I can see the *previous project manager*, but he's turning his back to us. Although I can see the *new project manager* and I have not contact with him.

Facilitator (to Mr M): Does this picture seem right to you?

Mr M: Absolutely. It's clear to me now why I'm being drawn into the accidents.

A test is now performed. The Facilitator holds a cataleptic hand over the position where the *previous project manger* is looking.

Facilitator: What changes for you, when something appears here?

Previous project manager: That feels good. I feel much, much better.

Facilitator: Say to that which appears to you here: 'It feels good to see you.'

A person from the group is placed in the position of the cataleptic hand. The *previous project manager* repeats the words as indicated by the facilitator.

Facilitator: Does anyone else feel any change?

Focus: That feels good to me too. Now I can also move my head to the left and can see the *team members*.

Mr K: The pressure is gone, and my heart is calm.

The facilitator rearranges the representatives so that the order in which they joined the team is respected and the *team members* can see each other better. We obtain the second picture, as follows:

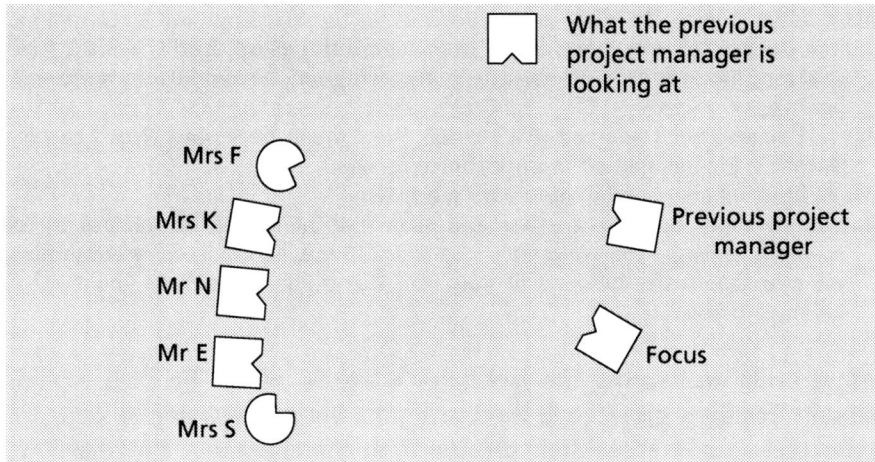

Figure 62

Facilitator: What has changed for the *focus*?
Focus: Now I'm seeing my *team* for the first time. They are completely new to me. It feels good to see my *predecessor* next to me. But I still feel somewhat wobbly.
Facilitator: Say to your *predecessor*: 'You came before me, and I came after you.'
Focus: 'You came before me, and I came after you'.... It feels good to say that, it makes things clearer.
Facilitator: Say to him now: 'I have taken over a heavy burden from you. It has nothing to do with me, and therefore I'm giving it back to you.' Then place this bag at his feet so that it touches both feet. (Gives the *focus* a bag to use.)

After repeating the facilitator's words, he lays the bag at the feet of the *previous project manager*, who takes the burden. The *focus* steps back again. In placing the bag at the feet of the *previous project manager*, the *focus* has to bow to his *predecessor*, albeit without this being mentioned directly. This act of deference occurs casually, without creating any resistance.

Facilitator: How does the *previous project manager* feel now?
Previous project manager: The burden belongs to me. I feel better with it.
Facilitator: How does the *focus* feel?
Focus: Much much better. I can breathe easily again. The pressure is completely gone and I can now see the *team members* much more clearly.
Facilitator: The *previous project manager* can now take a few steps backwards. How does that feel for the *focus*?
Focus: Now things can start. Now I can begin to act.
Facilitator: What has changed in the meantime for the other *team members*?
Mrs S: I feel much better now. Now I have contact with the *focus* and the other *team members*.

Mr E: I feel similar. I'm also seeing the *focus* for the first time. It felt really good that the burden was given back. That cleared things up. And when the *focus* said that he came only afterwards, it also felt good. I can take him more seriously now.

Mr N: I've also been relieved of a burden. I feel much freer now. Now I can see the *focus*. He has gained in importance for me.

Mr K: I think I also need to give back a burden.

Facilitator: Here, take this cushion and place it at the feet of the *previous project manager*, saying: 'You were very important to me. I tried to carry something for you that really belongs to you, and I'm giving it back to you now. It belongs to you.'

Mr K nods on hearing the facilitator's words, which he then repeats slowly. He then gives back the burden to the *previous project manager*, who picks up the cushion, presses it to his chest and breathes out, relieved.

Facilitator (to *previous project manager*): Say to *Mr K*: 'Its rightful place is with me, leave it here!'

The *previous project manager* repeats the words spoken by the facilitator. *Mr K* nods and begins to laugh.

Facilitator (to *Mr K*): How do you feel now?

Mr K: I feel stronger. My heart has calmed down completely and I'm beginning to sense for the first time that there are other people in the team. I'm also seeing the *focus* for the first time as a leader.

Facilitator (to Mr M): How do you feel now? Did that make sense to you?

Mr M: I'm surprised. So much of it made sense, but then there were also some completely new aspects that I'd never thought about before. It was very hard for me to establish contact with my colleagues. I also noticed how at the beginning they were suspicious of me and I didn't feel sufficiently respected. At the moment I can't imagine them acting differently.

The representatives are now given chairs and sit down maintaining their position. The facilitator joins them by sitting down opposite *what the previous project manager is looking at.*

Facilitator: There were some difficulties in your department after your previous project manager died so suddenly… and for some of you it was hard to adjust so quickly to a new person…and to accept the new project manager.

Some of the *team members* nod.

Facilitator: I assume it became easier for you, after the rituals we performed, to establish contact with each other.

The *team members* and the *previous project manager* nod in agreement.

Facilitator: Now I'd like to ask a somewhat difficult question, which each of you can answer just to yourself to start with … Afterwards, whoever wants to can tell their answers to the others … When you go home after this session … and maybe see your family again … eat an evening meal … and sometime during this night you become tired and go to bed … Assuming … during the night, between today and tomorrow … a miracle happens … just like that … and the miracle is that everything that brought you here today was solved … and that really would be a miracle … wouldn't it? … And when each of you wakes up tomorrow morning … and no one tells you that this miracle has occurred … how would you notice it? … What would be the first signs for you that the miracle had occurred? …

With a questioning look, the facilitator looks around the circle.

Facilitator: Who would like to begin?

Mr N: Well, a part of this miracle has already happened. I already feel better in the team… and now I'm able to respect the *focus*… What might also happen if the miracle occurred would be that we would once more be able to have trust in each other.

Facilitator: How would that show itself?

Mr N: Well, I'd share my ideas again, and I'd approach the new project manager when I needed something … He'd belong to us then … Yes, that would be different.

Facilitator: Anything else?

Mr N: Yes, *Mr K* would be there more often. That would make a big difference as we'd be able to work more consistently and not continually think about who can cover for *Mr K*.

Facilitator: Anything else?

Mr N: That's all.

Mr K: I'd like to continue … When I wake up in the morning, I'd already have more energy and look forward to the coming day … I'd have the feeling I could do what is required of me … and I also don't think I'd be absent as often. That would be a great relief. My bad conscience about my frequent absences would be gone.

Facilitator: And what would be there in its place?

Mr K: I'd be able to apply myself to my work, like before… and I'd have trust in the new project manager (*focus*)… It helped me a lot to give back the burden. Somehow I was still constantly orientated towards the *previous project manager*… Now I can turn towards the new one.

Facilitator: Anything else?

Mr K: That's it, basically.

Mr E: I hadn't seen the new project manager at all before… Now I can see him and he seems nice to me. I think I'll be able to work well with him now.

Facilitator: Anything else?

Mr E: (shakes his head)

Facilitator: Who wants to be next?

Previous project manager: The ritual was a great relief for me. It bothered me greatly that the others had carried so much of my burden. The ritual to me was the miracle.

What the previous project manager is looking at: I feel the same. For me the most important thing was being brought into the picture and being seen by the *previous project manager*. I'd have much connection with the others.

The facilitator nods and looks round the circle questioningly.

Mr S: I was very sceptical about the *new project manager*... and when the miracle happened I was able to relinquish my scepticism and listen to him.
Facilitator: How would this show?
Mr S: I'd talk to him, ask him things from time to time and no longer avoid him.
Facilitator: And?
Mr S: I'd approach him more...
Facilitator: Who else would like to speak?
Mrs F: I feel similar to *Mr S*. I'd see the miracle firstly in that I would be able to trust the *new project manager*.

The facilitator nods and looks from one representative to the other.

Focus: I'd also like to speak ... A lot of things have changed for me during the constellation as well as now during the conversation... A large part of the miracle has also occurred for me ... I've been relieved of a burden ... and it feels good to have my *predecessor* and *what he's looking at* in the picture ... and for the first time I've made contact with my colleagues. In the beginning I felt totally isolated, and didn't know how I'd be able to work with them ... It helped me a lot to hear what had changed for them when the miracle happened ... Now I have a picture of how things could go from here, and for the first time I can get to grips with the project ... Before, so many things were unexplained. Now we've become more of a group.
Facilitator (to Mr M): How do you feel hearing that?
Mr M: Many things are now a lot clearer to me, more concrete. I now also feel more a part of my team, and more present.

The facilitator asks Mr M to move into the position of the *focus*. Mr M does as instructed.

Facilitator: From this position, look at all the *team members*. Establish eye contact with them ... Look round at the *previous project manager*, and see how he is able to carry his burden and how it is in good hands there ... Look at *what he was looking at*, and see that that belongs to him ... Look at the individual *team members* ... take you time over each one.

Mr M follows the facilitator's instructions.

Mr M: It really moves me to be able to look at all of them. I feel now for the first time that I belong.
Facilitator: Absorb this picture. The rest will happen in the outside world.

Mr M's tendency to have accidents disappeared immediately after the constellation. He was able to work much better with his colleagues. The next time he went to work, Mrs S and Mrs F greeted him in a very friendly manner, as if they had experienced something of the atmosphere of the constellation.

IX.1.2 The solution lies in the constellation

As opposed to the previous example, exclusion plays no role in the following constellation. This shows itself in the feelings and arrangement of the representatives and allows us, after positioning the individual representatives, to move straight to the solution focused conversation.

IX.1.2.1 Case study 2: When cooperation fails

The following constellation was performed during a seminar on organisational structural constellations. Mrs B, whose colleagues were not present, wanted to work on the problem of how to improve cooperation in her department. No one had been sacked or left under duress. Since the other department heads were not participating in the seminar, I suggested that she first position herself and the absent department members, and then I would perform the interview with the representatives.

Facilitator: How many do colleagues do you work with?
Mrs B: There's four of us working together.
Facilitator: In what order did each of you join the department?
Mrs B: Mr L and Mrs W have been there the longest, then I joined, followed by Mrs N.
Facilitator: OK, now choose someone from among the participants for you … someone for Mr L … someone for Mrs W … and someone for Mrs N. Now go behind your representative, check that you have good contact to the floor with you feet, and feel how your hands touch your representative on the shoulder. Take a step forward and follow the direction that arises.

Mrs B chooses four representatives from among the participants and places them. The facilitator then places a chair behind each representative so that they can sit down for the interview. Afterwards, the facilitator also sits down facing the semi-circle, and we obtain the following picture:

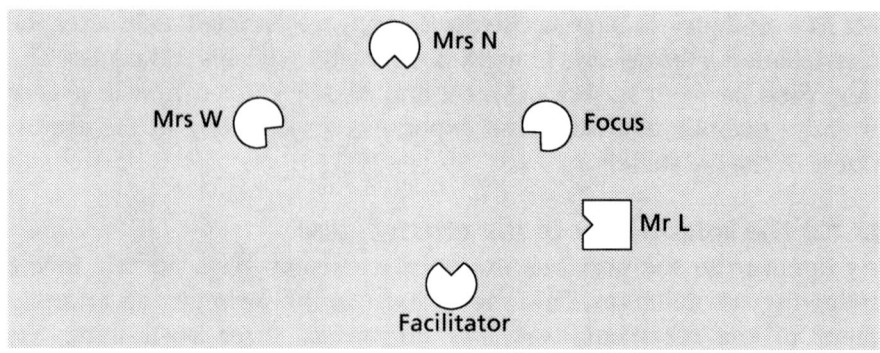

Figure 63

Facilitator: How does the *focus* feel?
Focus: I have contact with everyone, this is a good position.
Facilitator: How is *Mrs W*?
Mrs W: I can feel some ill-feeling between *Mrs N* and *Mr L*. I myself feel very good in this position.
Facilitator: How is *Mrs N*?
Mrs N: I'm happy that I'm not sitting next to *Mr L*. It's like he's disputing my position. I can feel a gentle nagging in my left foot, otherwise I feel good.
Facilitator: How is *Mr L*?
Mr L: I also feel hostility towards *Mrs N*: somehow I don't feel good, as if *Mrs N* were competing with me.
Facilitator (to Mrs B): Does any of that sound familiar to you? Does this picture fit?
Mrs B: Yes, very much so. Mrs N and Mr L have been competing with each other for a long time and they avoid each other. Otherwise we all get on well in the department. But we still find it hard cooperating.
Facilitator: First I'd like to ask *Mr L* and *Mrs N* to swap places so that the department members are sitting in the order in which they joined the department.

Mr L and *Mrs N* change places, giving the following picture:

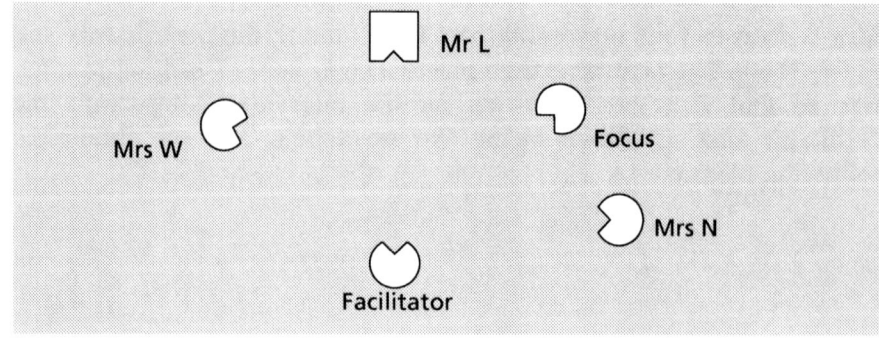

Figure 64

Facilitator: What has changed for the *focus*?

Focus: That feels better to me now.

Facilitator: What has changed for *Mrs W*?

Mrs W: It's also better for me like this.

Facilitator: How does *Mr L* feel now?

Mr L: I feel significantly better now.

Facilitator: Has anything changed for *Mrs N*?

Mrs N: The feeling in my foot is gone and, surprisingly, I feel much better now.

Facilitator: Now I'd like to ask quite a difficult question. You can each answer the question to yourselves ... Afterwards you can give your answers in turn ... Imagine that this constellation was successful and our seminar had already come to an end ... Tonight you go home and maybe see your family or friends again ... maybe you eat together ... and then you become tired, go to your bed and fall asleep ... Assuming ... during this night, i.e. the coming night ... a miracle occurs ... and the miracle was that all the problems that brought you here ... were solved in one fell swoop ... just like that... and no one tells you that this miracle has happened ... How would you be able to tell the next morning that this miracle had occurred? ... What would be different for you? ... What would be different at your work? ... Would anyone apart from you notice the miracle? ... What would be the reactions to your changed behaviour? ... Who would like to begin?

Mrs W: I could start.

Facilitator: Yes. How would you notice the next morning that the miracle had occurred for you?

Mrs W: I'd be much happier about going to work and would be pleased to see the others ...

Facilitator: What else would be different?

Mrs W: I'd be cheerful again ... tell jokes again ... I'd be more involved again ...

Facilitator: And what else would change?

Mrs W: I'd again find my work easier ... and we wouldn't have as much to do anymore.

Facilitator: How so?

Mrs W: We wouldn't get so many jobs all at once.

Facilitator: Assuming, one day, perhaps far in the future, the day came when you again got many jobs all at once. If the miracle had happened, how would you react to this?

Mrs W: ... We'd arrange things more among ourselves and consult each other about how we can solve it together.

Facilitator: Are there occasions when you already talk and consult each other?

Mrs W: We always want to, but never manage it. There's no time.

Facilitator: Would anything else be different after the miracle had occurred?

Mrs W: Yes, there'd be less pressure. We'd have more time to talk to each other ...

Facilitator: Anything else?

Mrs W: I think that's it, basically.

Facilitator: Who else would like to talk about their miracle?

Mr L: I'd like to continue.

Facilitator: Good.

Mr L: We'd be able to speak to each other again. The tension and the stress would be gone. I think we'd all notice it. We'd be more at ease with each other ...

Facilitator: And what else would be different?

Mr L: We'd discuss our work more ... talk more and find ways to tackle things together ...

Facilitator: When would you make time for that?

Mr L: During the breaks. We'd have breaks again.

Facilitator: Anything else different?

Mr L: Yes, there'd be less pressure coming from outside.

Facilitator: And assuming you again had so much to do, but the miracle had occurred, how then would you notice this?

Mr L: We'd consult each other more and close ranks more, together we'd be strong. I've been working on a new system that would be very helpful for cooperation. We could reduce the amount of work if we reorganised certain things. I've developed this program, it still needs some fine tuning, but I'm very optimistic ...

Facilitator: Anything else?

Mr L: I think that's all.

Focus: Then I'll continue ... For me the biggest difference would be that the pressure from outside would be less and we'd speaking to each other again ... we'd joke with each other again ... and take coffee breaks together again ...

Facilitator: Anything else?

Focus: I think that's about it, basically.

Facilitator: And in what would you notice the miracle, *Mrs N*?

Mrs N: I'd have the courage to leave. I don't think the pressure would be less, and then it'd be best if I went.

Facilitator: Anything else?

Mrs N: I agree with the others that it'd be good that we had more time to talk with each other. I just don't think this will be possible due to the external pressure.

Facilitator: Was there ever a time when the external pressure was less?

Mrs N: Yes, but that was a long time ago. We were working on another project then. I think the times have changed. It won't be like it used to be before.

Facilitator (to Mrs B): What is it like for you to hear this conversation?

Mrs B: I'm totally amazed! It's true: Mr L really does work all the time on his computer developing new systems. He believes we can solve our problem by completely reorganising ourselves. And Mrs N also said recently that she was planning to leave ... I'm completely taken aback by all these correlations.

Facilitator: Yes, it never fails to surprise ... I see that you feel a lot of pressure from outside but that you also have a lot of ideas about how things could be improved. You also have an idea, albeit vaguely, of how to bring this about. You agree that it would be better to consult each other more, exchange more. Assuming the miracle had already happened, when and how often in the coming week would you sit down together?

Focus: Well, we need to meet at least twice a week. (the others nod)

Facilitator: And what days would you do this?

Focus: I think Tuesday and Friday morning would be convenient.

Mr L: And we'd need to take half an hour.

The facilitator looks around the group with a questioning look. The other representatives nod.

Facilitator: How realistic do you consider this plan?

Mrs W: If we really put our minds to it, we could do it.

Mrs N: It wouldn't be easy, but we could give it a try. We have too much work as it is, so it won't make much difference if we lose a bit of extra time.
Facilitator: How would your boss react to it?
Mr L: He is very busy and often not there. He wouldn't notice it, not until he sees us achieving more. But I think if we reorganise, we'd get more done. We should give it a try. (The others nod in agreement.)
Facilitator (to Mrs B): What do you say to that?
Mrs B: I think it's an idea we could try. I think somehow we'd given up and therefore were unable to cope with the pressure. I'm more hopeful now. We should give it a go.
Facilitator: Where, on a scale of 0 to 10, would you place yourself now, where 0 represents the moment you decided to do this constellation, and 10 represents the miracle?
Mrs B: ... At 6
Facilitator: What helped you to move from 0 to 6?
Mrs B: It was encouraging to see that really we all want the same thing. It also became clearer to me that the pressure affecting us was coming from outside, and not from the work we do. In fact, I like my work a lot. The hectic situation spoilt it for me. That's clearer to me now. I'm no longer so confused ... and I can see way out.

This new perspective helped Mrs B to deal better with the hectic situation at work and to be friendlier with her colleagues. On her initiative, she and her colleagues began to meet once, and later twice, a week, which lead to an improvement to working atmosphere.

IX.2 Application: Mediation – The constellation of the absent conflict partner

A further application of the *solution geometric interview* is found in mediation. Although both conflict partners are normally present, there are some situations where it can an advantage to work with only one party. For example, when both partners refuse to speak to each other, a constellation allows us to develop the conditions for a joint discussion. When mediating between a married couple, for example, if the conflict is related to an entanglement of the partners vis-à-vis their respective families of origin, a constellation may help highlight the problem directly and then solve the disorder it gives rise to. An example of this is given in Chapter IX.3.1. The following case study shows how conflicts can be approached when only one of the partners acts as a referring agent and hence only this partner is present.

IX.2.1 Case study 3: Conflict solutions from afar
Mrs T was having trouble with three colleagues with whom she had worked on a previous project. She was now working on a new project with different colleagues. She still met her old colleagues frequently,

however, since they all worked in the same department, and as a result had found it difficult to distance herself from the old situation. The following constellation took place in one of my personal development groups.

Facilitator: What's your current problem?

Mrs T: Three colleagues of mine have been giving me a really hard time. When I meet them in the department, I get all tensed up inside. I want to be able to forget the problem I had with them.

Facilitator: What would it be like for you instead?

Mrs T: I'd be happy again

Facilitator: And assuming... during the night a miracle occurs... and the miracle was that everything that made you want to do this constellation was solved... and if this happened so suddenly that would be a miracle, wouldn't it?... How would you notice the next morning that the miracle had happened?

Mrs T: When I see the three of them it would no longer bother me.

Facilitator: What would be there instead?

Mrs T: Id be indifferent to them.

Facilitator: What else would be different?

Mrs T: I'd be able to dedicate myself fully to my new project.

Facilitator: Anything else?

Mrs T: I'd be less wary of my new colleagues.

Facilitator: How would you behave towards them instead?

Mrs T: I'd show them more trust.

Facilitator: Would anything else be different?

Mrs T: I think that's all.

Facilitator: Good, now select someone for you, for your goal, then for the miracle and for each of the three colleagues.

Mrs T chooses representatives from the group and places them in the constellation. We get the following picture:

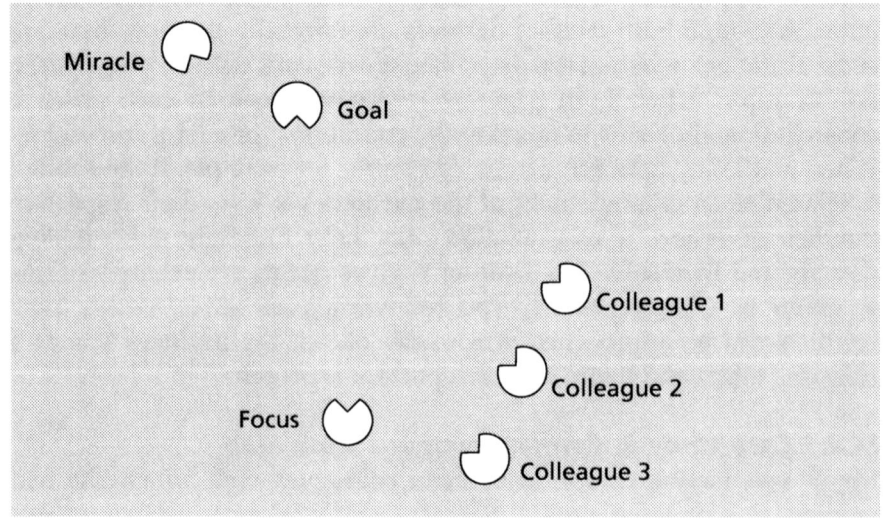

Figure 65

Facilitator: How does the *focus* feel?

Focus: I'm looking at my *goal* and am surprised it's so close. I don't notice the *colleagues*.

Facilitator: How does the *goal* feel?

Goal: I can see the *focus* and am very impatient: she should come to me quickly. The *miracle* behind me is doing me a lot of good, it gives me strength.

Facilitator (to *focus*): The *goal* is open-heartedly inviting you to go to her. Take a step towards your *goal*. What changes for you?

Focus: Now I feel a lot of resentment towards my *colleagues*.

Facilitator: Turn to your right and look at your *colleagues*. What has changed?

Focus: The resentment is gone. I am really surprised. I didn't expect that.

Facilitator: What is there instead of the resentment?

Focus: I can look at them like normal human beings.

Facilitator: Say to them: 'You were bad to me, but that is passed now. I'm going to turn towards my *goal* now.'

The *focus* repeats the facilitator's words.

Facilitator: Now turn towards your *goal*. How does that feel?

Focus: Now I can move towards my *goal*. The anger is gone. Now I can also see the *miracle*.

Facilitator: How does the *miracle* feel?

Miracle: Very good, since she turned back towards her *goal*.

Facilitator: We're now going to put chairs behind the representatives so they can sit down. The focus should sit down facing her *colleagues*.

The individual representatives are given chairs and they sit down. The facilitator also sits down in the circle, resulting in the following picture:

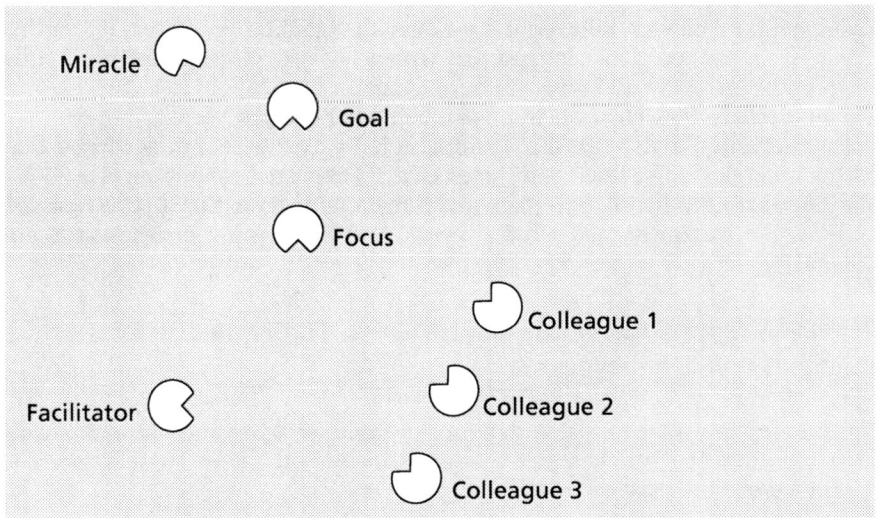

Figure 66

Facilitator: What has changed for *colleague 1*?

Colleague 1: I'm glad that the *focus* in the end turned towards her *goal*. It felt bad when she was looking in our direction. It was as if I were standing in a place of execution. I had the feeling that I needed to defend myself.

Facilitator: How did *colleague 2* feel?

Colleague 2: Somewhat the same. When she turned towards us it at first gave me a bit of a fright, but then I was relieved to hear her say that her resentment was gone. As she turned back to her *goal* I felt better.

Facilitator: How is *colleague 3*?

Colleague 3: When she looked at us I started to feel queasy. When she turned back to her *goal* I felt better.

Facilitator (to *focus*): How does it feel to hear them say these things?

Focus: I noticed that when I looked at them I felt angry and didn't hide it, I gave them a taste of how I felt. But I feel better when I leave them be and look towards my *goal*.

Facilitator (to *colleagues*): Assuming the *focus* continues in the direction she just began and goes back to her job happy, dedicating herself to her new project while the *miracle* continues to take shape. How would you notice this? ... Who would like to start?

Colleague 1: The focus would be friendlier to me again and no longer so uncommunicative.

Facilitator: And what would that change for you?

Colleague 1: I'd no longer be so prejudiced. The atmosphere would change. We could be more at ease.

Facilitator (to *colleague 2*): What would change for you?

Colleague 2: The tension would be gone, it would be much easier. The situation between us would become normal again.

Facilitator: And how would you notice that?

Colleague 2: We'd be able to greet each other normally again when we met and even exchange a few pleasantries.

Facilitator: Anything else?

Colleague 2: I'd be very relieved if it was like that again.

Colleague 3: Me too. This charged atmosphere is very stressful for me. I'd be happy if things would revert to normal again.

Facilitator (to *focus*): How do you feel when you hear that?

Focus: Actually I'd also like the resentment to be over with. I'm surprised that the *colleagues* don't think bad things of me. I expected something else.

Facilitator: Say to them: 'You have given me a hard time. But that has passed now. I'm leaving to you what is yours, and I'm turning now towards my goal.'

The *focus* repeats the words as instructed. The representatives of the *colleagues* nod in agreement.

Facilitator: Now all the representatives can stand up again and put their chairs to one side. The *focus* can turn so that it can see both the *goal* and the *miracle*. How does the *focus* feel now?

Focus: Now it's easier for me to move towards my *goal*. I no longer feel the *colleagues* behind me as a threat.

Facilitator (to Mrs T): You can now take the place of the *focus* ... and then take a further step towards the *goal* ... Then turn around and see how you perceive the *colleagues*.

Mrs T takes the place of the *focus* and her face begins to light up. She looks around and the *colleagues* nod with goodwill. She takes a step towards her *goal* and the *miracle* and absorbs the picture with a gesture (holds both hands to her heart).

Mrs T was very surprised that the resentment she had harboured for her colleagues could disappear so quickly. She said later that now they go to work with a happy feeling again, and, when she meets the colleagues she is able to communicate with them in a normal way again.

IX.2.2 Case study 4: A wonderful encounter

The following constellation took place during an adult education seminar.

It deals with a conflict between a mother and her son. It was the mother who participated in the seminar. The constellation highlights the ways in which the *solution geometric interview* can condense situations and how the quality of both procedures – the experience in the SySt constellation and the specification of actions in the solution focused discussion – can combine to form a new whole.

Facilitator: What is your problem?
Participant: I've been in a state of conflict with my son now for a long time, and I'd like to clear this up.
Facilitator: Choose someone from the group to represent you and someone for your son, then position both of them. Start with the representative for you.

The participant follows the instructions, placing two representatives in the constellation. Afterwards she sits back down in the circle and we have the following picture:

Figure 67

Facilitator: How does the representative of the *focus*, feel? What has changed
for you since you were put in this position?

Focus: I'm looking into the distance, I'm far away. I can't look at my *son*. He's
also standing in my way.

Facilitator: How is the *son*?

Son: I don't like looking at her, I'm just staring at the wall. I am not interested
in her.

Facilitator: OK, now we can perform the conversation with the representatives.
You can sit down for this.

The representatives are given chairs, allowing them to sit down in their
respective positions. The facilitator joins them.

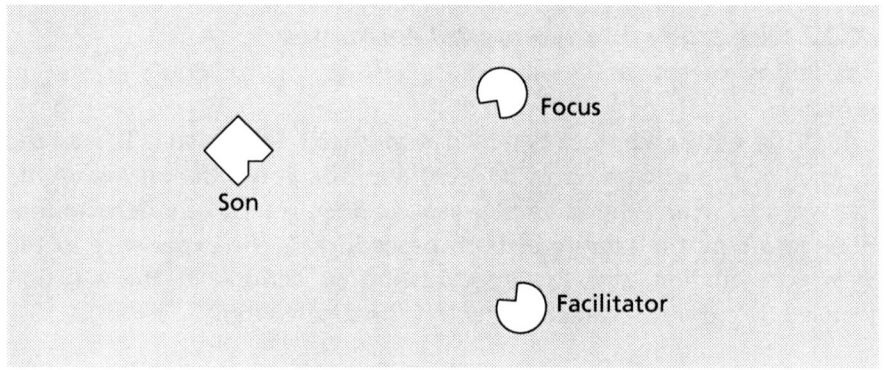

Figure 68

Facilitator: I'm going to ask quite a difficult question now, and you will need to
use your imagination to answer it ... Assuming ... our meeting today is
helpful to you, and later you go home ... do your day-to-day things ... and
sometime in the evening you become tired ... and you go to bed ...
Assuming ... during this night a miracle occurs ... and the miracle would be
... that everything... that brought you here today ... was solved ... in one
fell swoop ... and that really would be a miracle, wouldn't it? ... When you
wake up the next morning ... and nobody tells you that the miracle has
happened ... how would each of you notice that this miracle has happened?
... Who would like to give their answer first?

Focus: I can start ...

The *focus* begins to smile and looks at the *son*. The *son* looks back at the
focus, establishing eye contact, and both give each other a surprised and
heartfelt look.

Focus: (deeply moved) I can see him. And he's looking towards me. Before I
was unable to really see him.

Facilitator: What else is different?

Tears form in the *focus's* eyes.

Focus: We could talk now ... We could also do things together ... I can feel him now.
Facilitator (to *son*): How do you experience the miracle having happened?
Son: I can see her ... I'm happy to look at her. I'm more open towards her.
Facilitator: What else is different?
Son: We can talk like friends, no longer as mother and son.
Facilitator: What is different for you when you talk like friends instead of as mother and son?
Son: She'd stop constantly wanting something from me. There'd be no coercion anymore ... We'd be able to talk to each other effortlessly.
Facilitator (to the participant): Does this make sense to you? Do you recognise anything?
Participant: That was really moving, what my representative said ... Yes, we've been unable to look each other in the eye for a long time and unable to talk. And it's also true that I often try to make him do things: he has his head in the clouds so much, I'd like to shake him out of it.
Facilitator: (nods and turns back towards *focus* and *son*): Would anyone else apart from you notice the miracle?
Focus: Yes, my other son and my husband.
Facilitator: What would they notice?
Focus: They'd see that we were talking again ... Could my *son* come next to me now, so that we're looking in the same direction?
Facilitator: Yes, you can change your positions in that way. See if it feels better for you both.

The *son* shifts his chair closer to the *focus* and changes its direction so he can see the *focus* better, as shown in the following picture:

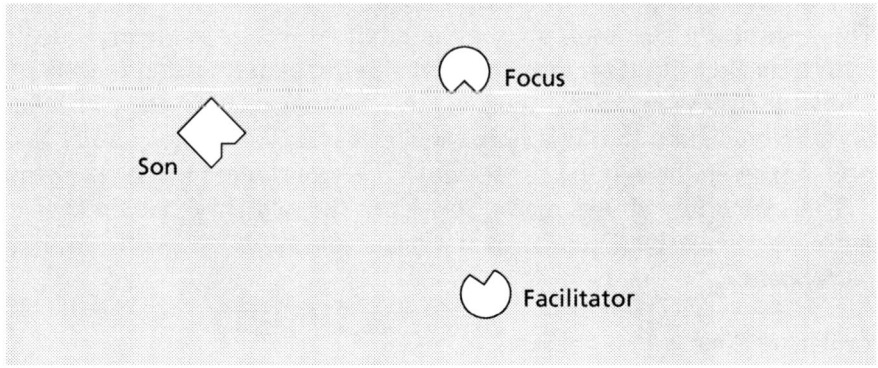

Figure 69

Facilitator: What things have changed for you?
Focus: It's better for me like this. We can both look in the same direction.
Son: It's better for me too. I can look at my *mother* when I want to, and I can also look in my own direction. I have the freedom to choose.

Facilitator: (to the participant): Now you take the position of the *focus*.

The woman takes the place of her *focus*.

Facilitator: How do you feel in this position?
Woman: Good, I can see my *son*. I perceive him in a totally different way now. I didn't see him in this way before.

Both the woman and her *son* are deeply moved and look at each other.

Woman: Everything that has happened before, was there in a condensed form in the constellation. Recently I saw him in a different way from how I normally do. I saw his beauty, which I normally don't notice. And this was taken further in the constellation.
Facilitator: Yes, that's good. Let that continue to work on you.

The constellation demonstrates well how the miracle is not dependent on the preceding conflict. An encounter between mother and son takes place in the constellation discussion. The relationship between them changes following the miracle question. The solution is found in this type of encounter. Mother and son both change their stance and consequently are able to deal with each other differently. For the client the conversation acted as a deeply touching encounter with her son. The **solution focused conversation** seems to also facilitate inclusion of the verbal reactions of the representatives, both among themselves and vis-à-vis the client.

IX.2.3 Case study 5: A difficult friend

This case study also took place at an adult education seminar. It deals with a conflict situation that one of the participants wanted to look at. Unlike the previous case, however, here it is revealed in the constellations conversation that it is only the client who views the conflict as a problem, even though the client thinks it is a problem for both of them.

This case study shows nicely how close the *solution focused interview* with representatives comes to a discussion situation with the real participants.

Facilitator: What is your problem?
T: There's a conflict between me and a man. We're actually friends, but recently he's been behaving erratically towards me, and I'm not sure how I should deal with it.
Facilitator: Is this conflict a problem for both of you, or just for you?
T: ... For both of us.
Facilitator: Good, now choose someone from the group to be your representative and someone for the man ... and then place both in the constellation.

The participant chooses two representatives and positions them so that we have the following picture:

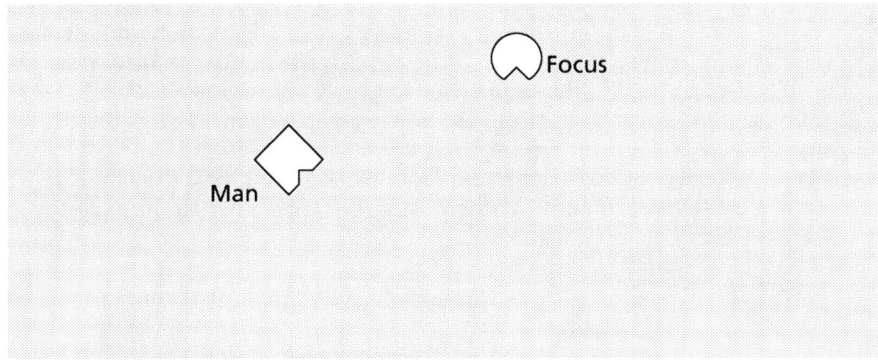

Figure 70

Facilitator: How does the *focus* feel? What has changed for you since you were placed in your position?
Focus: I'm looking past him. I don't feel anything particularly for him.
Facilitator: How does the *man* feel? What has changed for you?
Man: I can see her, but I also don't feel anything special.
Facilitator (to T): Is this how things are?
T: Yes, that's how it is.
Facilitator: Good, now you can take a seat where you are for the conversation.

The representatives are given chairs and sit down, joined by the facilitator.

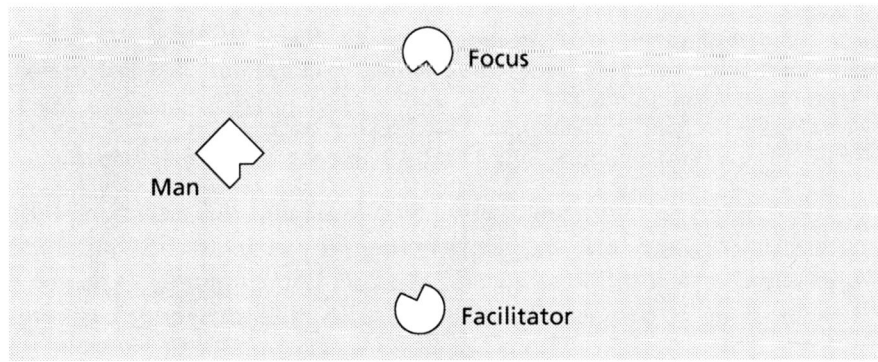

Figure 71

Facilitator: Now I'd like to ask you both a special question, which you can both answer afterwards ... Assuming the following conversation is helpful to both of you ... When you go home afterwards ... each to his own home ...

and there you see your family and return to you normal routine … and sometime during the evening you become tired and go to bed … Assuming during this night a miracle occurs … the miracle would be that everything that brought you here today were solved in one fell swoop… just like that … and that really would be a miracle, wouldn't it? … When nobody tells you that this miracle has happened … how would you notice the next morning that it had happened? Who would like to give their answer first?

Man: I couldn't follow the question. I don't see any problem. What is there to be solved?

Facilitator: OK, that's alright. (to *focus*) How would you notice the miracle?

Focus: We'd be able to talk to each other. We talk to each other on the same level, things would be better between us.

Facilitator: How would you notice that?

Focus: We'd be able to approach each other differently. We'd meet more, no longer be at cross-purposes.

Facilitator: And that's when you're at cross-purposes … but now the miracle has occurred … how would you react then?

Focus: Then I'd adopt a clear position, say more clearly where I stand, and maybe keep more distance.

Facilitator (to *man*): How does it feel when she says that?

Man: (angry) At last I can speak. I nearly exploded. I must be allowed to speak my mind. I can't keep checking carefully to see where she is and then adapt: that way I'm no longer myself. I can't keep saying things the way she wants, I need to be able have my own opinion, otherwise there's no longer any discussion. I'd like a clear counterpart. It'd be good for me if she adopts a clear position.

The facilitator looks at the client.

Focus: He can't just do as he wishes. He's behaving like a bull in a china shop.

Man: Now she's misunderstood me again. She wants to drag me onto her level. I want to be what I am. It'd be good for me if she said more clearly what she wants.

Focus: (contemplative): OK, I can express it more clearly.

Facilitator: If he continues doing as he wishes after the miracle has occurred, what would you do then?

Focus: I'd keep a greater distance and hold myself back.

Facilitator: Can you remember any situations like that before that helped?

At first it may seem unusual that the facilitator asks this question of the representative, and not the participant. However, in this situation representative perception allows the representative not only to perceive the sensations of the participant but also to give answers that correspond to the situation. This has been demonstrated in many previous *solution geometric interviews* and shows just how far-reaching representation can be.

Focus: … I can't think of any situation like that with him where I could have achieved that. I don't think that ever worked with him … I think it has something to do with the fact that he's a man. With women I've found it easier.

Facilitator (to T): Is this how it is?

T: I was very surprised by the question and curious how my representative would answer it. I was unaware of this. But what she says makes sense. This is very interesting for me.

Facilitator: Now take the place of the *focus*.

The participant takes up her position in the constellation.

Facilitator: How do you feel there?

T: It feels threatening. I'm afraid he's going to hit me. I don't trust him.

Facilitator: How can you protect yourself?

T: I'd need to move back, about a metre.

Facilitator: Then do so.

The participant shifts her chair about 20 centimetres backwards.

Man: (soft voice) I never wanted to do anything against you, and not at all to hurt you.

T: (touched) It feels good to hear you say that.

Man: I don't want you to distance yourself from me. I want to keep the closeness between us. I'm happy that you moved only 20 centimetres, and not a metre, back from me. If you need this, I feel it too.

T: It's nice that you say that.

Facilitator (to T): How do you feel now?

T: What he said made me feel good. Now I feel more myself.

Facilitator: I think we can leave it here. You can release your representative now.

The participant thanks her representatives and sits down again in her place in the circle.

This case study shows clearly how close a solution focused interview with representatives is to a conversation situation with the real participants. Compared with other SySt constellations, here the **representative perception is extended to include verbal reactions**. This vastly increases the opportunities of using systemic structural constellations and facilitates an even greater degree of solution focusing.

IX.3 Combining the solution geometric interview with a conflict constellation to solve accidental constellations

If, after the occurrence of conflict situations, one of the conflict partners would like to clarify the situation, this can also be done in the absence of the other conflict partner. The *solution geometric interview* can help to incorporate the absent conflict partner and clarify their role in the conflict.

In a conflict it it may be the case that one or more of the people involved have slid into the other partner's family system (as discussed above VII.3). We can understand this by imagining the excluded people from our family system being stored around us like vacant valence positions (as in a chemical compound) so that people we meet on a regular basis may begin to behave like these excluded people, despite not knowing them. In such cases, the behaviour of these people does not fit the current situation, but relates to the person they represent from the other's system. This behaviour often has absurd and harmful effects in the current situation. It can give rise to conflict that is incomprehensible and stressful for all those involved. It is therefore not very constructive to approach the problem in terms of 'how did this happen?' or 'why is this person so offensive?' The most helpful thing to do is to introduce a pattern disruption by breaking off the discussion and agreeing on a time for another meeting later.

We call these kinds of conflict **accidental constellations**. To solve this we use the **conflict constellation**. This is done in the form of a case reconstruction in which the real-life conflict events are treated like a constellation that was not guided towards an appropriate solution picture, but split into conflict and problem. By means of suitable interventions, the conflict events are guided towards a solution image. In this sense the conflict constellation works on three levels (the representative represents the actual person who in the original situation represents someone from an earlier time), whereas most other constellations only have two levels.

This type of conflict constellation can show *who* has slid into *whose* 'vacant valence position'. We can use it to look for a new context in which the initially mysterious behaviour would make sense and to which it relates. By seeing this new context, the people involved in the conflict are able to develop a new understanding between them. Both are able to see the other as entangled in the opposing system and no longer as the aggressor. This new perspective allows them to free themselves from the conflict and begin their relationship anew.

IX.3.1 Case study 6: When a friend becomes a representative

The following two constellations took place during an ongoing personal development group. Over the past six months, the client had been having a problem with a (female) friend she had known for the past four years. Despite their having discussed the issue many times together, neither was able to clarify the situation. (The names of the representatives are shown in italics.)

First constellation

Facilitator: What's your current problem?

Client: There's a conflict between me and my friend, and although we've discussed it many times, we haven't been able to sort it out.

Facilitator: How would you notice if the conflict were dissolved?

Client: We'd be able to talk to each other normally again, I'd no longer get so worked up and easily hurt ... it'd be like it used to be. My friend doesn't have a clue how to deal with me anymore.

Facilitator: I'm going to propose something now that might seem surprising at first ... Choose someone from the group as representative for yourself and someone for your friend, and place them in the constellation. We'll continue our conversation with the representatives.

Client: Yes, that does sound strange.

The client selects a representative for herself and one for her friend and positions both in the constellation before sitting down again. We obtain the following picture.

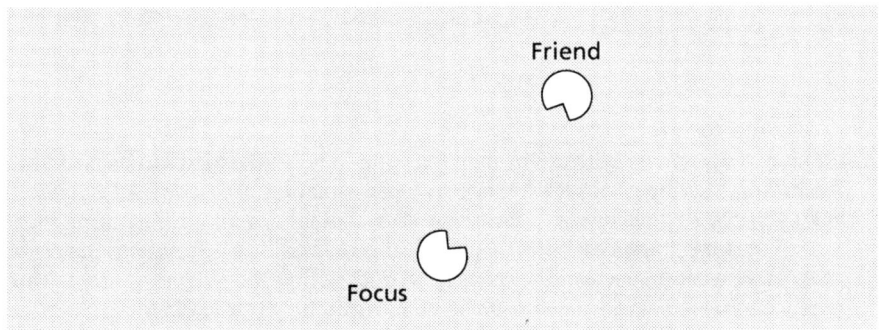

Figure 72

Facilitator: How have the feelings of the *focus* changed since she was positioned in the constellation?

Focus: My heartbeat has increased, I feel very worked up, I hardly dare look at her.

Facilitator: What has changed for the *friend*?

Friend: I feel very insecure, I feel uncomfortable when I look at her, and I'm slightly dizzy.

Facilitator (to client): Does that fit to your situation?

Client: Yes, precisely.

Facilitator: Then move into the position of your representative, and your representative can release herself from her role and rejoin the group.

The client follows these instructions. The facilitator then joins the client and the representative of the friend in the constellation and continues the conversation in this new arrangement, as show below.

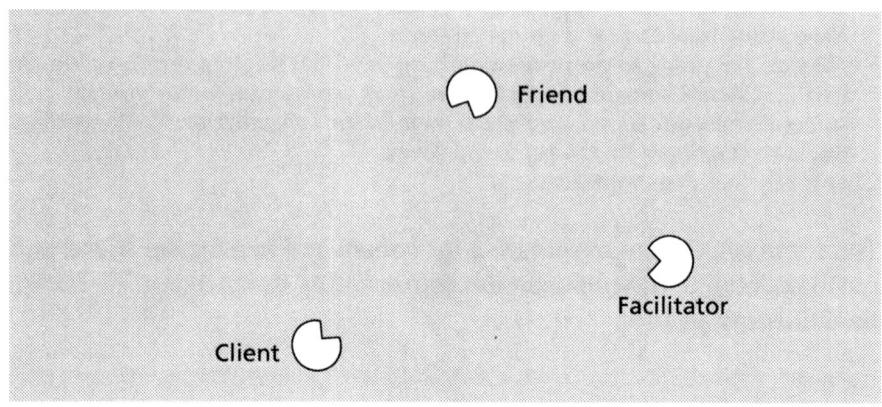

Figure 73

Facilitator: Now comes quite a difficult question that I'd like to ask to both of you: Assuming that the constellation and our conversation have come to an end ... and each of you goes home ... does something there ... eats your evening meal ... and at some stage you become tired and go to bed ... Assuming in the night ... a miracle occurs ... and the miracle would be that the reason we are sitting here together is solved ... and that really would be a miracle, wouldn't it? ... and then both of you wake up in the morning in your own beds ... and no one tells you that the miracle has happened ... from what things would you notice that the miracle had happened? ... Who would like to begin?

Client: I'd wake up and feel relieved, and when I think of my friend I'd no longer have that uneasy feeling ...

Facilitator: What would be there in its place?

Client: Things would be like before. We'd be able to talk to each other in a relaxed way again. I'd be able to concentrate on other things again. I'd feel freer ... we work at the same company ... I'd look forward to my work again and wouldn't be thinking about my friend all the time ... I'd have my concentration back.

Facilitator: Who else, other than you, would notice that the miracle had occurred?

Client: My friend, of course.

Facilitator: How would she notice?

Client: I'd be more relaxed and would have fewer expectations of her ... I'd be happier with things as they are.

Facilitator: How would your friend react to this?

Client: She'd be thoroughly relieved, I think. Things would be like before.

Facilitator: What was different then?

Client: We could just chat away freely. It used to be OK for me when we didn't see each other for a long time. I was calm and balanced, and I'd like to have that again now.

Facilitator: Who else would notice it?

Client: A friend, with whom I go out every now and again. He'd be really relieved. He notices that something's not right between me and her. I'd approach him more as well.

Facilitator: Who else would notice it?

Client: My colleagues at work.

Facilitator: What things would they see?

Client: I'd be more present, more approachable again. Recently I've been keeping more to myself.

Facilitator: How would they react to this?

Client: They'd say: 'At last you're back to normal again! What ever was the matter with you?'

Facilitator: How would you react to this?

Client: I'd laugh and say: 'I'm feeling better again.'

Facilitator: Would there be anyone else who would react to your miracle?

Client: I can't think of anyone else.

Facilitator (to *friend*): How would you notice the miracle?

Friend: I'd also be really relieved. I'd then know where I stand with her. Somehow things would be clearer between us. I'd think about her positively again and be pleased to see her. And, like her, I'd also be happier about going to work than I am now. That'd be a huge relief. We'd forge plans together again.

Facilitator: Who, other than you, would notice that the miracle had occurred?

Friend: Sabine (the client), of course. She'd notice how I'd again be pleased to see her.

Facilitator: Would anyone else notice the miracle?

Friend: Maybe some of my work colleagues?

Facilitator: How?

Friend: I'd be bright and cheerful again, especially when Sabine is with me. At the moment I avoid contact with her altogether.

Neither of the women speak of resentment or harm and both would be happy if the conflict passed. This and the intensity of the feelings, the broad lack of suitable causes, the many futile attempts at resolution and lack of understanding between them – all these indicate that an accidental constellation has taken place. I therefore now ask about any possible excluded people.

Facilitator (to client): Is there anyone in your family system that was not spoken of for a long time, or who suffered a difficult fate or died young?

Client: One of my mother's older sisters died when she was very young, just a few weeks after birth.

Facilitator: Then we can also add this aunt as well as your goal. What do you want to call your goal?

Client: 'well-balanced'

Facilitator: Now choose two more representatives from the group and add them to the constellation. Your *focus* can come back to her position.

The facilitator returns to the circle, the *focus* takes the place of the client and the client positions the two extra representatives. We obtain the following picture:

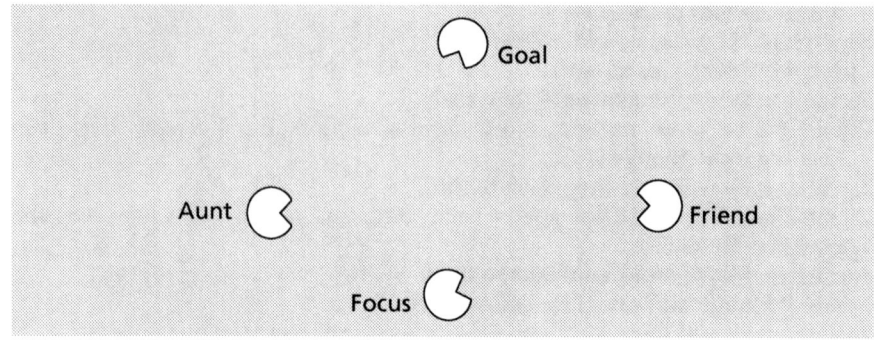

Figure 74

Facilitator: What has changed for the *focus*?
Focus: I'm only looking at her (the *friend*) and feel really worked up. I can't feel my *goal*.
Facilitator: How does the *goal* feel?
Goal: I feel insecure, weak and am shivering all over.
Facilitator: What has changed for the *friend*?
Friend: At first the dizziness got worse. When the *aunt* was added a feeling of deep sadness came over me.

That the *friend* reacts to a person from the system of the *focus* and the *focus* is only oriented towards the *friend* tells us that the friend could be representing the aunt. The facilitator therefore applies the test for partial pattern disruption by having *aunt* and *friend* change places (change of parameter as test).

Facilitator (to *friend*): Do you feel better or worse in this position?
Friend: Much better.
Facilitator: Then swap places again with the *aunt*.

Friend and *aunt* return to their original positions. The facilitator then performs a ritual to disrupt the partial pattern representation. The *friend* is instructed by the facilitator to move slowly towards the *aunt*. When standing very close to the *aunt*, the facilitator moves her to the side of the *aunt*. Finally, both go back to their original positions.

Facilitator (to *friend*): What has changed for you?
Friend: My increased heart beat and dizziness is gone. I also don't feel sad any more.
Facilitator (to *focus*): What has changed for you?
Focus: My heartbeat has also relaxed, and I feel more stable. Now I'm able to see

the *friend* in a completely different way. It's really amazing how it's changed.
Facilitator: Turn around so that you can see your *goal*. What does this change?
Focus: Now I have an orientation. But I dare not move towards the *goal*.
Facilitator: Look at your *aunt* and say to her: 'You are my *aunt* who I have got
to know. I give you a place in my heart.'

The *focus* repeats these words.

Facilitator: And now say to her: 'And in the future I will honour you differently, by moving towards my goal … and you can be happy for me.'

The *focus* repeats these words. At first she finds this hard, and only
during the last sentence does happiness begin to show.

Facilitator: What has changed for you now?
Focus: Now I find the *goal* much more attractive.
Facilitator: How is the *goal*?
Goal: I feel strong and balanced.
Facilitator (to *focus*): Then take a step towards your *goal*.

The *focus* laughs happily while carrying out the instruction.

Facilitator (to client): You can now move into the position of the *focus*.

The client follows this instruction.

Facilitator: How do you feel?
Client: It's really unbelievable. I see my *friend* in a completely different way
now … The view of my *goal* does me a lot of good.
Facilitator: Then look at everyone now and take a step forwards.
The client laughs while carrying out this instruction.
Facilitator: Take another step towards your *goal*, and absorb the picture while
doing so.

Second constellation
The same client returned to the group after a few weeks for another
constellation.

Facilitator: What has changed for you in the meantime?
Client: Things are better with my female friend, but I feel uncertain about my
male friend, in terms of what I actually want from him.
Facilitator: Then position someone for him and for yourself.

The client chooses two representatives from the group and places them in the constellation, and we arrive at the following picture:

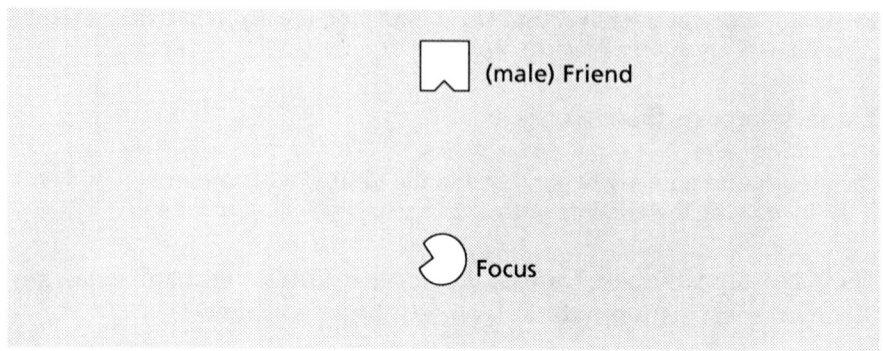

Figure 75

Facilitator: How does the *focus* feel?
Focus: I'm not looking at my *friend*. I'm looking past him instead.
Facilitator: How is the *friend*?
Friend: I am facing her, but she's not looking at me.

The facilitator holds a cataleptic hand over the position towards which the *focus* is looking.

Facilitator: What changes for you now?
Focus: That feels good.
Facilitator (to client): Place someone in this position. We'll call this person, 'what the focus is looking at.'

The client chooses a representative and places her in the position of the cataleptic hand. We then have the following picture:

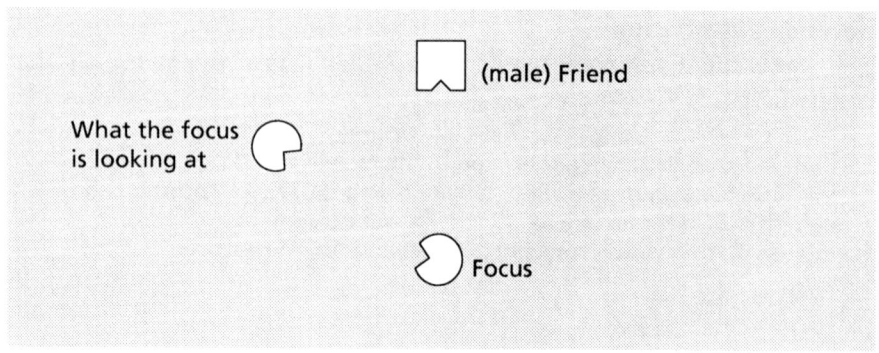

Figure 76

Facilitator: Is there anyone in your family who was unlucky in love?

Client: Before my mother, my father had a girlfriend, who he left. We were not allowed to talk about her. It was very hard for her at the time.

Facilitator (to *focus*): Say to *what the focus is looking at*: 'You were important to my father before my mother. You have a place in my heart. I will honour you as the person who was important to my father before my mother.'

The client repeats these statements, one after the other. *What the focus is looking at* is now renamed as the *father's girlfriend*.

Facilitator: And now say: 'Please look kindly on me if things work out better for me and I have more success than you with love.'

The client repeats these words. The *father's girlfriend* looks at her in a very friendly manner while she speaks.

Facilitator (to *focus*): What changes for you when you now look towards your *friend*?

Focus: Now I am able to see him properly for the first time. I see him in a new way.

Facilitator: How is the *friend*?

Friend: That makes me feel very good.

Facilitator (to client): Now you can move into the position of the *focus*. How do you feel?

The client moves into the position of the *focus*, laughing as she does so.

Client: I perceive my *friend* in a completely new way, and now I find him attractive.

Facilitator: Absorb this picture as it is, and let it take its effect. Carry on from there.

Chapter X

The advantages of combining SFT and SySt

In this chapter I will highlight some of the advantages of combining SFT and SySt. Though I have already described some of these in previous chapters, this chapter will serve to clarify and summarise the new aspects and perspectives of this approach anew.

X.1 Integrating the non-chosen with the chosen: The value of the problem

In the solution focused approach, although we ask questions about the client's problem, we do not learn the precise nature of the problem, or when, where and with whom it occurs, in which situation it appears or how it proceeds: in short, we do not perform a problem analysis. Since most other therapeutic methods deal with problems in considerable detail, it could be said that SFT lacks a fundamental component.

As shown in Chapter II.1.2, the reverse side of the problem can be found in the context of the miracle. This shows that while SFT does indeed take account of problems, it does not pay heed to the benefit the problem may afford the client and the opportunity for learning contained in the problem.

This aspect – the value of the problem – is key to constellation work. This allows us to deal with entanglements, as we see them in constellations pictures, in a respectful manner. A person's outwardly nasty or absurd behaviour can often be explained in terms of love for an excluded person. This positive side of this kind of behaviour becomes visible by observing the problem in its relational system. By looking at problems in this way, something that previously seemed bad can now be looked at with fresh eyes. And, in the same way, our attitude towards the outwardly 'bad' person also changes.

This teaches us to be less judgmental and to look on others more kindly. We will then adhere less to painful events – because rejection and judgment cause us to engage in rejecting behaviour ourselves, and we then find it harder to rid ourselves of the experience. The moment we reject something, that which we reject becomes part of our consciousness, and for as long as we continue to feel the rejection emotionally we remain connected with what we have rejected. The constellations method can help us enter into a different, new relationship with what has been rejected and to transform our contact with it into a respectful encounter.

This *transformation process* is rendered clearly in constellations. In solution focused work we take this process one step further by asking about what the world will look like after this transformation process. In doing so, although we may have integrated the process, we don't *experience* the transformation directly. Instead, we gain an experience of what it is like after the reconciliation has occurred.

The experience of the process of reconciliation may still be of considerable value in its own right: it shows us that what we initially rejected can also be looked at in a completely new way. Below I will use the tetralemma process to clarify the different ways of context expansion in the solution focused approach.

In the tetralemma process, the reconciliation process corresponds to the step from position 1 to position 2, and on to position 3. At this point it is important that what was learnt from the first step – the value of position 1 – is not left behind in order that we can move from position 2 to 3. This, for example, could involve the integration of what was not chosen (e.g. position 1) with what was chosen (position 2). Put another way: if, when at position 2, we have integrated the content of position 1, we have then in fact already arrived at position 3. At position 3 we have then reached a form of 'both'. Position 4 then corresponds to the inclusion of excluded members.

Solution focused questions, particularly the miracle question, take us directly from the problem to position 3. We then ask questions as to what it feels like in that position and how difficulties, should any appear in position 3, can be overcome. Position 4 then corresponds to the integration of the context of the miracle.

Through experiencing the transformation process, observers are able to change their inner attitude towards that which they have rejected, reconciling themselves with what they have previously despised, rejected or ignored. This change of inner attitude can have a healing effect, especially when viewed as a process that, despite being experienced in a specific situation, can be applied generally to rejected relationships. From this experience we learn what reconciliation really means and how we can relate to the world.

This type of reconciliation is often the first step in letting go of a difficult situation. As long as we deal with something in terms of anger or rejection, we are not, generally speaking, prepared to direct our attention towards anything else. In this sense, we are held prisoner by anger, hate and rejection. It is reconciliation that changes our motivation, enabling us to long for something new, which in turn helps us let go of past events and open new perspectives. And this is where the solution focused method comes into play. It helps us find a new direction and to formulate more clearly the destination.

By combining both methods we are able to discover the value of reconciliation in constellation work and (by focusing on the solution given by the SFT method) to steer what is experienced in the constellation in a clear direction and tackle it more directly and easily with the help of exercises.

X.2 Integrating the tetralemma with the goal approximation constellation as an integrated development model in the linear process of the solution focused method

The *goal approximation constellation*, as a form developed to combine the solution focused interview with constellation work, is already set up in a solution focused way. The *tetralemma constellation* is strongly process-oriented and serves as a model for expansion of the context. The tetralemma (and its negation), in the way we have reconstructed it in the *tetralemma constellation*, provides a general schema for the integration of opposites, and contains the basic schema of a canonical step sequence for systemic context expansion. In this respect, it can be used anywhere when combining opposites, overcoming blockages and transforming stagnation into processes.

The tetralemma can be understood as a general developmental model that is particularly applicable to learning processes. The systemic sequence of the different kinds of context expansion offers structural indications of how to find the next step. The way we find the next step here is different from the solution focused approach, which is entirely oriented towards the specific solution in the form of the client's miracle. It is the solution that provides the energy, and the new impulses, relayed by the newly-gained hope, that provide the action.

With the tetralemma there is no solution, only a continuous process. No one individual position is, in itself, better than the previous position. There is also nothing specific to be achieved. When we reach the 'fifth non-position', the process does not end – instead, we are more likely to have a new creative first position which, metaphorically speaking, lies on a different level. We can picture the tetralemmatic developmental process as a kind of never-ending spiral.

Since both the solution focused approach and the tetralemma process are useful methods of context expansion, it is worthwhile comparing both methods and applying the general schema of the tetralemma to the *goal approximation constellation*.

In the solution focused approach we are dealing with a process that leads us from a problem situation to a solution situation. In the tetralemma, this process corresponds with the path from position 1 to position 2 (from the perspective of position 1). This in no way means that position 2 already represents a final solution – what initially appears as a solution may later become a new task. Take, for example, graduation, which very soon turns into a new task: that of looking for a job.

If the choice of value for position 2 is to be stable, then the value of position 1 needs to be integrated with that of position 2, and we then reach position 3. In our graduation example, studying for an exam helps us pass it in order that we are later able to apply what we have learnt. When this knowledge is integrated into the new job, the exam will be experienced as something meaningful.

Stabilising this integration with the solution focused process involves questions about the context of the miracle. This brings us to position 4. The value of the non-solution (position 1) shows itself in things we are able to avoid while the miracle is yet to occur, as in the example above with job applicants or, in other situations, hostile reactions from partners, envy at work or damaged loyalty towards excluded people. Using the question

'If the miracle has happened, how do you now deal with this problem?'

the client is persuaded to integrate the obstacles that arise, for, by accepting the miracle as a resource, she is now in a position to master what was previously insurmountable, and her problems disintegrate. *Contemplation* of the miracle corresponds in the tetralemma to the acceptance of the existence of a *both* position. The answer to the miracle question contains elements of positions 3 and 4 of the tetralemma.

Position 4 is not systematically part of the solution focused approach. Instead it may feature, implicitly, in the answers to questions about the context of the miracle. Position 4 accounts for the context of the dilemma between position 1 and position 2. Here we are able to distinguish between four different forms of context, as follows:

– The past context: how does the question originate of the *one* or the *other*?

- The present context: for example, where do I currently have a blind spot such that I believe I must choose between the *one* and the *other*?
- The future context: what do I need to deal with, i.e. which context in the future is hindering me from solving, my problem (or dilemma)?
- The timeless context: for example, in which context does the problem (or dilemma) make sense?

The context in which the problem makes sense or which led to the question of 'the *one* (problem) or the *other* (goal)', is not addressed in the solution focused procedure, for this method does not involve problem analysis. In general, therefore, we learn nothing of the origin of the problem or the context in which it might have made sense. Answers to these kinds of context related questions may nonetheless occur in the context of the miracle, but this is in no way compulsory. The past, and the context in which the problem made sense, are, however, included in systemic structural SySt constellations. Hence, consideration of these contexts comes from the expansion by solution focused systemic structural constellations of SFT. In some cases, therefore, solutions arrived at through the application of solution focused SySt constellations may be more stable than those arrived at only through SFT. This difference may only become known when it is crucial for the client to find a context in which the problem made sense. Although this does not contribute to the content of a solution, it does help in leaving the past behind. This may be recognised by the fact that the client is then able to turn away from the problem *faster*.

Position 4, as the present or future context that is hindering the solution, is incorporated in the solution focused process by questions about the context of the miracle, when we get answers about what, after the problem is solved, we might expect to face in terms of difficulties, and what may cause us to be blind while in the problem-state. The induction of the solution-state through the miracle question helps us incorporate these blind spots despite being unable to put a name to them. They are thus included in the solution without having been known as part of the problem.

The fifth non-position is embedded directly in the tetralemma constellation, and indirectly in the solution focused procedure – for example, in the non-judgmental attitude of the therapist, in her silence, or in the experience of the miracle. The process of the tetralemma in the *tetralemma constellation* is, after a certain amount of movement back and forth between positions 1 and 2, mostly performed in the sequence of the positions.

This is equally true of the solution focused procedure: the back and forth movement between position 1 and position 2 is frequently seen in the client's 'but'-type objections, in her so-called 'relapses', and from the fact that the client may frequently 'lapse' back into her problem-state not yet daring to move to the solution-state. Position 3 corresponds to the answering of the first part of the miracle question, and position 4 to answers to questions about the context of the miracle, i.e. the reactions of the outside world and their consequences.

When using the *goal approximation constellation* as a solution focused constellation, we begin at position 1 of the tetralemma when the client creates the first picture. Position 2 is contained implicitly in the first picture through the positioning of the goal and, where applicable, the miracle.

The comparison with the tetralemma also indicates that, even though we may speak of a goal at this point, this is a preliminary goal, not a final one. Just as no one position in the tetralemma is better than any other, the goal in the *goal approximation constellation* is also no better than the thing to which the problem refers. It is precisely for this reason that we need to integrate the value of position 1 into position 2 if we are to move forwards in the tetralemma process. And then, even after successful integration (i.e. reaching the position), we continue with questions about the context. We remain in the process, never reaching a 'best' position: we can never possess the solution, we can only touch it repeatedly; we don't own the miracle, we can only keep on remembering it. It is always very close, even though in the problem-state we experience it as far away.

In the first picture of the *goal approximation constellation*, goal and miracle often can be perceived at a very low energetic level. This indicates that the client is still very much clinging to her problem and has little idea of the solution. In the process of the constellation, position 2 – goal and miracle – becomes increasingly clear and their representatives feel stronger and more stable. This process is often aided by the introduction of excluded people. We have then arrived at position 4, in the form of the past context, or at the least have made contact with it and included it.

Positions 3 and 4 are clarified during the entire process of the *goal approximation constellation* in the form of process work by, say, speaking ritual statements, clarifying relationships or including excluded people, and returning past burdens. This process work, at position 3, also includes the client's turning towards her goal (sometimes turning around in order to look at it directly). Both the reconciliation process and the turning towards the goal belong to position 3, and to position 4 if dealing with the inclusion of excluded people. Position 3 is also contained in the 'miracle'.

The fifth non-position is not explicitly contained in the *goal approximation constellation*, though the *miracle* often takes on this quality. If it is introduced at a later stage in the *goal approximation constellation*, it often acts as a particularly strong energy source, which makes the following processes much easier. In the *goal approximation constellation* we can position the 'miracle' as a free element, analogous to the fifth non-position of the *tetralemma constellation*. This gives the *goal approximation constellation* yet another dynamic, for now an additional mobile element may be used as an energy source and 'supervisor'.

Together with the *miracle*, however, the 'future context', as a form of position 4, may also come into play, and in such cases problematic aspects may mix in with the *miracle*. If this occurs, it can be helpful to split the *miracle* into 'miracle' and 'context of the miracle' bringing in a new representative for the *context of the miracle*.

By viewing the *goal approximation constellation* from the perspective of the tetralemma, we are able to allow for different types of context expansion in this constellation form more consciously, and, if needed, to add an extra free element to the *goal approximation constellation*.

We come across a completely different combination when we perform a *goal approximation constellation as a tetralemma constellation*. Here, next to the focus, we position the current state and the goal as the *one* and the *other*. *Both* and *neither* can be added to the subsequent picture as abstract positions and then the four positions can be rearranged to form a square (or rectangle).

The fourth position, *neither*, has both general and specific aspects. A specific fourth position includes, for example, excluded people and those who react negatively to the miracle. The latter appear in solution focused interviews as the context of the miracle. If we wish to clarify both aspects of the fourth position, we may also introduce additional specific excluded people, as part of the general form of *neither*. This has the advantage that, where in the fourth position excluded people have been 'forgotten', they may then emerge for the representative of the position of 'neither' in the guise of uncomfortable, strange sensations or as feelings of cold.

The miracle would then correspond to the fifth non-position in the tetralemma. The miracle is a broader context that cannot be described completely and which we are not in possession of. The symbol category of the *free element* may thus represent the *miracle* more adequately than, say, the symbol category *representative in the narrow sense*.

This comparison of the *goal approximation constellation* and the *tetralemma constellation* clarifies new aspects of the individually positioned elements. For example, we can learn to understand the 'miracle' positioned as a free element corresponding to the fifth non-position of the tetralemma, as a higher energy source; or we can begin to see the path between position 1 and position 2 as the way from the problem-state to the goal-state. Thus aspects of the solution focused approach can be translated into the purely process-oriented approach of the *tetralemma constellation*, and vice versa, and expanded within a given constellation form.

X.3 Integrating preparatory aspects in a willingness for change

When assigning an exercise in SFT, we distinguish between 'visitors', 'complainants' and 'customers'. When dealing with the visitor category, it is important that the therapist refrains from any interventions and acts politely, exerts no pressure and makes no suggestions. In SFT we try to allow the impulse to become a complainant or customer to arise on its own in the client. The therapist only offers support.

A visitor's goal-less state has certain consequences: it does not change. Nonetheless, in therapeutic conversations there is the expectation that something *will* change. If this change is a long time in coming, visitors often become impatient and start to expect advice. If the therapist perseveres, by remaining silent or asking solution focused questions, the visitor is thrown back on herself, and must develop her own impulses and find a goal for herself. The solution focused approach strongly encourages the individual development of future plans. It avoids making suggestions and imposing impulses from without. In situations lacking any orientation or impulse, however, an external impulse may still be helpful.

In such a situation, constellation work can be a great help. With systemic structural constellations parts can be positioned in the constellation that are unknown but which we have concluded must exist. In the goal approximation constellation, therefore, the goal and the miracle can be positioned, for example, without the client having a clear picture of them. It is thus possible for the client, when she moves into the position of the focus, to **experience how it is to have a goal**. This can help her to develop impulses to look for a goal or gain a clearer picture of her existing goal.

Constellations work is useful in yet another way. The client can observe the interaction between her focus and the goal or miracle from without. She can, for example, learn how a step by step approach towards her goal changes her own condition, what obstacles can appear and what can help her overcome them. This **anticipation of future events** can open up new paths for the client. Constellations work thus facilitates active learning.

Constellations work also helps clients who find it hard to picture the day after the miracle. **Experiences** can be had **vicariously** and **information obtained** via the representatives. By positioning the representatives, the client provides the first impulse in the constellation process. This makes it easier for her to accept information from the representatives.

Learning something from constellations also requires the client to be open to change, but this does not mean that the client must know in which direction the process of change will take place. This allows her goal to be unclear. In the case of visitors with a desire for change but no clear orientation, constellation work can be a very valuable addition to the solution focused interview, naturally including dissolving entanglements and the inclusion of excluded people, which often go unmentioned in the solution focused interview.

X.3.2 Case Study: How a visitor becomes a customer

This constellation took place during an experiential group. (The names of the representatives are shown in italics.)

Facilitator: What is your problem?
Client: I don't really know; it's all too much. I don't know at all where I should start.
Facilitator: What things are important to you at the moment?
Client: Nothing is important to me at all anymore.
Facilitator: What do you want in this moment?
Client: I don't know.
Facilitator: Hm.
Client (shaking head): ... A friend of mine recommended I do a constellation.
Facilitator: What things would you like to be different?
Client: That I didn't argue so much with others. Every time I talk to someone, we argue, and I don't know why.
Facilitator: What else would be different?
Client: My son would still be alive ... He took his life two years ago. Since then everything has been meaningless to me.
Facilitator: In what ways did you notice that your life was meaningful before?
Client: I took care of my son, and I liked that.
Facilitator: What about his father?
Client: He's no longer alive. He died in a car accident.
Facilitator: Do you have other children?
Client: No, I only had my son.
Facilitator: Do you reproach yourself for his suicide?
Client: I always ask myself, what else I could have done? But I don't know.
Facilitator: Now I'm going to ask a somewhat difficult question ... When today the group comes to an end and you go hom ... maybe you finish some work in the evening ... and suddenly you get tired and go to your bed ... Assuming ... during this night a miracle occurs ... and the miracle was ... that everything that brought you here today ... was solved for you ... and that really would be a miracle, wouldn't it? ... When you then woke up in

the morning ... and no one says to you that the miracle has happened... how would you notice this?

Client: ... I can't think of anything.

Facilitator: Hm.

Client: That's not possible.

Facilitator: It would have to make some kind of difference if your problem is solved?

Client: Yes, but I just can't imagine it. I've no idea.

Facilitator: OK, I suggest then that we begin the constellation. Maybe it will clarify things for you?

Client: (nods)

Facilitator: Then select someone for you, for your son and for the miracle, and place all three in the constellation.

The client chooses three representatives and positions them in the constellation one after the other and we obtain the following picture:

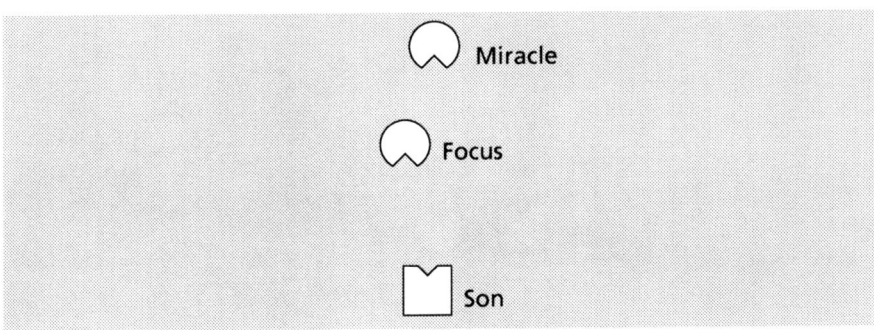

Figure 77

Facilitator: What has changed for the *focus* during the setting up process?

Focus: I feel completely weak, as if I was no longer there. I can only see my *son*, and that saddens me.

Facilitator: How does the *son* feel?

Son: I can see my *mother*. It worries me that she's so sad.

Facilitator: How is the *miracle*?

Miracle: I'm not being noticed – and like this I can't do my work.

Facilitator (to client): What do think about this?

Client: It feels really good to hear that my *son* does not reproach me with anything.

Facilitator: We'll make some statements now, and then we'll see what happens.

Facilitator (to *focus*): Now repeat the following statements to your *son*, and each time see that they feel right ... 'I could hardly cope with it ... I respect your decision ... and leave it [the decision] with you ... entirely ... You are my son, and I remain your mother ... Nothing there has changed ... You are already dead ... I will live for a while longer ... and I will do something with my life ... so that you will then be able to share in my happiness.'

The *focus* repeats all of the statements, word for word, despite some hesitation. She is very touched and cries. The client also begins to cry.

Facilitator: What has changed for the *focus*?
Focus: It feels good to say those things. As a result my connection with my *son* has become different.
Facilitator: How is the *son*?
Son: I want my *mother* to feel well, that's a relief. Now I feel better.
Facilitator (to *focus*): Now turn around to face the *miracle*. What changes do you notice?

The facilitator places the *son* on the left hand side of the *focus*. We have the following picture:

Figure 78

Facilitator: How does the *focus* feel now?
Focus: It's a really big surprise that there's something in front of me. I don't know what it is but it's pleasant.
Facilitator: How does the *miracle* feel now?
Miracle: It's good that she's looking at me. I'm starting to come alive.
Facilitator: How does the *son* feel?
Son: It's a relief for me when my *mother* looks towards her *miracle*.
Facilitator (to client): Move into the position of your *focus*.

The client swaps places with the *focus*.

Facilitator: How do you feel in this position? What's different now?
Client: This is very unfamiliar.
Facilitator: Yes, of course.
Client: It gives me strength, to see something of myself. I just don't know what it is.
Facilitator: Feel the difference it makes when there's something before you in the future.
Client (nods): I can see my *son* so well. That's nice for me. The questions that used to fill my mind are gone now. That's very nice.

Facilitator: Absorb this picture now, and let it take effect.

One week later the client called to say that she had regained the courage to face life and was feeling better. In the following months the client began to develop her own goals and became more active, and there was reduction in the number of conflicts she had with other people.

X.4 Integrating change by means of non-change: How behaviour changes when our inner attitude changes

Both SFT and SySt constellations contain examples of how to achieve change through the acceptance of non-change. In both methods, impulses for change are set in similar ways, and non-change is also accepted.

The fundamental principle of *constellation work* is the acceptance of 'what is'. All other basic principles and interventions can be derived from this meta-principle. If, for example, the facts of family relations and emotions are spoken of during process work, this then serves to express and recognise something that just 'is'. The only important thing here is that the statements be formulated in a respectful manner, and this is precisely what marks the difference between statements used to express the same things in everyday situations. On a daily basis, we express impulses, wishes and judgements instead of what shows itself in any given moment.

Instead of statements like:

'I hate you'
'I don't want to see you again'
'I'm going to destroy you'

during the process work of systemic structural constellations we say:

'That was very bad for me'
'You can never make up for that'
'I am angry with you'
'I resent you'
'I've still got a bone to pick with you'

The difference in this second list of statements is that they don't state anything about the other person. Instead they only give in words the emotions of the person speaking. While this still expresses the negative event, the culprit is not threatened with any consequences. This expresses and recognises that which 'is'.

I am often asked in seminars whether or not it is important for negative feelings to be expressed; whether, through the use of respectful expressions, the force is taken away from the negative impulse at the outset, and whether this excludes this darker side of life. If negative feelings are not reactively discharged, then we see something different from what usually occurs in daily life: the disruption of a generally unhelpful pattern. The acting out of negative feelings often creates new damage, rather than promoting reconciliation. If the opposite were true, clients would no longer come to us for therapy. It is necessary that negative aspects are recognised and find their place. It is, however, not recommended that those negative aspects are acted out.

The recognition of deeds takes place in the process work of systemic structural constellations through rituals such as:

- Stating family relations where these have been denied or abused
- Clarifying precedences where these have been forgotten
- Recognising commitment where this has not been seen
- Recognising performance and skills where these have not been appreciated

In all these cases, only that which already exists, but is not seen, is expressed. This allows something to become visible, appreciated and recognised that to a certain degree had been previously excluded. This recognition effects a change, even though it only what already exists to deal with.

The statements used in process work, therefore, do not anticipate anything. Instead, they describe something that exists already. Only after this has been expressed does a natural process of change occur within systemic structural constellations. Constellations work paves a way for us into the future through the inclusion of excluded contexts from the past. It is as if what is excluded is holding us back from any movement forward.

The process work within systemic structural constellations is wholly dedicated to the careful observation of that which 'is'. Only after this can statements be added that refer to future action, as, for example:

'In the future I will include you in a different way and make room for you in my heart.'

SFT, through its consistent use of questions about solutions, focuses more on the future. The recognition of that which 'is' occurs differently here. The therapist refrains from giving suggestions, personal opinions and impulses for change. The recognition of that which 'is' in SFT comes from this restraint. The strongest form of this recognition is seen in silences in which precisely no change is propagated and what exists is let be, even if its gravity calls for change. This 'letting be' is what allows a natural impulse for change to grow in the client.

Here we again meet the paradox in which changes occur spontaneously when we do not actively intervene. 'Letting be' in this way thus proves to be something of an art. It is important that this does not take on the form of 'You don't mean a thing to me'. Empathy and extreme restraint need to work here hand in hand.

Even when assigning an exercise at the end of a session, it is still important to leave to the client the matter of what it is she wants to change. Care needs to be taken that the level of difficulty of the exercises corresponds with the client's skills and willingness for change – i.e. that which 'is' is recognised. Steve de Shazer emphasises how we can recognise from the client's willingness to complete an exercise whether it has been set correctly. **This shows that the exercises, though provided by the therapist, are not ultimately an external impulse**, and that what the client is willing to do, and which change she herself is aiming for, will be seen through the exercise. To an extent, the exercise reflects externally what has already been shown by the way the client answered the questions. The setting of an exercise also incorporates:

- The way of combining the actions already mentioned by the client
- The addition of elements of chance (rolling dice, tossing a coin)
- The context in which the behaviour is placed (e.g. if something is done in a new way in a different place)

Thus with exercises we see the mixing of the element 'recognising that which is' with the establishing of a new impulses.

The exercises correspond in constellation work with the stepping into the solution picture with the instruction to allow this picture to take effect. This instruction is simultaneously passive and active. It is passive insofar as the client is not being called upon to perform any action; and active in as far as it is important that the client absorbs this picture and follows the impulses that arise out of it. In addition, an extra exercise can sometimes also be set.

Absorbing the picture does not imply doing nothing. It means 'allowing it to take effect'. This requires the acceptance of a non-change, since immediate action diminishes the effect. It is through this acceptance that our attitude changes, and out of this new attitude that new impulses can grow, which lead on to action. The turning point for change is thus a change in our attitude. When we change our attitude to the world, the borders of our world also change. This new world is a new context to us, in which new behaviour becomes possible; not one in which the individual changes, but one in which the whole changes. An internal change of attitude is followed externally by changed behaviour.

In SFT this change of attitude is effected by means of the miracle question, through acceptance that the solution is already there. From this question, we discover the ways in which the client's world changes and which changed behaviour this change of attitude – recognition that a solution is possible – brings with it. Here, again, the change in behaviour originates from a change in attitude. And, again, it is not important, when assigning an exercise in SFT, whether the client completes the exercise, **for this is not a matter of a change in behaviour**. If the client's attitude changes as a result of the miracle question, the exercise then helps to bring the internal change out in a certain form.

A change of attitude is often felt like a change in energetic state, like a state in which opportunities expand and as a result, the scope for activity is enlarged. The increase in willingness for change and mobility is experienced as increased energy. Solution focused systemic structural constellations mainly produce an increased energy-state of this kind in the client. In the solution picture, the client experiences what previously was problematic as ordered and reconciled and discovers a new direction in which she is able to move. What actions this changed state gives rise to often remains unclear at the end of a constellation session and often only becomes clear in further sessions.

On the other hand, in the solution focused interview exercises provide some initial orientation in terms of which actions could arise from the new attitude. This makes it easier for the client to act. While the process of change tends to be a passive one in which that which 'is' is recognised, the changes of attitude that follow give rise to the motivation to act. As soon as we are able to act, we are able to influence the change.

Change begins with a change in attitude, something often experienced as a gift. In order to use this gift, however, it is important to let the changed attitude take effect in our day-to-day lives through actions. Both aspects – the passive and the active – belong together. The first requires willingness, the second engagement.

The non-active or permissive components of the process of change for the therapist correspond with:

- The multi-directional attitude
- Refraining from making suggestions
- Parts of the process work in systemic structural constellations

The active elements for the therapist include:

- – The asking of the questions and the assigning of exercise to be completed at home
- – The rearrangement and adoption of parts of the process work, and the implementation of the tests in systemic structural constellations.

Just as non-active and active parts belong to the process of change for the client, this is also true on the part of the therapist.

When integrating both procedures, it is useful, in order to clarify the present state, to begin with solution focused questions before turning to constellation work. The latter is primarily aimed at reconciliation with the past, and therefore comes before SFT chronologically. The methods of SFT can be drawn on during the subsequent work.

A further type of combination involves starting with SFT and observing whether the results are stable. If this is not the case, a constellation may be able to show what has been forgotten. In terms of their approaches, both methods complement each other.

The more questions representatives are asked about differences in the constellation and, in particular, in process work, and the less clearly the expressions can be interpreted, the easier it is to combine the two methods since they then no longer contradict each other. The SFT attitude, as well as the different ways of configuring exercises, can be incorporated into process work. This allows the active and non-active components of the process of change to interact all the more intensely.

Chapter XI

Solution focused living

The solution focused attitude of SFT can become a way of life and have similar effects to those in therapy, counselling or any other field. In order to work in a truly solutions focused way, it helps if we also adopt this approach in our own lives. Only in this way can we learn to understand the idea of 'solutions focused' and what it can mean in different contexts. The following section will provide some everyday examples and exercises designed to help us think and act in a more solutions focused way.

XI.1 Changing your own attitude instead of the outside world

All components of SFT encourage, through their focus on the solution, a new approach to the world. This is especially true of its core element, the miracle question, which helps initiate the conversion from being problem focused to solution focused. In order to answer the miracle question, the addressee must change from a problem mindset to a solution mindset.

Let us recall a quotation from Wittgenstein (*Tractatus* No. 6.43) in Chapter II:

'If the good or bad exercise of the will does alter the world, it can alter only the limits of the world, not the facts – not what can be expressed by means of language.
'In short: the effect must be that it becomes an altogether different world. It must, so to speak, wax and wane as a whole. The world of the happy man is different from that of the unhappy man.'

For the addressee of the miracle question, it is not only individual aspects of her world that change; her world changes for her as a whole. The facts of the world remain the same – the people she deals with, spatial conditions etc. do not change. Rather, it is her attitude towards these that changes. The limits of her world change and therefore the opportunities open to her also change.

In terms of our everyday lives, this means we must recognise the facts and thereby change our stance towards them. Through this we change our relationship to existing things and also the scope of our opportunities. The actual change takes place in our attitude towards the world, not in the already existing world.

This 'recognition of what is' also forms the overall fundamental principal of constellations work. Only the recognition of existing facts – e.g. that we hold position A, that event B was bad for us, that we live in town C, that person D did a certain thing etc. – enable us to let go inside and move towards something new. Recognition is, in a way, the gate that opens onto change. By recognising that which 'is', we no longer try to change something intentionally and compulsively, rather we find internal peace. Turning towards the solution is a process of opening oneself to a new direction and not, initially, explicit action. The change of attitude may of course then show itself through new behaviour.

If I behave as if I had already changed my attitude this may sometimes be followed by a change in attitude. However, we mostly experience this as a gift and not an action.

In SFT, this change of attitude from problem to solution occurs as a result of the client's engaging with the miracle question; in systemic structural constellations it happens through the performance of the rituals, the externalised witnessing of our own relationship constellations and entering the solution picture. This 'engaging with' or 'entering into' begins the moment we start to believe a solution is possible. In our everyday lives this means that we need to allow for the fact that a solution *could exist*. You can ask yourself the following questions:

'From what would you notice that in this moment a miracle occurrs and that your current problem is solved? What would be the first indications that this miracle has happened?'

It is important at this stage to note that this miracle occurs inside us, not that other people, situations or material facts change. The question can be changed accordingly to:

'Assuming that the outside world does not change and that an even greater miracle occurs, namely that your problem is nonetheless solved, from what would you be able to observe this? And who, apart from you yourself, would notice that this has changed for you, and from what?'

Exercise 1

Ask yourself one of the above forms of the miracle question as soon as you experience a problem. Take note of all your answers and observe afterwards whether anything changes for you and if so, what.

Don't forget that this is a difficult question. Be patient and take your time with the answer.

If we ask ourselves this question as soon as something becomes a problem for us, we stay connected with the possibility of solutions existing and don't fall into a 'problem hole'. The question acts like a pattern disruption in many respects, for example:

- It interrupts problem orientation
- It diverts us from everyday stresses
- It installs in us a new attitude towards ourselves, i.e. an attitude of patience and acceptance
- We place ourselves in the position of others and perceive ourselves from the outside from different perspectives (a sort of 'constellation in our heads').

Exercise 2

Ask yourself where you would place yourself on a scale of 0 to 10, where 0 stands for 'You are not prepared to do anything' and 10 stands for 'You are prepared to do everything that is proposed to you in respect of a current problem.'

If you have placed yourself at 8 or higher on the scale then ask yourself the above questions once a day and observe whether this makes any difference to you.

If you are between 6 and 8 on the scale then ask yourself the questions every second day.

If you are below 6 but above 3 on the scale then perform this exercise only twice a week.

If you are at 3 or below on the scale then perform this exercise once a week at most.

Each time, observe if you notice any difference between days on which you asked the questions and days on which you didn't.

Let Exercise 2 become a sort of new habit, which you can draw upon in future at appropriate moments.

XI.2 Why a solution focused lifestyle does not mean avoiding problems

I am often asked during seminars whether we are running away from problems when we start to look for solutions so quickly. My answer is: on the contrary, and for the following reasons:

- We expose ourselves to future difficulties and don't get bogged down

- We act rather than spend time mulling things over
- We recognise facts, rather than denying them
- We recognise small levels of improvement, rather than rejecting them as negligible
- We deal with problems with the attitude that they are an exercise, rather than complaining
- We treat past emotions, attitudes and opinions just as we perceive them, rather than denying them

Focusing on solutions helps us to act. Focusing on problems helps us obtain an insight into past situations and to analyse problems. However, recognition of things that do not work by no means leads on to recognition of things that do, and therefore insights, while they may be of interest, do not always aid change.

A solution may be the opposite of a problem, but it is far from being the only opposite of the problem. From the negation of a problem, therefore, we are not yet able to infer a particular solution. The question

'Assuming your problem were solved, from what would you first notice this?'

is a far more rigorous way of hitting upon an appropriate solution.

Analysing problems is sometimes enjoyable and interesting. The best way to achieve a solution focused attitude, however, is to have an interest in solutions and to find problems in everyday life uninteresting. This is not valid for all fields: in thrillers and novel writing or screenplays this attitude is not what is wanted. But an interest in everyday problems can lead us all too easily to attract them.

Again, we say:

'Gain an interest in solutions!'

And not:

'You should find problems uninteresting.'

Otherwise, we adopt a problem oriented attitude when dealing with problems.

The following internal questions can be useful for focusing on solutions:

'What is good, what can be kept?'
'What can I be grateful for?'
'How I know that the current situation is expedient for me?'
'What was helpful in making something better?'
'How did I manage to change ... in the desired way?'

'When has this situations been better already?'
'In what ways have others been successful? And which of these would fit me?'
'What are the different ways of arriving at a solution?'
'From what do I observe improvements?'
'From what do I notice that my life has again become meaningful?'
'What gives me strength?'
'Which situations people or events are helpful to me?'

Exercise 3
In the evening, think back at the events of the day, and pick two of the above questions from a hat, from which you can then select just one question (a little cheating is allowed). Make a note of your answers. Work with the same question for a whole week. Then randomly choose another question.

 If you repeat this over a longer period of time your attitude will change as a result. For longer periods of time you should initially choose only one question. Later you can bring in other questions.

Exercise 4
Identify what proved most helpful to you, and do more of it.

Exercise 5
If something proves unsuccessful, or there are unwanted consequences, do something else.

These exercises help to direct your view back in the direction of a solution.

XI.3 Not judging and not denouncing

The solutions focused attitude involves the practice of 'Epoché', i.e. abstaining from judgments and valuations. Here we can see that the fifth, non-position in the tetralemma is a solutions focused position. This position is not easy to adopt on an everyday basis, since we are often required to take decisions and act, and this means adopting a position. However, what we can do is to adopt a temporary position, which we do not view as the only possible and correct position. We can take decisions for ourselves without judging others. The change starts with ourselves. This is highlighted by a Buddhist story (de Mello 1996, p. 41):

'To a pupil, who often complained of others, a Master said: 'If you want to find peace, change yourself, not other people. It is easier to protect your feet with shoes than to cover the entire world with a carpet."

It is often difficult to avoid casting judgments, since we are compelled to action by strong feelings. If we do not need to act straight away, however, it can help if we ask ourselves the following question:

'In which context would the behaviour that currently feels abhorrent to me or makes me angry make sense?'

By considering the possibility that the other person is not acting out of ill will, and that there might exist a context in which his or her actions make sense, changes our attitude to that person and to ourselves. Answering this question enables us to act less emotionally and more with an understanding for everyone involved. This question helps us achieve a multi-directional attitude, including towards some parts of ourselves.

Exercise 6
Ask yourselve the above question when you meet someone you spontaneously dislike, and observe what this changes for you.

We normally identify with the victim and consequently are not easily able to exert influence on the perpetrator, who sees us as being linked with the victim. Only a multi-directional attitude can enable us to engage and mediate with victim and perpetrator together. While this is a daily experience in therapy, in everyday situations we are often tempted to act imprudently.

A non-judgmental attitude also means not speaking badly of others. Speaking badly of others is often done in compensation for something and has many disadvantages:

- It reinforces our bad experience of others
- It blames our bad experience on other peoples' actions and attitudes
- It presupposed that we are able to judge the actions of others
- It assumes that it is not worthwhile appreciating the goodwill of others

Judging only strengthens what we are trying to combat.

Exercise 7
Choose one day of the week on which you will try not to speak badly about other people. If you can think of nothing positive to say, then try to speak about the person in question in a neutral way or say nothing. Observe whether on the days you try this there are any differences from the days on which you do not perform this exercise.

In education a solution focused attitude means we recognise, praise and reinforce improvement, progress and success. Pointing out mistakes often comes over as emphasis and can damage the person's self-esteem. It is more effective to establish consequences for particular actions than to reproach. Establishing consequences does not presume, however, that an action is bad; it simply shows what the consequences of that action are. We are thus able to avoid the judgment dilemma, and the other person is left to decide how to act. If necessary, the person must bear the consequences. As a Taoist wise man once said:

'Everything is permitted: the thief may steal, the person stolen from may report him, the police may throw him in jail, and the judge may sentence him. Everything is permitted.'

This way of dealing with 'bad' behaviour is effective and avoids our placing ourselves above others. As a consequence, the other person does not dispute whether his or her behaviour was correct or not, for this is not a matter of judging behaviour but a matter of the consequences that will follow as soon as a given action is performed.

Exercise 8
If you have children or are otherwise responsible for other people, try to establish consequences for what you see as negative actions, rather than reproaching or punishing your children. Observe what effect this has over a period of three months on your children or the people you are responsible for.

A non-judgmental approach is also an attitude in which we adopt an inquisitive view of the world, an attitude, therefore, in which we do not pretend to know everything. This may be very unusual in our cultural area, since we learn early on at school that knowledge is rewarded and ignorance is punished, which acts as a sort of training in pretending we know things.

In the solution focused attitude we are required to relinquish this approach and have the courage to admit when we don't know something.

Exercise 9
Imagine you came from a far away star and you had just now slipped into your body. How would this stranger experience your world in your body? How does the world change for you from his perspective? Spend a few hours in this new position. What difference does this image make to you in terms of your life so far?

An attitude of ignorance is a very open approach that allows us to learn something new from what is familiar, since everything is seen a s new and can be experienced as new. We learn again to be amazed.

XI.4 Motivated by goal orientation rather than suffering

We normally only consider change when something 'pushes' us, there is something absent or we feel something to be out of balance. In general, we are used to changing something only as a result of suffering. A change will only be successful if we have a positive goal towards which we can move. If we only recognise the disturbing or absent side of something, the motive to change may still exist, but we will not yet have an idea of what should be there in its place. A problem-oriented attitude can help create sufficient motivation for change, but this can sometimes become over-motivation. Knowing in what direction the change should take us is of more fundamental importance to change. It is only with a solutions focused attitude that we can create real opportunities for change and then go on to accomplish change.

How then do we become motivated to change something in the absence of suffering? As soon as we start to focus on successes and solutions, the desire for more successes and solutions can arise, providing the motivation for something to remain good or become even better. This motivation is obtained through picturing our goal. I can ask about something that is 'better', without having to categorise the here and now as 'bad'. We can ask ourselves the following questions:

'How do I notice that I'm happier?'
'How do I notice that I'm feeling better?'
'How do I notice that my life has become more meaningful?'
'What would then be different?'

These types of questions help focus our attention on solutions instead of problems and burdens. This has the advantage of being less draining, and motivating us with pleasant images.

Exercise 10
Choose one of the first three questions from the list given above and ask yourself this question and the last question on three nights each week. Make a note of your ideas and write down the difference between situations in which you feel better (or are happier or your life seems more meaningful) and situations in which you feel worse (or are unhappier or your life seems meaningless). Do this for three weeks, and notice if your condition improves as a result of this exercise.

This exercise helps us become conscious again of things that are often excluded from our consciousness, i.e. successes and all the things that make our lives easier and richer. However, it also requires that we refrain from our habit of analysing and emphasising problems, and that we adopt new habits. The following exercise can be of help with this.

Exercise 11
If you want to achieve a specific goal then make a note every night of your progress using a scale of 0 to 10, where:

- 0 stands for the state you were in when decided to pursue this goal
- 10 stands for achievement of the goal

Make a note of things that helped you move up a position on the scale.

Exercise 12
Choose symbols to represent your 'miracle' and make use of them. Create helpful belief statements. Symbols and belief statements will always remind you of your 'miracle' so that it is not forgotten.

XI.5 The solutions focused attitude in extremely restrictive and hostile environments

During a seminar, I was once asked if this type of solution focused approach needs a sympathetic context in which to exist, and whether a hostile environment punishes non-judgmental action. This question made me think of Nelson Mandela. Mandela survived a very hostile environment and went on to accomplish profound changes for his people. I would like to draw on a few excerpts from his book *The Long Road to Freedom* to show how a solution focused attitude is still possible, even under the severest of circumstances. This example illustrates particularly well how a solution focused attitude can be applied in extreme situations.

Nelson Mandela's worst years were the 18 years he spent as a political prisoner on Robben Island. The conditions were extremely hard: he lived in solitary cell three paces long with damp walls, a straw mat, three thin sleeping mats and a bucket for a toilet. All clocks were forbidden so that the prisoners would lose track of time. A letter from family members could only be received once every six months, and these were also heavily censored, with the censor's note sometimes being all that was left undeleted. Similarly, a letter could only be sent out once every six months, and this did not always get through.

Black South Africans were at the bottom of the social ladder in the prison: they got only boiled sweet corn to eat and a drink made of corn powder with a small amount of yeast. Some lunch times this was supplemented with a piece of carrot and gristle. Coloureds and Indians received better fare and enjoyed more privileges. Day and night, the light in the cell would be left on. News was generally not allowed. They were put to work in chalk pits, at times in extreme temperatures and in light so dazzling the eyes watered. An approval for sunglasses could take as long as three years. Years later, those who wanted to study were allowed to request individual books for their studies, but were hindered from getting them by many bureaucratic hurdles.

Small offences – a glance to the side, an undone button – received the maximum penalty: solitary confinement or the removal of food rations. From time to time, the prisoners were also tortured.

It is a wonder that anyone was able to survive in such a hostile environment. Nelson Mandela's survival was helped by his *goal orientation*. He transferred his fight against Apartheid to the prison. He writes (p. 546):

'For us, these kinds of battles – for sunglasses, long trousers, study privileges, equal food – were contributions to the battle we were fighting outside of prison. The battle for improved conditions in prison was a part of the battle against Apartheid. In this sense, everything was equal. We fought injustice wherever we encountered it, whether small or large, and we fought injustice in order to preserve our humanity.'

Nelson Mandela was able to *appreciate small improvements* and to put these down *as successes*. He achieved this by using the ever-worsening conditions:

- Since clocks were forbidden, he hung a calendar from the grooves of his cell wall
- Early each morning the prisoners had to 'slop out'. During this period, the prison guards would keep their distance, allowing the prisoners to engage in conversation, which was otherwise forbidden.
- In the evenings the prisoners would scatter sand on the corridors of the prison so that they could hear the footsteps of approaching guards earlier, thereby allowing discussions to be broken off and go undiscovered.
- When washing with the ice-cold water the prisoners would sing as this made the cold water easier to stand.
- Nelson Mandela used every legal opportunity to avoid any degrading new regulations. This enabled him, for example, to avoid being photographed in prison clothes (with one exception where he agreed) by insisting that he see the letter of authorisation from the prison commissioner, which was not normally to hand. The wardens normally did not know the regulations and could be overawed by better knowledge.

News and newspapers were forbidden (ibid. p. 557):

'Newspapers are more valuable to political prisoners than gold or precious stones, and they coveted them more than food or tobacco. On Robben Island they were the most valuable of smuggled goods. News was the intellectual raw material of the camp… The authorities tried to impose a complete blackout in terms of information. They didn't want us to find out anything that might lift our morale or give us assurance that people outside were still thinking about us.'

Still, Mandela and his friends did not give up, laying their trust in the fact that *small steps can give rise to large changes*. When, eventually, they were allowed to study, they used this opportunity to procure news materials (ibid. p. 555):

'One day, Mac Mharaj explained to a comrade who was studying economics that he should put in a request for the magazine *The Economist*. We laughed and said he might just as well ask for *Time* magazine, for the *The Economist* was also a news magazine. But Mac only grinned and explained that the authorities did not know that; they would judge a book by its cover. Within a month we received *The Economist* and devoured the news we had been so hungry for. However, the authorities soon discovered their mistake and cancelled the subscription.'

A solution focused attitude can be seen in Mandela's and his friends' refusal to give up, despite setbacks of this kind, and to make the best out of their situation. For example, they continually devised new methods of transmitting messages (ibid. p.565 et seq.):

'We noticed when the wardens would drop their guard. This was usually the case during and after meal times. We used to help each other handing out food and were thus able to devise a plan whereby comrades from the general wing, who worked in the kitchen, would put letters and notes in plastic bags and place them at the bottom of the food tubs. We sent news back in the same way, by placing them in the same plastic covers and leaving them under the mountain of dirty dishes that was brought back into the kitchen. We tried our hardest to create a mess on the food trays, spreading leftover food over all the plates. The wardens would complain, but they never bothered to inspect the dirty plates.

Our bathrooms and showers bordered on the solitary cells. Prisoners from the general wing were often given solitary confinement and thus used the same bathroom facilities, albeit at different times. Mac devised a method of packing notes in plastic and fixing them under the rim of toilet bowl. He encouraged our political prisoners in the general wing to condemn themselves to solitary confinement so that they could get hold of the messages and send replies. The wardens never went to the bother of searching the bathrooms…

However, of all these inventive methods, one of the best was also the simplest: getting admitted to the prison hospital. The island had only one hospital, and it was difficult, once we were admitted, to tell us apart from the normal prisoners. At times, prisoners from different wings had the same warden, and men from B wing and prisoners from F and G would meet and exchange information about political organisations, strikes, work to rule, whatever happened to be the newsworthy in the prison.'

This description of the camp from within the prison walls shows how Mandela and his friends were even *prepared to make greater sacrifices* if this served their goal. At an earlier stage in his book, Mandela writes of the necessity of being ready to make sacrifices and combating one's fear (ibid. p. 194):

'The ANC came out of the Campaign as an organisation with real mass support and an impressive group of experienced activists who had withstood the police, the courts and the prisons. The stigma normally associated with having been in prison was gone. That was an important step forward, since fear of imprisonment is a terrible impediment in every struggle for freedom. Ever since the Defiance Campaign, going to prison was viewed as an honourable distinction.'

To be able to survive in the hostile environment of the prison required the further step of *seeing the wardens as humans and understanding their perspective*. We find the perspective of the 'opponent' clearer and more intelligible if, during the solution focused interview, we answer questions like the following:

'Who, apart from you, notices the miracle?'
'From what might others notice that the miracle has happened to you?'
'How would others react to it?'
'What would you say?'
'What would you do?'
'What would you do afterwards?'
'Who do you expect to react afterwards, and how?'

These questions can only be answered if the person answering places himself or herself in the position of his or her 'opponent'. A solution focused attitude also always requires that allowance be made for interactions with the environment.

This approach to the opponent is also seen with Mandela (ibid. p. 525, p.562):

'The problem for every prisoner, especially a political prisoner, is how to survive the prison without sustaining any damage, how to come away unscathed, how to preserve your beliefs and even strengthen them. The first task consists of learning precisely what has to be done to survive. This requires knowing the intentions of the enemy, before adopting a strategy of undermining them. The purpose of the prison is, of course, to crush the prisoner's spirit and destroy his willpower...'
'I always tried to control my behaviour towards the wardens in my block. Animosity would have been self-destructive. It made no sense to make a permanent enemy of the wardens. It was ANC policy to try to educate all people, even our enemies: we believed that all people, even prison wardens, were capable of change, and we did our best to influence them. In general we treated the wardens as they treated us.'

Mandela instructed his comrades to make friends with particular wardens. This was not easy, 'for, in general, they found the idea of being polite to a black man repulsive' (ibid. p. 563). Mandela encouraged his comrades to show friendship towards the wardens (ibid.):

'One day the warden asked this comrade for his coat so that he could lay it on the floor and sit on it. Although I knew this ran right against the grain for this comrade, I nodded to him that he should agree.

   Some days later, we were eating our lunch in the shelter, when the same warden passed by. He still had a sandwich in his hand. He threw it on the grass next to us and said, 'There.' That was his way of being friendly.'

The dilemma of whether or not to swallow your pride and pick up the sandwich was less important as a goal than making friends with the warden, and for this reason Mandela encouraged his comrade to pick up the sandwich (ibid. p. 564):

'This strategy paid off, for the warden began to pay less attention to us. He even asked us questions about the ANC. A man working for the prison service probably underwent some obligatory brainwashing with government propaganda ... But if we calmly explained to him our non-racist attitude or our desire for equality or our plans to redistribute wealth, he would scratch his head and say, 'That makes a lot more sense than what the Nats (Nationalists) are saying.''

This is a very nice example of how enemies can become friends if we show them some respect. However, it also highlights the self-conquest and humility this at times requires. Although Nelson Mandela's many years spent in prison is an extreme example, it still goes to show that a solution focused approach, even under the most extreme of circumstances, will not fail us, and that this is not a matter of seeing everything through rose-tinted spectacles.

In conclusion

A miracle is by any measure an amazing thing, while the things we recognise the miracle by are mostly very simple, everyday matters. In solution focused work, the surprising and the everyday come together in the ability to see something as new.

Systemic constellations never stop affecting and amazing us, while the forms of perception they are connected with are simply there and given. Hence the coming together in constellations work of the incomprehensible *new* and the pre-existing *given*.

Why, then, are we still surprised that the marriage of solution focused work and constellations work enables, in an amazing way, the surprising and the familiar to be grouped together? Moreover, how could we be anything *but* surprised – for these types of miracles never diminish, they are happening every day.

End

Postscript: Recent Developments

Solution Focused Systemic Structural Constellations (SFSySt) have seen a number of **further developments** over the years.

Solution focused questions asked of representatives as an individual intervention:
I have generalised the *Solution Geometrical Interview (SGI)* by also asking solution focused questions to individual representatives in other systemic structural constellations. Interventions can then be devised based on the representatives' answers, and as such the system itself gives rise to further interventions.

Extension of the Solution Geometrical Interview with modular SySt fragments:
Here I use the representatives' answers from the *Solution Geometrical Interview* as suggestions for interventions that can then be performed immediately – for example, establishing contact by means of a shift in point of focus, dialogue between systemic parts, change of places or restitutions. Elements of structural constellations are thus incorporated modularly into an SGI. Consequently, SySt and the solution focused conversation increasingly interlock with each other, creating a new entity.

Context entanglement in the miracle:
With the *Solution Constellation, Goal Approximation Constellation* and *Twelve Square Constellation* the function of the miracle in a solution focused conversation is represented by a person and therefore becomes a *representative in the narrow sense*. Because the miracle represents an all-connecting entity, it may become entangled in SFSySt with things that have been forgotten (for example, people who is it forbidden to speak about, traumatic situations, someone to whom another is connected by

loyalty) and therefore may not display its power in the first picture.

In order to fully reveal itself, the miracle must first be released from entangled contexts – for example, by working with a cataleptic hand. If the entanglement is so intense that the miracle is effectively non-existent, i.e. the entanglement corresponds to a loss, what was formerly the miracle can be renamed as 'what emerged' and placed in its corresponding position. We call this a change of structure level. The miracle is then symbolised by a new representative.

Instead of *context entanglement* we used to speak about *pattern representations*. However, this term implies that particular patterns really are represented. The term *context entanglement*, on the other hand, only presupposes that contexts – for example, people or situations – are entangled, i.e. intermixed, with each other. This does not require the recognition of patterns and establishes no actor. An entanglement can be initiated from one or both sides, or may simply occur of its own accord. Consequently, the term *context entanglement* is less pre-supposing, something which helps reduce interpretation in SySt.

The miracle as free element:
If the miracle aspect needs to be represented, it can be symbolised using a free element. In this case the goal must then also be positioned in the constellation.

The miracle as thermostat:
An intermediary form between representative in the narrow sense and free elements is given by a symbolisation of the miracle as an intermittent free element, meaning that the representative in question changes his or her position after between one and three interventions, allowing for verification as to whether the miracle is moving away or coming closer. The miracle acts here as a kind of thermostat that displays improvements. The use of the miracle as an free element or intermittent free element gives rise to two new variations of the *Solution Constellation*, *Goal Approximation Constellation* and *Twelve Square Constellation*.

Modular SySt fragments:
By this I mean structural constellation fragments that can be incorporated into verbal conversations, such as adding rituals from SySt work into verbal conversations by using objects as symbols or the cataleptic hand. This enables the use of certain aspects of SySt in solution focused conversations. As a result, implicit knowledge about the body can be used in the conversation situation.

Constellation of the absent team with original members and representatives:
In these SySt absent team members are symbolised using chairs, which are positioned in the room. Representatives for the absent members are then selected, and these sit down on the chairs. The solution focused group conversation then takes place between the original members and the representatives in the constellation.

Differentiations between categories of representatives
The grammar of SySt has been developed over time so that even more differentiations between the different categories of representatives have been introduced. For example, among representatives in the narrow sense we now also differentiate between the following types:

- *Positioned* and *selected representatives*, depending on whether they are positioned or, after selection, remain seated. This, for example, allows for better differentiation between the actors in an event and the contextual factors in a given problem and leads to a reduction in the number of positioned representatives with no loss of information.
- *Deactivated and activated representatives*, depending on whether they, as selected representatives, remain seated or are instructed to stand up. This allows us to decide when selected representatives come into play. They can be introduced as test situations, in anticipation of in vivo conditions, to generate ideas about relevance and influences.
- *Representative differentiation* and *representative homogenisation*. With representative differentiation, the representative's body parts are used in different representations. For example, the representative's right and left shoulders may represent different elements. Homogenisation, on the other hand, removes differentiation, i.e. it is a simplification of a mode of symbolisation. This can be introduced where, during the course of a constellation, it becomes possible to do without the statements of some of the representatives.
- *Scaled representatives*. These move during the constellation, but only along a line on the floor, representing, for example, a scale from 0 to 10, and as such give some indication of the distance to the goal. This enables a direct translation of the work with scales in solution focused work to SySt.

We differentiate further between basic formats, combinations of formats, meta-formats and the application of formats to other formats.

This allows different formats to be combined with each other and the accuracy of the constellation picture to be increased. Supervening constellations, in which the pattern of a constellation format is discovered to be implicitly present in another format, enable the application of knowledge about one format in other formats.

Appendix 1:
The PeneTRANCE model

In terms of the fundamental logic of the approach, which transforms 'to have goals' into 'to be in the solution-state', the PeneTRANCE model developed in NLP by Thies Stahl (1988) comes closer to Steve de Shazer's application of the miracle question.

The well-formedness criteria with both extensions are helped by phrasing the goal definition in the indicative mood (the subjunctive 'I would like to ...' suggests an inner conflict in which only one part of the client wants to achieve the goal) as well as by making the feedback form as short as possible – i.e. the goal should be established such that the time that elapses between 'doing the decisive thing anew' and 'realising that it has been done' is kept to minimum.

In a 'penetrating' and context-free way, the question is asked: 'From what will you recognise that you have achieved your goal ... [meaning the last goal formulation by the client]?' This leads the client into the goal-state which she demonstrates progressively throughout the questioning process and visibly shows to the therapist through her 'physiology' – i.e. her collective bodily sensations. Thies Stahl's model is an implementation of John Grinder's requirement that the first step towards the goal should already contain features of the goal, helping the client not so much to 'have' the goal, than to 'be' in the process of achieving it.

The narrowing down to fixed goals is avoided in the PeneTRANCE model by applying the criteria so strictly that the client is able to let go of her 'goal schema', which she initially uses for her answers, and hence her fixation with a particular goal statement. Similar to SFT's use of the miracle question, by anticipating achievement of the goal (this has usually become clear again in this process) the client is able to anticipate from experience the state of being that will replace the problem-state.

In this respect, the process of goal definition in NLP can be combined with the logic of the questioning process used in SFT. When the client makes fixed goal statements, the well-formedness criteria, particularly when applied in their strictest form, give the therapist an additional set of questions for use in assisting the client to become more open to experiencing miracles.

The detailed miracle question can thus be complemented through the NLP approach in cases where the change to the client's physiology is not yet sufficiently clear. The miracle question could also be applied in NLP in order to verify whether the client's goal statements developed with the well-formedness criteria and the PeneTRANCE model are appropriate and complete. In this respect, it is both possible and desirable to enrich the questioning methods and procedures of both approaches simultaneously.

Bibliography

Andersen, H. a. H. Goolishian: Der Klient ist der Experte. Ein thera-peutischer Ansatz des Nicht-Wissens. In: Zeitschrift fuer systemische Therapie 10 (3), pp.176-189.

Andreas, C. a. T. Andreas (1996): Core Transformation: Reaching the Wellspring Within. Moab (UT).

Bandler, R. a. J. Grinder (1975): The Structure of Magic I: A Book about Language and Therapy. Palo Alto (Science and Behavior Books).

Bryant, M. (1993): The World´s Greatest Cat Cartoons. New York (Exley).

Bateson, G. (1972): Steps to an Ecology of Mind. New York (Ballantine).

Bateson, G. (1979): Mind and Nature: A necessary unity. New York (Dutton).

Boscolo, L., G. Cecchin a. P. Penn (2001): Milan Systemic Family Therapy: Conversations in Theory and Practice. (Basic Books).

Boscolo, L. a. P. Bertrando (1993): The Times of Time: A New Perspective in Systemic Therapy and Consultation. New York (Norton).

Boszormenyi-Nagy, I. (1987): Foundations of Contextual Therapy. Collected Papers of I. Boszormenyi-Nagy. New York (Brunner & Mazel).

Boszormenyi-Nagy, I. a. G. Spark (1973): Invisible Loyalties. Reciprocity in Intergenerational Family Therapy. New York (Harper & Row).

Brunner, E. J. (1990): Von der Familientherapie zur systemischen Perspektive. Berlin (Springer).

Buber. M. (2002): Between Man and Man. London (Routledge).

Buber, M. (1958): I and Thou. New York (Scribner & Sons).

Cecchin, G.: Zum gegenwaertigen Stand von Hypothetisieren, Zirkularitaet und Neutralitaet. Eine Einladung zur Neugier. In: Familiendynamik 13, pp. 190-203.

Chomsky, N. (1965): Aspects of the Theory of Syntax. Cambridge, MA (M.I.T. Press).

Drees, A. (1995): Freie Phantasien in der Psychotherapie und in Balint-Gruppen. Goettingen, Zurich (Vandenhoeck & Ruprecht).

Ende, M. (1985): Momo. London, New York (Puffin).

Erickson, M. H., E. L. Rossi a. S. L. Rossi (1976): Hypnotic Realities: The Clinical Hypnosis and Forms of Indirect Suggestions. New York (Irvington).

Erickson, M. H. (1954): Pseudo Orientation in Time as a Hypnotherapeutic Procedure. In: Journal of Clinical and Experimental Hypnosis, 2, pp. 261-283.

Essen, S.: Vom Problemsystem zum Ressourcensystem. In: Brunner, E. J. (1990): Von der Familientherapie zur systemischen Perspektive. Berlin (Springer), pp. 178-181.

Fiddy, R. (1990): The Fanatic´s Guide to Cats. New York (Exley).

Fischer, H. R. (1991): Sprache und Lebensform – Wittgenstein ueber Freud und die Geisteskrankheit. Heidelberg (Carl Auer).

Fischer, H. R. (1995): Die Wirklichkeit des Konstruktivismus. Zur Auseinandersetzung um ein neues Paradigma. Heidelberg (Carl Auer).

Foerster, H. von (1984): On constructing a Reality. In: P. Watzlawick (ed.): The Invented Reality: How Do We Know What We Believe to Know? New York (Norton).

Gendlin, E. T. (1978): Focusing. New York (Bantam).

Gilligan, S. G. (1987): Therapeutic Trances: The Cooperation Principle in Ericksonian Hypnotherapy. New York (Brunner & Mazel).

Gilligan, S. G. (1997): The Courage to Love: Principles and Practices of Self-Relations Psychotherapy. New York (Norton).

Glasersfeld, E. v. (1985): Konstruktion der Wirklichkeit und des Begriffs der Objektivitaet. In:

Grawe, K. (2002): Psychological Therapy. Goettingen et al. (Hogrefe & Huber).

Grinder, J. a. R. Bandler (1975): The Structure of Magic II: A Book about Communication and Change. Palo Alto (Science and Behaviour Books).

Gumin, H. a. H. Meier (eds.) (1992): Einfuehrung in den Konstruktivismus. Munich (Oldenbourg).

Hellinger, B. (1997): Die Mitte fuehlt sich leicht an. Vortraege und Geschichten Munich (Koesel).

Hellinger, B. (2002): Insights. Lectures and Stories. Heidelberg (Carl Auer).

Hellinger, B., G. Weber a. H. Beaumont (1998): Love´s Hidden Symmetry: What Makes Love Work in Relationships. Phoenix (Zeig,

Tucker & Theisen).

Hellinger, B., G. ten Hovel a. C. Beaumont (1999): Acknowledging What Is. Conversations with Bert Hellinger. Phoenix (Zeig, Tucker & Theisen).

Husserl, E. (1950): Husserliana. Gesammelte Werke. Bd.2: Die Idee der Phaenomenologie. Fuenf Vorlesungen. Dordrecckt et al. (Kluwer).

Husserl, E. (1950): Husserliana. Gesammelte Werke. Bd.3: Ideen zu einer reinen Phaenomenologie und phaenomenologischen Philosophie. Dordrecckt et al. (Kluwer). Husserl, E. (2001): Logical Investigations. (International Library of Philosophy). London (Routledge).

Husserl, E. (1985): Die phaneomenologische Methode. Ausgewaehlte Texte I. Stuttgart (Reclam).

Husserl, E. (1986): Phaenomenologie der Lebenswelt. Ausgewaehlte Texte II. Stuttgart (Reclam).

Husserl, E. (1992): Formale und transzendentale Logik. In: Gesammelte Schriften 7. Hamburg (Meiner).

Husserl, E. (2004): Ideas: General Introduction to Pure Phenomenology. (Muirhead Library of Philosophy).London (Routledge).

Isert, B. a. K. Rentel (2000): Die Wurzeln der Zukunft. Paderborn (Junfermann).

James, T. a. W. Woodsmall (1988): Time Line Therapy and the basis of personality (Meta Publications)

Jong, P. de a. I. Kim Berg (2001): Learner´s Workbook for Interviewing for Solutions. (Wadsworth).

Kim Berg, I. (1994): Family Based Services: A Solution-Focused Apporach. New York (Norton).

Kim Berg, I. a. S. D. Miller (1992): Working With the Problem Drinker: A Solution-Focused Approach. New York (Norton).

Kim Berg, I. a. S. D. Miller (1995): The 'Miracle' Method: A Radically New Approach to Problem Drinking. New York (Norton).

Lauterbach, M. a. E. Pfaefflin (1998): Familienaufstellung und Psychodrama. In: G. Weber (ed.): Praxis des Familien-Stellens. Heidelberg (Carl Auer).

Ludewig, K.: Systemische Therapie. Stuttgart (Klien-Cotta)

Mandela. N. (1994): The Long Walk to Freedom. London (Little, Brown).

Mayer, V. (1998): Unpublished Habilitation Lecture, Ludwig-Maximilian University, Munich.

Mello, A. de (1996): One Minute Wisdom. Anand, Gujarat, India.

Mello, A. de (1998): Zeiten des Gluecks. Freiburg (Herder)

Miller, G. (1997): Becoming Miracle Workers. New York (Aldine de Gruyter).

Milz, H. a. M. Varga von Kibéd (1998): Koerpererfahrungen – Anregungen zur Selbstheilung. Zurich (Walter).

Molzberger, P. (1993): Synergetische Zusammenarbeit – ein Schwimmkurs fuer uehrungskraefte. Munich.

Moreno, J. L. (1989): The Classics of Sociometry. London (Beacon House).

O'Hanlon, W. H. (1987): Taproots: Underlying Principles of Milton Erickson's Therapy and Hypnosis. (Norton Professional Books). New York (Norton).

O'Hanlon, W. H. a. A. L. Hexum (1991): An Uncommon Casebook: The Complete Clinical Work of Milton H. Erickson. New York (Norton).

Peirce, C. S. (1958): Collected Papers of Charles Sanders Peirce. (ed. by A. Burks). Cambridge (Harvard University Press).

Poppe, T. (1990): Der Loewe in uns allen. Die Tierfabel als Spiegel der Seele. Reinbeck (Rowohlt).

Prechtl, P. (1998): Edmund Husserl. Zur Einfuehrung. Hamburg (Junius).

Prekop, J. a. B. Hellinger: Satir, V. (1988): The New Peoplemaking. Palo Alto (Science and Behavior Books).

Satir, V., J. Banmen, J. Gerber, M. Gomori (eds.) (1991): The Satir Model. Family Therapy and Beyond.

Schlippe, A. v., J. Schweitzer (1996): Lehrbuch der systemischen Therapie und Beratung. Goettingen (Vandenhoeck & Ruprecht).

Schmidt, G. (1985): Systemische Familientherapie als zirkulaere Hypnotherapie. In: Familiendynamik 10, pp. 241-264.

Schuon, F. (1984): The Transcendent Union of Religions. (Quest).

Shazer, Steve de (1982): Patterns of Brief Family Therapy: An ecosystemic approach. New York (Guilford).

Shazer, Steve de (1985): Keys to Solution in Brief Therapy. New York (Norton).

Shazer, Steve de (1988):Clues: Investigating Solutions in Brief Therapy. New York (Norton).

Shazer, Steve de (1991): Putting Difference to Work. New York (Norton).

Shazer, Steve de (1994): Words Were Originally Magic. New York (Norton).

Sheldrake, R. (1995): The Presence of the Past: Morphic Resonance and the Habits of Nature. (Park Street Press).

Simon, F. B. (1997): Unterschiede, die Unterschiede machen. Berlin (Springer).

Singer, L. (1999): Des Rabbis Rat. Gütersloh.

Sparrer, Insa (1987): Grammatik der Koerpersprache. Ludwig-Maximilans-Universitaet Muenchen, Fakultaet fuer Psychologie (unpublished).

Sparrer, Insa (1997): Modifikationen der Grundprinzipien der Systemischen Familienaufstellungen beim Uebergang zu Systemischen Strukturaufstellungen. In: Hypnose und Kognition 4 (1/2).

Sparrer, Insa (1998): Aspekte des Systemischen – Wie systemisch ist die Aufstellungsarbeit? In: Praxis der Systemaufstellung 2, pp. 19-24.

Sparrer, Insa (1998): Loesungsaufstellung, Neunfelderaufstellung und Zielannaeherungsaufstellung: drei Formen der Verbindung von systemischer Aufstellungsarbeit und de Shazers loesungsorientierter Kurztherapie. In: G. Weber (ed.): Praxis des Familien-Stellens. Heidelberg (Carl Auer), pp. 360-364.

Sparrer, Insa (1998): Loesungsorientierte Kurztherapie und Strukturaufstellungsarbeit als zwei Formen der systemischen Therapie. In: J. Bley a. L. Lewitan (eds.): Leitfaden Psychotherapie in Muenchen. Munich (Goldschmidt).

Sparrer, Insa (1999): Heilsame Rituale und systemische Resonanz. In: W. Scheiblich (ed.): Bilder, Symbole, Rituale. Freiburg (Lamberus).

Sparrer, Insa (1999): Systemische Strukturaufstellungen zu psychosomatischen Erkrankungen. In: Praxis der Systemaufstellung 2, pp. 30-37.

Sparrer, Insa (2000): Die Organisationsstrukturaufstellung und andere Systemische Strukturaufstellungen fuer Fragestellungen im Organisationsbereich. In: Praxis der Systemaufstellung 1.

Sparrer, Insa (2000): Vom Familienstellen zur Organisationsaufstellung – zur Anwendung Systemischer Strukturaufstellungen im Organisationsbereich. In: G. Weber (ed.): Praxis der Organisationsaufstellungen. Heidelberg (Carl Auer).

Sparrer, Insa (2000): Loesungsfokussierte Systemische Strukturaufstellungen – Aufstellunge als Gespraech und Gespraech als Aufstellung. In: Praxis der Systemaufstellung 2.

Sparrer, Insa (2001): Konstruktivistische Aspekte der Phaenomenologie und phaenomenologische Aspekte des Konstruktivismus. In: G. Weber (ed.): Derselbe Wind laesst viele Drachen steigen. Heidelberg (Carl Auer).

Sparrer, Insa a. M. Varga von Kibéd (1995): Systemische Familientherapie: Strukturaufstellungsarbeit. In: B. Schwertfeger a. K. Koch (eds.): Der Therapiefuehrer. Munich (Heyne), pp. 243-349.

Sparrer, Insa a. M. Varga von Kibéd (1996): Theorie und Praxis der Systemischen Strukturaufstellungen (2 videotapes). Dortmund (vcr).

Sparrer, Insa a. M. Varga von Kibéd (1998): Wie Systeme Systeme wahrnehmen: Koerperliche Selbstwahrnehmung bei Systemischen Strukturaufstellungen. In: H. Milz a. M. Varga von Kibéd (eds.):

Koerpererfahrungen – Anregungen zur Selbstheilung. Zurich (Walter), pp. 114-141.

Sparrer, Insa a. M. Varga von Kibéd (1998): Vom Familien-Stellen zur Systemischen Strukturaufstellungsarbeit. In: G. Weber (ed.): Praxis des Familien-Stellens. Heidelberg (Carl Auer), pp. 394-404.

Sparrer, Insa a. M. Varga von Kibéd (2000): Aufstellungen lesen lernen. Part I: Die Tetralemmaaufstellung, part II: Interventionstypen und Grundprinzipien der Systemischen Strukturaufstellungen, part III: Interview vor der Aufstellungsarbeit und Demonstration einer Aufstellung, part IV: Aufstellungen zum Organisationskontext, part V: Das Experiment, part VI: Aufstellungen als transverbale Methode und die Aufstellung zum ausgeblendeten Thema, part VII: Von der Schuld zu den Schulden, part VIII: Demonstration mit Ebenenwechsel und Utilisation der Hilflosigkeit (8 videotapes). Dortmund (vcr).

Sparrer, Insa a. M. Varga von Kibéd (2000): Tetralemmaarbeit als eine Form Systemischer Strukturaufstellungen. In: H. Doering-Meijer (ed.): Die entdeckte Wirklichkeit. Paderborn (Junfermann), pp. 49-76.

Spencer Brown, G. (1994): Laws of Form. Portland, OR (Cognizer Co.).

Stahl, T. (1988): Triffst Du ´nen Frosch unterwegs ... NLP fuer die Praxis. Paderborn (Junfermann).

Sturm, H. P. (1996): Weder Sein noch Nichtsein. Der Urteilsvierkant (catuskoti) und seine Korollarien im oestlichen und westlichen Denken. Wuerzburg (Ergon).

Ule, Andrej: Operationen und Regeln bei Wittgenstein. Vom logischen Raum zum Regelraum. Ffm. (Lang) 1997.

Varga von Kibéd, M.: Wittgenstein und Spencer Brown. In: Weingartner, P. a. Schurz, G. (eds.): Philosophie der Naturwissenschaften. Akten des 13. Internationalen Wittgenstein-Symposiums, Kirchberg 1988 (1998), pp. 402-406.

Varga von Kibéd, Matthias: Aspekte der Negation in der buddhistischen und formalen Logik. In: Synthesis Philosophica 10, pp. 581-593.

Varga von Kibéd, M.: Wiedererkennen als Kontrolle und als Quelle von von Vergangenheit und Identitaet. In: Steinbrenner, J. a. Winko, U. (eds.): Bilder in der Philosophie und in anderen Kuensten und Wissenschaften. Paderborn et al. (Schoeningh) 1997, pp. 99-112.

Varga von Kibéd, M. (1998): Bemerkungen ueber philosophische Grundlagen und methodische Voraussetzungen der systemischen Aufstellungsarbeit. In: G. Weber (ed.): Praxis des Familien-Stellens. Heidelberg (Carl Auer), S. 51-60.

Varga von Kibéd, M. (1998): Die gemeinsame Form von Zeichen,

Unterscheidungen und Paradoxien. Lecture at the 1. World Congress of Psychotherapy in Vienna 1996. (audio tape). Muensterschwarzach.

Varga von Kibéd, M. (1998): Systemisches Kreativitaetstraining: Tetralemmaaufstellungen und Aufstellungsarbeit mit Drehbuchautoren. In: G. Weber (ed.): Praxis des Familien-Stellens. Heidelberg (Carl.Auer).

Varga von Kibéd, M. (2000): Unterschiede und tiefere Gemeinsamkeiten der Aufstellungsarbeit mit Organisationen und der systemischen Familienaufstellungen. In: G. Weber (ed.): Praxis der Organisationsaufstellungen. Heidelberg (Carl Auer).

Varga von Kibéd, M. a. I. Sparrer (2000): Ganz im Gegenteil. Tetralemmaarbeit und andere Grundformen Systemischer Strukturaufstellungen – fuer Querdenker und solche, die es werden wollen. Heidelberg (Carl Auer).

Waldenfels, B. (ed.): Edmund Husserl: Arbeit an den Phänomenen. Ausgewaehlte Schriften. Frankfurt (Fischer).

Walter, J. a. J. E. Peller (1995): Loesungsorientierte Kurztherapie. Dortmund (modernes Lernen).

Watzlawick, P. (1974): Change. Principles of Problem Formation and Problem Solution. New York (Norton).

Watzlawick, P. (1977): How Real Is Real? London (Vintage).

Watzlawick, P. a. G. Nardone (1993): The Art of Change: Strategic Therapy and Hypnotherapy Without Trance (Jossey Bass).

Watzlawick, P., J. H. Beavin a. D. D. Jackson (1967): Pragmatics of Human Communication. A Study of Interactional Patterns, Pathologies and Paradoxes. New York (Norton).

Weber, G. (ed.): Zweierlei Glueck. Heidelberg (Carl Auer).

Weber, G. (ed.): Praxis des Familen-Stellens. Heidelberg (Carl Auer).

Weber, G. a. B. Gross: Organisationsaufstellungen In: G. Weber (ed.): Praxis des Familien-Stellens Heidelberg (Carl Auer), pp. 405-420.

Weiss, T. a. G. Haertel-Weiss (1991): Familientherapie ohne Familie. Kurztherapie mit Einzelpatienten. Munich (Piper).

Wiest, F. a. M. Varga von Kibéd (1998): Homoeopathische Systemaufstellungen. In: G. Weber (ed.): Praxis des Familien-Stellens Heidelberg (Carl Auer), pp. 446-459.

Wiest, F. a. M. Varga von Kibéd (2000): Homoeopathische Systemaufstellungen. Anwendung und Analogien zu Organisationsaufstellungen. In: G. Weber (ed.): Praxis der Organisationsaufstellungen. Heidelberg (Carl Auer).

Wilhelm, R. (ed.) (1956): I Ging. Duesseldorf et al. (Diederichs).

Wittgenstein, L. (2001): Tractatus Logico-Philosophicus. London (Routledge Classics).

Wittgenstein, L. (2001): Philosophical Investigations. (Blackwell).
Wuchterl, K. (1999): Methoden der Gegenwartsphilosophie. Bern et al. (Paul Haupt, UTB).

About the author

Insa Sparrer, Dipl.Psych., is an acclaimed psychological psychotherapist. She has trained in client centred therapy, Ericksonian therapy, family therapy, behavioural therapy, systemic therapy and solution focused therapy. She has run her own clinics in Munich since 1989.

In 1996 she founded the SySt-Institute in Munich with Matthias Varga von Kibéd. They developed and teach about Systemic Structural Constellations (SySt) and offer certifications in Systemic Therapy/Systemic Consulting and in Solution focused Therapy/Consulting, as well as training in Hypnotherapy.

Insa Sparrer leads trainings in Systemic Structural Constellation Work and the Solution Focused approach at institutes for therapy and consulting in Germany, Austria, Italy, Slovenia, Greece, Netherlands, Hungary, Switzerland and the UK, as well as university courses in Austria and Germany.

Information about seminars and trainings;

SySt-Institute
Angererstr. 38
80796 München
Germany

Tel.: 0049-(0)89-363661
Fax: 0049-(0)89-36004880
Email: info@syst.info
Web: www.syst.info

The New Wave of Change is in SolutionsBooks!

In the 1960s, the legendary record label Impulse! launched itself with the motto 'The New Wave of Jazz is on Impulse!'. The label became the home of legends like John Coltrane and Charles Mingus, and led the way for a whole movement of new musical forms and talent.

In the same way, we now announce that The New Wave of Change is in SolutionsBooks. We will be promoting the developing movement around Solutions Focus and other positive, minimal change technologies including Narrative and Appreciative Inquiry, which value simplicity and pragmatism over complex models and ill-founded theory.

This New Wave is not a different model for change – it is a different kind of approach. We are not interested in finding grand designs. Instead, we seek ways to find the direct routes to progress, to explore the limits of what matters and what can be overlooked, in helping people and organisations move forwards in a complex and fluid world.

Solutions Focus is built on the successful field of Solution Focused Brief Therapy (SFBT) as developed by Steve de Shazer and Insoo Kim Berg at the Brief Family Therapy Centre, Milwaukee. Over the past fifteen years SFBT practitioners have discovered the power of finding what works, staying at the surface, careful listening and building on small successes, and bypassing conventional therapeutic tools such as diagnosis, cause analysis, 'talking through' the problem and searching for repressed feelings and thoughts.

This radically simple, skilful and subtle practice is found in randomised controlled studies to give as good or better results than more conventional methods, but in less time and with greater satisfaction from clients. Practitioners report fewer features of burn-out than with other approaches. We seek to continue this movement into the worlds of organisations, businesses and other settings.

Some people have found the ideas presented here to be simplistic – nice and positive, just like PollyAnna. We think this misses the point: simple is not simplistic. To be less simple, to take less direct routes involving a priori problem analysis, weakness diagnosis and any of the other myriad potential excursions and pitfalls, is to risk at best expending more resources and time than necessary, and at worst spreading confusion and making any problems significantly worse.

Ludwig Wittgenstein wrote that the aim of philosophy was 'to show the fly the way out of the fly-bottle'. In promoting the New Wave of change, our aim is show how simplicity and clarity can minimise confusion and futile effort. Readers will be able to find their own ways out of the bottle.

Mark McKergow and Jenny Clarke
SolutionsBooks

Also in SolutionsBooks

Also published by SolutionsBooks ...

Positive Approaches to Change: Applications of Solutions Focus and Appreciative Inquiry at Work, edited by Mark McKergow and Jenny Clarke (£13.99, ISBN 0-9549749-0-5)

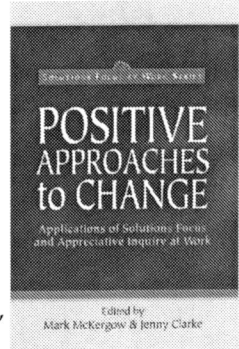

This collection of articles from the AMED journal Organisations & People describes international experience of applying the positive power of Solutions Focus and Appreciative Inquiry to strategic planning, coaching, performance management, feedback and much more.

Team Coaching with the SolutionCircle: A Practical Guide to Solutions Focused Team Development by Daniel Meier (£17.99, ISBN 0-9549749-1-3)

Applying the positive power of Solutions Focus to working with teams, Daniel Meier shows you how to:

- Apply Solutions Focus methods with groups and teams
- Choose and use the eight steps of the SolutionCircle
- Become an effective team coach - as a manager or external resource
- Engage team members in finding useful action steps
- Use challenges and difficulties in the team to build progress

Solutions Focus Working: 80 real-life lessons for successful organisational change by Mark McKergow and Jenny Clarke (£17.99, ISBN 978-0-9549749-4-7)

Fourteen organisations tell the stories of how Solutions Focus has helped them to change – and show you many ways to find what worked in the workplace. The organizations include Lufthansa, British Sky Broadcasting, the Ontario Medical Association and Freescale Semiconductor. Issues tackled include restructuring, strategy development, continuous improvement and team development.

Order these and other SF books from our online shop at

www.solutionsbooks.com

Index

Lightning Source UK Ltd.
Milton Keynes UK
21 March 2011

169613UK00004B/18/A